IMMERSION AT THE UNIVERSITY LEVEL

IMMERSION AT THE UNIVERSITY LEVEL
RETHINKING POLICIES, APPROACHES, AND IMPLEMENTATIONS

Edited by
Hélène Knoerr
and
Alysse Weinberg

University of Ottawa Press
2020

University of Ottawa **Press**
press.uOttawa.ca

The University of Ottawa Press (UOP) is proud to be the oldest of the francophone university presses in Canada and the oldest bilingual university publisher in North America. Since 1936, UOP has been "enriching intellectual and cultural discourse" by producing peer-reviewed and award-winning books in the humanities and social sciences, in French and in English.

Library and Archives Canada Cataloguing in Publication

Title: Immersion at the university level : rethinking policies, approaches and implementations / Hélène Knoerr, Alysse Weinberg.
Other titles: Immersion française à l'université. English
Names: Knoerr, Hélène, 1964– author. | Weinberg, Alysse, author.
Series: Politics and public policy (University of Ottawa Press)
Description: Series statement: Politics and public policy | Translation of: L'immersion française à l'université: politiques et pédagogies. | Includes bibliographical references and index.
Identifiers: Canadiana (print) 20190226927 | Canadiana (ebook) 20190226935 | ISBN 9780776628745 (softcover) | ISBN 9780776628868 (hardcover) | ISBN 9780776628752 (PDF) | ISBN 9780776628769 (EPUB) | ISBN 9780776628776 (Kindle)
Subjects: LCSH: French language — Study and teaching (Higher) — Canada — English speakers. | CSH: French language — Study and teaching as a second language — Immersion method. | CSH: French language — Study and teaching as a second language (Higher) — Canada.
Classification: LCC PC2068.C2 K6613 2020 | DDC 448.0071/171–dc23

Legal Deposit: First Quarter 2020
Library and Archives Canada
© University of Ottawa Press 2020

Copy editing	Christina Thiele
Proofreading	Elizabeth Schwaiger
Typesetting	Carleton Production Centre
Cover design	Édiscript enr.
Cover image	Untitled. All efforts have been made to ascertain the copyright holder of this image.

The University of Ottawa Press gratefully acknowledges the support extended to its publishing list by the Government of Canada, the Canada Council for the Arts, the Ontario Arts Council, the Federation for the Humanities and Social Sciences, and by the University of Ottawa.

uOttawa

Table of Contents

Acknowledgements vii

PREFACE: Post-Secondary French Immersion
    Graham Fraser 1

INTRODUCTION
    Aline Gohard-Radenkovic, Hélène Knoerr, and Alysse Weinberg 13

Chapter 1
    Solid Foundations:
    French Immersion Language Planning and Policies in Canada
    Sylvie A. Lamoureux 27

Chapter 2
    Political Interpretations and Institutional Arrangements for Immersion at the University of Ottawa
    Hélène Knoerr 43

Chapter 3
    From Applied Linguistic Theories to Language and Culture Teaching: Origins of Immersion
    Jérémie Séror, Aline Gohard-Radenkovic, and Hélène Knoerr 65

Chapter 4
    From Informal to Formal Immersion
    Alysse Weinberg and Sandra Burger 81

Chapter 5
    Immersion in Canada in Its Multiple Forms:
    From Vision to Reality
    Bettina B. Cenerelli, Eva Lemaire, and Françoise Mougeon 99

Chapter 6
    The Resources for French Immersion at the University of Ottawa
    Hélène Knoerr 123

Chapter 7
    Learning Modes and Situations in the *Régime d'immersion en français*:
    A Holistic Approach
    Alysse Weinberg and Catherine Elena Buchanan 151

Chapter 8
    Content Learning and Language Support
    Hélène Knoerr 167

Chapter 9
Collaborative Practices between Actors in Immersion:
Mentoring, *parrainage*, Tandem Work
    Alysse Weinberg, Hélène Knoerr, and Aline Gohard-Radenkovic 189

Chapter 10
The Role of Testing in Immersion Programs
    Alysse Weinberg and Amelia Hope 209

Chapter 11
Training Modalities for Immersion Stakeholders
    Catherine Elena Buchanan, Hélène Knoerr, and Sandra Burger 227

Chapter 12
Biographical Interviews with the RIF Administrators:
Potential Mediators of a Linguistic and Cultural "In-between"
    Aline Gohard-Radenkovic 249

Chapter 13
Language Ideologies of Immersion Stakeholders:
The Case of Language Instructors
    Jérémie Séror and Alysse Weinberg 269

Chapter 14
Experiences of Immersion Stakeholders at the University of Ottawa:
Content Instructors
    Hélène Knoerr 285

Chapter 15
The Student Experience in the *Régime d'immersion en français* at the
University of Ottawa: From Spaces of Tensions to "In-Between" Spaces?
    Sylvie A. Lamoureux 299

Chapter 16
RIF Students' Self-Narratives on Their Itineraries and Experiences
    Aline Gohard-Radenkovic 313

SYNTHESIS
    Hélène Knoerr, Alysse Weinberg, and Aline Gohard-Radenkovic 329

About the Editors 337

Acknowledgements

The two co-editors of this volume, Hélène Knoerr and Alysse Weinberg, have worked in close collaboration to offer this updated English translation of their 2016 collaboration (with Aline Gohard-Radenkovic) *L'immersion française à l'université: politiques et pédagogies*, giving international readers the opportunity to learn about immersion at the university level in Canada.

The co-editors gratefully acknowledge the financial support of the Canadian Centre for Studies and Research on Bilingualism and Language Planning (CCERBAL) and the Post Secondary Immersion Interdisciplinary Research Group (PSIRG). Without the generous support of these two research centres of the Official languages and Bilingualism Institute (OLBI) at the University of Ottawa, this project could not have been completed.

There are many people we would like to thank. First and foremost, we thank all the authors, who undertook the translating of their own chapters from French into English. Without their expertise and commitment, this book would never have materialized.

Thank you to our scrupulous, indomitable, eagle-eyed editor, Christina Thiele, for her hard work, grace, dedication, and patience during the production of this book. She was responsible for the copyediting phase, with the added layer of addressing translation issues arising from the original 2016 French edition. In particular, confirming the accuracy of citations and their sources, which have been identified, located, and updated (including URLs, many of which had changed since 2016), also fell to her, to yield consistent bibliographies across all chapters.

We would also like to thank Elizabeth Schwaiger for a final read-through and careful proofreading of the manuscript. Elizabeth had helped to shepherd the original French edition through publication and we were pleased that she was available to work with us on this edition as well.

And finally, thank you to the many individuals — too many to name — who supported and reviewed this work and helped improve the translation over the past two years.

Hélène Knoerr
Alysse Weinberg
January 2020

PREFACE
Post-Secondary French Immersion

Graham Fraser*

CANADA, AS AN OFFICIALLY BILINGUAL COUNTRY, is in a distinct position in comparison with several other countries with the same status. Here, contrary to Belgium and Ireland, the federal government is not responsible for education. Thus, Canadian federalism has resulted in each province having a different language regime: one bilingual province (New Brunswick); one province with French as the official language (Quebec); several provinces with a French-language services act (Ontario, Nova Scotia, and Prince Edward Island); others with a policy on French-language services (Newfoundland and Labrador, Manitoba, and Saskatchewan; and finally, two provinces that are, de facto, unilingual English (Alberta and British Columbia).

1. THE ORIGINS OF THE DEBATE ON BILINGUALISM

Despite this asymmetry. the unilingualism of the English-speaking majority has always been a preoccupation for some members of the English-Canadian elite. Throughout Canada's history, a certain number of people have recognized the importance of the mastery of the second language. Robert Baldwin,[1] one of the key players in the struggle for responsible government[2] during the 1840s, asked Louis-Hippolyte Lafontaine to recommend a school for his son: "I must not expose him to the miserable embarrassment that I labour under myself for want of French" (Fraser, 2006, p. 17). A century later, at the beginning of the 1960s, a group of young Anglophones enrolled in law in French at Laval University, including Brian Mulroney, Michael Meighen, Peter White, and Conrad Black.[3] Other Anglophones have studied in French at Laval, such as Andrew Molson, whose foundation finances scholarships for young Anglophones wanting to study at Laval. But these examples are the exceptions rather than the rule.

However, the Canadian school system's desire to produce bilingual graduates is not recent. The Royal Commission of Inquiry into Bilingualism and Biculturalism (RCBB)[4] quotes from a report of the Manitoba Department of Education (Canada, RCBB, 1968):

---

* Mr. Fraser was Commissioner of Official Languages from 2006 to 2016.
[1] Robert Baldwin shared the Prime Ministership of the United Canada with Louis-Hippolyte Lafontaine from 1842 to 1843 and from 1848 to 1851.
[2] In Canada, responsible government "originated in the 1830s and became an important part of Confederation. It's the method by which Canada achieved independence without revolution" (*The Canadian Encyclopedia*, 2006, "Responsible government").
[3] Brian Mulroney was Prime Minister of Canada from 1984 until 1993 and Peter White was his principal secretary; Michael Meighen is a former Canadian senator, lawyer, and philanthropist; Conrad Black is a former newspaper owner, financier, and author.
[4] Also known as the Bi and Bi Commission or the Laurendeau–Dunton Commission.

> The good effect of the new course in French is very noticeable and the policy of requiring the students to become acquainted with French, a living tongue, and to use it in speech as well as for reading, has already been amply justified. It is safe to say that within a year or two high-school students on leaving school for business or the University will carry with them a real training in French which will prove vastly more useful to them than a mere grammar and reading course in that language could possibly be. Many teachers are making an effort to live up to the ideal of using French as the language of instruction during the teaching periods in that branch. (Book II. para. 512, p. 199)

This statement, which the Commissioners describe as "optimistic," dates from 1919 or 1920. *Plus ça change* ...

The question of education and linguistic duality was dealt with largely in terms of the rights of the minority to access to education in the official language of its choice. It is one of the anomalies of Canadian history. These rights were abused for almost a century, following the elimination of French-language education in Manitoba, Alberta, Saskatchewan, and Ontario (see Martel, 1997, pp. 25–42). The impact of these decisions on minority language communities was dealt with by the Royal Commission in the first volume of its report (Canada, RCBB, 1967):

> Almost without exception, it has been impossible for a French-speaking student outside Quebec to complete his education in French through the elementary and secondary public schools. But in Quebec, Anglophones have access to a complete education through the public schools of the province — elementary, secondary, and university. (Book I, para. 387, p. 122)

The recommendation of the Royal Commission was clearly intended to correct this injustice (Canada, RCBB, 1967):

> Therefore, *we recommend that the right of Canadian parents to have their children educated in the official language of their choice be recognized in the educational systems, the degree of implementation to depend on the concentration of the minority population.* (Book I, para. 389, p. 123; emphasis in original)

Thus, the right was conceived as a minority right and was limited in its application by the size of the minority community. This faithfully reflected the commissioners' principal concern: the need to establish or restore the equal status of the minority Francophone communities and the Anglophone majority.

It was also the same approach taken by the drafters of the Canadian Charter of Rights and Freedoms (1985) in article 23, and in the interpretation given to this by the Supreme Court of Canada in the *Mahe v. Alberta* (1990) and *Arsenault–Cameron v. Prince Edward Island* (2000) decisions.[5] From a legal point of view, "the official language of their choice" meant the choice made by parents living in a minority situation. Thanks to this recommendation by the Royal Commission, its inclusion in the Charter and the Supreme Court's interpretation, this right has been recognized and established. There are now French-language schools in every province and territory and universities which

---

[5] These decisions confirmed that article 23 established not only the right to instruction, but also the right to control and manage public school boards.

offer programs in French in eight provinces. However, there has never been recognition of the right to be educated in the minority language. Nevertheless, it was clear that the Royal Commission was in favour of second-language education, as indicated by these quotations from Book II of its report (Canada, RCBB, 1967):

> ... most Canadians believe that a second language should be taught in the schools, and that it should be the second official language of the country. (para. 517, p. 201)

> ... Today, on all continents with the possible exception of North America, the study of a second language is as much taken for granted as the study of geography or mathematics. (para. 522, p. 203)

> ... Today's child will live in a mobile and highly competitive society. What parent in 1968 can know with any certainty where his child will live in the year 2000, or even what career opportunities his child will have? It is apparent, however, that the child who learns French or English as a second language will have career opportunities that other children will not. Learning a second language is also a valuable educational experience because it brings the child into contact with a different culture. In Canada, such contact can provide our children with knowledge and appreciation of the culture of many other Canadians. (para. 526, p. 204)

> ... Language learning can increase the number of bilingual Canadians and so reduce the language barrier in our country. It can play a significant role in increasing the mutual understanding ... of the two cultural groups. (para. 527, pp. 204–205)

> The need for second language teaching cannot be seriously questioned. The majority of Canadians are aware of this need and feel that all children should study French or English as a second language in school. The national interest also underlines the need for Canadian school children to study the second official language. The question, therefore, is not so much whether it should be taught but rather how it can be better taught. (para. 533, p. 206)

The Commissioners also saw the negative effect of Anglophone unilingualism on the role of Francophones (Canada, RCBB, 1968):

> ... As long as most bilingual Canadians are of French mother tongue, many members of this group will be absorbed in interpreting their society to English-speaking Canadians and interpreting English-speaking Canada to their compatriots. The potential benefits of their other talents will be lost and Canadian society will be the poorer as a result.... More Anglophones must become bilingual if French-speaking Canadians are to play a more creative role in Canadian society. (Book II, para. 531, p. 206)

2. THE CREATION OF FRENCH IMMERSION PROGRAMS

It was also during the 1960s that French immersion began. The creation of immersion programs was not a response to an elitist theory developing an experiment and using children as guinea pigs but rather a reaction to a desire from parents. They knew that the traditional teaching of French had not been particularly effective for them and they wanted something better for their children. Twelve parents in Montreal's South Shore started to hold meetings and formed the Study Group of the Bilingual School of St. Lambert. They reached out to Wallace Lambert and to Dr. Wilder Penfield, the well-known neurologist of the Montreal Neurological Institute: "The parents had the impression that their children were being deceived and that they should have the possibility of becoming 'bilingual' inside the school system, since it was so difficult to do so outside of school," recalled one of the parents almost ten years later (Melikoff, 1972, p. 220).

As Genesee said (1987):

> These parents felt that their lack of competence in French contributed to and indeed was attributable in part to the two solitudes[6] which effectively prevented them from learning French informally from their French-speaking neighbors. Their inability to communicate in French, they felt, was also attributable to the inadequate methods of second language teaching in the English schools. (p. 9)

It is worth recalling the climate in Quebec in 1965: the Quiet Revolution was well underway; the *Front de libération du Québec* (FLQ) had set off bombs three years earlier, in 1962; Pierre Bourgault was drawing large crowds to meetings of the *Rassemblement pour l'indépendance nationale* (RIN).[7] The English-speaking community of Quebec was uneasy and perplexed: the unwritten rule — that Anglophones were not required to learn French but that Francophones had to learn English — was disappearing. In Quebec City and Sherbrooke, in 1964, the members of the Royal Commission on Bilingualism and Biculturalism were heckled during public meetings that crackled with anger. The commissioners produced a preliminary report in 1965, saying that Canada was passing through the greatest crisis in its history.

A dozen parents from Montreal's South Shore community — appealing to university experts such as Lambert and Penfield, in order to learn what to do so that their children would speak better French than they could — were making a noble civic act. In their own way, they were stating their determination to live in Quebec as part of a minority. In this way, they were echoing Frank Scott who, during a meeting in Sherbrooke where it was said that the Anglophone community should leave Quebec as soon as possible, responded: "*J'y suis, j'y reste*" ['I'm here, I'm staying']. These parents were not leaving — they were at home in Quebec and determined to make a better life for their children (Canada, OCOL, 2011).

It is unnecessary to discuss the success of immersion at the primary and secondary level in Canada; since the introduction of the Saint Lambert experiment in the mid-1960s (Lambert & Tucker, 1972), the model has been used everywhere in Canada and around the world. What is more, since the beginning, the phenomenon has been the constant subject of studies.

But the question of teaching French as a second language remains problematic. First, enrolment in French immersion has plateaued at 342,000 for 25 years (Fraser, 2006, p. 189). Its success has had a perverse effect on the traditional teaching of French; that

---

[6] *Two solitudes* (1985) is a novel by Hugh MacLennan that has become the symbol of the tensions in the relations between English and French Canadians.

[7] Pierre Bourgault (1934–2003) was a politician, university professor, and radio host; he is considered one of the pioneers of the Quebec independence movement. He joined the *Rassemblement pour l'indépendance nationale* (RIN) in the early 1960s and became its president. When René Lévesque (1922–1987) founded the *Parti Québécois* in 1968, Bourgault dissolved the RIN, urging its members to join the PQ.

is to say, Core French.[8] Immersion attracts the best instructors and committed students, which has the effect of undermining Core French programs.

There is also an inequity of access across the country. French is not an obligatory subject in all of the provinces west of Ontario, while it is for Grades 4 to 9 in Ontario, Prince Edward Island, Nova Scotia, and Newfoundland and Labrador, from Grades 5 to 8 in the Yukon, and Grades 4 to 10 in New Brunswick.[9] The situation in Alberta is more complicated. There is a requirement to study a second language from Grades 5 to 8, but not necessarily French. However, the immersion program offered by Edmonton public schools has often been cited as exemplary in Canada. There continues to be great interest in immersion in the West. British Columbia parents often line up all night outside school board offices to get an immersion school place for their child. This asymmetry of access to quality instruction has produced a range of high school graduate skill levels in French, from a total lack of knowledge to an impressive mastery of the second language.

3. A NEW STEP FORWARD: POST-SECONDARY IMMERSION

The post-secondary immersion experience is completely different. English-speaking institutions have been slow to recognize the needs of students who did their primary and secondary schooling in French to continue to have access to courses and programs in French. The exception has been York University's Glendon College, founded soon after the creation of immersion programs, and created with the explicit goal of shaping a bilingual Canadian elite (King, 2004):

> Escott Reid arrived at York University's Glendon College in early January 1965. He was charged with creating a unique and intimate place of learning that would be fully bilingual, fully residential, and offer a small but demanding curriculum: a liberal arts college in the Oxford tradition. (p. 101)

John Ralston Saul played a key role in pressuring for post-secondary immersion. As an activist intellectual, he was one of the founders of French for the Future/*Le français pour l'avenir*, an organization created to give immersion students a cultural contact and inspiring models. At the same time, he encouraged Canadian universities to recognize their responsibilities toward linguistic duality in Canada. Finally, as the spouse of Governor-General Adrienne Clarkson, he used the opportunities that were available to him to promote bilingualism as a Canadian value (Ralston Saul, 2001, 2004).

The experience varies a great deal across the country, and immersion is often handled by a minority institution with a Francophone mandate. As an example, l'Université Sainte-Anne in Nova Scotia has become for all intents and purposes an immersion establishment specializing in the training of immersion teachers in the Atlantic provinces. The University of Ottawa, on the other hand, has developed an immersion program

---

[8] Core French is a basic second language program in which French is taught as a subject or a course. It is available in elementary schools at various points of entry depending on the provinces, typically offering an average of 90 minutes of French instruction per week. [Eds.]

[9] In Quebec, English is obligatory from kindergarten to Grade 11.

which will be described in greater detail elsewhere in this book. And the Campus Saint-Jean of the University of Alberta has a majority of its students coming from immersion schools.

Even if the government of Canada is the country's largest employer and requires a certain level of bilingualism from its employees and senior executives, the faculties of public administration have been slow to respond to this need.

4. "TWO LANGUAGES, A WORLD OF POSSIBILITIES"

Following this realization, the Office of the Commissioner of Official Languages (OCOL) published a study in 2009 entitled *Two Languages, a World of Possibilities: Second-language learning in Canada's universities*. The study found that "while many universities in Canada offer a range of second-language learning programs and courses, there are serious gaps and unmet needs" (p. III).

Among these gaps, we concluded that:

> opportunities for intensive second-language study are limited — for example, to enroll in immersion programs, to take subject-matter courses taught in the second language or to take second-language courses tailored to different academic disciplines. (p. III)

We developed an interactive map which served to illustrate the location of courses offered in the second language, the support available, the networking possibilities, and the possibilities of exchanges.

The knowledge of our two official languages is fundamental for the growth and development of Canadian youth, particularly in light of the international knowledge economy and the intensification of international competition.

It is just as important that a larger number of Canadians can learn French and English. It would prove Canada's commitment to linguistic duality. In the context of the continual renewal of the public service, it is also essential that the government have access to a larger pool of bilingual recruits.

In general, access to regular programs and courses allowing students to continue their second-language learning is adequate. However, the opportunities for intensive second-language learning (for example, studying in the second language) are limited. At the present time, only a limited number of courses in a limited range of disciplines is offered in the second language. Few universities have policies or requirements concerning the second language. Those that are in place are minimal and usually apply to a few courses offered only in a language other than French in Quebec, and other than English in the rest of the country. Moreover, there is very little collaboration between French-language and English-language educational institutions. This collaboration is essential for offering an increased number of exchange opportunities and a better contact with the second language. While many Canadian universities offer or facilitate exchanges with other countries, the opportunities for exchanges with other Canadian universities are very limited.

5. CONTRIBUTIONS AND LIMITS

In the context of our 2009 study, we made a number of observations on ways to improve second-language learning in our universities.

First, the students we consulted told us that the professor remains the most important factor. They also indicated that small classes are essential to allow increased interaction in the second language. They added that second-language courses based on content—including content of a cultural nature or adapted to the area of learning—makes the experience much more stimulating.

From their vantage point, university professors and administrators who participate in second-language learning programs are of the opinion that the leadership and commitment of the senior administration are essential. The universities should demonstrate that they value teaching in the second language. That includes planning, co-ordination, and negotiation with other faculties and establishments, which results in additional costs for the universities which cannot be fully covered by the current per-student financing formula.

Students, professors, administrators, experts, and government representatives all agree that access to real opportunities to use and practice one's second language as well as exchanges and other possibilities of interaction with people who speak the other language is absolutely essential. Indeed, it is impossible to learn to speak another language well simply by taking a course: one has to live in the language.

6. RECOMMENDATIONS AND NEW CHALLENGES

In order for universities to be able to offer our young people the tools that they need in the context of their second-language learning, the federal and provincial governments have an important role to play and they should collaborate closely with universities. In this regard, we have developed numerous recommendations directed at the federal government and Canadian universities. To the Canadian government and to provincial and territorial governments, we have recommended the creation of a new fund to offer financial aid to universities. Such a fund would enable them to develop and put into place new initiatives intended to improve the possibilities for second-language learning. In the study, we also recommended that the Public Service Commission[10] develop, in collaboration with universities, a working framework for language skills, such as the Common European Framework of Reference for Languages, in order to establish equivalencies between the examinations administered by the public service and those used by universities. The ultimate goal of this working framework would be to give universities the job of evaluating students in advance, according to the different levels of language competence required to fill a position in the public service, The Office of the

---

[10] The Public Service Commission (PSC) is responsible for promoting and safeguarding a merit-based, representative and non-partisan public service that serves all Canadians, in collaboration with its stakeholders. It also manages the tools for public service recruitment, providing applicants and managers with a single portal to access all public service job opportunities (Canada, n.d.).

Commissioner currently participates in discussions with the Public Service Commission on this subject.

In this regard, there are two somewhat discouraging elements.

The first is that these recommendations of additional investment did not bear fruit. Nevertheless, they did result in a pilot project during which the Canada School of the Public Service shared its training tool and the Public Service Commission's procedure for language evaluation with eleven universities, thus allowing a student interested in a career in the public service to know his or her language level before entering. Unfortunately, the program was not renewed in the last *Roadmap for Official Languages, 2013–2018* (Canada, Canadian Heritage, 2013). In general, universities responded positively to the study, on condition of receiving additional funding; for their part, the governments did not respond.

A second disappointment came to mind when I reread the second volume of the Report of the Royal Commission on Bilingualism and Biculturalism. What is striking is the similarity of its recommendations with those that the Office of the Commissioner developed forty years later. For example: *"We recommend that the federal government meet the cost of a one-year transfer programme for university students specializing in the other official language"* (Canada, RCBB, 1968, Book II, p. 257; emphasis in original). The recommendations I made in my annual report for 2012–2013, to the effect that the federal government should invest more in exchange programs, are, sadly, strikingly similar (Canada, OCOL, 2013, p. 48).

The new challenges are considerable. Often, the universities do not benefit from an increase in financing for these programs, and any change in priorities demands difficult choices. Universities that already have a language immersion program in place have to deal with a climate of competition, which means that students hesitate to enrol for fear of compromising their chances of being admitted to a professional program or a graduate program by taking courses that would be more difficult in an institution where they would be studying in their second language. Innovative solutions have nevertheless emerged to meet these challenges, as will be seen in different chapters of this book.

As Commissioner of Official Languages, I had the opportunity to speak with many students across the country. I met some who had done their primary and secondary studies in immersion and were frustrated to realize that they were losing their mastery of French because of the lack of university courses in their second language. I met others who had strategically used summer programs such as *Explore*[11] to perfect their French. Some found that the experience of immersion in an environment where English predominated was inadequate and pursued their studies in a French-language university. Here are some of the comments that we received (Canada, OCOL, 2009, section 4.1):

> The learning of another language opens many doors and makes you discover a new world ... It allows you to develop connections with others ... It is an immense advantage.

---

[11] "*Explore* is a five-week, intensive language immersion bursary program that is offered by the federal government during the spring or summer. The program provides opportunities for English-speaking students to study French, and for French-speaking students to study English" (Canada, Department of Canadian Heritage, n.d.).

It seems trivial but learning another language eliminates obstacles. It enlarges your way of thinking and gives you access to another way of seeing the world.

The knowledge of another language allows you to understand other people, another culture, another way of life ... It's like a bridge, another way of getting close to others.

This learning offers many possibilities; you are not confined to a region, a city, or a culture ...

You can't separate the learning of a language from the learning of the culture with which it is identified ... That is what gives a meaning and substance to language learning.

I want more than linguistics and literature.

I would like very much to take a second-language course related to my discipline, like a business or engineering course. Many young people would benefit!

The reaction of the students at Simon Fraser University who shared their experiences with me was extremely positive. "Finally, being part of the Cohort[12] was really the best decision that I ever made as far as my studies are concerned," a 2008 graduate told me (personal communication, 2016). For her, the best aspect of the program was the entire year that she spent at *Sciences Po* in Paris.[13] In addition, the fact that the program had a small number of students allowed them to develop strong ties.

A graduate of the same program in 2007 felt the same way, while recognizing the challenge of writing reports, projects, and essays at a university level in his second language. For him as well, the obligatory aspect of studying in a French-language university was an essential part of a program that transformed his life: "The time that I spent in Quebec City at Laval University had an immeasurable effect on my life, and because of that I will always be grateful to the French Cohort Program" (personal communication, 2016).

A 2004 graduate particularly appreciated the practical application of what he had learned, and the commitment demanded by the minority language community, whose vitality he had discovered: "You leave the program not only with a university degree but useful skills in research and project management experiences lived in the real world. From the perspective of a student, it is perhaps the most important element of the program (personal communication, 2016).

These are the pioneers, just like the young people who were the guinea pigs during the first experience of French immersion at the primary level in Saint Lambert in the mid-60s. One can hope that what these young people have experienced will produce a model of university education that is just as fruitful as the primary and secondary models of immersion.

We already have a good knowledge of the second-language learning programs at the primary and secondary levels, but we have very little information concerning this type of program at the university level. Thus, in order to ensure a learning continuum from primary to the job market, we need to focus on this question and make sure that this

---

[12] The program in Public and International Affairs at SFU, or French Cohort Program.

[13] More formally known as the *Institut d'Études Politiques de Paris* [Paris Institute of Political Studies].

information is available to the public. It is one of the objectives of this work, which intends to collect and analyze the practices underway, in order to propose a successful model of French immersion at the university level.

REFERENCES

Arsenault-Cameron v. Prince Edward Island. (2000). 1 S.C.R. 3. scc-csc.lexum.com/scc-csc/scc-csc/en/item/1762/index.do

Canada. (n.d.). Public Service Commission. www.canada.ca/en/public-service-commission.html

Canada. Department of Canadian Heritage. (n.d.) Explore — Second language bursary program. www.canada.ca/en/canadian-heritage/services/funding/explore.html

Canada. Department of Canadian Heritage. (2013). *Roadmap for Canada's Official Languages, 2013–2018*. Ottawa: Minister of Canadian Heritage and Official Languages. www.canada.ca/content/dam/pch/documents/services/official-languages-bilingualism/roadmap/roadmap2013-2018-eng.pdf

Canada. Constitution Act, 1982. (1982). Canadian Charter of Rights and Freedoms. laws-lois.justice.gc.ca/eng/Const/page-15.html

Canada. Office of the Commissioner of Official Languages (OCOL). (2009). *Two languages, a world of opportunities: Second-language learning in Canada's universities*. Ottawa: Minister of Public Works and Government Services Canada. www.languesofficielles.gc.ca/sites/default/files/uni_e.pdf

Canada. Office of the Commissioner of Official Languages (OCOL). (2011, March). The quiet evolution of language and culture relations in Canada: A tribute to the work of Professor Wallace Lambert [Notes presented at tribute symposium]. Montreal. www.clo-ocol.gc.ca/en news/speeches/2011/2011-03-17

Canada. Office of the Commissioner of Official Languages (OCOL). (2013). *Annual Report, 2012–2013*. Ottawa: Minister of Public Works and Government Services Canada. www.languesofficielles.gc.ca/sites/default/files/uni_e.pdf

Canada. Royal Commission on Bilingualism and Biculturalism (RCBB). (1967). *Report of the Royal Commission on Bilingualism and Biculturalism*, Book I: *The Official Languages*. Ottawa: Queen's Printer. [second half of Book I, pp. 89–212]. publications.gc.ca/collections/collection_2014/bcp-pco/Z1-1963-1-5-1-2-eng.pdf

Canada. Royal Commission on Bilingualism and Biculturalism (RCBB). (1968). *Report of the Royal Commission on Bilingualism and Biculturalism*, Book II: *Education*. Ottawa: Queen's Printer. [second half of Book II, pp. 133–305]. publications.gc.ca/collections/collection_2014/bcp-pco/Z1-1963-1-5-2-2-eng.pdf

Fraser, G. (2006). *Sorry, I don't speak French: Confronting the Canadian crisis that won't go away*. Toronto: McClelland and Stewart.

Frenette, Y. (1998). *Brève histoire des Canadiens français*. Montreal: Boréal.

Genesee, F. (1987). *Learning through two languages: Studies of immersion and bilingual education*. Cambridge, MA: Newbury House.

King, A. (2004). The Glendon College Experiment. In G. Donaghy & S. Roussel (Eds.), *Escott Reid: Diplomat and scholar* (pp. 1-1–121). Montreal: McGill-Queen's University Press.

Lambert, W.E., & Tucker, G.R. (1972). *Bilingual education of children: The St. Lambert experiment*. Rowley, MA: Newbury House.

MacLennan, H. (1945). *Two solitudes*. Toronto: Macmillan.

Mahe v. Alberta. (1990). 1 S.C.R. 342. scc-csc.lexum.com/scc-csc/scc-csc/en/item/580/index.do

Martel, M. (1997). *Le deuil d'un pays imaginé: rêves, luttes et déroute du Canada français*. Ottawa: University of Ottawa Press.

Melikoff, O. (1972). Appendix A: Parents as change agents in education: The St. Lambert experiment. In W.E. Lambert & G.R. Tucker (Eds.), *Bilingual education of children: The St. Lambert experiment* (pp. 219–236). Rowley, MA: Newbury House.

Ralston Saul, J. (2001, April). *Speech on the occasion of the opening of the French for the Future National Conference*. Winnipeg, MB.

Ralston Saul, J. (2004, March). *The unheralded success of bilingualism in Canada*. Paper presented at the Inaugural Joseph Howe Lecture, Halifax, NS.

Responsible government. (2006). *The Canadian Encyclopedia*. www.thecanadianencyclopedia.ca/en/article/responsible-government

Simon Fraser University. (n.d.). About the French Cohort Program. www.sfu.ca/fassfr/en/frcohort.html

INTRODUCTION

Aline Gohard-Radenkovic, Hélène Knoerr, and Alysse Weinberg

1. RATIONALE FOR THIS BOOK

FRENCH IMMERSION FIRST APPEARED in a primary school in suburban Montreal in the 1960s, to meet the needs of Anglophone children living and working in the new Francophone context of Quebec (Lambert & Tucker, 1972). While it spread rapidly to the primary and secondary schools throughout Canada, and was at the same time abundantly studied and researched, it is today still practically non-existent at the university level, as the Commissioner of Official Languages, Graham Fraser, stated in his 2009 report (Canada, The Office of the Commissioner of Official Languages [OCOL], 2009, pp. 5–10): basically, only four main universities were offering university-level immersion, namely the University of Ottawa, Glendon College at York University, Campus Saint-Jean at the University of Alberta, and Simon Fraser University in British Columbia. It should also be stated that the Commissioner, in his annual reports as well as in his presentations, routinely recommends that the immersion offer be extended to the post-secondary level.

To echo his recommendation, a scientific event entitled *International Forum on French Immersion at the University Level: Models, Challenges and Prospects* was organised at the University of Ottawa (henceforth uOttawa[1]) in February 2012 by two of the authors of this introduction (Hélène Knoerr and Alysse Weinberg), along with the third author, Aline Gohard-Radenkovic, who was the guest speaker. In her closing lecture, Gohard-Radenkovic wished to set up specific teaching methods for French immersion at the university level. The forum led to the collaboration by all three researchers in a pioneer book, written in French, *L'immersion française à l'université: politiques et pédagogies* (Knoerr, Weinberg, & Gohard-Radenkovic, 2016). Indeed, as the Commissioner of Official Languages pointed out in the present foreword, there was no other reference work on French immersion at the university level.[2] The present book is not simply an English translation of the original—it is an updated and augmented version, taking into account the many changes that have happened since the original 2016 edition and their repercussions and implications.

The title of this book, *University-level Immersion: Rethinking Policies, Approaches, and Implementations*, is not accidental at all. Immersion "at the university level" immediately clarifies that the scope is beyond compulsory schooling and also specifies

---

[1] In the book, the authors sometimes use 'uOttawa' to refer to the University of Ottawa. The two terms are used interchangeably at times to reflect the fact that the RIF is an important marketing and recruitment tool for the institution.

[2] In 2013, vol. 6 of the *OLBI Working Papers* (Knoerr & Weinberg, 2013) included a collection of articles from the 2012 forum (University of Ottawa, n.d.) but it was not a reference work.

the different types of contents: specialized theoretical content, as well as university and discipline cultures. As politics have a certain impact, especially regarding decisions on funding or legislation, we chose the word "policies": it explains the eminently political nature of all dispositions and developments concerning language, especially in a bilingual or multilingual environment. It implies choices and decision-making at different operational levels. Moreover, "policies" in the plural describes programs and targeted actions. Next, the word "approaches" refers to the development and the "implementations" of such decisions to teaching and learning methods. The intention of this book is to point out that any institutional environment for French immersion at the university level must make choices based on its specific contexts and challenges. In other words, our aim is not only to think but to rethink all the dimensions of such a complex *dispositif* (see p. 19 of this chapter for an elaboration of this term) at the post-secondary level: the best practices must therefore be sought out to successfully implement these choices through an immersion program and structure so that its graduates may work effectively in their second language.

Mr. Fraser, the sixth Commissioner of Official Languages of Canada,[3] was kind enough to preface this book, thus greatly emphasizing its relevance. The Commissioner is an agent of Parliament, appointed for a seven-year term by commission under the Great Seal,[4] after approval by resolution of the House of Commons and the Senate. He reports directly to Parliament (Canada, OCOL, n.d., "Mandate"). As a federal spokesman for the promotion of Canada's two official languages and the protection of linguistic rights, the Commissioner oversees the publication of case studies, annual reports, speeches, and press releases on various subjects dealing with linguistic duality in order to "inform the people and Parliament of Canada about how the federal government is fulfilling its responsibilities under the *Official Languages Act*" (Canada, OCOL, n.d., "Annual reports"). His mandate, as defined by Section 56 of the 1969 Act, states that:

> It is the duty of the Commissioner to take all actions and measures within the authority of the Commissioner with a view to ensuring recognition of the status of each of the official languages and compliance with the spirit and intent of this Act in the administration of the affairs of federal institutions, including any of their activities relating to the advancement of English and French in Canadian society. (Canada, Justice Laws Website, n.d.)

The Commissioner must therefore strive to achieve the three main objectives of the Official Languages Act (Canada, OCOL, n.d., "Mandate"):

- Ensure the equality of English and French in Parliament, the Government of Canada, the federal administration and the institutions subject to the Official Languages Act;

---

[3] Since 1969, six Commissioners have each brought their personal touch to the position: Keith Spicer (1970–1977), Maxwell Yalden (1977–1984), D'Iberville Fortier (1984–1991), Victor Goldbloom (1991–1999), Dyane Adam (1999–2006), and Graham Fraser (2006–2016) — and one Interim Commissioner: Ghislaine Saikaley (2016–2018). The 7th (and current) Commissioner is Raymond Théberge, in office since January 2018.

[4] The Great Seal of Canada is affixed on all State documents such as proclamations and commissions of cabinet ministers, senators, judges, and senior government officials (Canada, The Governor General of Canada, n.d.).

- Support the preservation and the development of official minority language communities;
- Promote the equality of status and use of English and French in Canadian society.

Hence, the Commissioner's involvement in this book expresses his confidence in its potential role as a tool to reach the goals of the Official Languages Act. It is indeed an important mission since, even though both founding peoples have lived together in Canada for five centuries, the two languages have sometimes followed chaotic paths, which the federal institutions are still trying to regulate.

2. OVERVIEW: FRENCH AND ENGLISH IN CANADA AND AT uOTTAWA

The relationship between Francophones and Anglophones has constantly evolved since the creation of Canada, and it is characterized by an alternating series of dissensions and reconciliations, depending on the policies put forward by the federal government in office.

The great explorers introduced French and English to Canada in the early 16th century. At the time, language acquisition was made solely through contact. The French only settled permanently in New France (*Nouvelle France*) in the 17th century. Then, contacts with the native people and their various languages became commonplace. After the conquest,[5] linguistic contacts occurred not only between settlers and natives but also between Europeans.

In Canada, including in Quebec, English became the language of business until the 1960s.[6] Following the Quiet Revolution[7] and Quebec's subsequent language laws,[8] the

---

[5] From *The Canadian Encyclopedia* (Miquelon, 2006):

The Conquest (*La conquête*) was a term used to designate the acquisition of Canada by Great Britain in the Seven Years' War and, by extension, the resulting changed conditions of life experienced by Canada's 60,000 to 70,000 French-speaking inhabitants and numerous Indigenous groups.

[6] As shown in the preliminary report of the Laurendeau–Dunton Commission (1965; cited in Mills, 2007, p. 30):

- 83% of administrators and managers in Quebec were Anglophones;
- the average income of Francophones in Quebec was 35% lower than that of Anglophones;
- Francophones ranked 12th on the income scale depending on their ethnic origin;
- Francophones earned less than all other linguistic groups with the same level of education;
- unilingual Anglophones earned more than bilingual Anglophones or Francophones;
- even when assimilated, Francophones were not more successful;
- the situation has only grown worse in 30 years.

[7] From *The Canadian Encyclopedia* (Durocher, 2013):

The Quiet Revolution (*la Révolution tranquille*) was a time of rapid change experienced in Québec during the 1960s.

[8] Specifically:

- Bill 63 (*Bill for the promotion of the French language in Quebec*, 1969)

pendulum swung in the opposite direction and Anglophones in Quebec saw the relevance of mastering French. The federal Official Languages Act (1969) generalized this duality throughout Canada.[9]

In this context — indeed, since its foundation in the 19th century — uOttawa has played a specific role, which makes it the oldest and largest bilingual university in North America. The University of Ottawa was first established as the College of Bytown, a bilingual college founded in 1848 by Bishop Guigues, who was both Bishop of Bytown and a member of the Congregation of the Oblates of Mary Immaculate. The first mission of this new institution was religious, aimed at bringing together the Francophone and Irish Catholic communities, thus making bilingualism a fundamental value. Classes were given in French in the morning and in English in the afternoon, with a view to "reconciling Anglophones and Francophones by forcing them while at the College not only to live together but also to study together in the same classroom, sometimes in one language, sometimes in the other" (Prévost, 2008, p. 13 [trans.]).[10]

This idealistic vision could not always be pursued and, depending on the circumstances, the two linguistic groups did not always coexist peacefully — sometimes French was more dominant; at other times, English took over. In 1874, for fear of losing its Anglophone students, the College started to favour English and the only courses offered in French were religious studies and French literature, attended solely by Francophone students. But, as a result of a demographic shift at the end of the century, there were again more Francophone students; courses in French became more prominent, thus allowing the College "to restore the teaching of Humanities in French without reducing the English curriculum. On the other hand, Science was only taught in English" (Guindon, 1995, p. XI [trans.]). From the early part of the 20th century until the 1960s, the number of Francophones increased again, representing 56% of the student body. The ratio remained stable until the 1990s, when it shifted again and the number of Anglophone students (70%) exceeded that of Francophone students (30%). It was then that the university adopted the concept of "Francophile" — an Anglophone student able and/or willing to study in French — so as to continue to be true to the mission conferred by the *Act* (University of Ottawa, 1965, paragraph 4(c)): "to further bilingualism and biculturalism and to preserve and develop French culture in Ontario." In 2016, the university had a student population of 42,000, of whom 31% were Francophones and 69% Anglophones. Among the latter, about 1,950 Francophile students were enrolled in the immersion program in the fall of 2016 (University of Ottawa, 2016).

3. DEFINITION OF CONCEPTS

It is important at this stage to precisely define the various terms which will be used in this book. According to the Canadian approach, immersion takes place in the second language, which is the other official language of the country. As Stern (1984) points out,

---

- Bill 22 (*Official Language Act*, 1974)
- Bill 101 (*Charter of the French language*, 1977)

[9] For a comprehensive overview of the legal scope of immersion in Canada, see Chapter 1.

[10] Quoted material translated from French into English by the authors is marked "[trans.]."

"immersion in French began in the Anglo-Canadian school systems ... Consequently, immersive classes are meant for children whose mother tongue is English or any other language than French and who are prepared to study mostly in French" (p. 4). Cummins and Swain (1986) emphasize its cultural dimension: "Immersion describes a situation where children from a similar linguistic and cultural background who have never been in contact with the language of the school find themselves in a classroom where the second language is the language of instruction" (p. 8).

Another characteristic of immersion is that, while language is the "end" or the purpose of instruction, school subjects are the means:

> a method designed for students who are not proficient in the second language when they enter the program. It allows them to acquire this second language through the subjects taught in it from the beginning of the program until they leave school. (Toupin, 1986, p. 7 [trans.])

Consequently, this approach stands out from current European methods such as CLIL (Content and Language Integrated Learning) and ICHLE (Integration of Content and Language in Higher Education), which, at least initially (and in any case, in practice) consider language as an essential tool to acquire professional skills, which are, indeed, the goal of education (for a discussion of this matter, see Chapter 4).

It is also necessary to recall the definitions of such terms as "Francophone" and "Anglophone,"[11] which are now commonly used by English Canadians but which are not part of the standard vocabulary of Americans, for instance, who say "French-speaking" and "English-speaking" (used in formal language). Onésime Reclus (1837–1916), a French geographer from Béarn, the son of an evangelical protestant minister, employed the word "Francophone" for the first time in his book, *France, Algérie et colonies* (1880), to refer to "all those who are or intend to remain or become participants in our language" (p. 423). According to the *Larousse* dictionary, the word means "someone who speaks French" and "it refers to a country where French is the official language, exclusively or among others, or where it is one of the languages spoken there." The same source describes the term "Anglophone" as "someone who speaks English," reverting to the French Academy's original definition in 1986. *Merriam-Webster* further develops the meaning of the term: "consisting of or belonging to an English-speaking population especially in a country where two or more languages are spoken" and traces its first recorded usage back to 1900. According to the same source, the term "Francophone" means "having, or belonging to a population using French as its first or sometimes second language," and appeared for the first time in 1962. As for the term "Allophone" — again referring to *Larousse* — "In Canada, it refers to someone whose mother tongue is neither French nor English."

However, according to Corbeil and Lafrenière (2010), these definitions need further explanation:

> There is no established definition of Francophone. For historical reasons, Statistics Canada has generally used the criterion of mother tongue, that is, the first language learned at home

---

[11] [Translations of dictionary entries are by the authors.]

in childhood and still understood at the time of the census. Statistics based on mother tongue have the advantage of being roughly comparable going back more than half a century.

Other criteria are also used, opening the way for either more inclusive or more restrictive definitions of French-speaking persons. Thus, does the definition of a Francophone in Ontario apply to some 510,000 persons with French as their mother tongue,[1] 540,000 persons with French as their first official language spoken, or 544,000 persons[2] who speak French most often (322,000) or on a regular basis (222,000) at home? Or should a broader definition be considered? Such a definition might include all of the approximately 1.4 million French speakers, or indeed more if we include young children who do not speak French, but who have at least one parent whose mother tongue is French.

[1] The number is 533,000 if all single and multiple responses mentioning French are included.

[2] This number includes all single or multiple responses mentioning French. (p. 7)

In this book, these three terms — Francophone, Anglophone, and Allophone — are generally used according to the dictionary definition, even if, as will be seen on several occasions, Corbeil and Lafrenière's (2010) differentiations qualify their acceptance.

On the other hand, even if the *Trésor de la langue française* defines the term "Francophile" as early as 1919 as "someone who loves France, the French and all things related thereto," its use here is completely different and corresponds to the definition given by the founders of the French Immersion Stream at uOttawa, François Houle: "a group of students from the Anglophone community who enjoy and value living in the French language and culture" (p. 46 [trans.]).[12] In the Canadian context, it indeed mainly concerns Anglophones, but the term also covers Allophones who have settled in Canada and whose second language is English.

Finally, the notions of "majority" and "minority" should be defined as, in many ways, they play a major role when it comes to linguistic groups in Canada. The 2016 census showed that, out of Canada's 34.7 million inhabitants, Anglophones were the majority group, with 56% of the population. Francophones, with 20.6% of the population, no longer represented the largest linguistic minority in Canada. Allophones accounted for almost 21% of the Canadian population (Statistics Canada, 2016).

We recall here the repeated statements and recommendations by Commissioner Fraser to extend the immersion offer to the post-secondary level. Although in this book we focus essentially on uOttawa, since immersion, according to the definition, is exclusively aimed at non-Francophones (Anglophones or Allophones), we should not exclude, however, the other types of programs that, despite being originally intended for Francophones, also accept students from the immersion program. And indeed, given the demolinguistic development and the unequal geographical distribution of Francophones throughout Canada, even at the primary and secondary levels (where education in French is nevertheless guaranteed by law), the small number of students does not allow for the creation or preservation of university programs in French at all Canadian universities:

[12] Interview conducted on November 6, 2012. See Chapter 2.

Students wishing to pursue their university education in French in a minority Francophone environment encounter a few practical obstacles. On the one hand, the university can only integrate those who have already acquired certain skills in French, i.e., mainly students who have attended a Francophone or an immersion school, and/or have mostly spoken French at home. On the other hand, the few Francophone post-secondary institutions outside of Quebec and, especially the only two in Western Canada, are rather underdeveloped compared with Anglophone or Francophone universities in Quebec. Therefore, insufficient skills in French or perceived as such by students, the distance from the chosen university, the limited number of programs and services offered compared with Anglophone universities are key factors of the minority university structure which tend to influence the choice of English as the language of instruction at this academic level. Much like their Francophone feeder schools, attendance at Francophone universities is quite low, exacerbated by the fact that they do not benefit from the support given to Francophone and immersion schools. (Lemaire & Montgomery, 2003 [trans.])

Educational institutions must therefore deal with this reality, which explains why there are many different institutional environments, or *dispositifs*. This notion of *dispositif* has been recognized for some years in educational studies (Charlier & Henri, 2010) as well as in studies relating to languages and culture pedagogy (Derivry-Plard, Alao, Yun-Roger, & Suzuki, 2014; Gohard-Radenkovic, 2006, 2010, 2013b), mostly within the Francophone context.[13] According to the *Dictionnaire de didactique du français langue étrangère et seconde* (Cuq, 2003), a *dispositif* is:

> an intellectual, technical or material set whose function is to ensure the achievement of a project and define the role played by the actors, the associated tools and the steps needed to achieve a previously identified, and possibly pedagogical, task. (p. 74 [trans.]).

Quite a few authors have tried to define the notion of *dispositif* in terms of various fields (philosophy, sociology, communication, etc.) as a concept of "in-between," acting as "a go-between" (Peeters & Charlier, 1999, p. 14). The focus here is on the "hybrid" nature of the notion they proposed, which we define as follows:

> It could be the work product of the analyst and the practitioner who tries to find correlations, links. The term *dispositif* allows for the description of a field comprising heterogeneous elements (for instance, "the explicit" and "the implicit") and for dealing with this heterogeneity.

Foucault, who introduced the concept, described it in these terms: "The *dispositif* itself is the network that can be established between [the] elements" (cited in Defert & Ewald, 2001, p. 299 [trans.]). "To talk about a *dispositif* ensures therefore that entities traditionally regarded as incompatible exist within the argumentation" (Peeters & Charlier, 1999, pp. 15–16 [trans.]).

---

[13] Very early on, Anglophone educators abandoned the notion of "device," considered too static and restrictive—and quite rightly so—and chose the term "institutional environment," initially linked specifically to new technologies but nowadays with a broader meaning to describe any socio-educational *dispositif*.

In the fields of languages and culture pedagogy, one defines *dispositif* as a complex field, made of multiple and interdependent dimensions, in constant co-construction. This conception of the institutional environment as an area "to read" where dynamics operate, involves, on the one hand, the analysis of structures, means, materials, places, technical equipment, programs, steps, methods, etc., brought together by the various stakeholders (actually "actors"), in order to attain their common goal. On the other hand, this understanding of the institutional environment would be incomplete if the researcher did not question the issues, values, legacies, speeches, ideologies, representations, practices, logics, struggles, and so forth, as well as the mutual effects on and between the various actors involved in this institutional environment at different levels. Identifying the relationships between alliance and opposition, concordance and discrepancy, processes of legitimacy and non-legitimacy, remediation and non-remediation, which fall within *de facto* asymmetrical institutional relationships, helps, at the core of these crossed dimensions, to gain a better insight of the various embedded processes at stake in the institutional environment (Gohard-Radenkovic, 2013a, 2013b).

One final word regarding terminology: we have choses to use the term "instructors," as opposed to "professors" or "teachers" for two reasons: first, it is generic; and second, it is derived from "content-based instruction." For that same reason, we have chosen "content" over "discipline." There is no value judgment implied.

4. STRUCTURE OF THE BOOK

The objectives of this book are threefold, unchanged from its 2016 original:

1. Assess what the Canadian government has set up for French immersion at the university level in terms of linguistic policies and their implementation.
2. Identify existing French language immersion structures and programs (*dispositifs*) at the post-secondary level in Canadian universities, and more specifically, at uOttawa.
3. Ask the various actors—that is, students, language and content instructors, plus administrators—about their personal experiences in the *Régime d'immersion en français* (RIF) at uOttawa.

4.1. Framework for Reflection and Analysis

The chosen approach stems from these three objectives, illustrated in Figure 1.

The first part of this book deals with French immersion at university at the macro level, which involves "social determinations in its broadest sense, such as: education policies, linguistic policies of the countries concerned and their education systems themselves" (Porquier & Py, 2004, p. 59 [trans.]).

Jumping ahead, the third part concerns immersion viewed from the inside, as it is experienced daily by its various actors – students, instructors, administrators — and how it affects their personal and professional itineraries. It stands, therefore, at the micro level, which "corresponds to variable-sized moments or sessions but which include unity of time, place and interaction" (Porquier & Py, 2004, p. 59 [trans.]).

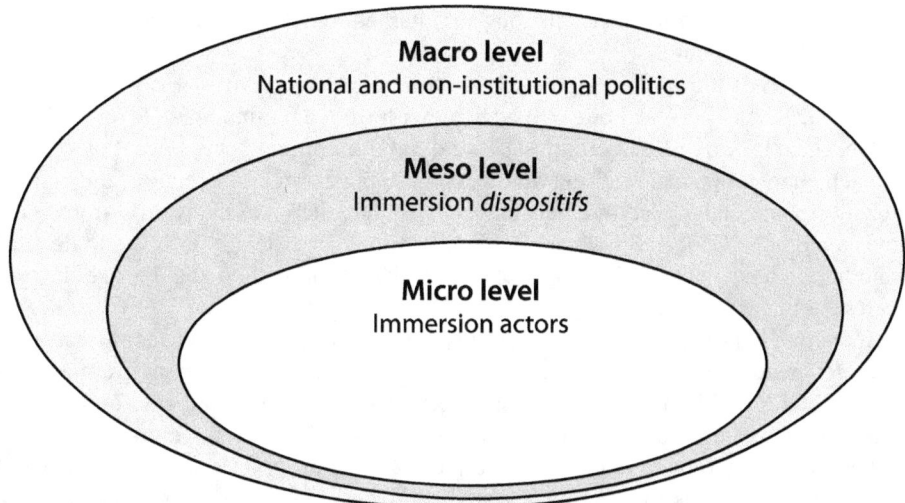

Figure 1: Threefold objectives of this book

However, from a macro/micro perspective, a significant level is missing in order to grasp the complex processes at stake in tertiary institutions — the meso level. In the second part of this book, this missing level will be examined and the ways in which the institutional and political decisions are implemented at the meso level will be explained: how do universities achieve the objectives set by their governing bodies in terms of courses and program offers, pedagogical and methodological choices, financial, logistic and human resources, technical equipment, administrative structures — in other words, *dispositifs*. To this end, Shiosé (1995)[14] marked a paradigmatic turning point when she suggested that both institutional and individual logics be analyzed from a co-constructionist perspective, thus putting actors again at the heart of these strained processes. But again, a "reading" level was missing, namely the meso level, already discussed by researchers in other disciplines[15] in the late 1970s, but which was only introduced into cultural anthropology and sociolinguistics in the early 2000s (Eder, 1991; Helmes Hayes, 2003; Levy, 2002; to name just a few). This meso level was analyzed and clearly revealed the various interacting levels between social micro-processes and macro-processes. Hence, Gohard-Radenkovic's assumption (2003, 2010, 2013a) that this intermediate level covers the whole implementation of educational, migratory, linguistic policies, as well as measures and (usually state-controlled) recommendations, namely their applications and interpretations through what is called "institutional

---

[14] In research conducted at a primary school in the Sherbrooke region, Shiosé showed how the children in one class that she observed for a year came to grips with French while, at the same time, developing their own strategies in response to the discourse and behaviour of the teacher, who "relayed" the official position of the government (who will, in turn, interpret the *doxa* or dominating discourse), to newly arrived pupils.

[15] Particularly in industrial economics, see Marchenay & Morvan (1979).

environments": these three levels in constant interaction have entailed an analytical approach via "embeddedness."[16]

Within each of these three dimensions — macro, meso, micro — various facets will therefore be discussed. Each one will be dealt with from a particular angle, even if they overlap, since they question certain issues and provide common processes. For this reason, each chapter is an autonomous entity, comprising enough information and contextualization to be considered independently. Of course, there are many cross-references between chapters, especially when a topic is covered superficially in one and detailed in another. Indeed, each reader is free to choose their own method and does not have to adhere to a linear reading.

On the one hand, this book will hopefully show how the various academic actors — and more specifically, those in immersion — perceive the immersion program and, on the other hand, highlight the discrepancies between the institutional environments offered by universities and the expectations and needs of immersion actors. The aim of this book is to make recommendations to facilitate the program's sustainability and it will hopefully serve as the reference framework for other universities in Canada and around the world.

REFERENCES

Allophone. (n.d.). *Dictionnaire de français Larousse* [Larousse French dictionary]. www.larousse.fr/dictionnaires/francais/allophone/2427?q=allophone#168109

Anglophone. (n.d.). *Merriam-Webster*. www.merriam-webster.com/dictionary/anglophone

Canada. Canadian Charter of Rights and Freedoms — 1982 Constitution Act. (1985). Canadian Charter of Rights and Freedoms Examination Regulations, SOR/85-781. laws-lois.justice.gc.ca/PDF/SOR-85-781.pdf

Canada. Governor General of Canada. (n.d.). *Great Seal of Canada*. www.gg.ca/en/great-seal-canada

Canada. Office of the Commissioner of Official Languages (OCOL). (n.d.). Annual reports. www.clo-ocol.gc.ca/en/publications/annual_reports/index

Canada. Office of the Commissioner of Official Languages (OCOL). (n.d.). Mandate and roles. www.clo-ocol.gc.ca/en/aboutus/mandate

Canada. Office of the Commissioner of Official Languages (OCOL). (2009). *Two languages, a world of opportunities: Second-language learning in Canada's universities*. Ottawa: Minister of Public Works and Government Services Canada. www.languesofficielles.gc.ca/sites/default/files/uni_e.pdf

Canada. Official Languages Act. (1969). Official Languages Act (1969) 1970, R.S.C, chapter 0-2. www.uottawa.ca/clmc/official-languages-act-1969

Canada. Justice Laws Website. (n.d.). Part IX: Commissioner of Official Languages (continued), section 56(1). laws-lois.justice.gc.ca/eng/acts/O-3.01/page-6.html

---

[16] As proposed by Granovetter (1995). See also the concepts of *Einbettung*, developed by Giordano (1992), or the term *emboîtements successifs*, used by Thiesse (1997, p. 17).

Canadian Centre for Studies and Research on Bilingualism and Language Planning (CCERBAL). (2012, February). International forum: *Immersion at the university level: Models, challenges and prospects*, University of Ottawa. ccerbal.uottawa.ca/en/immersion-2012

Charlier, B., & Henri, F. (2010). *Apprendre avec les technologies*. Paris: Presses universitaires de France.

Corbeil, J.-P., & Lafrenière, S. (2010). *Portrait of official-language minorities in Canada: Francophones in Ontario*. Catalogue no. 89-642-X — No. 001. Ottawa: Statistics Canada. www150.statcan.gc.ca/n1/pub/89-642-x/89-642-x2010001-eng.pdf

Cummins, J., & Swain, M. (1986). *Bilingualism in education: Aspects of theory, research, and practice*. London: Longman.

Cuq, J.-P. (Ed.). (2003). *Dictionnaire de didactique du français langue étrangère et seconde*. Paris: CLE International.

Defert, D., & Ewald, F. (2001). *Michel Foucault: Dits et écrits II, 1976–1988*. Paris: Gallimard.

Derivry-Plard, M., Alao, G., Yun-Roger, S., & Suzuki, E. (2014). *Dispositifs éducatifs en contexte mondialisé et didactique plurilingue et pluriculturelle*. Bern: Peter Lang.

Durocher, R. (2013). [The] quiet revolution. In *The Canadian Encyclopedia*. www.thecanadianencyclopedia.ca/en/article/quiet-revolution

Eder, K. (1991). Au-delà du sujet historique: vers une construction théorique des acteurs collectifs. *L'homme et la société*, *25*, 121–140.

Francophile. (n.d.). *Trésor de la langue française*. www.cnrtl.fr/definition/francophile

Francophone. (n.d.). *Dictionnaire de français Larousse* [Larousse French dictionary]. www.larousse.fr/dictionnaires/francais/francophone/35064?q=francophone#350342016

Francophone. (n.d.). *Merriam-Webster*. www.merriam-webster.com/dictionary/francophone

Giordano, C. (1992). *Die Betrogenen der Geschichte: Überlagerungsmentalität und Überlagerungsrationalität in mediterranen Gesellschaften*. Frankfurt: Campus Verlag.

Gohard-Radenkovic, A. (2003). Politique ethnoculturelle du gouvernement malaisien et ses effets sur le statut des langues dans le supérieur: réflexions à partir d'une expérience. In A. Akkari & S. Perez (Eds.), *Debates in education: Comparative analysis* (pp. 29–42). Biel/Bienne: HEP-Bejune.

Gohard-Radenkovic, A. (2006). *La relation à l'altérité en situation de mobilité dans une perspective anthropologique de la communication*. Post-doctoral degree in communications, Université Lumière-Lyon II.

Gohard-Radenkovic, A. (2010). Politiques de gestion de la pluralité linguistique: leurs effets sur les logiques des institutions et les logiques des individus. In F. Ruegg & A. Boscoboinik (Eds.), *From Palermo to Penang: A journey into political anthropology/Hommage à/for Christian Giordano* (pp. 119–135). Berlin: Freiburg Studies in Social Anthropology/LiT Verlag.

Gohard-Radenkovic, A. (2013a). L'émergence d'une pédagogie de l'immersion. *OLBI Working Papers*, *6*, 143–149. uottawa.scholarsportal.info/ojs/index.php/ILOB-OLBI/article/view/1136/988

Gohard-Radenkovic, A. (2013b). Politiques de rétention au Canada: écarts entre logiques des acteurs de l'institution et logiques des étudiants étrangers en situation de transition. In C. Hauser, P. Milani, M. Pâquet, & S. Skenderovic (Eds.), *Sociétés de migrations en débat. Québec–Canada–Suisse: approches comparées* (pp. 97–112). Quebec: Presses de l'Université Laval and Société jurassienne d'émulation.

Granovetter, M. (1985). Economic action and social structure: The problem of embeddedness. *American Journal of Sociology, 91*, 481–510. www.jstor.org/stable/2780199

Guindon, R. (1995). *La dualité linguistique à l'Université d'Ottawa: coexistence féconde, 1936–1965.* Ottawa: University of Ottawa Press.

Helmes Hayes, R. (2003). L'analyse des classes sociales dans la sociologie canadienne de langue anglaise (1895–1965). *Cahiers de recherche sociologique, 39*, 15–53.

Knoerr, H., & Weinberg, A. (Eds.). (2013). *OLBI Working Papers* [thematic issue: *French immersion at the university level*], 6.

Knoerr, H., Weinberg, A., Gohard-Radenkovic, A. (Eds.). (2016). *L'immersion française à l'université: politiques et pédagogies.* Ottawa: University of Ottawa Press.

Lambert, W.E., & Tucker, G.R. (1972). *Bilingual education of children: The St. Lambert experiment.* Rowley, MA: Newbury House.

Laurendeau, A., & Dunton, A.D. (1965). *Rapport préliminaire de la Commission Laurendeau–Dunton sur le bilinguisme et le biculturalisme.* Ottawa: Queen's Printer.

Lemaire, M., & Montgomery, C. (2003). Exogamie et choix de la langue d'enseignement au niveau universitaire au Canada: six études de cas. *DiversCité Langues, 8.* www.teluq.uquebec.ca/diverscite/entree.htm

Levy, R. (2002). Meso-social structures and stratification analysis: A missing link? *Revue suisse de sociologie, 28*, 193–216.

Marchesnay, M., & Morvan, Y. (1979). Micro, macro, meso. *Revue d'économie industrielle, 8*, 99–103. www.persee.fr/doc/rei_0154-3229_1979_num_8_1_1931

Mills, S. (2007). *The empire within: Montreal, the sixties, and the forging of a radical imagination.* (Unpublished doctoral dissertation). Department of History, Queen's University, Kingston, ON. qspace.library.queensu.ca/bitstream/handle/1974/900/Mills_Sean_W_200710_PhD.pdf

Miquelon, D. (2006). [The] conquest. In *The Canadian Encyclopedia.* www.thecanadianencyclopedia.ca/en/article/conquest

Peeters, H., & Charlier, P. (1999). Contributions à une théorie du dispositif. *Hermès, 25*, 14–23.

Porquier, R., & Py, B. (2004). *Apprentissage d'une langue étrangère: contextes et discours.* Paris: Didier.

Prévost, M. (2008). *L'Université d'Ottawa depuis 1848.* Ottawa: University of Ottawa.

Quebec. (1969). *An Act to promote the French Language in Quebec* (Bill 63; *Loi pour promouvoir la langue française au Québec*). www.oqlf.gouv.qc.ca/50ans/images/Bill_63.pdf

Quebec. (1974). *Official Language Act* (Bill 22; *Loi sur la langue officielle.* National Assembly of Quebec. web.archive.org/web/20041120120718/http://www.oqlf.gouv.qc.ca/charte/reperes/Loi_22.pdf

Quebec. (1977). *Charter of the French language* (Bill 101; *Charte de la langue française*. www.legisquebec.gouv.qc.ca/en/showdoc/cs/C-11

Reclus, O. (1880). *France, Algérie et colonies*. Paris: Hachette.

Shiosé, Y. (1995). *Les loups sont-ils québécois? Les mutations sociales à l'école primaire*. Quebec: Presses de l'Université de Laval.

Statistics Canada. (2016). *Language highlight tables, 2016 Census: Mother tongue by age (Total), % distribution (2016) for the population excluding institutional residents of Canada, provinces and territories, 2016 Census — 100% Data*. www12.statcan.gc.ca/census-recensement/2016/dp-pd/hlt-fst/lang/Table.cfm?Lang=E&T=11&Geo=00&SP=1&view=2&age=1

Stern, H.H. (1984). The immersion phenomenon. *Language and Society*, *12*, 4–7.

Thiesse, A.M. (1997). *Ils apprenaient la France*. Paris: Éditions de la Maison des Sciences de l'homme.

Toupin, L. (1986). Une terminologie en immersion propre à l'ACPI [Association canadienne des professeurs d'immersion]. *Les Nouvelles de l'ACPI*, *9*, 7. www.acpi.ca/journaux/V9N2.pdf

University of Ottawa. (n.d.). CCERBAL: Immersion 2012. ccerbal.uottawa.ca/en/immersion-2012

University of Ottawa. (1965). Administration and governance: 1965 University of Ottawa Act. www.uottawa.ca/administration-and-governance/1965-university-of-ottawa-act

University of Ottawa. (2016). Institutional research and planning: Quick facts 2015: Students. www.uottawa.ca/institutional-research-planning/resources/facts-figures/quick-facts

CHAPTER 1

Solid Foundations:
French Immersion Language Planning and Policies in Canada

Sylvie A. Lamoureux

INTRODUCTION

IN THE CANADIAN EDUCATIONAL CONTEXT, there are clearly defined standards when it comes to the official languages and the right to education. Article 23 of the Canadian Charter of Rights and Freedoms (1982) specifically outlines the legal guarantee regarding access to education in the minority official language: as it stands, English in Quebec, and French in the other provinces and territories. This legal right applies to a large portion, if not the entirety of compulsory schooling, depending on the relevant school authority, where enrolment numbers warrant. Case law precedents, such as *Mahe v. Alberta* (1990; see also Foucher, 2011), specify that this guarantee includes not only the right to education in the minority language, but also the management of educational institutions. The appellants in the Mahe case requested that the Supreme Court of Canada determine whether the rights referred to in Article 23 of the Charter grant speakers of the minority official language the full management and control of educational institutions as well as the curriculum and, where applicable, the right to outline the scope and nature of this management and control. Ultimately, the Court was faced with the decision of ruling on the incompatibility of certain articles of Alberta's School Act (2000) with Article 23 of the Charter. In a historic decision, the Supreme Court ruled in favour of the appellants, which led to the creation of independent school boards in 1994, with full managerial oversight in Alberta. This precedent recognized the right of speakers of the official minority languages of Canada to manage and control education and their educational institutions, where numbers warrant.

However, this constitutional guarantee does not include the right to post-secondary education in the language of the minority (Giroux, 2017), nor the right to access schooling in the second language in Canada, whether for primary, secondary, or post-secondary education. This raises the following question: Which language plans or policies determine Canadians' access to French immersion programs for second-language learning, in elementary, secondary, or post-secondary education?

Before answering this question, it is necessary to define the terms "language policy" and "language planning." Eloy (1997) distinguishes between both notions: "It must, however, be acknowledged from the outset that lexicon causes confusion, given that these comprehensive terms both specifically define a 'policy' or 'policies' " (p. 7 [trans.]). According to Labrie (cited in Eloy, 1997), " 'language planning' designates deliberate efforts to influence, or that have the effect of influencing, the behaviours of others, with regard to the acquisition, structure, and functional distribution of their linguistic codes" (p. 7 [trans.]).

Both authors synthesize the various rhetorical propositions regarding a decisional process (particularly based on Rubin, 1971); they propose a five-step descriptive framework that Eloy (1997) summarizes as follows:

- studies conducted
- policy formulation
- decision-making
- implementation
- assessment

Eloy continues: "This plan calls for a fairly literal interpretation, thus confirming the predominance of the 'deliberate' nature of language planning" (1997, p. 8 [trans.]).

Daoust and Maurais (1987), on the other hand, have defined "language plan" as "various general plans or definitions of language planning, as a method of government intervention on languages" (p. 29).

We must therefore be aware of the fact that the relationship between the terms "language policy" and "language planning" is unclear. However, although they cover different situations and measures, they also imply different levels and degrees of intervention on the part of governmental bodies, as well as levels and degrees of application — or interpretation — by their various institutional, educational, or academic intermediaries, onto language speakers, their practices, behaviours, and sociolinguistic "choices."

Whereas the availability of immersion in universities for students of French as a second language (henceforth FSL) or those enrolled in Francophone programs[1] aimed at graduates of elementary and secondary schools, has increased in almost all Canadian provinces, the answer to the aforementioned question has remained less studied

---

[1] It is important to distinguish between these two types of programs:

a. Post-secondary French immersion programs, such as the *Régime d'immersion en français* (RIF) at the University of Ottawa, are open to all French learners, no matter what FSL programs they participated in during their compulsory schooling (Core, Extended, or Immersion), as long as they achieve a minimal passing grade on a French-language test. Students are registered for programs in English, take academic courses in French with Francophones as well as FSL courses, and have access to a significant number of support resources. An "Immersion" designation appears on the post-secondary diploma for those who meet the program's requirements.

b. There are also Francophone post-secondary programs in French or bilingual institutions that target graduates of French immersion secondary school programs. These students are registered in French programs and integrated into French classes; they take FSL courses, without having access to the support structures that are an integral part of a program such as the RIF.

than the K–12[2] immersion classroom experience or teaching methods. First, we will briefly situate the origins of French immersion in Canada in its socio-historical context. Second, we will identify the language policies and plans at various levels of government that oversee or support this type of program. The goal is to provide some possible answers that demonstrate the importance of the relationship between provincial and territorial governments, on the one hand, and federal bodies, on the other, in the context of second-language learning in Canada, while shining a light on a fundamental fragility.

1. BRIEF HISTORY

The immersion model of teaching FSL is a Canadian innovation that has proved its worth across the country and abroad, whether for the teaching of French or of other languages. Its origins, in 1965,[3] in the Montreal suburb of Saint Lambert—where a group of Anglophone parents appealed to bilingualism experts from McGill University to develop and test a teaching program for FSL—have been thoroughly researched and documented, and feature prominently in any history of immersion in Canada (see Swain & Johnson, 1997). These parents wanted to afford their children, who were in kindergarten at the time, the opportunity to acquire sufficient proficiency over the course of their education to allow them to easily communicate with their fellow Francophone Quebecers and to actively participate in the political and economic development of the province. In other words, they wanted their children to be bilingual; hence, their desire for functional bilingualism as an educational objective (Ouellet, 1990). This initiative emerged during a period of great sociolinguistic tension throughout the country between what MacLennan (1945) had referred to as "the two solitudes." The era was marked by the Quiet Revolution[4] in Quebec and the launch of the Commission on Bilingualism and Biculturalism in 1963, led by Laurendeau and Dunton.

It is important to remember that Francophone–Anglophone relations have been in near constant flux since Confederation in 1867, alternating between dissent and reconciliation, depending on the policies spearheaded by the federal government. In the 1960s, while Quebec was shaken by the Quiet Revolution and influenced by controversial remarks made by French President Charles de Gaulle,[5] the emergence of Quebec nationalism and the recognition of the French language in the economic, political, social, and cultural spheres played a crucial role in its relationship with Canada. At the federal

---

[2] Kindergarten to Grade 12; that is, ages 5 to 17.
[3] While the Saint Lambert project is cited as the origin of immersion in Canada, this attribution is the subject of some controversy. According to Ouellet (1990, p. 22), the Toronto French School, a private institution, and therefore one that did not receive government funding, would have been the model for the Saint Lambert project. This school, which emerged in Ontario in 1961–1962, had a balanced bilingual education as its primary goal.
[4] This period (roughly 1960 to 1979) was marked by profound changes led by the government in power, changes emerging from a desire for modernization and for Quebecers to reclaim leadership of their province (*The Canadian Encyclopedia*, 2013, "Quiet revolution").
[5] De Gaulle's controversial "*Vive le Québec libre*" phrase in July of 1967 was an endorsement of Quebec's sovereignist [independence] movement.

government level, Prime Minister Lester B. Pearson launched the Royal Commission on Bilingualism and Biculturalism (RCBB), with the mandate (Canada, RCBB, 1967):

> to inquire into and report upon the existing state of bilingualism and biculturalism in Canada and to recommend what steps should be taken to develop the Canadian Confederation on the basis of an equal partnership between the two founding races, taking into account the contribution made by the other ethnic groups to the cultural enrichment of Canada and the measures that should be taken to safeguard that contribution ... (Book I, p. xxi)

Some of the commission's recommendations were subsequently implemented by Pierre Elliott Trudeau's government, particularly the 1969 Official Languages Act (OLA), which formally recognized English and French as Canada's official languages, and imposed new linguistic requirements on certain sectors of the federal government.[6] This political sea change allowed for the emergence of immersion in Quebec (Lambert & Tucker, 1972). The teaching of French through immersion soon spread throughout Quebec and, subsequently all of English Canada, contributing to the rise of elementary and secondary immersion programs nationwide, thereby promoting bilingual education. Consequently, bilingualism entered the core of Canadian political discourse, emerging as a "Canadian value" (Canada, Standing Senate Committee on Official Languages, 2013). Through immersion, Canadian society advocates a politically, economically, and ideologically motivated reconciliation that promotes the pursuit of a higher rate of bilingualism. At present, the Canadian government's policy aims to give Canadian students the opportunity to acquire skills, knowledge, and international specialization related to employment, notably language skills and cultural understanding from a Canadian perspective.

2. LEGISLATIVE FRAMEWORK

2.1. The Official Languages Act

It is within this law that we find elements of language planning that address access to second-language learning in Canada. We must bear in mind that Canada is a federation, where education falls under the jurisdiction of provincial and territorial governments.

The primary aim of the Official Languages Act is not the education of Canadians. Rather, this law reiterates the status of English and French as the two official languages of Canada and provides clarification regarding the use of the official languages "in all the institutions of the Parliament and government of Canada," as well as in the "laws of Canada and the courts established by Parliament" (Canada, OLA, 1985, p. 1). The law's objective was not to render all Canadians bilingual, but to allow "guarantees relating to the right of any member of the public to communicate with, and to receive available services from, any institution of the Parliament or government of Canada in either official language" (p. 1). Furthermore, the preamble declares the federal government's commitment to:

---

[6] This law was then enforced by the Canadian Charter of Rights and Freedoms, which was adopted in 1982.

cooperating with provincial governments and their institutions to support the development of English and French linguistic minority communities, to provide services in both English and French, to respect the constitutional guarantees of minority language educational rights and to enhance opportunities for all to learn both English and French. (p. 2)

The stipulations that allow the federal government to support the teaching of the official languages are found in Part VII of the Official Languages Act (Canada, OLA, 1988), alongside the responsibility of the territorial and provincial governments on the matter of education. Paragraph 41(1) outlines the federal government's commitment with regard to:

(a) enhancing the vitality of the English and French linguistic minority communities in Canada and supporting and assisting their development; and
(b) fostering the full recognition and use of both English and French in Canadian society. (p. 20)

The practical application of these concrete measures is implemented "while respecting the jurisdiction and powers of the provinces," as specified in paragraph 41(2) (p. 20). Article 42 delegates the coordination of these measures to the Minister of Canadian Heritage, and paragraph 43(1) specifies the implementation mandate (Canada, OLA, 1988):

43 (1) The Minister of Canadian Heritage shall take such measures as that Minister considers appropriate to advance the equality of status and use of English and French in Canadian society and, without restricting the generality of the foregoing, may take measures to

...

(b) encourage and support the learning of English and French in Canada;
(c) foster an acceptance and appreciation of both English and French by members of the public;

...

(e) encourage and assist provincial governments to provide opportunities for everyone in Canada to learn both English and French; ... (pp. 20–21)

Aside from the mention of positive measures, no additional guideline or stipulation defines expectations with regard to the teaching of the official languages, nor the type of training to favour in order to support second-language learning.

2.2. Positive Measures

The positive measures implemented by the Minister of Canadian Heritage to outline the learning of French and English as second languages are de facto funding opportunities through the Official Languages Funding Program, which is divided into five parts:

(i)   Development of Official Language Minority Communities
(ii) Minority Language Education
(iii) Second Language Learning
(iv) Promotion of Linguistic Duality
(v)   Bilingual Advantage Initiative (Canada, Department of Canadian Heritage, n.d., "Official languages support programs")

Part (iii), regarding second language learning (Canada, Department of Canadian Heritage, n.d., "Official languages support programs") states that it:

> supports programs and activities offered by the provinces and territories for the instruction of English and French as first and second official languages at all levels of learning. This component also aims to increase the production and dissemination of knowledge and innovative methods and tools, to support language instruction.

Funding opportunities for the official languages also include a Language Learning and Exchange Programs component, which is administered in cooperation between provinces and territories, and the Council of Ministers of Education, Canada (CMEC) (n.d.). These include:

- *Odyssey*: language assistants to work full-time for a year in a different part of the country (salary)
- *Destination Clic*: French enrichment for Francophone students in minority environments (bursary)
- *Explore*: second-language summer program (bursary)

These one-time programs complement the learning of first and second languages in compulsory schooling and post-secondary environments (Canada, Department of Canadian Heritage, n.d., "Official languages support programs").

Other programs include the *Young Canada Works in Both Official Languages Initiative*, managed by Canadian Heritage, as well as the *Languages at Work* program (Canada, Department of Canadian Heritage, n.d. "Official languages support programs"). The latter is reserved for the *Explore* program, and offered collaboratively by the *Explore* and *Young Canada Works in Both Official Languages* initiatives. Managed by the Fédération de la jeunesse canadienne-française (FJCJ), this program offers students opportunities to continue learning their second language and gain summer job experience.

2.3. Federal and Provincial Government Agreements

The federal government's contribution to the provinces and territories to support official language teaching takes the form of intergovernmental collaborative agreements that support access to official language teaching in minority language communities and access to second-language learning. The provinces and territories must devote a sum that is at least equal to the federal government's commitments.

Intergovernmental cooperation in minority language education (Canada, Department of Canadian Heritage, n.d., "Intergovernmental cooperation") consists of two parts: one agreement coordinated by the CMEC, and another with each of the provincial and territorial governments. Once again, each party must ensure funding at least equal in sum to the amount allotted by the federal government. Both agreements must be carried out within a common strategic framework, wherein each objective involves six areas of results pertaining to education, for which provinces and territories establish plans of action with targets and performance indicators (CMEC, 2013, pp. 4–5; emphasis added):

- student participation
- *provisions of program*
- student performance
- enriched school environment
- *access to post-secondary education*
- support for educational staff and research

Highlighted in this list are the first two mentions of language planning with respect to the availability of second-language learning programs and access to post-secondary education. The last collaborative agreement was concluded in 2013 (for more details on this agreement, see CMEC, 2013). But which programs receive this funding in the Canadian provinces and territories?

3. DEMOGRAPHIC CONTEXT

Before addressing the FSL programs made available through federal funding, we must keep in mind the demolinguistic situation in Canada. The 2016 census shows that, of Canada's 34.7 million inhabitants, 19.4 million declared English as their mother tongue, while 7.1 million declared French, and 7.3 million declared another, non-official language (Statistics Canada, 2016b). Therefore, if Anglophones represented Canada's linguistic majority (about 57%), the "majority" linguistic minority is made up of Francophones (about 21% according to 2016 census data).

But this situation must be considered within the context of the specific provinces and territories: whereas in Newfoundland and Labrador, Prince Edward Island, and Nova Scotia, Anglophones make up 90% of the population, this proportion decreases to 65% in New Brunswick, 28% in Nunavut, and slumps to just 8% in Quebec. Francophones, for their part, are mainly present in Quebec (86%), in New Brunswick (around 35%), and in Ontario (7%) (Statistics Canada, 2016b).

Therefore, while Anglophones are numerically the majority in Canada, they are the minority in Quebec, where the population is mainly Francophone. However, Francophones outside of Quebec (Franco-Ontarians, Franco-Manitobans, Franco-Saskatchewanians, and others) are a double minority, both in their country and in their province.

Furthermore, the number of Anglophones has been steadily declining (more sharply than the number of Francophones) in favour of Allophones (those whose mother tongue is neither English nor French) from 1996 to 2016. In Ontario, this evolution is especially significant since, from 1951 to 2016, the proportion of Anglophones went from 81.7% to 68.2%; Francophones, from 7.4% to 3.8%; and Allophones, from 10.9% to 25.6%. The increase in Allophones is even more marked in Quebec, where they now outnumber Anglophones (17.3% compared to 7.6%). The majority mother tongue declared by Allophones is Chinese (more than a million speakers of Mandarin and Cantonese, according to the 2016 census), followed distantly by Punjabi, Tagalog, and Spanish (about half a million speakers each), and then Arabic, Italian, and German (400,000 to 485,000 speakers) (Leclerc, 2019).

Given this demolinguistic evolution, the official language that Allophones choose and the possibility for Anglophones to enter the post-secondary immersion program have been key factors for linguistic balance in Canada. Institutional intervention is crucial in this regard, since it can influence this choice. It is therefore important to question the role of institutional actors in their various manifestations, notably legal and educational, in the adoption of linguistic behaviours—particularly the language shift toward French or English. Thus, Quebec has chosen the path of legislation (Charter of the French Language, 1977) to impose French on Allophones as the language of schooling, by reserving access to English schools only for children of Canadians who have attended Anglophone schools in Canada, while making French the official language of institutions, business, and administration. One of the main consequences of this legislation has been a spectacular increase in the rate of attendance of French schools by Allophones, from 14.6% to 87.5% between 1971 and 2012. Furthermore, the rate of language shift among Allophone students toward French increased from 21.0% in 1983–1984 to 67.3% in 2012–2013 (Quebec, MELS, 2014). Thus:

> The Charter of the French Language has had a significant impact on education. The reversal of the traditional tendency of allophone students to attend English school, their shift toward French, and the decrease in the proportion of these students who are eligible to attend school in English are direct results of the enforcement of the Charter in educational environments. (p. 3 [trans.])

Corbeil and Lafrenière (2010) emphasize the role of schools in Ontario in the choice and continued use of French in non-Francophones—Allophones as well as Anglophones:

> Knowledge of French among non-Francophones is usually more widespread among persons with English as their mother tongue than among those with a mother tongue other than French or English, except for the 10 to 14 age group. Knowledge of French is also much more widespread among young persons, because of their attending programs of French immersion or French as a second language. Because the learning of French usually takes place at school, the bilingualism rate peaks in the 15 to 19 age group, which covers the period when young people are completing their secondary education. (p. 38)

The importance of the educational option seems to highlight another fact pointed out by Corbeil and Lafrenière (2010), who state that:

> the ability of young Anglophones to maintain their knowledge of French as a second language diminishes over time.... [W]hen we consider youths aged 15 to 19 in 1996, we observe that their bilingualism rate as reported in that census (18%) falls to 14.8% in 2001, whereas this cohort are aged 20 to 24 years, and to 13.2% in 2006 when the same cohort is aged 25 to 29 years. A similar trend is observed among youths who were 15 to 19 years of age in 2001 and who are between 20 and 24 years of age five years later. (p. 39)

More recent data from the 2016 census show that, although the bilingualism rate seems to peak, the decline over time persists. Although 24.7% of young Canadians aged 15 to 19 report a knowledge of both official languages, this figure declines with age: 23.4% in the 20 to 24 age group, 21.7% in the 21 to 44 age group, 16.8% in the

45 to 64 age group, and only 14% in the 65+ age group (Statistics Canada, 2016a).[7] In fact, this rupture coincides with the end of the immersive option after secondary school, when students, no longer having the possibility to pursue studies in the second language, turn to post-secondary education in English. Hence, without the opportunity to practice their French, they progressively lose their working knowledge of the language.

4. THE STATUS OF FSL LEARNING IN THE PROVINCES AND TERRITORIES

4.1. Overview

In Canada, education falls under provincial jurisdiction, but in general terms, the teaching of FSL is divided into two types of programs: Core French, on the one hand, and immersion programs on the other.

- *Core French:* also known as French as a second language (FSL) in Alberta and British Columbia, and as Basic French in Manitoba; a French as a second language program where the French language is taught as a subject in the classroom according to the established number of minutes per week or per term.

- *French Immersion:* A French as a second language program where French is used as the language of instruction for certain subjects as well as art classes for the entirety or for a significant portion of the school day.

There are are some alternatives to these two major trends: on a Canada-wide scale, the approach to *Intensive French* is an enrichment of the basic French program, with three to four times the number of hours regularly scheduled during a concentrated period (five months) in Grade 5 or 6 (students aged 11 and 12) (see also Canada, Office of the Commissioner of Official Languages, n.d., "Accessing").

A memorandum presented in November 2013 to the Standing Senate Committee on Official Languages by Canadian Parents for French (CPF) establishes the status of the FSL programs available in the provinces and territories of Canada. CPF is of the opinion that, in spite of significant financial support from the federal government, these programs do not have enough influence to affect the development of official policies on the matter of mandatory FSL, or access to various kinds of FSL learning programs (2013, p. 3). This inevitably leads to unequal access to these kinds of programs more generally, notably immersion programs, whether early or late.

The participation rate of Canadian students registered in FSL programs in English-language schools, regardless of program type, ranges from 1.8% of the student population in Nunavut to 85.8% in New Brunswick,[8] for a national average of 46% (if we include Quebec). As for participation in immersion programs,[9] the rate ranges from 6.9% in Alberta to 29% in New Brunswick (CPF, n.d., "FSL enrolment").

---

[7] Note that immersion in Canada became widespread from the 1970s onward.
[8] New Brunswick is the only officially bilingual Canadian province. This status is written in the Canadian Charter of Rights and Freedoms (1982).
[9] Immersion is not an educational option in Nunavut.

In the Francophone minority context (that is, outside of Quebec), while all Canadian provinces and territories offer access to an FSL program, learning French is optional in Alberta, British Columbia, Manitoba, Nunavut, the Northwest Territories, and Saskatchewan. In Manitoba and British Columbia, students must study a language other than English in Grades 5 through 8, yet French is but one choice among other languages (CPF, 2013, p. 9).

Moreover, no policy explicitly mentions that French immersion programs are mandatory. Immersion is therefore but one option among others for learning FSL and does not benefit from any Canadian government language planning to ensure access, whether for elementary, secondary, or post-secondary education.

4.2. The Case of Ontario

4.2.1. The FSL Situation

In Ontario, Canada's most populated province, which boasts the largest Francophone population outside of Quebec, teaching of French is mandatory from Grades 4 to 8 (for children aged 9 to 14 years).[10] Ontario legislation outlines three types of programs: Core French, Extended French and French immersion. In addition, school boards are free to choose the types of programs offered in each of their schools (Ontario, Ministry of Education, 2014):

- *Core French:* Students learn French as a subject. At the elementary level, they must accumulate at least 600 hours of French instruction by the end of Grade 8. At the secondary level, academic, applied and open courses are offered for Grades 9 and 10; university preparation and open courses are offered for Grades 11 and 12.
- *Extended French:* Students learn French as a subject and French serves as the language of instruction in at least one other subject. At the elementary level, at least 25 per cent of all instruction is provided in French. At the secondary level, academic courses are offered for Grades 9 and 10; university preparation courses are offered for Grades 11 and 12. In the Extended French program, students accumulate seven credits in French: four are FSL language courses and three are other subjects in which French is the language of instruction.
- *French Immersion:* Students learn French as a subject and French serves as the language of instruction in two or more other subjects. At the elementary level, at least 50 per cent of all instruction is provided in French. At the secondary level, academic and applied courses are offered for Grades 9 and 10; university preparation and open courses are offered for Grades 11 and 12. In the French Immersion program, students accumulate ten credits in French: four are FSL language courses and six are other subjects in which French is the language of instruction.

In Ontario, in 2016–2017, 51.9% of students were enrolled in FSL programs: 39.8% in Core French (which also includes Extended French) and 12% in French immersion,

---

[10] Educational policies in Ontario grant the management of a school the power to replace the compulsory study of French by that of another subject, notably for First Nations, Métis, and Inuit students who choose to study their ancestral language.

which represented, respectively, 985,970 and 229,062 students, from kindergarten to Grade 12 (CPF, n.d. "FSL enrolment").

These statistics do not take into account students registered in the RIF program at uOttawa, which welcomes young Canadians who have studied in any type of FSL program.[11]

4.2.2. Legislative Framework

Whereas the Canadian Charter of Rights and Freedoms does not extend the legal guarantee of access to French education in minority environments to include college and university studies, access to post-secondary education in French is a priority for the Canadian Heritage funding programs for official languages. In Ontario, access to university studies in French is a current issue, as evidenced in 2011 by the launch of Ontario's *Politique d'aménagement linguistique* (PAL) (MTCU, 2011a). This policy concerns the two French-language colleges in the province, La Cité (in Ottawa) and the Collège Boréal (in Sudbury), as well as various bilingual university institutions or those which offer programs in French: uOttawa, Laurentian University (Sudbury), Saint Paul University (Ottawa), York University's Glendon College (Toronto), Dominican University College (Ottawa), the Université de Hearst, the University of Sudbury, and the University of Toronto's Ontario Institute for Studies in Education (OISE).

Ontario is the only Canadian province that has adopted a language planning policy extending beyond the secondary level, which makes PAL a unique document in Canada. Although this policy does not guarantee any new financial investment to support the development or the increase in available French-language training or post-secondary programs, it does, however, recognize the participation of Francophiles in post-secondary and French-language training programs in Ontario, as well as the need to support students developing their language skills. It must be mentioned that the teaching of FSL in elementary and secondary schools in Ontario occurs in English-language institutions overseen by Anglophone school boards.

While immersion students at these levels take content courses in their second language, they no longer have this possibility at the post-secondary level, where their only option is to take these courses in programs designed for native speakers of French. They therefore constitute a significant critical mass to support the availability of French programs in a minority context. As stated in PAL (MTCU, 2011a):

> The policy is designed to encourage students from these [Francophone and Francophile] groups to enter the province's French-language and bilingual postsecondary education and training institutions. Higher enrolments will foster an increase in the number, range, and quality of French-language programs; will strengthen the ability of these institutions to attract and retain students from across Canada and from other countries; and will provide improved access to lifelong learning opportunities for francophones and for all Ontario residents. (p. 7)

PAL therefore places post-secondary studies and French-language training at the heart of promoting continuity with regard to recruitment and retention within

---

[11] Chapters 6 through 11 are devoted to the description and analysis of RIF.

French-language establishments (Ontario, MTCU, 2011b), a concept that shares parallels with "institutional completeness" (Breton, 1964).[12] If we apply this principle to French education in Ontario, it appears that the possibility of pursuing studies at this level in one's mother tongue (in this case, French) encourages the public to choose education in French right from the beginning. Thus, the availability of programs in French at the post-secondary level promotes the presence of Francophones at all levels of compulsory education. Could the same logic of continuity, of institutional completeness, apply to FSL learning in the context of college and university French immersion programs?

CONCLUSION

Our analysis of language policies and planning for FSL education in Canada demonstrates not only the fragility of the availability of French immersion programs at the elementary and secondary levels in the territories and provinces, but also that of the access to post-secondary studies in French. We note that half of the Canadian provinces and territories, in spite of federal government funding designated as part of "positive measures" by virtue of paragraph 43(1) of Canada's Official Languages Act, do not impose any FSL learning requirement in compulsory education. This is despite the existence of various kinds of programs in elementary and secondary school.[13] It is worth noting that no legal guarantee protects access to education in French at the post-secondary level in communities where French is the minority language. These two findings illustrate the precariousness of access to immersion programs supporting FSL learning in Canada.

Rethinking French-language post-secondary studies for FSL learners in light of the concept of Breton's "institutional completeness" (1964) and PAL (Ontario, MTCU, 2011a) raises three questions:

1. Without increased access to post-secondary French programs and support to guide students learning French in their transition from a context in which they study in French with other Anglophones toward a context in which they study in French with Francophones, why would young people and their families invest in French immersion studies at the secondary level, let alone in elementary school?

2. Without access to a job market, in both the public and private sectors, that demands and values bilingual employees, why would students pursue post-secondary studies in French and develop their professional skills in French?

3. What language policies or planning initiatives must be implemented by provinces and territories to ensure access to French immersion programs at the elementary, secondary, and post-secondary levels?

---

[12] Charron (1997) quotes Dallaire (1995), who explains that, according to Breton (1964), institutional completeness "refers to the social organization of an ethnic group and its capacity to mobilize resources in order to provide itself with a network of institutions. (...) In other words, institutional completeness is the element that ensures the maintenance of community" (p. 141 [trans.]).

[13] The type of program offered is left to the discretion of school boards.

Canada's Official Languages Act, as well as provincial laws such as the French Language Services Act of Ontario (1990), are public policies that make it mandatory for governments to ensure that, where numbers warrant, civil servants must respond to requests from the public who have the right to communicate with the administration in the official language of their choice. Without an explicit provincial educational policy that institutes the learning of FSL in an immersion context continuously from primary to post-secondary education, how can we guarantee that Canadians have the possibility to exercise their constitutional and linguistic rights at various levels of government?

For the moment, the current language planning context in Canada for second-language learning—paragraph 43(1) of the Official Languages Act—is subject to the interpretation of the government in power. Only the Act, through the Department of Canadian Heritage, can in fact promote, first, the implementation of funding programs to support the positive measures that it deems appropriate, and second, the implementation of collaborative intergovernmental agreements to ensure implementation in all the provinces and territories of the country. It would therefore be ideal for the legal framework to specify the conditions of its application, ensuring a solid foundation to build on.

REFERENCES

Alberta. (2000). *School Act: Revised statutes of Alberta 2000*, Chapter S–3. Edmonton: Alberta Queen's Printer. www.qp.alberta.ca/documents/Acts/s03.pdf

Breton, R. (1964). Institutional completeness of ethnic communities and personal relations of immigrants. *American Journal of Sociology*, 70, 193–205.

Canada. Canadian Charter of Rights and Freedoms — 1982 Constitution Act. (1985). Canadian Charter of Rights and Freedoms Examination Regulations, SOR/85-781. laws-lois.justice.gc.ca/PDF/SOR-85-781.pdf

Canada. Department of Canadian Heritage. (n.d.) Intergovernmental cooperation on minority language education. www.canada.ca/en/canadian-heritage/services/funding/official-languages/minority-language/intergovernmental.html

Canada. Department of Canadian Heritage. (n.d.). Official languages support programs. www.canada.ca/en/canadian-heritage/services/funding/official-languages.html

Canada. Department of Canadian Heritage. (n.d.). Young Canada Works in Both Official Languages program. www.canada.ca/en/canadian-heritage/services/funding/young-canada-works/employers/official-languages-employers.html

Canada. Office of the Commissioner of Official Languages (OCOL). (n.d.). Accessing opportunity: A study on challenges in French-as-a-second-language education teacher supply and demand in Canada. www.clo-ocol.gc.ca/en/publications/studies/2019/accessing-opportunity-fsl

Canada. Official Languages Act (OLA). (1988). Official Languages Act R.S.C., 1985, c. 31 (4th Supp.). laws-lois.justice.gc.ca/PDF/O-3.01.pdf

Canada. Royal Commission on Bilingualism and Biculturalism (RCBB). (1967). *Report of the Royal Commission on Bilingualism and Biculturalism*, Book I: *The Official Languages*. Ottawa: Queen's Printer. [first half of Book I, pp. i–87]. publications.gc.ca/collections/collection_2014/bcp-pco/Z1-1963-1-5-1-1-eng.pdf

Canada. Standing Senate Committee on Official Languages (2013). *Issue 19 — Transcript of Proceedings, April 29, 2013* [statement by Graham Fraser, Commissioner of Official Languages]. sencanada.ca/en/Content/SEN/Committee/411/ollo/19ev-50109-e

Canadian Parents For French. (n.d.). *French as a Second Language enrolment statistics: 2012–2013 to 2016–2017.* Ottawa: Canadian Parents for French. cpf.ca/en/files/Enrolement-Stats-2018-web.pdf

Canadian Parents For French. (2013). *An overview of French-second-language education in Canada.* CPF submission to the Standing Senate Committee on Official Languages — Addendum, November 6, 2013. cpf.ca/en/files/Senate-Brief-Addendum.pdf

Charron, M. (1997). Le sens des institutions, *Revue du Nouvel-Ontario, 21,* 137–158.

Council of Ministers of Education, Canada (CMEC). (n.d.). Language learning and exchange programs. www.cmec.ca/155/Language_Learning_and_Exchange_Programs.html

Council of Ministers of Education, Canada (CMEC). (2013). *Protocol for agreements for minority-language education and second-language instruction.* www.cmec.ca/156/Official_Languages_in_Education_Protocol.html

Corbeil, J.-P., & Lafrenière, S. (2010). *Portrait of official-language minorities in Canada: Francophones in Ontario.* Catalogue no. 89-642-X — No. 001. Ottawa: Statistics Canada. www150.statcan.gc.ca/n1/pub/89-642-x/89-642-x2010001-eng.pdf

Daoust, D., & Maurais, J. (1987). L'aménagement linguistique. In J. Maurais (Ed.), *Politique et aménagement linguistiques* (pp. 5–46). Québec: Conseil de la langue française.

Eloy, J.-M. (1997). "Aménagement" ou "politique" linguistique? *Mots: les langages du politique, 52* (Sept.), 7–22. www.persee.fr/doc/mots_0243-6450_1997_num_52_1_2462

Foucher, P. (2011). L'Affaire Mahe: le jugement de la décennie en droits linguistiques. *Forum constitutionnel/Constitutional Forum, 3,* 10–12.

Giroux, M. (2017). Le droit à une université franco-ontarienne: au-delà du positivisme juridique. In N. Labrie & S. Lamoureux (Eds.), *L'accès des francophones aux études postsecondaires en Ontario: perspectives étudiantes et institutionnelles* (pp. 114–135). Sudbury: Prise de parole.

Lambert, W.E., & Tucker, G.R. (1972). *Bilingual education of children: The St. Lambert experiment.* Rowley, MA: Newbury House.

Lamoureux, S. (2013). L'expérience étudiante au Régime d'immersion en français: perspectives et constats. *OLBI Working Papers, 6,* 109–121.

Leclerc, J. (2019). Données démolinguistiques: Recensement de 2016. *L'aménagement linguistique dans le monde.* Québec: Université Laval, Chaire pour le développement de la recherche sur la culture d'expression française en Amérique du Nord (CEFAN). www.axl.cefan.ulaval.ca/amnord/cnddemo.htm

MacLennan, H. (1945). *Two solitudes.* Toronto: Macmillan.

Mahe v. Alberta. (1990). 1 S.C.R. 342. scc-csc.lexum.com/scc-csc/scc-csc/en/item/580/index.do

Ontario. (1990). French Language Services Act, R.S.O. 1990, c. F.32. www.ontario.ca/laws/statute/90f32

Ontario. Ministry of Education. (2014). *French as a second language: What are some of the benefits of learning French as a second language (FSL)?* www.edu.gov.on.ca/eng/amenagement/FLS.html

Ontario. Ministry of Training, Colleges and Universities (MTCU) (2011a). *Politique d'aménagement linguistique (PAL): A policy framework for French-language postsecondary education and training in Ontario*. Toronto: Queen's Printer. www.tcu.gov.on.ca/pepg/publications/PAL_Eng_Web.pdf

Ontario. Ministry of Training, Colleges and Universities (MTCU) (2011b, Sept.). *Politique d'aménagement linguistique de l'Ontario pour l'éducation postsecondaire et la formation en français*. Slideshow presentation at ACELF (Association canadienne d'éducation de langue française) conference [based on print version, MTCU, 2011a]. www.acelf.ca/c/fichiers/Actes2011_A1.pdf

Ouellet, M. (1990). *Synthèse historique de l'immersion française au Canada suivie d'une bibliographie sélective et analytique*. Quebec: Centre international de recherche sur l'aménagement linguistique.

Quebec. (1977). *Charter of the French language* (Bill 101; *Charte de la langue française*. www.legisquebec.gouv.qc.ca/en/showdoc/cs/C-11

Quebec. Ministère de l'éducation, du loisir et du sport (MELS) (2014). *Indicateurs linguistiques: secteur de l'éducation*, Édition 2013. Quebec: Gouvernement du Québec. www.mels.gouv.qc.ca/fileadmin/site_web/documents/PSG/statistiques_info_decisionnelle/PSG_indicateurs_linguistiques_2013.pdf

Quiet revolution. (2013). *The Canadian Encyclopedia*. www.thecanadianencyclopedia.ca/en/article/quiet-revolution

Rubin, J. (1971). Evaluation and language planning. In J. Rubin & B.H. Jernudd (Eds.), *Can language be planned? Sociolinguistic theory and practice for developing nations* (pp. 217–253). Honolulu: University of Hawaii Press.

Statistics Canada. (2016a). *Language highlight tables, 2016 census: Knowledge of official languages by age (15 to 19), % distribution (2016) for the population excluding institutional residents of Canada, provinces and territories, 2016 census % data*. www12.statcan.gc.ca/census-recensement/2016/dp-pd/hlt-fst/lang/Table.cfm?Lang=E&T=21&Geo=00&SP=1&view=2&age=7

Statistics Canada. (2016b). *Language highlight tables, 2016 census: Mother tongue by age (Total), 2016 counts for the population excluding institutional residents of Canada, provinces and territories, 2016 Census — 100% data*. www12.statcan.gc.ca/census-recensement/2016/dp-pd/hlt-fst/lang/Table.cfm?Lang=E&T=11&Geo=00&SP=1&view=2&age=1

Swain, M., & Johnson, R.K. (1997). Immersion education: A category within bilingual education. In R.K. Johnson & M. Swain (Eds.), *Immersion education: International perspectives* (pp. 1–16). Cambridge: Cambridge University Press.

CHAPTER 2

Political Interpretations and Institutional Arrangements for Immersion at the University of Ottawa

Hélène Knoerr

INTRODUCTION

CHAPTER 1 DESCRIBED the situation of French in the context of an officially bilingual Canada and outlined the conclusions and recommendations of the Royal Commission on Bilingualism and Biculturalism (1963–1969)—a defining moment for the status of French in Canada. More specifically, the commission made it clear that the teaching of French as a second language is crucial from an economic, social, cultural, and political perspective:

> Today's child will live in a mobile and highly competitive society. What parent in 1968 can know with any certainty where his child will live in the year 2000, or even what career opportunities his child will have? It is apparent however that the child who learns French or English as a second language will have career opportunities that other children will not have. Learning a second language is also a valuable educational experience because it brings the child into contact with a different culture. In Canada, such contact can provide our children with knowledge and appreciation of the culture of many other Canadians....
>
> ... Language learning can increase the number of bilingual Canadians and so reduce the language barrier in our country. It can play a significant role in increasing the mutual understanding of the attitudes and aspirations of the two cultural groups. (Canada, 1968, pp. 204–205)

Fifty years later, this statement is still valid (Canada, Office of the Commissioner of Official Languages [OCOL], 2019):

> A 2016 survey conducted by Nielsen for the Office of the Commissioner of Official Languages (the Office of the Commissioner) showed that roughly 8 in 10 Canadians agree that:
> - both languages should be taught to some extent in all elementary schools across Canada;
> - more needs to be done so that young people can become bilingual;
> - provincial governments should make more spaces available in immersion programs. (p. 1)

Chapter 1 also mentioned that the French immersion programs, a uniquely Canadian invention, "aimed at developing native-like skills in a second language by having that language used as the main medium of instruction during the elementary school years" (Lambert & Tucker, 1972, p. 2). But as the former Commissioner of Official Languages, Graham Fraser, writes in the preface to this book:

> The post-secondary immersion experience is completely different. English-speaking institutions have been slow to recognize the needs of students who did their primary and secondary schooling in French to continue to have access to courses and programs in French. (p. 5)

The Commissioner of Official Languages concluded in his 2009–2010 report (Canada, OCOL, 2010a) that:

> Other students have had to give up on the idea of perfecting the language skills they acquired in primary and secondary school at university, because very few post-secondary institutions give their students the opportunity to take courses within their field in the official language of their choice. (p. 3)

And finally, Chapter 1 provided a detailed account of the main Canadian laws and policies with respect to second languages.

In this chapter, we will examine how the University of Ottawa implemented these laws and policies via its unique response to the dual challenge — linguistic and political — reported by the commissioner: The *Régime d'immersion en français* (RIF, French Immersion Stream).

The RIF is the brainchild of a single individual, François Houle, then Provost and Vice-President, Academic Affairs, but first and foremost, an expert in political science at the Faculty of Social Sciences at the University of Ottawa. Based on an in-depth interview with this key administrator, this chapter describes his vision in the context of its time, details the components of the proposal he designed and implemented, and presents the reactions of the various stakeholders. We also draw on an interview with his successor as vice president, Sylvie Lauzon, as well as an interview with a key player at the political level, Hilaire Lemoine, Executive Director of the Official Languages Support Program (OLSP) at the time, in order to give a complete and accurate picture of the scope of the project.[1] We then analyze the key elements of the RIF, and conclude with recommendations for the successful implementation of a university-level immersion program, as well as suggestions to address the challenges such a program poses.

1. POLITICAL AND INSTITUTIONAL CONTEXT

As already noted, French immersion graduates, whether in primary or secondary school, do not feel adequately equipped to continue their post-secondary education in French and have no other option but to enrol in English-language universities, forfeiting the benefits of years of schooling in French. The University of Ottawa, through Mr. Houle, saw the potential of this situation and was able to turn it to everybody's advantage thanks to a new academic option targeting this increasing segment of the Canadian student population: the RIF. This option is the result of two independent contexts — political and institutional — whose combination produced the conditions necessary for its

---

[1] François Houle (FH) was interviewed on November 6, 2012. Sylvie Lauzon was interviewed first on August 27, 2013 (SL-1) and again on December 11, 2013 (SL-2). Hilaire Lemoine (HL) was interviewed on December 13, 2013. All interviews were conducted in French; all translations are the author's.

emergence: "There was a will from both the government and the University to increase immersion, to extend it to the University level" [FH].

1.1. Political Context

As discussed in the previous chapter, the federal government makes significant investments to support official languages in primary and secondary education programs. In Ontario, this financial support is exclusively devoted to school boards: the amounts allocated for the Francophone minority are used to fund projects put forward by French-language primary and secondary schools affiliated with either the Catholic or the public school boards. If universities want to have their share in this funding for their own French-language programs in a minority context, they must wage a fratricidal war— Francophone against Francophone — against the province's school boards. And it is a battle they are unlikely to win, since the boards are a powerful lobby. As a result, Ontario universities do not attempt to seek funding through the minority French-language channel since they know their chances are slim.

In March 2003, under the auspices of then-Prime Minister Jean Chrétien, the Minister for Intergovernmental Affairs, Stéphane Dion, issued a policy statement on official languages, entitled "The Next Act: New Momentum for Canada's Linguistic Duality" (Canada, 2003). Its pivotal element, the Action Plan for Official Languages, aimed to promote the learning of French in Canada from coast to coast and "to ensure that in 10 years one young Canadian out of two will master both official languages" (p. 28). This significant undertaking was given the resources to match its ambition: a massive budget of 751 million dollars over five years. And unlike the usual funding envelopes, this one was not restricted to primary and secondary education. The Department of Canadian Heritage was the project manager of Minister Dion's Action Plan, but the funds were administered by their recipients, the largest allocation — over 400 million dollars — being awarded to the Action Plan.

Education in Canada is a provincial jurisdiction. Consequently, the federal government's official languages policy usually takes the form of partnerships with the provinces and territories. Since 1971, the Official Languages in Education Program, which regulates education in the minority language and second language teaching, has been a key instrument in this partnership. In this context, federal funds are transferred within the framework of a 5-year agreement protocol with the Council of Ministers of Education, Canada, regarding overall objectives, as well as through bilateral agreements with each government. This process ensures respect for provincial and territorial jurisdictions and their different circumstances. Each government develops a multi-year action plan that includes minority-language education activities, second-language instruction, and awareness of the culture of the other official-language community.

1.2. Institutional Context

As of 2000, uOttawa, the largest French–English bilingual university in the world, found itself in a situation of linguistic imbalance: although the number of Francophone students was stable or even slightly up, their percentage was in constant decline while the number of Anglophone student registrations rose steadily rise. This threat to the linguistic balance was also a threat to the very mandate of the university — "to preserve and develop French culture in Ontario" (University of Ottawa, 1965, "Administration and governance ...," section 4c). Recruiting more students to populate the French programs became a necessity. But how to achieve this goal when the university was already recruiting 55% of the young Franco-Ontarian students enrolled in university programs (Labrie, Lamoureux, & Wilson, 2009), knowing that the French-language pool in the province was limited?

Around the same time, the university engaged in an academic strategic plan, *Vision 2010* (University of Ottawa, 2005), which established its major orientations and funding priorities for the next few years. The main goal was:

> [t]o play a leadership role in promoting Canada's official languages ... By 2010, we will have improved our linguistic balance and have become the standard among Canadian universities in the areas of acquisition, development, evaluation and promotion of the official languages. (p. 2)[2]

2. THE RIF AT THE CROSSROADS OF GOVERNMENTAL AND INSTITUTIONAL WILLS

In this context, the newly appointed Vice-President Houle came up with a plan which addressed the concerns of both the university and the federal government: the *Régime d'immersion en français*.

2.1. Institutional Objectives and Political Resources

For the vice-president, the answer to the challenge did not consist in attempting to attract more Francophones, whether majority or minority, but rather, to tap into the vast and prolific pool of the Anglophone majority, via an innovative concept — "Francophile" — which Houle defined as follows: "a group of students from the Anglophone community who enjoy and value living in the French language and culture."

> [FH] Politically speaking, the University is the microcosm of Canada, with the two linguistic groups staring at one another like statues ... As vice-president, I felt that if we could create a buffer group of 10, 12 or 15% of the student population that would go back and forth between the two linguistic groups, it could generate a lot more exchanges between the two communities.

For uOttawa, having this buffer group enrol in courses delivered in French presented the added benefit of increasing the supply of programs and courses taught in French. But more importantly, it allowed the university to delve into the funds from Minister Dion's Action Plan. In the long term, the RIF would provide both the federal and the provincial governments with the pool of bilingual senior management they would need in order to fulfill their linguistic obligations under Canadian language laws (see Chapter 1), as pointed out by the Commissioner of Official Languages of the day (Canada, OCOL, 2010b):

---

[2] The Anglophone/Francophone ratio was 70/30, as of 2013.

by increasing its efforts to help university students become bilingual, the federal government will find it much easier to recruit the 5,000 bilingual employees it will need each year in order to renew its workforce and, ultimately, to adequately serve the Canadian public. (p. 9)

Houle shares this vision: "One can easily imagine that within 15 years a huge number of senior management public servants in both the federal and provincial will be graduates of the RIF."

Let us not forget that, in Canada, education is under provincial, not federal, jurisdiction. In Ontario, universities must submit proposals to the Ministry of Training, Colleges and Universities, advised by the *Consortium des universités de la francophonie ontarienne* (CUFO[3]). However, although the boundaries between these two levels of government are strictly defined, individuals within them are in frequent contact and make sure they stay abreast of proposed projects, so as to better advise the province when it comes to making funding decisions — approved projects receive 50% of their funding from the consortium and 50% from the province.

Coincidentally, at the time CUFO's rotating presidency was held by uOttawa, represented by Mr. Houle, who was able to convince the consortium to support his project, which he would then be submitting to the OLSP. As for the province, the fact that the university was funding a substantial proportion of the project, thereby reducing the contribution required from the province, was a definite asset.[4]

The OLSP executive director himself, Hilaire Lemoine, was very favourably impressed by the proposal: "It was well thought-out and well laid out." One of its many strengths was its long-term vision: providing young Francophiles with an option to pursue their studies in French after their primary and secondary education. Another asset was the fact that Lemoine was familiar with the immersion project that uOttawa had pioneered in the 1980s with sheltered courses (see Chapter 8), a concept which he found appealing.

This concept also struck a nerve at a time when more and more research studies were indicating that investing in French as a second language was a waste of money since these young Anglophones, after graduating from high school, enrolled in English-language universities, thereby sending their French — and the billions of taxpayer dollars spent on it down the drain:

---

[3] CUFO was founded in 1995. The University of Ottawa is among its founding members. Other members include: Laurentian University, the University of Sudbury, Saint Paul University, Glendon College (York University), Hearst University College, and the Dominican University College. The consortium advises the ministry and acts as a coordinator between the bilingual universities to help identify and prioritize projects eligible for funding under the Canada–Ontario Agreement on Minority Language Education and Second Official Language Instruction.

[4] In order to receive funding from the OLSP, proposals must obtain a contribution from the province, whether directly through the government or indirectly through the universities and colleges.

[HL] We found it very sad that the federal government would spend so much money on language courses in the school system. After Grades 10 or 11, students do not see the point of continuing, whether in Core French, Intensive French, or French Immersion,[5] since there is no similar option at the post-secondary level. It does not make any sense. We felt there was a desperate need for continuity, and we were very happy to see the University's proposal. It was easy to sell it to our management. I believe they still talk about it every time there is a presentation to the parliamentary Standing Committee on Official Languages.... We were thrilled to ... launch an initiative that met a clear and compelling need. We knew that to implement such a project, a strong political will from the University was necessary but not sufficient — it would also take language courses, a student population, and collaboration.

The proposal received full approval and full funding from the OLSP:

[HL] We knew that the proposal required an administration and an administrator, with a salary, that it required funding for curriculum development. We were eager to get started so we convinced the province to act quickly. And I believe that the federal government also made a generous contribution.... So I believe that the project was funded at the requested level.

2.2. Implementing the RIF

The RIF received approval as a development priority by uOttawa in 2005 and, as such, was included in the *Vision 2010* strategic plan (University of Ottawa, 2005) and officially launched in September 2006, at a time when the university was undergoing profound changes, not only because of the restructuring of its bachelor's degrees, but also because of the arrival of the double cohort:[6] as 80% of the programs were being restructured, the number of Ontario high school students registering in first-year programs at the university increased by a third, with 4300 new registrations.

2.2.1. Step-By-Step Implementation

As soon as he took office, Houle put into place the winning conditions for his project, making use of his political science background: "The first thing I did was to strike a

---

[5] **Core French:** also known as FLS in Alberta and British Columbia; in this French-as-a-second-language program, language is the subject of study, taught for a set number of minutes per week or per cycle.
  French Immersion: in this French-as-a-second-language program, language is the medium used for teaching other subjects for part or all of the school day.
  Intensive French: this French-as-a-second-language program is literacy-based; it is incorporated in the Core French program for five months over the course of a school year, in Grades 5 or 6 (11- or 12-year-old students); classroom activities are project-based.

[6] In June 1997, Ontario's Ministry of Education and Training announced that it would eliminate Grade 13 with the introduction of a new four-year secondary school curriculum, effective September 1999. The new curriculum was phased in, one year at a time, but the plan also created a situation in which two cohorts would graduate from high school in 2003: one from the old five-year secondary program and one from the new four-year program. This caused the highest increase (+47% from 2002 and almost 70% from 2001) in registrations in post-secondary institutions in over a generation.

committee. I made sure that the committee members all agreed. If you turn potential opponents into allies ... "

Step 1: Identifying the Target Audience

The university was aware of the dwindling percentage of French-speaking students. To be able to tap into the English-speaking student population, it had to make sure there was a sufficient number of Francophiles amongst its ranks. Houle examined the student records and noted that, out of the 2000 immersion graduates on campus, fewer than twenty (less than 1%) were enrolled in classes taught in French. When he met with them in order to find out why, their answers reinforced his belief in the RIF project:

> The Anglophone students all said that they came to Ottawa because it is bilingual, but they did not want to study in French because they would be lost in a majority French language group, they would jeopardize their scholarships and their grades, and they didn't feel competent enough to handle a class taught entirely in French. So ... we had to come up with a program that would allow them to overcome that hurdle.

There was definitely a pool of Francophiles large enough for the RIF to draw from.

Step 2: Reinstituting the language support classes

In Houle's vision, the success of the RIF depended on a pivotal element: sheltered courses, an innovative concept tested at the university in 1983 and in which he had participated himself as a newly hired professor. As such, he viewed them as the answer to many problems faced by the immersion graduates he had met: such courses would allow them to take a content course in French alongside French-speaking students, and to receive language support specifically targeting the particular content course they were taking. Unfortunately, the university had discontinued them: they were very expensive, due to the very small number of students in each of them: "That meant one instructor for fifteen students, but also sometimes six, four or two" [FH].

But there is (emotional) safety in (small) numbers: immersion students, who felt intimidated by French-language content courses, where they drowned in a sea of Francophones, felt reassured by the sheltered environment of the small-size language support classes. So the vice-president brought them back, because "obviously, for all the introductory courses in Political Science, Sociology, History, these students needed a course to support the learning of the language and the content" [FH].

As an additional precautionary measure, he decided to house the RIF in the central administration, in the Office of the Vice-President, rather than in a faculty, to prevent the language support classes being slashed in the event of budget cuts.

As a bilingual institution, uOttawa has been offering programs in both French and English since its founding. Houle established that only content courses offered in both languages could be included in the RIF, so that in the event that a student felt unable to continue in French, he or she could switch to the English-language corresponding course without any academic cost. This further helped allay the fears voiced by the immersion students he had met.

Step 3: Setting up a Pass/Fail system

Another student fear was related to grades. Here again, Houle left the beaten track and introduced an approach which, although implemented by major American universities such as Johns Hopkins, was a novelty at uOttawa: the Pass/Fail system instead of alphanumeric grades: "RIF students take several courses in their second language, and around the beginning of November, they determine whether they want a grade or a Pass/Fail for each of them" [FH]. Under this system, immersion students would no longer worry that their GPA (grade point average) would suffer and they would lose their scholarships if they took the risk of enrolling in a content course taught in French, since they could designate up to 24 credits as Pass/Fail. Their stress levels would decrease and the quality of their university experience would be enhanced.

In theory, they had no further reasons to stay away from taking university courses in French.

Step 4: Adding advanced communication courses

Introductory courses in several disciplines draw hundreds of students each term, thus ensuring a sufficient number of immersion students to make language support classes viable. Typically, these courses are lectures delivered in large halls. Therefore, the most effective language support for immersion students focuses on listening and reading comprehension, since they must be able to understand the instructor's lecture and the many assigned readings.

But the RIF went beyond comprehension: in the vice-president's vision, its graduates would be able to work in French in their area of expertise, which implies the ability to communicate orally and in writing. However, research showed that, although the receptive skills of immersion students in primary and secondary schools were as developed as those of their French-speaking peers (Swain & Lapkin, 1986), their productive skills, and particularly their writing skills, were significantly lower (Bibeau, 1984; Lyster, 1987).[7] Consequently, Houle complemented the comprehension-based courses with more advanced production-based courses (see Chapters 6 and 8 for extensive details), a move that was made possible by the introduction of majors, minors, and specializations, following restructuring of the bachelor's programs.[8]

---

[7] Interestingly, immersion students themselves perceived their ability to express themselves in French as very inadequate. Wesche (1993) and Genesee (1990) reported that immersion students were satisfied with their ability to perform listening- or reading-comprehension-based tasks; however, their level of satisfaction declined when it came to performing speaking- or writing-based tasks.

[8] In order to end the excessive specialization of undergraduate programs, the reform restructured all 4-year bachelor's programs so as to impose two fields of study by combining majors, minors, and specializations (University of Ottawa, n.d., "About uOttawa: Academic regulations"):

   a) Honours bachelor's with specialization: in-depth training in a single discipline or in an interdisciplinary area of studies with a minimum of 54 credits in the discipline or interdisciplinary area.

Step 5: Recognizing the second language proficiency level

To fulfill its objective — producing graduates who would be able to work in French in their area of expertise — the RIF needed more than courses in French and about French; it needed official validation and formal recognition, particularly by prospective employers: "We also wanted something that would be quickly recognized by the government and by major companies" [FH]. To that effect, Houle invested money in the Testing and Evaluation Service of the Faculty of Arts, which had stopped producing new tests for lack of financial resources. This new funding resulted in the Second Language Certification Test (a standardized proficiency test) and its companion distance-learning course (see Chapter 13). As described on the university's website, the test:

> gives students an opportunity to have their abilities in English or French formally recognized. This certificate will be a definite asset when entering the job market.
>
> To take the test, students must first enrol in an online self-study course (FLS 3500 for French as a Second Language and ESL 3100 for English as a Second Language). This self-study course allows students to practice and to perfect their skills in the language.... (OLBI, n.d., "Second Language Certification")
>
> Students who receive at least a level 2 in each of the four test components will receive a final grade of P (pass). (OLBI, n.d., "Second Language Certification ... Final Grade")

Initially, the RIF requirements (2005) were as follows:

1. complete the requirements of their program of study
2. complete at least 36 credits (12 courses) in courses taught in French
3. pass the Second Language Certification Test

They were modified in 2009, adding two more courses in French and limiting the number of lower-level courses (University of Ottawa, n.d., "French Immersion Stream" [Diploma requirements]):

1. complete the requirements of your program of study
2. complete at least 42 credits (14 courses) in courses taught in French, of which:
   - a maximum of 6 credits (2 courses) at the 1000 level
   - a maximum of 12 credits (4 courses) for accompanying language courses (FLS 2581, 3581, 4581 and 4781), of which a maximum of 6 credits (2 courses) for FLS 2581

---

b) Honours bachelor's with specialization and a minor: a combination of the honours bachelor's with specialization and of a minor, which introduces students to a field or sub-field within a discipline or particular area and consists of 30 credits.
c) Honours bachelor's with double major: intensive training in two main disciplines/ areas and consisting of 42 credits in each.
d) Honours bachelor's with major and minor: both intensive training in one discipline or in one interdisciplinary area and an introduction to a field or sub-field within a discipline or subject.

- at least 6 credits (2 courses) taught in French at the 3000 or 4000 level, other than FLS courses
3. pass the Second Language Certification Test

Step 6: Appointing a high-ranking director

The new structure only needed one more element: a top administrator. Again, Houle's vision prevailed. He felt that the position should be at a high-ranking level in the university's administrative hierarchy, not only to confer the authority, independence, and legitimacy necessary to approach deans and other senior administrators, but also to serve as an incentive to remain in the position long enough to acquire experience and knowledge and to ensure continuity in the RIF:

> [FH] In the university's classification of administrative positions [levels 6 through 14], the committee [I had formed] had ranked the position as a 12. I wasn't happy with it. I appealed the decision and argued that it should be a 13. The highest-ranking position in the faculty is a 14, the dean's Executive Assistant. The second highest-ranking position is the Academic Administrator, at 12. The person in charge of all the academic services is a 12. Moreover, there are lots of 12, one in each faculty. A 13 would be distinctive. I emphasized the autonomy, the budgets, and the institutional prestige. And in the end I got a 13, which would be attractive enough in terms of salary, career prospects, and status within the institution. I said, "If this fails, the whole university fails." So the position comes with a lot of institutional responsibilities ... The director must meet with at least the vice-deans each year, meet with as many professors as possible, and raise awareness of the RIF. That is why he needs the legitimacy of a 13, a senior administrator, and the status associated with it.

Step 7: Ensuring administrative autonomy

The RIF had a structure, courses, a certification process, and a senior administrative director. The next step consisted in taking the necessary precautions to ensure that this administration would be completely independent from the Official Languages and Bilingualism Institute (OLBI) and the Faculty of Arts, who were very keen on taking this flagship program under their wings. Once again, Houle's views prevailed: the RIF should not be exposed to budget cuts, and the only way to achieve that was to house it not in a department or in a faculty but directly in the central administration:

> [FH] The big issue was to have the RIF director answer directly to the central administration. I had to fight the OLBI director on this.... I said, "No, that is unacceptable, that is impossible." He had his reasons, but I had mine. The OLBI director answers to the dean of Arts. For me, it was unacceptable that the Faculty of Arts should have control over the RIF because historically, Arts had never supported immersion or the OLBI. But more importantly, we should not allow the faculty to apply its financial logic to the RIF because the RIF will never be profitable financially although it will pay off politically in terms of reputation.

Step 8: Anchoring the RIF in the community

The program envisioned by Houle gave an answer to the concerns voiced by primary and secondary school immersion students, but their parents, their schools, and their communities also had to be persuaded. This was achieved through financial incentives, promotional tools, and cultural experiences:

> [FH] Language support classes and the Pass/Fail system preserving the GPA were two attractive features. We added several others, such as special immersion scholarships;[9] competitions; we were actively involved with associations, giving them scholarships to award during their annual competitions so that parents would get to know us — at the provincial and national level, for primary and secondary education [see Chapter 17 for more details]. These associations of parents of immersion students have been around for a long time, the parents are typically from privileged backgrounds, who went to university, who are more knowledgeable. Will they send their kids to Toronto, UBC [University of British Columbia] or Ottawa? ... The immersion scholarships and competitions were incentives for those parents.

The RIF became actively engaged in the community fabric of its target population, partnering with many national associations promoting French and giving presentations in the province's high schools for Grades 10 to 12.[10] Lastly, the RIF gave its students opportunities to get immersed not only in the French-speaking academic world but also in the French-speaking community at large, thanks to cultural programming and a short study-abroad option at a French university, with courses tailored to the RIF, taught by faculty from the host university, and credited to their programs. As Houle pointed out, "the RIF's objective is to play a part in the development of *la francophonie* in Canada. It goes beyond the language, it is also the culture, there are trips, shows, excursions abroad." This was also the vision of the central administration, as noted by Sylvie Lauzon, who succeeded him as vice-president:

> [SL-1] The immersion club, the trip to the Quebec City Carnival, many activities anchored in the French-speaking communities allow them to get to know the culture. Learning the language is important, but discovering and understanding the culture takes them to the next level. We tried early on to make sure that we created opportunities for them to get acquainted with the culture.

---

[9] The $1000-a-year French Studies Bursary is awarded automatically to all full-time, first-year French Immersion Stream and Extended French Stream students who are taking at least 6 credits (2 courses) in French per term and maintaining a minimum CGPA of 5.5. Students can earn $4,000 over four years. This bursary can be combined with a regular admission scholarship (University of Ottawa, n.d., "Scholarships ... French Studies Bursary").

[10] The RIF is also taking over the *Concours de français langue seconde*, which was previously organized and funded jointly by uOttawa and Carleton University. The *Concours* is open to Grade 11 and 12 students from all English-language school boards in the province.

Step 9: Building in an evaluation process

This step was implemented by Lauzon, who took over as Houle accepted a new position within the university. She understood how vital a follow-up program was, in order to quickly identify and correct any potential issues:

> [SL-1] I requested it. From the very beginning we implemented an evaluation process. After two years into the RIF we evaluated it because we wanted to intervene right away. Then we instituted a periodic evaluation process, every five or ten years.... It is crucial for any new program. Research, that step always gets overlooked. We had budgeted it to make sure we would have a foundation. We knew it wasn't perfect, but we wanted to intervene as soon as possible. And we did. Our operating mode was a formative evaluation after two years, and then a summative evaluation.[11]

3. RESPONSES TO THE RIF

Vice-President Houle's master plan met with a mixed response: while the central administration was highly favourable, some faculties were more reluctant. Admittedly, the RIF challenged well-established preconceptions and traditions.

3.1. An Overall Positive Reaction

The RIF received immediate support, both institutionally and politically. The Undergraduate Studies Committee voted almost unanimously in favour:

> [FH] Institutionally, the president and the vice-president never questioned the importance of immersion. For two years it was part of every single speech the president made. And the president always attended the several immersion competitions and awards ceremonies. So there was very strong support from the institution.

Support from the central administration was clear from the very start: including the RIF in the *Vision 2010* plan (University of Ottawa, 2005) was key in obtaining funding to create new language instructor positions for the language support classes. The number one goal of the strategic plan was to "play a leadership role in promoting Canada's official languages" (p. 2) through two main instruments: the OLBI and the RIF — both initiated by Houle.

To Houle's surprise, the Faculties of Arts and of Social Sciences wanted to be involved right away, and very few departments refused to join in, although they had the right to do so. Some sectors of the Faculty of Health Sciences also decided to participate. The Faculty of Science joined in later, but with special accommodations (mainly due to the structure of its programs):

> [FH] I think it was a success within the institution, because there was such strong support in spite of some reluctance — even toward the end of the process, some departments in the Faculty of Arts were begging me to abolish the Pass/Fail system, which I always refused to do.... Strong support from the institution and steady growth in enrolment. I no longer am vice-rector so I cannot give figures but I believe we are now at 1000, 1100, 1200 students, which is considerable.[12]

---

[11] For a complete description of evaluation and assessment, see Chapter 5.
[12] As of September 2019, there were over 2000 students registered in the RIF.

Immersion students are the cream of the crop: their grades upon admission place them in the top quartiles, above the general student population of uOttawa.[13] The university can justifiably be proud of its iconic program:

> [FH] Some of the positions created for the RIF are technically funded by the federal government, but I am positive that the university would take over if that funding disappeared. I cannot imagine that, if the federal government withdrew its financial support, the university would not fund the RIF.

His successor, Lauzon, concurs:

> [SL-2] The RIF is extremely popular with the central administration, no one questions its importance for the university.... It is a great source of pride, so there is a lot of support. Sometimes we would request more money than was allocated in our budget because we had to hire more language teachers to meet the demands, and we would never be turned down.

There is also long-term political support, even though the RIF must reapply for funding every five years, as evidenced by Lemoine, the former OLSP executive director:

> [HL] Initially, there were agreements for education between the federal and provincial government. What we achieved with immersion is that the province requests funding for French proposals in post-secondary education and the federal government provides it. A substantial part of the costs associated to the RIF comes from those funds. The funding is for 5-year periods, but I don't think it will stop.

3.2. Administrative and Ideological Tensions

Still, there are a few flies in the ointment, for two main reasons: the resentment caused by the RIF's flagship status and its independence from the faculties, and the little secret around the existence of another, less advertised, immersion "model."

The RIF is the envy of everyone because of its privileged situation: housed directly in the central administration, it is safe (or safer) from budgetary cuts in effect in all faculties and departments. As the number one objective of *Vision 2010* — and still prominent in *Destination 2020* and *Transformation 2030*, the next two strategic plans (University of Ottawa, 2013, 2019) — the RIF is the crown jewel of the university. As such, it overshadows other academic units.

However, despite the overwhelmingly positive response given to the RIF, some of its features were met with resistance and sometimes fierce opposition. Admittedly, it went against a number of well-established academic traditions and values, particularly with its grading system (Pass/Fail versus alphanumeric grades). The Faculty of Science rejected the system, claiming that it favoured immersion students since it allowed them to take the more difficult courses in French without any risk to their grade average, whereas their peers enrolled in the same courses in English would get a low grade, which would negatively impact their GPS. The resistance was so fierce that it forced

---

[13] The number of students admitted with an 85% average has consistently been twice as high for immersion students than the number of students with an equally high average admitted in English-medium programs.

the creation of a different model: the Extended French Stream (*Français enrichi*; see Chapter 3 for details):

> [FH] The Faculty of Science demanded a different model, with language support classes but without the Pass/Fail system. They never bought into the idea that 24 credits would not receive any grades. So we had to give in. I didn't support that, I didn't want that to be associated with the RIF. My view is that studying in a second language was enough of a disadvantage. But the science faculty did not believe that.

Today, this is still a bone of contention, and the RIF has abolished the confusing distinction in the terminology while still maintaining the two models — advertising a single option but automatically adjusting it depending on the faculty and the program.

Another issue comes from the RIF's excessive growth: Houle had been aiming for a "buffer group" of about two thousand immersion students, but not everyone — administrators and instructors — believed that it was a good thing.[14] Lauzon was one of the sceptics:

> [SL-1] The university's goal was 50/50: 50% Anglophones, 50% Francophones, including the Immersion students. We started with 125 students and within five years we were at almost 1000. My view was: I'd better grow slowly but surely, instead of having a growth spurt but failing our students. I favoured a conservative approach over a "let's open the floodgates" policy, with the risk of not being able to deliver on our promise.

4. IDENTIFYING THE KEYS TO SUCCESS

Several recurrent, common themes emerged from analyzing the interviews with Houle and Lauzon, the two vice-presidents, and Lemoine, the OLSP executive director, suggesting a number of key factors in designing and implementing a successful university-level immersion program.

4.1. A Strong Vision and Leadership

Arguably, one of the RIF's most commendable traits is that it was designed not by a second-language teaching or language pedagogy specialist but by an expert in political science, a member of the central administration, who brought in a team of specialists and made good use of his network of connections, particularly within senior management, at both the federal and provincial levels.

Although he had no formal training in second language teaching/learning, education, or curriculum development, Houle designed and implemented a program of unprecedented scope, drawing solely on his political intuition, his vision, his beliefs, and his experience with the sheltered courses at uOttawa in the 1980s (see Chapter 4). The former vice-president is used to thinking outside the box: at the same time as he was working on the RIF, he had just successfully reformed the undergraduate programs despite fierce opposition from the Faculty of Arts and, more importantly, from the Faculty

---

[14] Language support instructors have echoed this concern: they report a decrease in the level of competence of students compared to the RIF's early years. This decline has not been due to lower levels of admission but rather to a general trend among students.

of Sciences—the Faculty of Social Sciences, his home, had not been too hard to convince. He had also applied to OLSP for funding for another of his visions: the OLBI, which would eventually be approved and embedded, alongside the RIF, in *Vision 2010*, as one of the university's top priorities.

Houle had studied at Laval University in Quebec and obtained his doctorate from the University of Kent (England). A full professor at uOttawa since 1981, he has taught Canadian politics and contemporary political thought, his areas of research. He has held several administrative positions: active within the Canadian Political Science Association, president of CUFO, and vice-president for undergraduate studies with the Faculty of Social Sciences from 2001 to 2015 (University of Ottawa, n.d., "Administration ... Houle"). He defines himself as follows: "I am from the old school of structuralism, but I discovered that the key element in structures is the individuals. If someone comes up with a project, a structure can do amazing things to make the project happen."

With such leadership, the RIF was bound to be successful.

4.2. Support from Within the Central Administration

Just as the RIF was launched, Houle took up the position of vice-president, the highest-ranking officer after the president. Amongst his numerous responsibilities, he would be in charge of:

- setting the university's broad academic directions, in collaboration with the faculties' deans
- designing and evaluating programs
- recruiting and retaining instructors
- establishing student-recruitment strategies
- co-chairing of the Standing Committee on Francophone Affairs and Official Languages
- overseeing the ten faculties and their schools, departments, and programs, as well as the library network (in short, all sectors that play a strategic role in the university's Francophone mission)
- presiding over CUFO, thus gaining even more authority

The RIF could count on support from the highest levels, as well as from most faculties and department, as mentioned earlier.

4.3. Language Support to Facilitate Comprehension in the Content Courses Taught in French

In high school, French immersion students were taking many courses in French, at both the primary and secondary levels. But, as they had explained to Houle, they felt that the gap between secondary school and post-secondary education was so huge (Lamoureux, 2007) that they did not want to make it worse by adding a linguistic challenge to the academic one:

[FH] To me, the concept of sheltered courses was front and centre in implementing the RIF. We knew from the Anglophone students already on campus that they didn't feel competent enough in French — they had no language support — so these support classes were pivotal.

4.4. Community-Based Programming to Take Language Learning Beyond the Classroom

Language is acquired as much as it is learned. Consequently, the language learning experience should not be limited to the classroom. Of course, students need to learn the discipline-specific vocabulary and culture. But to be fully functional in their second language, they must experience it in everyday life. In that respect, bilingual uOttawa offers students the unique opportunity of mingling with members of French-speaking communities and to use French in all aspects of their lives (media, shopping, culture, etc.). But, as Houle explained, in practice, it doesn't happen this way: "Even though we are a bilingual institution there is virtually no bilingual community; the Francophones are on one side and the Anglophones on the other side" [FH].

To break the ice, the RIF included a community-based component in its structure, both on campus and beyond. The *Club d'immersion*, operated by immersion students for immersion students, offers extensive programming in French such as movie nights, theme-based nights, and field trips to Montreal and Quebec City. For a number of years, the RIF organized a three-week program at the University of Lyon, France (see Chapter 7 for more details). During these three weeks, students, accompanied by a language instructor from the RIF, had a chance to experience studying at a French university, take courses taught by professors from the host university, and take part in a variety of cultural activities. Research has shown the critical importance of study-abroad programs in the successful acquisition of linguistic, sociolinguistic, personal and intercultural skills (Meunier, 2013; Mougeon, Rehner, & Nadasdi, 2004; Regan, Howard, & Lemée, 2009; Thomas, 2002).[15]

4.5. Language Support in Small Class Sizes

The feelings of insecurity that immersion students experience about their language proficiency and their identity are widely documented (see Chapters 12 and 13). The vice-president had heard it directly from them. To convince them to take the plunge and study in French at the university level, it was essential to build a sense of safety and emotional security. That is exactly what the language support classes were meant to do: capped at twenty students, but often only taught for groups as small as four, they not only bring together the Anglophone students, who can get to know and support each other, they also bring in a mentor — the language instructor — who guides them on their immersion path, advises them, and goes with them through the process of learning the disciplinary content in French (these instructors attend the lectures with the students).

---

[15] The study-abroad option was discontinued in 2011 for financial reasons.

4.6. Cooperation Between Funding Sources: Educational Institutions, Provinces, Federal Government

Funding new projects is a complex proposition since it involves several levels of government. Provinces defend tooth and nail their areas of jurisdiction against any intrusion, perceived or real, from the federal government. But there is also competition from within: in each province, federal funding for the development of French-language projects is reserved exclusively for the Francophone school boards, in charge of primary and secondary education. Post-secondary institutions have to fight the boards for a piece of the financial pie and are more than likely to get only crumbs.

But the successful implementation of a major project relies on adequate funding. In this case, cooperation is better than competition. This is precisely what happened with the RIF: all stakeholders at the educational, provincial, and federal levels rallied together behind the proposal and its mastermind. In the words of Lemoine himself:

> [HL] It was truly a fine example of cooperation between areas of government, with one having jurisdiction and the other providing funding and maybe some guidelines. The RIF is a fine example of that, an example of a project that worked and that met a real need. It never met with a single criticism as a waste of money. On the contrary.

The educational stakeholders also presented a united front, as pointed out by Lauzon:

> [SL-2] First, we acted as a single unit, CUFO, instead of as individual representatives of different universities, and I think it was an important factor. Second, because our proposal presented an educational continuum for immersion, from preschool to university, it was easy to see the overall structure and organization — which level did what. Finally, we worked together with the colleges and the school boards in order to take their needs and requirements into account. The Ministry liked our openness.

Clearly, a proposal of the scope of the RIF is costly and requires funding that matches its ambitions. Houle recalls: "When I took office, there were surpluses.... I quickly used them all to start the immersion project, and the university added funds as well. The federal government also contributed to the RIF, but it did not start it."

The winning conditions identified here are similar to those stated by Fraser in his 2009 report (Canada, OCOL, 2009):

> Key findings about what works and what is effective in second-language learning include the following:
> - *Content*-based learning can be very effective and provide good results. [emphasis in original]
> - Opportunities to use and practice the second language outside the classroom and interact with persons from the other language group are critical.
> - Good teachers, smaller classes and learning supports such as tutors and help with grammar and writing are important.
> - Key success factors for structuring effective second-language programs include financial and funding issues; leadership and commitment from the highest levels of university administration; and planning, organization and coordination. (p. III)

5. CHALLENGES AND RECOMMENDATIONS

5.1. Divergent Models

Although this book is about *the* French immersion studies program at uOttawa, the RIF, in reality there is not one but two programs, in spite of Mr. Houle's hard work. One of the RIF's main features, the Pass/Fail system, has been a consistent stumbling block for a number of faculties, which has led to the creation of the less-advertised *Régime de français enrichi* (*RFE*, Extended French Stream).

However, qualitative versus quantitative grades need not be a bone of contention. First, world-class universities, such as Johns Hopkins, use a Pass/Fail in their first years of studies, proving that the system is compatible with high-calibre education. Second, as noted by the RIF director, if it is required for admission to a graduate program it is always possible to "unmask" a passing grade and change it back to its alphanumeric value. Therefore, the Pass/Fail system would not appear to be valid grounds to justify rejecting the RIF model.

The co-existence of these two paths is also a source of confusion for students, who are often not sure which one they should be enrolled in, and why one is called immersion and the other is not.

5.2. Lack of Faculty Training, Information, and Recognition

The RIF is based on a unique philosophy and a distinct methodology. Consequently, all the stakeholders should be familiar with this unique approach and actively promote it. Unfortunately, this is far from being the case, for a variety of reasons.

The university's demographics have led to massive hirings in recent years. The cohort of newly hired faculty is not familiar with the university's unique culture and priorities, as stated in *Vision 2010* and *Destination 2020*, particularly with respect to immersion:

> [FH] There is a potential challenge caused by faculty renewal. A good 70% of professors have less than 15 years of seniority on campus. We hired massively in the past seven, eight, ten years. As dean, in four years I hired 120 new professors. This is a significant change, and we should not take it for granted that these new professors are aware of how important immersion is for the University.... Not to mention part-time teachers.

Sessional instructors make up about 75% of the teaching staff at uOttawa, and many introductory courses in most disciplines are taught by part-time instructors. The same goes for the language support classes: due to their sheer numbers (over 70), they are mostly taught by part-time instructors, most of them newly hired. Awareness and training are therefore major challenges for the RIF (see Chapter 6 for information on training and professional development in the RIF).

The university's Teaching and Learning Support Service offers orientation sessions to the new instructors and teaching assistants at the beginning of each session, and provides ongoing professional development opportunities. But there are no such provisions in the RIF.

Content instructors receive an email with a form letter informing them that the course they are teaching has been designated an immersion course.[16] The form letter is identical for all instructors, regardless of whether they have taught in the RIF for several years or they have just been hired, whether they are regular faculty or sessional instructors who have just signed their part-time contract, whether they had been enrolled in immersion in Canada themselves or they have come from abroad:

> [FH] If you just got your PhD from the United States or from France or from the University of Toronto and you are given an introductory Canadian History course with immersion students in it, you still only get a one-page document.

Houle offers a very simple solution to this problem: The central administration should make it very clear to each dean and to each instructor they hire that immersion is of strategic importance for the university. This can be achieved through formal recognition of the contributions made by all immersion stakeholders: a reception, awards, etc.:

> [FH] Maybe the vice-president should have a reception for all the immersion professors at the beginning of the year, and raise their awareness of how important immersion is. When I was dean, I created writing awards. Now, each session, the Faculty of Social Sciences offers three awards in English and three in French for best essay. That's twelve awards per year, $1000 for first place, $800 for second, and $600 for third. Maybe there should be something similar for immersion students and teachers. It is certainly worth investing in little ways of recognizing the importance of immersion courses for the university. Discipline professors don't need to do much to help immersion students and language support instructors: meet with the instructors for a couple of hours at the beginning of the session, give them the readings or textbooks, answer a few questions before and after class. I never felt it was more demanding than that.

Such recognition should come from the highest levels in the central administration, in order to validate the RIF and to assert its importance, as well as to reaffirm the university's commitment to teaching excellence:

> [FH] It should come from the central administration. Of course, we need people in the faculties who promote and advocate the RIF, but people come and go, so it should be done at the institutional level, by the vice-president or the associate vice-president, to make it very clear to the deans how important the RIF is.

Nor is there any specific training for language instructors teaching in the RIF. Although they are language specialists and educators — they need to have a master's degree in second language teaching, applied linguistics, or equivalent — they are not trained in the RIF's unique approach, methodology, and pedagogy. This is a cause for concern, especially for sessional instructors, who are not required to take any of the immersion workshops designed and facilitated by the RIF's pedagogical advisors.

---

[16] This is further addressed and developed in several other chapters. See more specifically Chapters 13 and 14.

5.3. Lack of Methodological Expertise

The RIF was born out of the vision of a political science expert, not of a specialist in second language teaching or methodology. For ten years, its executive director was an administrator holding an MBA, not an academic with a degree in education or second language teaching. This manager was the sole decision maker for all aspects of the RIF — whether administrative, financial, pedagogical, or methodological — without the benefit of guidance from experts and researchers in the field, many of them on campus, in the same building. He appointed pedagogical advisors (*responsables pédagogiques*), but their selection was based on his personal preferences and agenda rather than on the informed decision of a committee of experts in the field. This is clearly a weakness for the RIF, one of the very few oversights made by Houle, as stated by Lauzon, his successor:

> [SL-2] I am shocked to find out that there is no committee. I thought there was some sort of committee with the RIF director and some professors to talk about strengths and weaknesses in the program ..., an executive committee, an advisory committee, something like that, to oversee the implementation of the RIF across programs. I was really sure there was something ... I am stunned. It is essential to have a body to address pedagogical issues, both for professors and for students. Initially, there were requirements, then the requirements were changed, the number of credits and type of courses were changed.[17] Of course, things can be changed, but only by a committee, not by a single individual. All the programs in this university have a committee.

Some of the decisions made by RIF directors and their pedagogical advisors regarding pedagogical issues have been challenged by experts in university-level French immersion and by language instructors, to no effect. The lack of an advisory committee within the RIF's administrative structure has caused a failure in governance, and some decisions have been made without the benefit of consultation and debate. Following a change in leadership in 2018, the interim director is a language specialist holding a master's in education and has years of experience as an educator and an administrator in high school immersion programs. The advisory committee has been revived and its statutes revised in order to ensure good governance. The committee is now very active, meeting twice a month. A new vision has been developed, with an ambitious goal: "[to produce] graduates who are functional in both official languages and are able to hold a bilingual position or pursue graduate studies in French" (University of Ottawa, n.d., "French Immersion Stream: About: Our vision"), and the advisory committee is currently working on a "2.0" version of the RIF to meet this goal.

CONCLUSION

As shown in this chapter, the RIF enjoys unprecedented institutional and political support. It can count on the federal government's policy on bilingualism and second language development and it is the flagship program of uOttawa. Although it is facing real challenges, these can be overcome if the political will is there. The RIF has many strengths and a few weaknesses, as evidenced by the accounts given by the people who

---

[17] The number of credits required in French increased from 36 to 42.

played a key role in its design and implementation: Vice-Presidents Houle and Lauzon, and the executive director of OLSP, Lemoine.

The goal of this chapter has been to identify the winning conditions for university-level immersion programs and to offer suggestions to overcome the potential challenges. It is hoped that this contribution will assist the RIF in pursuing its original vision and inspire other post-secondary institutions to implement similar initiatives.

REFERENCES

Bibeau, G. (1984). Tout ce qui brille.... *Language and society*, 2, 46–49.

Canada. Office of the Commissioner of Official Languages (OCOL). (2009). *Two languages, a world of opportunities: Second-language learning in Canada's universities*. Cat. no. SF31-100/2009E-PDF. Ottawa: Minister of Public Works and Government Services Canada. www.clo-ocol.gc.ca/sites/default/files/uni_e.pdf

Canada. Office of the Commissioner of Official Languages (OCOL). (2010a). *Annual report 2009–2010: Beyond obligations*, vol. 1 [Summary: Promoting linguistic duality, p. 3]. Cat. no. SF1-2010. Ottawa: Minister of Public Works and Government Services Canada. www.clo-ocol.gc.ca/sites/default/files/uni_e.pdf

Canada. Office of the Commissioner of Official Languages (OCOL). (2010b). *Annual report 2009–2010: Beyond obligations*, vol. 1 [Summary: Linguistic duality: A value and an advantage to harness, p. 9]. Cat. No. SF1-2010. Ottawa: Minister of Public Works and Government Services Canada. www.clo-ocol.gc.ca/html/ar_ra_2009_10_p9_e.php

Canada. Office of the Commissioner of Official Languages (OCOL). (2019). Accessing opportunity: A study on challenges in French-as-a-second-language education teacher supply and demand in Canada. Cat. No. SF31-142/2019. Ottawa: Minister of Public Works and Government Services Canada. www.clo-ocol.gc.ca/sites/default/files/accessing-opportunity-fsl.pdf

Canada. Privy Council Office. (2003). The next act: New momentum for Canada's linguistic duality: The action plan for official languages. Cat. no. CP22-68/2003E. Ottawa: Privy Council Office. publications.gc.ca/site/eng/9.686463/publication.html

Canada. Royal Commission on Bilingualism and Biculturalism (RCBB). (1968). *Report of the Royal Commission on Bilingualism and Biculturalism*, Book II: *Education*. Ottawa: Queen's Printer. [second half of Book II, pp. 133–305]. publications.gc.ca/collections/collection_2014/bcp-pco/Z1-1963-1-5-2-2-eng.pdf

Centre for Research and Information on Canada (CRIC). (2002). *Portraits of Canada 2001*. Montreal: CRIC. library.carleton.ca/find/data/centre-research-and-information-canada-cric

Genesee, F. (1990). Beyond bilingualism: Sociocultural studies in immersion. In B. Fleming & M. Whitta (Eds.), *So you want your child to learn French!* (pp. 96–107). Ottawa: Canadian Parents for French.

Labrie, N., Lamoureux, S., & Wilson, D. (2009). *L'accès des francophones aux études postsecondaires en Ontario: le choix des jeunes*. Toronto: Ontario Institute for Studies in Education (OISE).

Lambert, W.E., & Tucker, G.R. (1972). *The bilingual education of children: The St Lambert experiment*. Rowley, MA: Newbury House.

Lamoureux, S. (2007). *La transition de l'école secondaire de langue française à l'université: questions de changements identitaires* (Unpublished doctoral dissertation). Department of curriculum, teaching and learning, OISE/University of Toronto.

Lyster, R. (1987). Speaking immersion. *Canadian Modern Language Review, 43*, 701–717.

Meunier, D. (2013). Mobilité et apprentissage linguistique: des représentations contrastées? In E. Yasri-Labrique, P. Gardies, & K. Djordjevic (Eds.), *Didactique contrastive: questionnements et applications* (pp. 131–140). Montpellier: Cladole.

Mougeon, R., Rehner, K., & Nadasdi, T. (2004). The learning of spoken French variation by immersion students from Toronto, Canada. *Journal of Sociolinguistics, 8*, 408–432.

Official Languages and Bilingualism Institute (OLBI). (n.d.). Second Language Certification. olbi.uottawa.ca/programs/register-credit-course/second-language-credit-courses

Official Languages and Bilingualism Institute (OLBI). (n.d.). Second Language Certification: Final exam: Results: Final grade. olbi.uottawa.ca/programs/register-credit-course/second-language-credit-courses

Regan, V., Howard, M., & Lemée, I. (2009). *The acquisition of sociolinguistic competence in a study abroad context*. Bristol: Multilingual Matters.

Swain, M., & Lapkin, S. (1986). Immersion French in secondary schools: The goods and the bads. *Contact, 5* (3), 2–9.

Thomas, A. (2002). La variation phonétique en français langue seconde au niveau universitaire avancé. *AILE, 17*, 101–121.

University of Ottawa. (n.d.). About uOttawa: Academic regulations. www.uottawa.ca/about/governance/academic-regulations#r8

University of Ottawa. (n.d.). Administration and governance: François Houle. www.uottawa.ca/governance/biography_3.html

University of Ottawa. (n.d.). French Immersion Stream [Diploma requirements]. immersion.uottawa.ca/en/diploma-requirements

University of Ottawa. (n.d.). French Immersion Stream: About: Our vision. immersion.uottawa.ca/en/about

University of Ottawa. (n.d.). Scholarships and bursaries: Admission scholarships 2019–2020: French Studies Bursary. www.uottawa.ca/financial-aid-awards/scholarships-and-bursaries

University of Ottawa. (1965). Administration and Governance: 1965 University of Ottawa Act. www.uottawa.ca/administration-and-governance/1965-university-of-ottawa-act

University of Ottawa. (2005). *Vision 2010—Academic Strategic Plan*. web5.uottawa.ca/vision2010/pdf/strategic_plan.pdf

University of Ottawa. (2013). *Destination 2020—Discover the future*. www.uottawa.ca/about/sites/www.uottawa.ca.about/files/destination-2020-strategic-plan.pdf

University of Ottawa. (2019). *Transformation 2030: Building the university of tomorrow*. transformation2030.uottawa.ca/sites/default/files/DCG19-1135-TwoPager-EN-GENERIC-ACS.pdf

Wesche, M. (1993). French immersion graduates at university and beyond: What difference has it made? In J. Alatis (Ed.), *Georgetown University Roundtable on Languages and Linguistics* (pp. 208–240). Washington: Georgetown University Press.

CHAPTER 3

From Applied Linguistic Theories to Language and Culture Teaching:
Origins of Immersion

Jérémie Séror, Aline Gohard-Radenkovic, and Hélène Knoerr

INTRODUCTION

FRENCH IMMERSION PROGRAMS IN CANADA are arguably one of the most famous implementations of a content-based language instruction approach that integrates content, language, and socio-cultural objectives (Lyster & Ballinger, 2011). In so doing, immersion programs represent a shift away from traditional forms of language teaching focused exclusively on learners' acquisition of the various systems of a language (grammar, vocabulary, and discourse, amongst others). By broadening the field of study to include disciplinary knowledge embedded within a specific discourse community populated by authentic speakers, students are given the chance to increase their exposure to a language and the opportunity to use, practise, and acquire the language through authentic interactions and language-mediated activities.

There are several variants of content-based language teaching worldwide (see Chapter 4 for details), each with its own label — CBI (Content-Based Instruction), CLIL (Content and Language Integrated Learning), ICLHE (Integrating Content and Language in Higher Education) — each with their own underlying pedagogical and sociohistorical framework (Stoller & Grabe, 1997), unique qualities, and needs based on the specific contexts in which they are embedded. Still, they all share the goal of simultaneously fostering the advancement of learners' content knowledge and language skills (Brinton, Snow, & Wesche, 2003; Lyster, 2007; Mohan, 1986).

This rise of content-based language learning practices across the world stems in part from the growing emphasis placed on the competitive advantages of multilingualism in an age of global exchanges and communication. Throughout the world, governments have recognized the value of encouraging educational systems that will enable their citizens to master the ability to function in more than one language in both academic and professional settings.

Content-based language learning has emerged as a core initiative that can play a complementary role to traditional language courses by allowing students to achieve impressive levels of bilingualism. In this, the Canadian immersion model continues to stand as one that inspires both local educators, parents, and researchers as well as stakeholders in other countries who have made second- and foreign-language education a national priority.

To better understand and situate the impact of the immersion approach, this chapter seeks to provide an overview of the research, theories, and concepts in the fields of language and literacy education and applied linguistics (de Courcy, 2002) that have underpinned the field of content-based language teaching. The chapter will also review the socio-political factors that contributed to the evolution of French immersion in Canada and will conclude by examining unexplored avenues in second- and foreign-language education in order to advance immersion pedagogy at the university level.

1. THEORETICAL AND PEDAGOGICAL FOUNDATIONS OF IMMERSION

1.1. At the Crossroads of Several Disciplines

Many of the theoretical currents and concepts that laid the groundwork for immersion are linked to the rise of a relatively new field of research: applied linguistics and its subbranches, second language pedagogy and second language acquisition.

Emerging in universities in the middle of the last century (Harris, 2002), applied linguistics is situated at the crossroads of multiple older disciplines related to the humanities and social sciences (Fazel, 2014). These include psychology, cognitive sciences, linguistics, sociology of language, anthropology, and ethnography of communication, to name but a few. This interdisciplinarity is a source of both strengths and tensions. Applied linguistics' cross-disciplinary nature makes it possible to adopt multiple and, at times, conflicting perspectives. Still, these theories can help study "language and language-related problems in specific situations in which people use and learn languages" (Vercoe, 2017, "Language journals").

The specific study of the problems linked to language teaching and learning is associated with different labels, according to specific regions and contexts. In the Canadian context, immigrants need to master one or both of the two official languages of their adopted country (traditionally French in Quebec and English in the rest of Canada). This emphasis on the acquisition of what are primary national languages has resulted in the common use of the terms "English as a second language" (ESL) or "French as a second language" (FSL) or "second language acquisition" (SLA) as key descriptors of the language learning needs found in Canada.

Europe, where languages taught are not always the national languages of the countries where the learning occurs, has more frequently adopted the term "foreign" to help define the study of language learning. In France, one can find references to the *didactologie des langues et cultures étrangères* (Galisson, 2002; Galisson & Porcher, 1985; Porcher, 1987), and the term "FLE" (*Français langue étrangère*) refers to the work of teaching French to Allophones. In addition, the term "*français langue seconde*" is used in three situations:

- when it is the language of instruction for immigrants
- when it is the official language of the former colonized countries
- when it is one of the national languages in a bi- or multilingual context, such as Switzerland or Belgium

Whatever the context or label adopted, second language pedagogy traditionally has two main objectives. It seeks to explore and define key concepts and approaches for implementing and understanding socio-educational practices and their impact on institutional and pedagogical innovation; it also seeks to produce specific recommendations and guidelines regarding best practices and strategies, to help respond to the needs of language learners.

1.2. From a Linguistic Approach to an Integrated Approach

The field of applied linguistics saw an important turn as it moved from a didactic approach rooted principally in linguistics and cognitive theory to a more integrated approach, which sought to establish a stronger link between language, its socio-cultural context, and its functional role within specific discursive communities (Hinkel, 2006). Johnson (2004) described this shift from a cognitive and purely linguistic orientation to a more sociolinguistic and socio-historical approach to language learning. He noted that, for language courses, the consequence was the adoption of a more naturalistic and ecological approach (van Lier, 1996) that emphasized the importance of learners' social interactions, identities, and ideologies for successful language learning.

With this development, the notion of language acquisition as a predominantly individual process divorced from context was replaced by a shift in emphasis toward the social dimension of language and literacy development (Firth & Wagner, 1997; Wang & Vasquez, 2012). This new epistemological posture in the field of second language pedagogy has been defined in several ways. For example, in English-language research, this shift has been referred to as "the social turn" (Block, 2003), while in French-language research, it has been tied to the notion of *complexité* (Morin, 1990) as a core component of any act of communication and learning (Zarate & Gohard-Radenkovic, 2004).

This social turn has its roots in the ground-breaking work of Hymes (1974) and his notion of "communicative competence" as a concept developed to apply a more ethnographic and sociolinguistic lens to the study of language behaviour in society. For Hymes, seeking to understand language use meant examining language in context, with its related set of implicit referents, values, codes, and ideologies, which were most often conveyed unconsciously by the actors involved. This complex interrelationship between language and context has to be navigated — if not mastered — by any individual seeking to become an expert user of a language.

With this in mind, applied linguists and language teachers have promoted a more interactive and constructed vision of the language-mediated activities that emphasizes the multidimensionality of language use and the need to take into account a wider range of socio-cultural factors (e.g., identity, power relations, agency, and community of practice) that contribute to the situated, dynamic co-construction of interactional competence (Galaczi & Taylor, 2018; Kramsch, 1986).

Pedagogical recommendations have also emerged, linked to the detailed analysis of language-mediated activities and learning situations and the discursive actions and positions taken by various actors involved directly or indirectly in these exchanges (Duff & Talmy, 2011). These recommendations emphasize the importance of presenting and teaching a language within a precise communicative situation while considering the political context in which it is situated.

On a pedagogic level, this desire to reconnect language to its context and its functions is at the heart of a content-based language learning approach which emphasized that:

- language and content cannot and should not be kept separate, since language is more than simply a linguistic code to master
- language should be learned through tasks which allow learners to participate more fully in their learning, since language is at the heart of human socialization and empowerment

This push for a more integrated and balanced focus on meaning and form with a focus not only on language learning but also learning through language was essential as a source of inspiration for the first attempts at immersion pedagogy in Canada (Swain, 1996). This more naturalistic approach "immersed" learners in a language in order to promote its active use and unconscious acquisition by incorporating the teaching of content disciplines in the target language (Krashen 1981, 1987).

1.3. From a Linguistic to a Naturalistic and Communicative approach

Krashen stood out as an influential voice in second language acquisition, stressing the importance for learners to be exposed to meaningful environments and comprehensible input in the target language. For maximum acquisition, Krashen proposed that the input should be at a level slightly above the developmental level of the language learner, a hypothesis known as "i + 1" ("input + 1," Krashen, 1977). Krashen also stressed the need for learning contexts that lowered any affective filters that might impede students' ability to absorb input through their negative impact on learners' anxiety, self-confidence, and motivation (Krashen, 1987). In such environments, students would be able to engage in the natural, unconscious process of acquisition (i.e., learning to use a language through exposure) versus the less natural and conscious learning of a language.

Krashen's principles, later extended to the so-called natural didactic approach, developed with Terrell (Krashen & Terrell, 1983), were found to be both appealing and inspiring for language teachers (Lightbown & Spada, 2013) and had a significant impact on the design of immersion programs:

- *Focus on the input*: Teaching would promote language acquisition by exposing the learner to optimal input, preferably through a discussion in the target language on a non-linguistic subject.
- *Limit the focus on grammar*: Since the goal was to promote natural unconscious acquisition, attention to grammar was limited, to ensure that conscious rule learning would not interfere with the unconscious acquisition.
- *Foster students' emotional security*: Students' language acquisition would be enhanced by encouraging their confidence, allowing them to remain silent if necessary and limiting error correction.

Indeed, these same principles were the basis for the introduction of immersion-like "sheltered content courses" for language learners at the University of Ottawa, an experiment conducted in 1981 during a sabbatical term Krashen spent on campus (Burger, Weinberg, & Wesche, 2013). The goal remained to create safe places for language learners to be exposed to rich meaningful academic input in naturally occurring social situations with the help and guidance of language instructors.

These principles — and the insights gained from early experimentations with university-based immersion programs — led to the development of the "adjunct model" (Ready & Wesche, 1992); the structure and approach remains in place today in the French immersion stream at uOttawa.[1]

It is worth noting that, over time, Krashen's theories were expanded and adapted, and other theoretical frameworks came to guide the design of immersion programs. This included research which proposed that, in addition to comprehensible input, learners could benefit from explicit focus on form-meaning relationships (Larsen-Freeman, 2003) and contextualized activities that fostered interaction (Long, 1996), negotiation of meaning (Long, 1981), and scaffolded opportunities to produce output in the target language (Swain, 1985) as a means of allowing them to formulate, test, and, if necessary, adapt their interlanguage system. The greater emphasis on students' output emerged directly from early studies conducted on French immersion students in Canada. They showed that, in spite of impressive language gains, after many years of exposure to naturalistic language settings and quality input, such students frequently displayed a lack of accuracy and mastery of certain target forms including fossilized errors (e.g., failure to mark 3rd person plural) and pronunciation (Nadasdi, 2001; Swain, 1985, 2000a, 2000b). It was thus deemed important to allow students to note more explicitly specific target forms through form-focused instruction (Tipurita & Jean, 2014) and form-focused corrective feedback (Lyster, 2004), while providing opportunities for learners to both encounter and produce structures in natural settings with meaningful tasks that could include a focus on both language and content (Ellis, 2001, 2003). In other words, the challenge was to balance opportunities for quality input, focus on form, and meaningful output (Nassaji & Cumming, 2000). Attempts to achieve this balance were often associated with the adoption of another core component of immersion programs: the "communicative approach" (Somers & Surmont, 2012; Spada, 2014)).

A central pillar of immersion in Canada, the communicative approach emphasized the importance of function and meaning, helping learners acquire language by placing them in situations of spontaneous and natural communication (Swain, 1996). By involving learners in authentic communication, tasks which centred on creating a real need to convey a message through language, the communicative approach also rejected decontextualized approaches to language learning whereby grammar points would be presented to students without any specific communicative function or precise objective. Recommending the use of natural settings, personal involvement, and relevant/motivating topics, the approach promoted, first, the authenticity of input and, in later stages, the authenticity of the language output asked of students (Savignon, 1991). In perfect alignment with a content-based approach, a core objective of the communicative approach was to give students the opportunity to practise their target language *in vivo*, in situations as realistic as possible, with a strong emphasis on having meaning and content conveyed through language (Madrid & Sánchez, 2001).

---

[1] French language learners are integrated into regular French content courses with native speakers, while taking a separate "adjunct" credit language course designed to allow them to work with a language expert on content and language elements associated with the discipline being studied (Knoerr, 2010).

In traditional language classrooms, students would thus be encouraged, for example, to carry out group projects, engage in role-play, and achieve objectives which went beyond the simple acquisition of target language features. In so doing, students would be best prepared to use and reinvest acquired L2 skills outside the walls of the L2 classroom. Immersion courses, with their emphasis on the lived experience of using language in context to achieve real-world demands and satisfy real needs and interests connected with a disciplinary content (e.g., social studies in L2) provided an ideal educational setting for communicative language learning while promoting the learner's socialization into new linguistic and disciplinary communities.

Research on content-based language teaching continues to evolve. A new trend allows students to draw on their own various linguistic repertoires (Cummins, 2008; Zarate, Levy, & Kramsch, 2011). For instance, Lyster and Tedick (2014) argue for a "cross-lingual pedagogy" as a means of enhancing learners' ability to draw on their biliteracy and awareness of the similarities and differences across their languages. They noted "students' positive reactions to biliteracy instruction" (p. 218) and their pleasure at being able to establish connections across languages. This reflects a growing interest in plurilingual and biliteracy approaches in content-based language learning contexts as a means of further strengthening form-meaning connections and metalinguistic awareness (Gajo, Grobet, Serra, Steffen, Müller, & Berthoud, 2013; Steffen, 2015).

2. SOCIO-POLITICAL ROOTS OF IMMERSION

The growing popularity of content-based instruction (immersion) approaches are in part the result of theoretical and pedagogic gains in the fields of applied linguistics and second language pedagogy. This popularity is also rooted in socio-political factors that served as a catalyst for the rise of this approach and justified the investments necessary for their development and implementation. Modern-day societies are increasingly defined by notions of mobility and dynamic interactions across cultural and linguistic borders, such that "multilingualism is enmeshed in globalization, technologization, and mobility" (Douglas Fir Group, 2016, p. 19). This reality has significantly increased interest in individuals' ability to develop a wide range of language skills. Applied linguistics and second language pedagogy have been called on to serve as a platform for innovative means of achieving this goal. Second language programs are a response to various socio-political pressures from stakeholders, including governments, policy makers, and also parents seeking to ensure that their children have a chance to acquire the linguistic resources required to navigate an increasingly multilingual world.

In the case of French immersion programs, the pressure came from Canadian English-speaking parents, reacting in the late 1960s to the advent of the new official bilingualism policies in Canada (Lambert & Tucker, 1972). They pressured local school boards and politicians to create and support more effective language programs that would ensure their children could become proficient enough in their second official language to be able to study and work in both French and English (Genesee, 1988), and thus access positions in the public sector in their adult lives. The response to this pressure generated the first immersion programs in public schools (see Chapter 1).

These programs were designed almost immediately in conjunction with a systematic and rigorous process of evaluation and research to assess their impact and the educational outcomes of the first generations of students who participated in them (Mejía, 2008). The goal was to reassure parents that the immersion approach would not negatively affect their children academically or impact their English language proficiency. The overall positive nature of the results of these studies and the impressive levels of French proficiency compared to more traditional approaches ensured that the call for these programs from parents would spread across Canada (Hayday, 2015). Evidence was found that immersion programs generated more openness to cultural and linguistic diversity (Lapkin & Swain, 1984). The promise of educational programs that could promote bilingualism and thus help close the gap that had long separated the French and English communities in Canada also encouraged the federal government to invest heavily in encouraging all Canadian provinces to offer second language programs. These investments were tied to the political objective of raising the levels of bilingualism in Canada in the hope of establishing greater understanding between linguistic minority and majority communities (Saindon, Landry, & Boutouchent, 2011). This would contribute to social cohesion and national unity at a time when the province of Quebec had threatened to separate from Canada.

Similar situations have been found across the world, wherever immersion programs have been adopted. In the Basque Country for instance, Basque immersion classes were developed at a language policy level, with the main aim of fostering the use of Basque as a minority language. The programs, however, attracted large numbers of Spanish L1 students whose parents perceived an advantage for their children by learning Basque. As well, the rise of English as a global language both for business and scientific communication is linked to the complicated and yet largely unavoidable dominance of English-speaking countries (particularly the United States) as well as the development of CLIL English programs in Europe (especially in university settings). These come as a response to students who seek to develop English language and literacy skills that will allow them to participate fully on the global stage (Doiz, Lasagabaster, & Sierra, 2011). In Europe, CLIL as a powerful means of promoting advanced forms of multilingualism is also deeply tied to the political objectives of the Council of Europe, which advocates strengthening the linguistic and cultural "capital" of citizens and encouraging greater mobility, intercomprehension, and economic development through language education (Lefever, 2005).

As suggested above, the rise of immersion is thus both the result of the evolution of key theories in the fields of applied linguistics and second language pedagogy and the consequence of unique local and international socio-political pressures linked to national interests, political standing, and economic and social aspirations. Multilingual education, policies, and programs effectively foster the acquisition of a wider range of languages.

3. ASSESSING THE IMMERSION APPROACH: WHERE ARE WE TODAY?

3.1. The Contributions

Investigations of the benefits and outcomes associated with immersion programs have shown that, under the right conditions, these programs do make it possible for students to make significant progress, successfully combining the acquisition of both a second/additional language and content/disciplinary knowledge (Lazaruk, 2007; Meyer, 2010; Swain, 1991), all while "maintaining and developing their proficiency in the first language" and with no harm to "their educational development" (Stern, 1972, cited in Swain, 2000a, p. 199). As Wesche and Skehan argue (2002), this ability to achieve so many desirable pedagogical objectives simultaneously is at the heart of the contribution of this approach.

> In successful CBI, learners master both language and content through a reciprocal process as they understand and convey varied concepts through their second language ... CBI may be seen as particularly relevant to learners who are preparing for full-time study through their second (or weaker) language, at any level of education. (pp. 220–221)

More than one thousand studies have been conducted exploring this particular educational approach (Baker, 2001). This research has largely demonstrated to policy makers that immersion is a viable approach with a positive impact on the linguistic, academic, cognitive, and attitudinal dispositions of students (Mejía, 2008), while reassuring politicians and parents of the value of these programs. Results have underscored the positive impact on the language skills of students, particularly in terms of comprehension (Burger & Weinberg, 2014), the development of sociolinguistic competence (Lyster, 1994; Van Compernolle & Williams, 2012), strategic competence (Chamot & O'Malley, 1994), the literacy development of both plurilingual students (Gohard-Radenkovic, 2013; Zarate, Levy, & Kramsch, 2011) and immigrant language minority students (Dagenais & Day 1998; Dagenais & Jacquet, 2001; Mady, 2017).

While this work continues to evolve, its greatest contribution has been the broadening of our understanding of language learning processes and the close ties between content, language, and the specific settings and practices that shape how language skills are developed and ultimately used in specific discursive communities. Efforts continue to better document the specific pedagogical practices that can support content-based language learning (Gajo & Berthoud, 2008; Lyster & Tedick, 2014), teacher education and professional development (Cammarata & Tedick, 2012), institutional-level immersion pedagogy beyond the classroom, and the collaborations between content and language instructors (Knoerr, Weinberg, & Gohard-Radenkovic, 2016). Finally, research continues to explore the impact of new technologies and their potentialities as a means of supporting students' exploration of language and content connections through technology-mediated tasks, web-based tools (e.g., podcasting), and the use of multiliteracies (Knoerr & Weinberg, 2014; Marenzi & Zerr, 2012; Taibi, Kantz, & Fulantelli, 2014).

3.2. The Limits

Despite its proven effectiveness as a method whose results largely exceed those obtained by traditional language teaching methods (Lazaruk, 2007), immersion pedagogy is not without its limits.

Indeed, research has consistently noted immersion students' grammatical inaccuracies when speaking (Harley, 1992; Lapkin, 1984; Lyster, 1987) and writing (Lapkin, 1984). Some authors (Lyster, 1999; Lyster, Saito, & Sato, 2013) point out that these weaknesses may result from traditional approaches that favoured message and communication (content) at the expense of form, making it difficult to raise students' awareness of their errors. In a similar manner, a narrow interpretation of the communicative approach emphasizing message (content) while downplaying form and grammatical competence may have conveyed to students that grammatical accuracy could be sacrificed without harming their chances to communicate—resulting in error fossilization (Harley, 1989). Others have also noted that an emphasis on linguistic development in immersion classes was not always matched with an equivalent effort to sensitize students to sociolinguistic variation and help them connect with target language speakers and cultures through activities that went beyond interactions with classroom peers (Mandin, 2008).

The simple fact is that it is not easy to properly balance and integrate language and content (Stoller, 2004). Indeed, research shows that even if this integration represents the key to immersion pedagogy at all levels, according to Wesche and Skehan (2002), in practice, one dimension frequently takes over the other. As Lyster (2010) notes, this exemplifies a central "weakness in second-language proficiency among French immersion students in elementary or secondary schools" (p. 13). The challenge thus remains to create a classroom experience that can systematically integrate language and content through tools and approaches that support students and teachers as they shuttle back and forth from a focus on language to content-oriented discourse.

While the goal is still the communicative competence of the immersion learner, it has become more essential to adopt a counterbalanced approach that more explicitly plans for and combines form-focused and content-focused interventions (Lyster & Mori, 2006). The learner can explore more actively and consciously the socio-cultural elements of the target language. This echoes calls for bilingual education programs to adopt a more socio-cultural lens (Byrnes, 2006; Kramsch, 2007; Swain & Lapkin, 2013) that moves beyond a focus on simple acquisition through exposure to input and context. More emphasis is needed on designing learning to encourage learners' output as they negotiate meaning and form in the target language (Pica, 2013; Swain, 2000b).

CONCLUSION

Immersion pedagogy has both a theoretical and political resonance. Through its ability to produce language learning outcomes that surpass those achieved through more conventional approaches, content-based language learning has continued to gain in popularity, spreading around the world, especially in bilingual or multilingual countries. Its key principles are clear but it also offers a great deal of flexibility in its implementation, and each education context can adapt the approach to its needs, resources, and structures. In Canada, immersion is implemented from primary to secondary school and increasingly in universities (Séror & Weinberg, 2013). In Europe, the Content and language integrated learning (CLIL) approach is popular (Pérez-Cañado, 2012) and has also been linked to heritage and indigenous language revitalization programs (Feinauer & Howard, 2014; Reyhner, 2010; Reyhner & Johnson, 2015). Immersion pedagogy thus continues to represent an important topic for all interested in a language education experience that can help promote bi/plurilingual education.

REFERENCES

Baker, C. (2001). *Foundations of bilingual education and bilingualism* (3rd ed.). Clevedon: Multilingual Matters.

Block, D. (2003). *The social turn in second language acquisition*. Washington, DC: Georgetown University Press.

Brinton, D.M., Snow, M.A., & Wesche, M.B. (2003). *Content-based second language instruction*. Michigan Classics Edition. Ann Arbor: University of Michigan Press.

Burger, S., & Weinberg, A. (2014). Three factors in vocabulary acquisition in a university French immersion adjunct context. *Journal of Immersion and Content-Based Language Education*, *2*, 23–52.

Burger, S., Weinberg, A., & Wesche, M. (2013). Immersion studies at the University of Ottawa: From the 1980s to the present. *OLBI Working Papers*, *6*, 21–43.

Byrnes, H. (2006). *Advanced language learning: The contribution of Halliday and Vygotsky*. New York: Continuum.

Cammarata, L., & Tedick, D.J. (2012). Balancing content and language in instruction: The experience of immersion teachers. *Modern Language Journal*, *96*, 251–269.

Chamot, A.U., & O'Malley, J.M. (1994). *The CALLA handbook: Implementing the cognitive academic language learning approach*. Reading, MA: Addison-Wesley.

Cummins, J. (2008). Teaching for transfer: Challenging the two solitudes assumption in bilingual education. In J. Cummins & N.H. Hornberger (Eds.), *Encyclopedia of language and education: Vol. 5. Bilingual education* (pp. 65–75). Boston: Springer. doi.org/10.1007/978-0-387-30424-3_116

Dagenais, D., & Jacquet, M. (2001). Valorisation du multilinguisme et de l'éducation bilingue chez des familles immigrantes. *Journal of International Migration and Integration*, *1*, 389–404.

Dagenais, D., & Day, E. (1998). Classroom language experiences of trilingual children in French immersion. *Canadian Modern Language Review*, *54*, 376–393.

De Courcy, M. (2002). *Learners' experiences of immersion education: Case studies of French and Chinese*. Clevedon, UK: Multilingual Matters.

Doiz, A., Lasagabaster, D., & Sierra, J.M. (2011). Internationalisation, multilingualism and English-medium instruction. *World Englishes*, *30*, 345–359.

Douglas Fir Group. (2016). A transdisciplinary framework for SLA in a multilingual world. *Modern Language Journal*, *100* (Supplement 2016), 19–47.

Duff, P.A., & Talmy, S. (2011). Language socialization approaches to second language acquisition. In D. Atkinson (Ed.), *Alternative approaches to second language acquisition* (pp. 95–116). New York: Routledge.

Ellis, R. (2001). Investigating form-focused instruction. *Language Learning, 51*, 1–46.

Ellis, N. (2003). Constructions, chunking, and connectionism: The emergence of second language structure. In C. Doughty & M. Long (Eds.), *Handbook of second language acquisition* (pp. 63–103). Malden, MA: Blackwell.

Fazel, I. (2014). Current issues and debates in SLA. *Journal of ELT and Applied Linguistics (JELTAL), 2*, 82–91.

Feinauer, E., & Howard, E.R. (2014). Attending to the third goal: Cross-cultural competence and identity development in two-way immersion programs. *Journal of Immersion and Content-Based Language Education, 2*, 257–272.

Firth, A., & Wagner, J. (1997). On discourse, communication, and (some) fundamental concepts in SLA research. *Modern Language Journal, 81*, 285–300.

Gajo, L., & Berthoud, A.-C. (2008). *Rapport final: Construction intégrée des savoirs linguistiques et disciplinaires dans l'enseignement bilingue au secondaire et au tertiaire.* PNR 56. Bern: Swiss National Science Foundation. www.snf.ch/SiteCollectionDocuments/nfp/nfp56/nfp56_schlussbericht_gajo.pdf

Gajo, L., Grobet, A., Serra, C., Steffen, G., Müller, G., & Berthoud, A.-C. (2013). Plurilingualisms and knowledge construction in higher education. In A.-C. Berthoud, F. Grin, & G. Lüdi (Eds.), *Exploring the dynamics of multilingualism: The DYLAN project* (pp. 287–308). Amsterdam: John Benjamins.

Galaczi, E., & Taylor, L. (2018). Interactional competence: Conceptualisations, operationalisations, and outstanding questions. *Language Assessment Quarterly, 15*, 219–236.

Galisson, R. (2002). Préambule: Est-il fou? Est-il sage? *ELA: Études de linguistique appliquée* [thematic issue: *Comment peut-on être didactologue?*], *127*, 261–271). www.cairn.info/revue-ela-2002-3.htm

Galisson, R., & Porcher, L. (Eds.). (1985). *ELA: Études de linguistique appliquée* [thematic issue: *Didactologies et idéologies*], *60*.

Genesee, F. (1988). L'immersion française: une histoire à succès. *Québec français, 70*, 28–32.

Gohard-Radenkovic, A. (2013). L'émergence d'une pédagogie de l'immersion. *OLBI Working Papers, 6*, 143–149. uottawa.scholarsportal.info/ojs/index.php/ILOB-OLBI/article/view/1136/988

Harley, B. (1989). Functional grammar in French immersion: A classroom experiment. *Applied Linguistics, 10*, 331–359.

Harley, B. (1992). Aspects of the oral second language proficiency of early immersion, late immersion and extended French students at Grade 10. In R.J. Courchesne, J.I. Glidden, J. St. John, & C. Thérien (Eds.), *L'enseignement des langues secondes axé sur la compréhension* (pp. 317–388). Ottawa: University of Ottawa Press.

Harris, T. (2002). Linguistics in applied linguistics: A historical overview. *Journal of English Studies, 41*, 99–114. dialnet.unirioja.es/descarga/articulo/720765.pdf

Hayday, M. (2015). *So they want us to learn French: Promoting and opposing bilingualism in English-speaking Canada.* Vancouver: UBC Press.

Hinkel, E. (2006). Current perspectives on teaching the four skills. *TESOL Quarterly, 40*, 109–131.

Hymes, D.H. (1974). *Foundations in sociolinguistics: An ethnographic approach*. Philadelphia: University of Pennsylvania Press.

Johnson, M. (2004). *A philosophy of second language acquisition*. New Haven: Yale University Press.

Knoerr, H. (2010). L'immersion au niveau universitaire: nouveaux modèles, nouveaux défis, pratiques et stratégies. *OLBI Working Papers, 1*, 89–110.

Knoerr, H., & Weinberg, A. (2014). Stratégies d'écoute: les étudiants d'immersion en français au niveau universitaire ont la parole. *Dossiers des sciences de l'éducation, 32*, 110–130.

Knoerr, H., Weinberg, A., Gohard-Radenkovic, A. (Eds.). (2016). *L'immersion française à l'université: politiques et pédagogies*. Ottawa: University of Ottawa Press.

Kramsch, C. (1986). From language proficiency to interactional competence. *Modern Language Journal, 70*, 366–372.

Kramsch, C. (2007). In search of the intercultural. *Journal of Sociolinguistics, 6*, 275–285.

Krashen, S. (1977). Some issues relating to the Monitor Model. In H.D. Brown, C. Yorio, & R. Crymes (Eds.), *On TESOL'77: Teaching and learning English as a second language: Trends in research and practice* (pp. 144–158). Washington, DC: TESOL.

Krashen, S.D. (1981). *Second language acquisition and second language learning*. Oxford: Pergamon Press.

Krashen, S.D. (1987). *Principles and practice in second language acquisition*. New York: Prentice-Hall International.

Krashen, S.D., & Terrell, T.D. (1983). *The natural approach*. New York: Pergamon Press.

Lambert, W.E., & Tucker, G.R. (1972). *The bilingual education of children: The St. Lambert experiment*. Rowley, MA: Newbury House.

Lapkin, S. (1984). How well do immersion students speak and write French? *Canadian Modern Language Review, 40*, 575–585.

Lapkin, S., & Swain, M. (1984). Faisons le point/Research update. *Language and Society, 12*, 48–54.

Larsen-Freeman, D. (2003). *Teaching language: From grammar to grammaring*. Boston: Thomson & Heinle.

Lazaruk, W. (2007). Linguistic, academic, and cognitive benefits of French immersion. *Canadian Modern Language Review, 63*, 605–627.

Lefever, S. (2005). The role of language teaching — Looking to the future. *Málfríður* [magazine for language teachers in Iceland], *21*, 1–6. archive.ecml.at/mtp2/lea/results/Othermaterials/Articles/role.pdf

Lightbown, P.M., & Spada, N. (2013). *How languages are learned* (4th ed.). Oxford: Oxford University Press.

Long, M. (1981). Input, interaction and second language acquisition. *Annals of the New York Academy of Sciences, 379*, 259–278.

Long, M. (1996). The role of the linguistic environment in second language acquisition. In R. Ritchie & T. Bhatia (Eds.), *Handbook of second language acquisition* (pp. 413–468). San Diego: Academic Press.

Lyster, R. (1987). Speaking immersion. *Canadian Modern Language Review, 43*, 701–717.

Lyster, R. (1994). The effect of functional-analytic teaching on aspects of French immersion students' sociolinguistic competence. *Applied Linguistics, 15*, 263–287.

Lyster, R. (1999). La négociation de la forme: la suite … mais pas la fin. *Canadian Modern Language Review, 55*, 355–384.

Lyster, R. (2004). Differential effects of prompts and recasts in form-focused instruction. *Studies in Second Language Acquisition, 26*, 399–432.

Lyster, R. (2007). *Learning and teaching languages through content: A counterbalanced approach*. Amsterdam: John Benjamins.

Lyster, R. (2010). Le "contrepoids" dans la pédagogie immersive. *Immersion Journal, 32*, 13–20.

Lyster, R., & Ballinger, S. (2011). Content-based language teaching: Convergent concerns across divergent contexts. *Language Teaching Research, 15*, 279–288.

Lyster, R., & Mori, H. (2006). Interactional feedback and instructional counterbalance. *Studies in second language acquisition, 28*, 269–300.

Lyster, R., & Tedick, D.J. (2014). Research perspectives on immersion pedagogy: Looking back and looking forward. *Journal of Immersion and Content-based Language Education, 2*, 210–224.

Lyster, R., Saito, K., & Sato, M. (2013). Oral corrective feedback in second language classrooms. *Language Teaching, 46*, 1–40.

Madrid, D., & García Sánchez, E. (2001). Content-based second language teaching. In E. García Sánchez (Ed.), *Present and future trends in TEFL* (pp. 101–134). Almería, Spain: Universidad de Almería.

Mady, C. (2017). The bilingual advantage for immigrant students in French immersion in Canada: linking advantages to contextual variables. *International Journal of Bilingual Education and Bilingualism, 20*, 235–251.

Mandin, L. (2008). Transmettre le flambeau: L'avenir de l'enseignement des langues secondes est entre nos mains. *Canadian Journal of Applied Linguistics, 11*, 5–19.

Marenzi, I., & Zerr, S. (2012). Multiliteracies and active learning in CLIL — The development of LearnWeb2.0. *IEEE Transactions on Learning Technologies, 5*, 336–348.

Mejía, A.-M.D. (2008). Researching developing discourses and competences in immersion classrooms. In K.A. King & N.H. Hornberger (Eds.), *Encyclopedia of language and education: Vol. 10. Research methods in language and education* (2nd ed.) (pp. 217–228). Boston: Springer.

Meyer, O. (2010). Towards quality CLIL: Successful planning and teaching strategies. *Pulso, 33*, 11–28.

Mohan, B. (1986). *Language and content*. New York: Addison-Wesley.

Morin, E. (1990). *Introduction à la pensée complexe*. Paris: Seuil.

Nadasdi, T. (2001). Agreeing to disagree: Variable subject–verb agreement in immersion French. *Canadian Journal of Applied Linguistics, 4*, 87–101.

Nassaji, H., & Cumming, A. (2000). What's in a ZPD? A case study of a young ESL student and teacher interacting through dialogue journals. *Language Teaching Research, 4*, 95–121.

Pérez-Cañado, M.L. (2012). CLIL research in Europe: Past, present, and future. *International Journal of bilingual education and bilingualism, 15*, 315–341.

Pica, T. (2013). From input, output and comprehension to negotiation, evidence and attention: An overview of theory and research on learner interaction and SLA. In M.P. García Mayo, M.J. Gutierrez Mangado, & M. Martínez Adrián (Eds.), *Contemporary approaches to second language acquisition* (pp. 49–69). Philadelphia: John Benjamins.

Porcher, L. (1987). *Champs de signes: États de la diffusion du français langue étrangère.* Paris: Crédif/Didier.

Ready, D., & Wesche, M. (1992). An evaluation of the University of Ottawa sheltered program: Language teaching strategies that work. In R.J. Courchesne, J.I. Glidden, J. St. John, & C. Thérien (Eds.), *L'enseignement des langues secondes axé sur la compréhension* (pp. 389–405). Ottawa: University of Ottawa Press.

Reyhner, J. (2010). Indigenous language immersion schools for strong Indigenous identities. *Heritage Language Journal, 7*, 138–152.

Reyhner, J., & Johnson, F. (2015). Immersion education. In J.Reyhner (Ed.), *Teaching Indigenous students: Honoring place, community and culture* (pp. 157–172). Norman, OK: University of Oklahoma Press.

Saindon, J., Landry, R., & Boutouchent, F. (2011). Anglophones majoritaires et français langue seconde au Canada: effets complémentaires de la scolarisation et de l'environnement social. *Revue canadienne de linguistique appliquée, 14*, 64–85.

Savignon, S.J. (1991). Communicative language teaching: State of the art. *TESOL Quarterly, 25*, 261–278.

Séror, J., & Weinberg, A. (2013). Personal insights on a postsecondary immersion experience: Learning to step out of the comfort zone. *OLBI Working Papers, 6*, 123–140.

Somers, T., & Surmont, J. (2012). CLIL and immersion: how clear-cut are they? *ELT Journal, 66*, 113–116.

Spada, N. (2014). Instructed second language acquisition research and its relevance for L2 teacher education. *Education Matters: The Journal of Teaching and Learning, 2*, 41–54.

Steffen, G. (2015). Enseignement bilingue et apprentissage intégré des disciplines et des langues. In X. Gradoux, J. Jacquin, & G. Merminod (Eds.), *Agir dans la diversité des langues: Mélanges en l'honneur d'Anne-Claude Berthoud* (pp. 191–208). Louvain-la-Neuve: De Boeck.

Stoller, F.L. (2004). Content-based instruction: Perspectives on curriculum planning. *Annual Review of Applied Linguistics, 24*, 261–283.

Stoller, F.L., & Grabe, W. (1997). A six-Ts approach to content-based instruction. In M.A. Snow & D.M. Brinton (Eds.), *The content-based classroom: Perspectives on integrating language and content* (pp. 78–94). White Plains, NY: Addison Wesley Longman. www.carla.umn.edu/cobaltt/modules/curriculum/stoller_grabe1997/6Ts.pdf

Swain, M. (1985). Communicative competence: Some roles of comprehensible input and comprehensible output in its development. In S. Gass & C. Madden (Eds.), *Input in second language acquisition* (pp. 235–256). Rowley, MA: Newbury House.

Swain, M. (1991). French immersion and its offshoots: Getting two for one. In B. Freed (Ed.), *Foreign language acquisition: Research and the classroom* (pp. 91–103). Lexington, MA: Heath.

Swain, M. (1996). Integrating language and content in immersion classrooms: Research perspectives. *Canadian Modern Language Review, 52,* 529–548.

Swain, M. (2000a). French immersion research in Canada: Recent contributions to SLA and applied linguistics. *Annual Review of Applied Linguistics, 20,* 199–212.

Swain, M. (2000b). The output hypothesis and beyond: Mediating acquisition through collaborative dialogue. In J. Lantolf (Ed.), *Sociocultural theory and second language learning* (pp. 97–114). Oxford: Oxford University Press.

Swain, M., & Lapkin, S. (2013). A Vygotskian sociocultural perspective on immersion education: The L1/L2 debate. *Journal of Immersion and Content-based Language Education, 1,* 101–129.

Taibi, D., Kantz, D., & Fulantelli, G. (2014). Supporting formative assessment in content and language integrated learning: The MWS-Web platform. *International Journal of Technology Enhanced Learning, 6,* 361–379.

Tipurita, M.E., & Jean, G. (2014). Enseignement explicite du genre des noms en français: expérimentation au primaire en classe d'immersion. *Canadian Modern Language Review, 70,* 279–302.

Van Compernolle, R.A., & Williams. L. (2012). Teaching, learning, and developing L2 French sociolinguistic competence: A sociocultural perspective. *Applied Linguistics, 33,* 184–205.

Van Lier, L. (1996). *Interaction in the language curriculum: Awareness, autonomy, and authenticity.* New York: Longman.

Vercoe, T. (2017). Language journals: *Applied Linguistics.* www.tesolgames.com/language-journals

Wang, S., & Vasquez, C. (2012), Web 2.0 and second language learning: What does the research tell us? *CALICO Journal, 29,* 412–430.

Wesche, M., & Skehan, P. (2002). Communicative, task-based, and content-based language instruction. In R. Kaplan (Ed.), *The Oxford handbook of applied linguistics* (pp. 207–228). Oxford: Oxford University Press.

Zarate, G., & Gohard-Radenkovic, A. (2004). *La reconnaissance des compétences interculturelles: de la grille à la carte.* Paris: Les Cahiers du CIEP/Didier.

Zarate, G., Levy, D., & Kramsch, C. (2011). *Handbook of multilingualism and multiculturalism.* Paris: Éditions des archives contemporaines. (Original work published 2008)

CHAPTER 4

From Informal to Formal Immersion

Alysse Weinberg and Sandra Burger

INTRODUCTION

T**HIS CHAPTER** offers various models of immersion for the acquisition and learning of a language. Figure 1 summarizes the dimensions of immersion and will serve as a guide throughout this chapter.

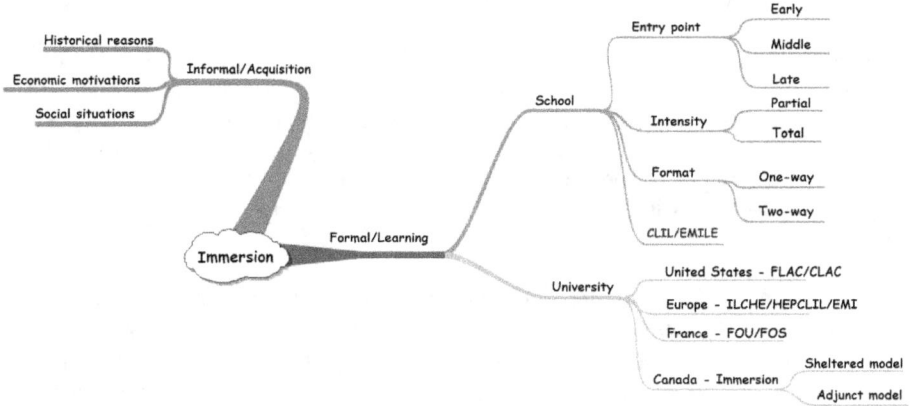

Figure 1: Summary of the different models of immersion

The horizontal reading of Figure 1 traces the diachronic evolution of immersion from an informal to a formal context. Informal context here refers to those daily situations of language interaction a person will have that will eventually lead to his or her acquisition of the language. Formal context points to institutionalized learning situations in school or university.[1]

The vertical reading of Figure 1 describes the different teaching options available within the paradigm of models in institutionalized learning situations. Here the student learns a second language for academic and professional purposes through disciplinary content taught in that second language. Thus, immersion is defined as "the teaching of content through the medium of a second language" (Rebuffot, 1993, p. 203 [trans.]).

First, a historical overview of the different forms of immersion will be presented in relation to their context: informal and formal. Then, within the formal contexts, the main models of content-based second language teaching will be differentiated. Finally, the French Immersion Stream at the University of Ottawa will be described and, based on this case, conclusions will be drawn regarding the choice of an immersion model at the university level.

---

[1] We will come back to these concepts in more detail in Chapter 7.

1. INFORMAL IMMERSION

Since the first contacts between different language groups, the acquisition of another language has regularly happened in a natural, informal way for practical purposes of a historical, geographical, political, economic, or social nature.

Empires have always exported their national language(s) through territorial conquest. From ancient Greece and Rome right up to the ex-Soviet Union, through England, France, Spain, the Netherlands, and Portugal, these great powers have imposed their respective languages on the conquered territories. Thus, with the arrival of the first explorers, French and English were introduced to Canada at the beginning of the 16th and 17th centuries, respectively. At this time, the assimilation of languages took place only through personal contact:

> Cartier went back home bringing furs in his baggage as well as 6 words of Micmac which he finally understood ... Either the French must learn the local native American language or the indigenous must learn the French language. Cartier decided the latter, that the natives would take on the heavy load. As Cartier could not count on their good will, he captured two Iroquois and brought them to France. From there, the following year they could come back knowing enough French to serve as interpreters. (Trudel, 2003, p. 10 [trans.])

It is only in the 17th century that the French settled permanently in New France and contacts with the indigenous population and their different languages became more common. This inaugurated "a system which will be in play in the 17th century: immersion in a foreign language" (Trudel, 2003, p. 10 [trans.]). Missionaries, especially Récollets and Jesuits, contributed to the expansion of French while the French in the fur trade also learned the Amerindian languages. These same Amerindian languages enabled the French and the English to understand one another: "The French and the English can communicate with each other through one or another indigenous language that they became comfortable with" (p. 21 [trans.]). After the conquest of New France by the English, linguistic exchanges took place not only between the colonists and the indigenous population but also between Europeans as well, "not so much through an Amerindian language but ... because they more or less learned each other's language" (p. 21 [trans.]). This was a time when French served as the diplomatic language of Europe, while the British Empire simultaneously introduced English as the language of business in its colonies. As the British Empire declined, the importance of the American economy expanded and thus strengthened English as the language of business in the 20th century. Today, with globalization, English has become the *lingua franca*.[2]

In Canada and even in Quebec, up until the 1960s, English was the language of business (see p. 15 in the Introduction) and Francophones had to master this language if they had any hope of participating in the economic life of the country. After the Quiet

---

[2] A *lingua franca*: "a shared language of communication used between people whose main languages are different" (Oxford Advanced Learner's Dictionary, 2019).

Revolution,[3] and the introduction of strong pro-French language laws in Quebec,[4] the pendulum swung back and the Anglophones of Quebec saw the necessity of mastering French. At the federal level, the Official Languages Act (Canada, 1969) introduced a new requirement for bilingualism for the federal government. Learning French would now have an economic benefit for anybody working in the civil service throughout Canada.[5]

The need to speak the language of prestige or of business has always existed. The elite had the means to hire language tutors for their children (Kok-Escalle & Bellassen, 2011),[6] whether in a semi-formal or formal context with private instructors, or in informal situations, with a governess. Informal immersion was not limited to the elite:

> [For the speakers] living on different sides of linguistic borders and areas of contact or exchange, knowing the language of the other group would allow them to connect not only within their own micro social-environment but also to wider language groups. These included farmers, crafts people, small business owners, service providers in the transport, food, and domestic service sectors. (Caspard, 1998, p. 112 [trans.])

This situation has existed since time immemorial and is still found today in border areas of numerous countries where several languages exist side by side, whether within the country (French, German, and Italian in Switzerland; Catalan, Basque, Occitan, and Castilian in Spain; French and English in Canada) or outside the country — Swedish and Finnish in Finland, for example. Day-to-day contacts in the economic sphere favour the acquisition of a language.

Interlanguage marriages also favour the acquisition of a language, within either a natural or adopted family unit. In general, for example in Canada, marriage outside your own linguistic group is a question of individual choice. On the other hand, in Amazonia, exogamy forbids a person to marry someone who speaks his or her own language (Gomez-Imbert, 1992, p. 540; 1996, p. 442). The language of a family unit may change where a child, who speaks a different language, is adopted into it. For example, in Switzerland in the Middle Ages, there was the practice of the linguistic "*change,*" when families would welcome a child from another language:

> A Neuchatel family, for example, would take charge of a child from Basel or Zürich or Schaffhausen instead of its own child who was sent to the other family. This applied to boys or girls. But this exchange only lasted as long as the families were satisfied with it. (Caspard, 1998, p. 115 [trans.])

---

[3] From *The Canadian Encyclopedia* (Durocher, 2013):

> The Quiet Revolution (*la Révolution tranquille*) was a time of rapid change experienced in Québec during the 1960s.

[4] These included: Bill 63 (Law to promote the French language in Quebec, 1969), Bill 22 (Law on the official language, 1974), and Bill 101 (Charter of the French language, 1977).

[5] For a complete overview of the legal dimension of immersion in Canada, see Chapter 1.

[6] Based on the work of researchers specializing in the history of languages, Kok-Escalle and Bellassen (2011) present an overview of language learning and teaching in Europe and go beyond a diachronic and synchronic perspective.

Caspard compares this practice to "boarding school within a family but as a free exchange" (p. 115 [trans.]).

Informal immersion also occurs in the case of immigration, when immigrants, forced to integrate, must make linguistic adjustments to survive daily life. Bouillon (2010) speaks in this case of "submersion" because immigrant populations find themselves submerged in a foreign language environment and have to "sink or swim." Canada has always been a land of immigration and continues to pursue an active immigration policy. Until the beginning of the 20th century, immigrants to Canada — mainly from England and Ireland — usually spoke English upon their arrival. Since that time, immigration has diversified and Canada has been welcoming immigrants with varied language profiles who would have to learn English. Only after 1969 and the passing of the Official Languages Act could immigrants choose to learn English or French, which had become the two official languages of their new country.

According to the National Household Survey of 2011 (Statistics Canada, 2013, p. 4), among the G8 countries, Canada boasted the strongest proportion of the population born abroad (20.6%), far ahead of Germany (13% in 2010) and the United States (12.9% in 2010). Outside of the G8, only Australia surpassed Canada (26.8%). The country is becoming more and more a multilingual society as the number of immigrants whose mother tongue[7] is other than French or English has risen to 72.8% of the immigrant population by 2011 — more than 200 mother languages have been identified. The linguistic landscape of Canada has evolved with different waves of immigration. Prior to the 1970s, the most common mother tongues were English, Italian, German, and Dutch, and about 78.3% of immigrants came from Europe. Since that time, immigrants will still have English, but more arrive speaking Chinese (Cantonese or Mandarin), Tagalog from the Philippines, Spanish, Punjabi, followed by Arabic, Italian, German, Portuguese, Persian (Farsi), and Polish. More than two hundred different ethnic origins were reported in 2011 (Statistics Canada, 2013, p. 4).

The linguistic practices of these immigrants vary, from informally learning the host province's language through natural submersion to participating in formal language learning programs available through numerous educational and community facilities. Newcomer classes for children are designed to integrate them into their school environment, while courses for adults are geared to socioprofessional integration.

2. FORMAL IMMERSION

The rise of the nation state and obligatory schooling in the official language used as instruments of national unification marked a paradigm change in Europe in the 19th century. As Gohard-Radenkovic (2013, p. 6 [trans.]) says, "the passage from informal to formal immersion resulted in a transition from natural to institutionalized immersion."

---

[7] A mother tongue is defined as the first language that a person learns at home as a child and still understands.

2.1. Definition

Formal immersion occurs when an institution is in charge of education and implements a *dispositif*[8] or an immersion program. Stern (1984) points out that many primary or secondary schools have immersion programs that target students who do not know the second language at the time of their entry into it:

> French immersion is a phenomenon of English-speaking educational systems in Canada.... Therefore, immersion classes are intended for children whose home language is English (and, in some instances, e.g. in the case of immigrants, a third language) and who, with the consent of their parents, are willing to undergo a large part of their schooling through the medium of French in French. (p. 4)

Cummins and Swain (1986) reiterate that definition and clarify it:

> Immersion designates a situation where children from an identical linguistic and cultural milieu who have had no previous contact with the language of the school are placed together in a class where the second language is the language of instruction. (p. 8)

2.2. Immersion at the School Level

In the 1960s, for political, economic, and cultural reasons, French immersion at the primary level began in Canada in a school in Saint-Lambert, a suburb of Montreal (Lambert & Tucker, 1972). Following the success of this experiment, French immersion spread across the whole country (for a complete description, see Burger, Weinberg, & Wesche, 2013; Knoerr 2010). French immersion is found in all Canadian provinces: in 2015–2016, there were 428,625 students enrolled in immersion (Statistics Canada, 2017).

Immersion at the primary and secondary levels follows an approach where content material is taught through the other official language. Although all programs are classified as formal immersion at school, there are disparities in its implementation. These differences lie in the intensity of the program, the point of entry, and how the immersion program is implemented:

- With reference to intensity, we speak of total immersion when 100% of the instruction is done in French and partial immersion when at least 50% of the instruction is given in French (Genesee, 1987, p. 1).
- As for the point of entry, students can choose between early immersion (which begins in kindergarden), middle immersion (which starts after the first year but before Grade 6), and late immersion (offered in Grades 6, 7, and 8, and in secondary school).
- Finally, there are two directions among the immersion models:
    - Immersion can be one-way, which targets additive bilingualism (which can be beneficial to the two languages). Students enrolled in this stream come from the dominant linguistic milieu and already know the basics in their mother tongue at the beginning of their schooling. The knowledge of this

---

[8] A *dispositif* refers to a complete teaching and learning system, including stakeholders, programs, and resources (Gohard-Radenkovic, Knoerr, & Weinberg, 2014, p. 9 [trans.]).

language continues to develop outside the school situation. As for the second language, these students usually form a homogenous group which progresses in one direction toward a common goal, bilingualism (Fortune & Tedick, 2008).

- Two-way immersion is a variation of the one-way model, which favours "the use in school of two languages spoken locally, most often the dominant language and the minority language, and uses both languages in instruction" (Meier, 2012, p. 7). Two-way immersion was initially introduced in the United States, in particular in Florida, so that the children of Cuban refugees who wanted their children schooled in English in the American schools could acquire literacy and bilingual competence in Spanish because they expected to return to Cuba (Fortune & Tedick, 2008). Nowadays, two-way immersion is very common in the United States and, according to the National Dual Language Immersion Research Alliance (2011, p. 5), more than 450 programs offer dual language immersion programs in secondary schools across the United States.

In the best-case scenario, this type of immersion places children of different mother tongues in the same classroom in equal proportions and provides program content in those two languages (Tedick, Christian, & Fortune, 2011). The proportion of time dedicated to the target language can vary from 90% at the beginning, down to 50% later on during the children's schooling. Two-way immersion is less widespread in Europe, but when it is implemented, it fosters the development and survival of regional languages. In fact, two-way immersion is firmly established in regions where two or several languages are in contact, such as Finland, Switzerland, Wales, Friesland, Brittany, or Corsica (Meier, 2012).

As a result, this type of formal immersion approach has been implemented in different variations in Europe, North America, and Asia, placing more or less emphasis on language or content. Therefore, the term "Content and language integrated learning" (CLIL) is used. While in Canada it is always a question of a second language, in Europe, in contrast, the target language is essentially a foreign language — in most cases, English.

In the English version of his 2002 historical review of the development of the teaching of foreign languages, Marsh (2003) pointed out that, "In the 1990s the European Commission made a recommendation that all school leavers should have some competence in both the mother tongue and two community languages (MT+2)" (para. 9). CLIL was the European response to the language needs created by this new requirement. Several European researchers (Coyle, Hood, & Marsh, 2010; Dalton-Puffer, Nikula, & Smit, 2010) have proposed definitions of CLIL. They all follow from the early work of Marsh and his 2002 definition:

> Content and language integrated learning (CLIL) refers to any dual-focused educational context in which an additional language, thus not usually the first language of the learners involved, is used as a medium in the teaching and learning of non-language content. It is

dual-focused because whereas attention may be predominantly on either subject-specific content or language, both are always accommodated. (Marsh, 2003, para. 3)

In the beginning, this approach was limited to the secondary level, but later on it spread to the whole European school and university system in different formats, depending on the country and the level of students. As with French immersion in Canada, there are differences in the implementation and intensity of this approach. Nevertheless, there are notable differences between immersion and CLIL. Lyster (2012), drawing on the work of Dalton-Puffer (2011) and Swain and Johnson (1997), summarized the two approaches in his closing talk at the CLIL 2012 conference, "From practice to visions," in Utrecht (see Table 1).

Table 1: Differences between immersion and CLIL (Lyster, 2012)

	CLIL	Immersion
Target language	Foreign language (not second language, generally English)	Second, foreign, regional, heritage, and indigenous language
Instructor	In general, non-native speaker	Native or non-native speaker
Language context	Discipline courses separate from language courses	Discipline and language courses often integrated at the beginning but later separated
Curriculum	50% or less taught in the target language	50% or more taught in the target language
Starting point	Often at the secondary level but also at the beginning of primary	Often as soon as kindergarten but also later in the school program

As the table shows, in contrast to Canadian immersion, CLIL puts more emphasis on the teaching not of a second language but of a foreign language, in particular English. Often it is called EMI (English as medium of instruction). Learners encounter the language mainly in the context of the school curriculum and not in their daily lives. In general, the instructors are not native speakers. Finally, in most cases the instructors are not language teachers but content specialists. Dalton-Puffer et al. (2010) describe CLIL as follows:

> an educational approach where subjects such as geography or biology are taught through the medium of a foreign language, typically to students participating in some form of mainstream education at primary, secondary but also tertiary level. (p. 1)

2.3. Immersion at the University Level

The immersion approach has also spread to university level. Wesche proposes the following definition:

> University immersion targets content teaching and language teaching concurrently. The curriculum of the adjunct language course is determined by the specific linguistic requirements of the discipline content course. (personal communication, September 28, 2007)

This later extension began in the 1980s. It stems from theories developed for the teaching of language for specific purposes (LSP) (Strevens, 1977; Widdowson, 1983) and the theory of the comprehensible input developed by Krashen (1982, 1984).[9] University immersion as a follow-up to secondary school immersion allows university students to integrate their learning of content and language at the same time. In some cases, students can take a content course taught in their second language accompanied by an adjunct language course.

In the United States, by the end of the 1970s, a sheltered model linking a language course with a content course was put in place at the University of California in Los Angeles. This seven-week summer intensive program was geared to facilitating Asian students' entry into the university and the language instruction was at the heart of this model (Brinton, Snow, & Wesche, 1989). Other variations of immersion can be found in the United States, such as FLAC (Foreign language across the curriculum) or CLAC (Culture and languages across the curriculum). They are quite different from immersion and simply represent adapted versions of language teaching through content (Content-based language teaching, or CBT). In this approach, content is taught in the mother tongue with a language component designed to reinforce the material taught. For example, at St Olaf's College in Minnesota, students can expand their linguistic knowledge of French, Chinese, German, Russian, or Spanish by taking an optional language course linked to the discipline they are studying. The teaching can take different forms:

- a pairing of a content and a language instructor
- one instructor teaches both content and language
- one content instructor leads discussion groups, where students read texts in their second language while examining and analysing them in their native language.

These variations also offer a study-abroad semester where students can refine their knowledge of the language and culture. Soltero (2018) describes a fully bilingual tertiary dual-language immersion model in Puerto Rico as well as in Florida.

In Europe, at the university level, CLIL is known by different names: ILCHE (Integrating learning and content in higher education), HEPCLIL (Higher education perspectives on content and language integrated learning), and EMI (English medium instruction). They generally refer to the instruction through English. Although, in theory, CLIL can be carried out in a variety of languages, English instruction is predominant. This approach is called CEIL (Content and English integrated learning; Dalton-Puffer et al., 2010, p. 286). The term "EMI" has become more common to describe this approach (Doiz, Lasagabaster, & Sierra, 2013; Macaro, 2018). The focus of these approaches is content taught in a foreign language by non-native speakers for non-native-students. There is almost no foreign language teaching and the linguistic objectives are less clearly defined (Dalton-Puffer et al., 2010). "Certain immersion approaches have been criticized

---

[9] "Comprehensible input" refers to Krashen's theories, according to which the linguistic input must be comprehensible to the learner at or slightly above his/her level of competence and it is in this non-threatening context that the acquisition of a given language can take place. For more details, see Chapter 3.

because they emphasized content more than form which has been associated with a lack of precision in language production" (Muñoz, quoted by Meier, 2012, pp. 7–8).

Following the Bologna Declaration (1999),[10] universities made major changes to their programs to facilitate the movement of Erasmus exchange students[11] and to allow them to continue their studies in a common language, English, the new *lingua franca* of the European Union. Universities offered more and more graduate programs (masters and doctorates) in English—in particular, in the pure sciences and business administration. At the undergraduate level, this European policy of mobility should in theory allow students to acquire languages other than English but in practice, English is the common language in the internal Erasmus group.

French universities offer a different path: FOS (French for specific purposes),[12] where students are taught French for business, agriculture, tourism, and FOU (French for university purposes).[13] These two programs are geared to non-Francophone learners who want to enter and be integrated into French universities and the French work force. The goals are to develop competence based on four components—linguistic, discursive, cultural, and disciplinary (Gohard-Radenkovic, 2004)—along three axes (Mangiante & Parpette, 2011; Yasri-Labrique, 2013):

- modules accompanied by language courses
- intensive language and content training courses
- a university diploma.

Each university uses its own methodology, framework (particularly immersion) models, and procedures. Some French universities are also introducing EMI courses.

Finally, there are bilingual universities teaching programs with two languages in parallel, such as the Catalan and Basque universities or the University of Freiburg in Switzerland (French and German). Catalan students leaving high school and entering the Catalan universities are usually fluent in both Catalan and Spanish. In order to complete their diplomas, students must take a certain number of courses in the two teaching languages of the university and write exams in both languages (Brohy, 2008; Vila 2018). Mutual understanding between the two groups in Freiburg is facilitated by the constant, authentic, and meaningful contact. For example, in the *Bilingue Plus* program at the University of Freiburg, cooperation between students of both linguistic groups is fostered by having them work on tasks and topics to be prepared together in small mixed

---

[10] In 1999, 29 countries of the European Higher Education Area (EHEA) adopted a system of comparable degrees, and enhanced and facilitated mobility of students and professors throughout the European university system (European Higher Education Area, 1999, "The Bologna Declaration").

[11] Students in Erasmus programs travel and study in the different countries of the European Community and very often find themselves studying in English in the countries where they stay. These exchanges are named in honour of Erasmus of Rotterdam, who advocated travel and stays in different parts of Europe.

[12] For more information on FOS, see Agito (n.d.), "Le FOS."

[13] To consult research done on FOU, see the Centre de ressources et d'ingénierie documentaires (2017).

groups (Gohard-Radenkovic, 2013, p. 15; Racine, Keller-Gerber, & Burkhalter, 2018, p. 23). Professors may be required to deliver their courses in both teaching languages of the university. In fact, every new professor hired into the University of Freiburg must be able to work and teach fluently in French, German, and English. According to Gajo (2018), formal immersion is not used as a teaching method at Swiss universities; instead, they have plurilingual environments with parallel monolinguism.

Bilingual programs at European universities have increasingly come to mean the national language plus English.

3. IMMERSION AT THE UNIVERSITY OF OTTAWA

The following section describes the implementation of French immersion at uOttawa. This initiative dates from the 1980s. From its beginnings, this approach was reserved exclusively for non-Francophone students (Anglophones or Allophones) who wished to pursue immersion at the university level; Francophones were not allowed into the courses. In the course of its history, the university has applied two models in succession: the sheltered, and later, the adjunct models (Brinton, Snow, & Wesche, 1989; Knoerr, 2010).

3.1. Historical View of French Immersion At uOttawa

The University of Ottawa has been a bilingual university since its founding in 1848. It offers two course streams in the two official languages of Canada (English and French) and encourages both institutional and personal bilingualism. It has always supported students wanting to take courses in their second language with the possibility of writing their reports and papers and fulfilling other course requirements in their first language. Nevertheless, few students were taking advantage of this opportunity, even though they had reached an advanced level in their second language. In the 1980s, two researchers at the Second Language Institute, P. Hauptman and M. Wesche, along with a visiting professor, S. Krashen,[14] proposed an initial immersion project. This project, which took shape in 1982 with the cooperation of the School of Psychology, was designed to bridge the passage of second language students into content courses offered in the other official language.

French immersion at uOttawa has its roots in Krashen's Comprehensible Input theory and in the teaching of languages for specific purposes (Krashen, 1985). This approach, implemented as early as the 1980s, was described later by Burger, Wesche, and Migneron (1997), yielded two successive models: the sheltered model and the adjunct model.

3.2. The Sheltered Model

Definition: According to this model, one section out of the many offered in a content course is reserved for second language students. All students were required to complete the same readings, assignments, and examinations and were subject to

---

[14] Krashen is a linguist, specializing in second language acquisition and bilingual education who spent a sabbatical term at uOttawa.

the same evaluation criteria as the other sections. The instructor of the section, designated "sheltered," would arrange for a time within class sessions to address linguistic issues (Edwards, Wesche, Krashen, Clément, & Kruidenier, 1984). This support was aimed at fostering students' receptive skills.

The Content Course: In the sheltered model, all the sections of the content course had a common course outline and were extremely structured. The textbook was the same for the other non-sheltered sections and chapter summaries were provided. Supplementary documents providing extra support, such as tables, graphs, illustrations, photos, and videos complemented the course. This lecture-style course did not require much oral participation from the students. Students in all sections were evaluated using a multiple-choice format. This applied to the weekly tests on content, and the common mid-term and final examinations

Language Support Course: Second language students also received linguistic support from the Second Language Institute (now the Official Languages and Bilingualism Institute) instructor for twenty minutes during each content course. The main objective was to ensure that students understood the content course and, if not, to answer their questions. The second goal was to create a relaxed atmosphere and reduce anxiety and any affective blockages the students might have in order to encourage them to communicate in their second language (Krashen, 1984). This support was assigned the same value as a regular second language course, as students who passed their content courses in French automatically obtained the credits normally attributed to a second language course (Burger, Chrétien, Gingras, Hauptman, & Migneron, 1984).

The Content Instructors: Content instructors were full-time, experienced professors, specialists in their domain, who had volunteered to participate in the project. In the same trimester, they taught both a sheltered section and a section for native speakers, to ensure they were following the same progression in both courses. Still, sometimes the content instructors made accommodations in their lecture presentations for the second language students. The research on the psychology lectures showed that they spontaneously made adjustments in their teaching style in the sheltered sections, but that these adjustments differed from one instructor to the next. Thus, one wrote more on the blackboard, gave more illustrative examples and more concrete examples, and suggested exercises to apply the material; other instructors sometimes reverted to translation for certain terms or expressions. Others unconsciously modified their verbal and non-verbal style, slowing their spoken delivery, adding more pauses and making fewer elisions, simplifying the syntax of sentences, and exaggerating facial expressions (see Wesche & Ready, 1985). The content instructors accepted the presence of a language instructor in their courses and allowed them to devote 15–20 minutes of the course to language activities (Burger, Chrétien et al., 1984; Burger et al., 2013).

The Language Instructors: The language instructors, too, were full-time experienced teachers who had volunteered for this project and were interested in the content material. In the beginning, there was neither an existing methodology nor any special material created to respond to the special needs of these students. Instead, the approach relied on the flexibility of the language instructors and their sensitivity to the students' language difficulties. They had to develop language material based on the content of the content course and create activities adapted to the particular needs of the learners. During that time, thanks to a cordial rapport and close collaboration, the two instructors (content and language) were usually comfortable intervening during the course. The language instructor might also suggest to the content instructor ways of adapting their teaching style to the needs of their students:

> Because of being in close communication with the students, sometimes, the language teacher could more easily detect difficulties, resolve particular problems and then indicate to the content professor adaptations to make and suggest techniques which would stimulate communication and foster a climate of confidence (Burger et al., 1984, p. 401 [trans.]).

Students: The students were a homogenous group of language learners, strong enough to understand the content course. All the students had chosen to participate in immersion, knowing full well the risks they might face. When they registered in the section, they signed a contract in which they promised not to use English textbooks or attend the course in English and to do the examination in French. From the beginning, they knew that the course would have the same requirements as regular courses. Nevertheless, as there was a small number of students in the sheltered section, it gave the instructors the opportunity to offer them extra support. The students studied in their own cocoon with no direct contact with French-speaking students who were studying the same subject matter.

3.3. The Adjunct Model

Definition: The adjunct model[15] offered a content course in the target language with the second language students integrated with native speakers, who formed the majority of learners. The course was no longer tailored to the language level of the second-language learners. In addition, each content course was accompanied by a weekly ninety-minute adjunct language course (Burger et al., 1997; Burger et al., 2013; Knoerr, 2010; Ready & Wesche, 1992).

The content course: Five courses from the Faculties of Arts and of Social Sciences (*Histoire générale du Canada*, *Introduction à la psychologie*, *Introduction au language*, *Sociologie de la famille*, and *Introduction aux sciences politiques*) were offered in the adjunct format. For two of these courses, students had to participate in discussion groups (Ready & Wesche, 1992). Evaluation varied from one course to another. Some only had a mid-term and final exam with multiple choice questions, while others required both written assignments, such as critical reviews of articles, and exams with short or long essay questions.

---

[15] See Chapter 3 for further information on the implementation of the adjunct model at uOttawa.

Research done on this model (Burger et al., 1997) showed that certain courses required more advanced language competence than others. For example, the psychology course was based on a very structured textbook and required mostly receptive skills. As such, it did not need a very high level of second-language competence. On the other hand, the political science course, where the readings consisted of scientific articles and in which the students had to participate in discussions with their Francophone peers as well as write papers and essays for their assignments or their final exams, required a more advanced language competence. Research by Ready and Wesche (1992) indicated that the social science courses which were added in the adjunct format were cognitively more demanding and that this style of teaching presented a real challenge for second-language students.

Language support: The first objective of the adjunct course was to increase students' confidence[16] and to teach them some strategies for understanding the content course and learning the material in French — all activities for receptive skills. The second objective focused on language development, oral production activities, and then writing activities.

The content instructors: These instructors were specialists in their field, with native speakers preferred but normally without training in second-language teaching. They had volunteered to participate in this project and had accepted to work with the language instructor by participating in a pre-session meeting. They also provided information on upcoming lectures at regular intervals.

The language instructors: The language instructors were bilingual native speakers with an excellent mastery of French. They were full-time professors with extensive experience in second-language teaching at the university level. They all held a master's degree in applied linguistics or second-language teaching. They, too, had volunteered for the courses, as they were very interested in the discipline taught and were ready for a long-term commitment to teach in the adjunct course (Burger et al., 1997). Finally, they believed strongly in this approach.

In this model, the language instructors were not teaching assistants for the content instructors and their teaching was different from regular FLS courses (Burger et al., 1994; Knoerr, 2010). Language instructors were expected to attend all content courses in order to prepare the material for each language course. Their presence in the content course served to reassure the students who would not feel abandoned in their journey toward bilingualism. The themes of the lectures, the content vocabulary as well as comprehension and note-taking strategies, formed the basis of the pedagogical material for their language course.

The students: Since the students were taking the content course with Francophones in the adjunct model, a higher language competence level was required than for the

---

[16] Using Krashen's terminology, it was a question of lowering the students' affective filter; for a description of Krashen's theory, which served as the basis of this model, see Chapters 3 and 8.

sheltered courses. This situation offered students direct contact and communication with their Francophone peers in the course. Table 2 describes the difference between the two models.

Table 2: Characteristics of the sheltered and adjunct models

	Sheltered model	Adjunct model
Immersion students	• Low intermediate level[a] (A2+ or B1−) • Separate section • Homogeneous group	• High intermediate level (B2 or C1) • Integrated with Francophones
Credits	• Six credits (content plus language) when the content course was successfully passed	• Three credits for content • Three credits for language
Linguistic adjustments	• 15 minutes during the content lecture	• 90 minutes outside the content lecture
Language teaching	• Provided within the content course by the language instructor (and perhaps by the content instructor)	• Provided outside the content course in a special adjunct course
Weekly schedule	• Three hours	• Three hours for the content course • 90 minutes for the adjunct language

[a]For the levels, see Council of Europe (2001, p. 24).

The sheltered and adjunct models allow students to succeed in their academic courses and to become more confident and make significant gains in their second language (Edwards et al., 1984; Hauptman, Wesche & Ready, 1988).

CONCLUSION

We have seen that immersion is multifaceted in both formal and informal contexts. Education systems around the world integrate content teaching with second or foreign language teaching. In this chapter, we have attempted to outline a typology of its implementations by focusing on university models and their characteristics. Each formal model develops according to its specific contexts. Two-way immersion is the preferred model when two equally strong language groups are present—for example, within regional language (e.g., Catalan, Swedish) situations in Europe. In France, FOS follows a holistic approach and is particularly useful for professional needs since it targets a designated content goal (such as tourism). Since 2000, FOS has been expanded to other learning groups with other goals. FOU is an offshoot of FOS and was developed in France to integrate foreign students into the French university environment. Due to globalization, the integration of content and language instruction (CLIL) and EMI has emerged as a means of fostering the spread of English as a *lingua franca* both in Europe and beyond. In Canada, immersion at the university level is still quite rare. The University of Ottawa has offered classes in the sheltered format, an appropriate approach for students with limited competence, which focus mainly on content. The university has also offered classes in the adjunct format, which were more suitable for stronger students whose focus in on both language improvement and content. It is incumbent upon each institution to analyze its own situation and adopt the most appropriate approach.

REFERENCES

Agito. (n.d.). Le FOS: Français sur objectifs spécifiques. agi.to/enseigner/carnets-pedagogiques/fos-francais-sur-objectifs-specifiques

Bouillon, H. (2010, February). Quel enseignement des langues pour les besoins de demain? Immersion ou submersion? Presentation made at the monthly debate, Ville et Société, Cercle gaulois artistique et littéraire, Brussels. ffue.org/archive/PDF/CERCLE_G_100224_EXPOSE_Bouillon.pdf

Brinton, D.M., Snow, M.A., & Wesche M. (1989). *Content-based second language instruction*. Boston: Heinle and Heinle.

Brohy, C. (2008). Und dann fliesst es wie ein Fluss… L'enseignement bilingue au niveau tertiaire en Suisse. *Synergies: pays germanophones, 12*, 51–66.

Burger, S., Chrétien, M., Gingras, M., Hauptman, P., & Migneron, M. (1984). Le rôle du professeur de langue dans un cours de matière académique en langue seconde. *Canadian Modern Language Review, 41*, 397–402.

Burger, S., Weinberg, A., & Wesche, M. (2013). Immersion studies at the University of Ottawa: From the 1980s to the present. *OLBI Working Papers, 6*, 21–43.

Burger, S., Wesche, M., & Migneron, M. (1997). Late, late immersion: Discipline-based language teaching at the University of Ottawa. In R.K. Johnson & M. Swain (Eds.), *Immersion education: International perspectives* (pp. 65–84). Cambridge: Cambridge University Press.

Canada. Official Languages Act. (1969). Official Languages Act (1969) 1970, R.S.C, chapter 0-2. www.uottawa.ca/clmc/official-languages-act-1969

Caspard, T. (1998). Les "changes" linguistiques en Suisse: XVIIe–XIXe siècles. *Documents pour l'histoire du français langue étrangère ou seconde* [anniversary issue: *Hommage à André Reboullet*], *21*, 111–129. fle.asso.free.fr/sihfles/Documents/Documents%2021%20corrig%E9/Documents%2021%20on-line%20PDF%20corrig%E9/l%20D21%20caspard.pdf

Centre de ressources et d'ingénierie documentaires (CRID). (2017). Le français sur objectifs universitaires. Paris: Centre international d'études pédagogiques (CIEP). www.ciep.fr/sites/default/files/atoms/files/bibliographie-francais-sur-objectifs-universitaires.pdf

Council of Europe. (2001). *Common European Framework of Reference for Languages: Learning, teaching, assessment*. Cambridge: Cambridge University Press. rm.coe.int/1680459f97

Coyle, D., Hood, P., & Marsh, D. (2010). *CLIL: Content and Language Integrated Learning*. Cambridge: Cambridge University Press.

Cummins, J., & Swain, M. (1986). *Bilingualism in education: Aspects of theory, research and practice*. London: Longman.

Dalton-Puffer, C. (2011). Content-and-language integrated learning: From practice to principles? *Annual Review of Applied Linguistics*, *31*, 182–204.

Dalton-Puffer, C., Nikula, T., & Smit, U. (Eds.). (2010). *Language use and language learning in CLIL classrooms*. Amsterdam: John Benjamins.

Doiz, A., Lasagabaster, D., & Sierra, J.M. (Eds). (2013). *English-medium instruction at universities: Global challenges*. Bristol: Multilingual Matters.

Durocher, R. (2013). [The] quiet revolution. In *The Canadian Encyclopedia*. www.thecanadianencyclopedia.ca/en/article/quiet-revolution

Edwards, H., Wesche, M., Krashen, S., Clément, R., & Kruidenier, B. (1984). Second language acquisition through subject-matter learning: A study of sheltered psychology classes at the University of Ottawa. *Canadian Modern Language Review*, *41*, 268–282.

European Higher Education Area (EHEA). (1999). The Bologna Declaration of 19 June 1999. www.ehea.info/media.ehea.info/file/Ministerial_conferences/02/8/1999_Bologna_Declaration_English_553028.pdf

Fortune, T.W., & Tedick, D.J. (2008). One-way, two-way and indigenous immersion: A call for cross-fertilization. In T.W. Fortune & D.J. Tedick (Eds.), *Pathways to multilingualism: Evolving perspectives on immersion education* (pp. 3–21). Clevedon: Multilingual Matters.

Gajo, L. (2018). Bilingual modes in higher education: Didactic and sociopolitical issues. In H. Knoerr, A. Weinberg, & C.E. Buchanan (Eds.), *Current issues in university immersion* (pp. 1–27). Ottawa: Groupe de recherche en immersion au niveau universitaire (GRINU).

Genesee, F. (1987). *Learning through two languages: Studies of immersion and bilingual education*. Cambridge, MA: Newbury House.

Gohard-Radenkovic, A. (2013). Radiographie de l'immersion dans l'enseignement supérieur en Suisse et à l'Université de Fribourg: les prérequis nécessaires. *OLBI Working Papers*, *6*, 3–19.

Gohard-Radenkovic, A., Knoerr, H., & Weinberg, A. (2014). Introduction. In H. Knoerr, A. Weinberg, & A. Gohard-Radenkovic (Eds.), *L'immersion française à l'université: politiques et pédagogies* (pp. 1–20). Ottawa: University of Ottawa Press.

Gohard-Radenkovic, A. (Ed.). (2004). *Communiquer en langue étrangère: de compétences culturelles vers des compétences linguistiques* (2nd ed.). Bern: Peter Lang.

Gomez-Imbert, E. (1992). Force des langues vernaculaires en situation d'exogamie linguistique: le cas du Vaupés colombien, Nord-Ouest amazonien. *Cahiers des sciences humaines*, *27*, 535–559.

Gomez-Imbert, E. (1996). When animals become "rounded" and "feminine": Conceptual categories and linguistic classification in a multilingual setting. In J.J. Gumperz & S.C. Levinson (Eds.), *Rethinking linguistic relativity* (pp. 438–469). Cambridge: Cambridge University Press.

Hauptman, P.C., Wesche, M.B., & Ready, D. (1988). Second-language acquisition through subject-matter learning: A follow-up study at the University of Ottawa. *Language Learning*, *38*, 433–475.

Knoerr, H. (2010). L'immersion au niveau universitaire: nouveaux modèles, nouveaux défis, pratiques et stratégies *OLBI Working Papers*, *1*, 89–110.

Kok-Escalle, M.-C., & Bellassen, J. (2011). History, practices and models. In G. Zarate, D. Lévy, & C. Kramsch (Eds.), *Handbook of multilingualism and multiculturalism* (pp. 365–372). Paris: Éditions des archives contemporaines. (Original work published 2008)

Krashen, S.D. (1982). *Principles and practice in second language acquisition*. Englewood Cliffs, CA: Prentice Hall.

Krashen, S.D. (1984). Immersion: Why it works and what it has taught us. *Language and Society, 12*, 61–64.

Krashen, S.D. (1985). *The Input Hyphothesis: Issues and implications*. New York: Longman.

Lambert, W.E., & Tucker, G.R. (1972). *Bilingual education of children: The St. Lambert experiment*. Rowley, MA: Newbury House.

Lingua franca. (2019). *Oxford Advanced Learner's Dictionary*. www.oxfordlearnersdictionaries.com/definition/english/lingua-franca

Lyster, R. (2012, April). *Connections and complementarity across CLIL and immersion contexts*. Paper presented at the CLIL 2012 conference — From Practice to Visions, Utrecht.

Macaro, E. (2018). *English medium instruction*. Oxford: Oxford University Press.

Mangiante, J.-M., & Parpette, D. (2011). *Le français sur objectif universitaire*. Grenoble: Presses universitaires de Grenoble.

Marsh, D. (2003). Report: The relevance and potential of content and language integrated learning (CLIL) for achieving MT+2 in Europe. Berlin: European Language Council (ELC) Information Bulletin 9. userpage.fu-berlin.de/elc/bulletin/9/en/marsh.html

Meier, G. (2012). Introduction. *Synergies Europe* [thematic issue: *Éducation bilingue en Europe et ailleurs: statu quo et itinéraires de recherche possibles*], *7*, 5–16.

National Dual Language Immersion Research Alliance. (2011). [Position paper]. Washington, D.C.: American Councils for International Education. www.americancouncils.org/sites/default/files/DLI-portfolio.pdf

Quebec. (1969). *An Act to promote the French Language in Quebec* (Bill 63; *Loi pour promouvoir la langue française au Quebec*). www.oqlf.gouv.qc.ca/50ans/images/Bill_63.pdf

Quebec. (1974). *Official Language Act* (Bill 22; *Loi sur la langue officielle*. National Assembly of Quebec. web.archive.org/web/20041120120718/http://www.oqlf.gouv.qc.ca/charte/reperes/Loi_22.pdf

Quebec. (1977). *Charter of the French language* (Bill 101; *Charte de la langue française*. www.legisquebec.gouv.qc.ca/en/showdoc/cs/C-11

Racine, R., Keller-Gerber, A., & Burkhalter, K. (2018). Créer un espace bilingue et interdisciplinaire: ein Sprachlernprojekt zwischen Sprachen, Disziplinen, Perspektiven. *Language Learning in Higher Education, 8*, 21–44. doi.org/10.1515/cercles-2018-0002

Ready, D., & Wesche, M. (1992). An evaluation of the University of Ottawa sheltered program: Language teaching strategies that work. In R.J. Courchesne, J.I. Glidden, J. St. John, & C. Thérien (Eds.), *L'enseignement des langues secondes axé sur la compréhension* (pp. 389–405). Ottawa: University of Ottawa Press.

Rebuffot, J. (1993). *Le point sur l'immersion au Canada*. Anjou, Québec: Centre éducatif et culturel.

Soltero, S.W. (2018). Dual language higher education: Post-secondary discipline-based bilingual Immersion. In H. Knoerr, A. Weinberg, & C.E. Buchanan (Eds.), *Current issues in university immersion* (pp. 29–54). Ottawa: Groupe de recherche en immersion au niveau universitaire (GRINU).

Statistics Canada. (2013). *Immigration and ethnocultural diversity in Canada: National Household Survey, 2011*. Cat. no. 99-010-X2011001. Ottawa. www12.statcan.gc.ca/nhs-enm/2011/as-sa/99-010-x/99-010-x2011001-eng.pdf

Statistics Canada. (2017). *Enrolments in French immersion programs, public elementary and secondary schools, Canada*. www150.statcan.gc.ca/n1/daily-quotidien/171103/cg-c001-eng.htm

Stern, H.H. (1984). The immersion phenomenon. *Language and Society, 12*, 4–7.

Strevens, P. (1977). Special purpose language learning: A perspective. *Language Teaching and Linguistics Abstracts, 10*, 145–163.

Swain, M., & Johnson, R.K. (1997). Immersion education: A category within bilingual education. In R.K. Johnson & M. Swain (Eds.), *Immersion education: International perspectives* (pp. 1–16). Cambridge: Cambridge University Press.

Tedick, D.J., Christian, D., & Fortune, T.W. (Eds.). (2011). *Immersion education: Practices, policies, possibilities*. Bristol: Multilingual Matters.

Trudel, M. (2001, 2003). *Les mythes et la réalité de notre histoire du Québec*. Saint-Laurent: Québec loisirs.

Vila, F.X. (2018). Linguistic models in higher education in Catalonia: Origins, rationale, achievements, and challenges. In H. Knoerr, A. Weinberg, & C.E. Buchanan (Eds), *Current issues in university immersion* (pp. 55–88). Ottawa: Groupe de recherche en immersion au niveau universitaire.

Wesche, M., & Ready. D. (1985). Foreigner talk in the university classroom. In S.M. Gass & C.G. Madden (Eds.), *Input in second language acquisition* (pp. 89–114). New York: Newbury House.

Widdowson, H.D. (1983). *Learning purpose and language use*. New York: Oxford University Press.

Yasri-Labrique, E. (2013). Le français sur objectif universitaire: une approche multifocale. In E. Yasri-Labrique, P. Gardies, & K. Djordjevic (Eds.), *Didactique contrastive: questionnements et applications* (pp. 67–81). Montpellier: Éditions Cladole.

CHAPTER 5

Immersion in Canada in Its Multiple Forms:
From Vision to Reality

Bettina B. Cenerelli, Eva Lemaire, and Françoise Mougeon

INTRODUCTION

IMMERSION TAKES ON MULTIPLE FORMS in Canada. The three examples presented below, which are located in Ontario (French Second Language Program, Glendon College), Alberta (Campus Saint-Jean, University of Alberta), and British Columbia (French Cohort Program, Simon Fraser University), respectively, will provide the reader with some institutional solutions that illustrate the necessity to adapt programs to local realities and challenges. Student populations have changed, challenging these three institutions to put new *dispositifs* in place to continue to promote students' bilingualism. This brings us to questioning the original definition of "immersion": initially, it was a program "intended for children whose home language is English ... and who are willing to undergo a large part of their schooling through the medium of French" (Stern, 1984, p. 4). In this book, immersion refers to a pedagogical approach that "allows the learning of that second language by being taught in that second language" (Toupin, 1986, p. 7). However, the multiplication of a variety of approaches to learning French and non-linguistic disciplines in French also opens the door to including student groups that are increasingly diversified, but who all want to pursue their undergraduate studies in French. The demographic changes among our student populations have prompted post-secondary institutions to adapt to this new reality, if only to respond to institutional visions or goals established decades ago.

While challenges remain similar for all three institutions, solutions put in place as a response vary:

- Different labels ("campus," "college," "program") are a first indicator of differences in origins, size, and goals.
- Campus Saint-Jean (in Alberta) can look back on a tradition as a bilingual academic institution of over a century; by contrast, Simon Fraser University's (SFU) Program in Public and International Affairs (also called French Cohort Program, FCP) will celebrate its 15th anniversary in 2019.[1]

Even where bilingualism was an integral part of an organization's vision at the time of its founding/inception, the institutional response to a changed reality varies from one to the next:

---

[1] The name was changed in the fall of 2018 from Program in Public Administration and Community Services to Program in Public and International Affairs, in response to growing student interest in the international side and a change of focus in political science research in general.

- At Glendon College, the original goal was to encourage French–English bilingualism in a predominantly Anglophone context. However, programs need to adjust to changing student populations as well as socio-economical and demographic changes. As student profiles became more and more plurilingual — a plurilingualism which may or may not include the French language — a new upgrading program for bilingualism was put in place, allowing students to acquire the necessary language proficiency level in order to meet the college's bilingual requirements.

In other situations, conversely, immersion becomes a question of defending speakers' minority rights in the context of a dominant second language.

The pool of Francophone speakers is shrinking; however, the inclusion of Francophile speakers in French-stream courses has two explanations: the need to increase the number of students in French-medium classes and the need to respond to changes in the socio-demographic makeup of the student body. For example:

- Glendon College and Campus Saint-Jean are able to offer a whole range of postsecondary programs.
- By contrast, at SFU, teaching in French is restricted to courses in political science and history in the French Cohort Program, to a teacher training program in the Faculty of Education, and to courses given in the Department of French.

This chapter will present three adaptations of immersion to the new sociodemographic reality: a program with French language training in response to institutionalized bilingualism (Glendon College);[2] an institution where an entire university campus is dedicated to education in French (Campus Saint-Jean); and a program that allows students to study in French in three disciplines (FCP). The presentation of each institution will start with a short historical overview, continue with a summary of the administrative structure, and conclude with a presentation of the program, its learning objectives, and challenges ahead.

1. GLENDON COLLEGE: ADAPTING TO A NEW STUDENT POPULATION

1.1. Historical Overview

Glendon is the birthplace of York University. It was created in 1965 to relieve overcrowding at the University of Toronto by accepting a large number of its undergraduate students. In 1966, York University moved out to a more spacious location while Glendon College remained on site. Escott Reid, its first principal, defined the mission of the college as training the next generation of bilingual Canadian public servants and diplomats, in line with then Prime Minister Lester B. Pearson's vision (see Preface and Chapter 1). Historically, Glendon is a traditional liberal arts college, committed to the official bilingualism policy of Canada. Over time, it has evolved to include a wider selection of global fields of interest, to respond to changes in the job market. Political

---

[2] Glendon allows students from both linguistic groups to enrol, whether the course is offered in English or in French.

science and international studies may still reflect the preferred choice of many undergraduate students, but more and more are attracted to economics, which in turn tends to trigger an increased interest in modern languages, including French, although often in competition with Spanish or other languages. Finally, in an increasingly multicultural and multilingual society, acquiring other languages of more immediate applicability has proved detrimental to the importance of French.

In order to achieve its bilingual mission, Glendon offers courses in both English and French in all disciplines of specialization. All administrative and teaching staff are bilingual or multilingual. Students must meet linguistic requirements in order to obtain their degree from Glendon College (i.e., they must pass a six-credit course at any level, in their second language — French, for most of them). Alternatively, they may opt for a six-credit FSL course at the second-year level — a "safer" choice, since this option includes any other prior FSL course. All in all, institutional requirements differ substantially from the college's bilingual mandate, which aims to prepare students to use their second language in their academic life in order to fully participate in that language in debates and discipline-related activities. The college linguistic requirements, as defined some 50 years ago, remain unchanged.

1.2. Current Student Population

Since its founding, the student population has become more diverse. Originally, Glendon students were mainly unilingual Anglophones. Today, most incoming students are already bilingual and often speak several languages (although French may not be one of them). One might think that learning yet another language would therefore not seem too difficult for them, and that being multilingual might even give them an edge over their unilingual predecessors. However, while it gives them a fresh sense of the changing value/weight of languages, it also leads them to minimize the importance of French as they plan for their future — contrary to the expectations of the college.

Like other post-secondary institutions, Glendon College has defined its identity based on its surrounding community. The minority status of the local French-speaking community and the intensity of the contacts between the communities speaking the two official languages have had a critical influence on the bilingualism of Franco-Ontarians, which school boards and universities have had to acknowledge in the design of their curricula. A small proportion of the students admitted to Glendon come from immersion programs and have received between 30% to 100% of their education in French, some as early as kindergarten, and others from Grade 1 or later. However, most incoming students come from regular programs in Ontario schools, with a maximum of 50 minutes of daily Basic French instruction, starting in Grade 3 or 4. Some students come from other provinces or countries, sometimes with no knowledge of French. In sum, Glendon caters to high school graduates, most of them English-speaking, and whose competence in French varies greatly from non-existent to advanced. Incoming students also include Quebec Francophone students attracted to the big multicultural city of Toronto and wishing to brush up on their English.

In such a context, Glendon's bilingual *raison d'être* is justified. Its bilingual mission was inspired by the recommendations of the Royal Commission on Bilingualism and Biculturalism (Laurendeau & Dunton, 1967),[3] which redefined Canadian language policy, based on the idea of a country united around the two languages of its founding peoples and around its multiple cultures. Given its small size (about 3000 students), this liberal arts faculty facilitates easier contacts between students and staff, and fosters the hope and goal of mutual comprehension between the two linguistic groups. About 80% of students are English-speaking, outnumbering French-speaking students. This being said, the presence of French native speakers on campus provides FSL students with genuine experiential opportunities to use French in real-life situations and gives them a valuable learning edge while creating a common ground for good mutual understanding.

1.3. Administrative Context

The redesigned program of French as a second language (FSL) is housed in a separate, autonomous administrative unit, the Centre for Studies in French, whose mission is to teach French to university students. New faculty were hired to develop a new curriculum for the programs and to coordinate a team of tutors and language teachers in charge of smaller classes.

In addition to faculty, other resources for the centre include the *Salon francophone*, a social and cultural space where unstructured activities are organized by senior French-speaking students acting as language monitors, and available for free to FSL students on a drop-in basis in a relaxed atmosphere. The same language monitors also manage in-class structured discussion groups under the class instructor's supervision. Additionally, the centre benefits from the presence of an exchange student from France, hired as a language monitor and coordinator of the language monitor team, who proposes original activities in French outside class hours. The critical need for contact opportunities with the French-speaking community in the acquisition of certain aspects of the target language has already been stressed by many researchers, but most remarkably by a group of Glendon students in linguistics (Alleyne, Chow, Famula, Rodrigues, & Thiang, 2010).

Apart from FSL courses, English-speaking students may also take courses taught in French, and interact in French with Francophone students, faculty, and staff on campus. Moreover, a few bilingual jobs are available on campus for students. Finally, a number of placements are offered in French-speaking community and governmental agencies of the greater Toronto area, as will be discussed later.

Because of the linguistic regulations in place at Glendon College, students must meet some basic language requirements in their second language — French, for most students — in order to graduate. To reach the desired French competency level, most students[4] choose to enrol in FSL courses that the centre offers to English-speaking

---

[3] Established in 1963 by the Pearson government, the Royal Commission on Bilingualism and Biculturalism, also known as the Laurendeau–Dunton Commission, provided an opportunity for a fundamental debate on Canadian identity, the situation of French Canadians, and Canada's future. It led to the adoption of the Official Languages Act in 1969. More details are available in Chapter 1.

[4] Some students taking courses in their second language demonstrate that they already meet the college's linguistic standards. Others may also have scored high on the placement test taken

students majoring in disciplines other than French. Prior to being admitted, students must take a placement test,[5] to assess their level in French and determine their learning profile and an individualized learning path through a set of FSL courses. The placement test is used at various stages of the learning process to assess progress and potentially redesign the student's learning path. Alternatively, in order to meet the college's second language requirements, students may take a content course in their second language and obtain a passing mark.

1.4. The Program

1.4.1. Organization

The new FSL program was implemented in 2012, following several years of intense preparation and development. The research team benefited from financial support through York University's Academic Innovative Fund (AIF) to design an innovative and efficient way for students to become better bilinguals and meet their academic and future professional goals in French in the four-year time frame of their undergraduate studies. The research team drew upon the findings of Alleyne et al. (2010), which examined student, faculty, and staff perceptions regarding the efficiency of the previous FSL program. Most of the main findings and recommendations identified in the study have served as guidelines to design a new curriculum and approach to FSL learning and teaching at Glendon.

The linguistic requirements of the college are based on the overarching principle that graduating students should be able to participate in debates and discuss issues related to their area of specialization in both official languages, although they may perform better in one of them. Indeed, it would be unrealistic and naïve to expect students to become balanced bilinguals within four years while meeting other discipline-related requirements. The purpose of the new program is to prepare students to use their linguistic skills efficiently to perform the academic tasks required in their fields of study.

The new curriculum comprises four levels; a passing mark is needed to progress from one level to the next. The most advanced level offers three options during the last term:

- enrolling in a course taught in French in the student's major (with language support)
- a bilingual placement in a community or government agency
- a second-year FSL course

Upon completing one of these options, in addition to the previous term's second-level FSL course, students will have obtained the six French-language credits required by the college.

---

after their admission to Glendon. In both cases, students from these categories do not need to enrol in FSL courses.

[5] The assessment and evaluation test in FSL — a task-based and effect-driven tool — was developed between 2011 and 2012 by a team of researchers from the Department of Human Development and Applied Psychology at the Ontario Institute for Studies in Education (OISE) in Toronto, in cooperation with the Glendon team of FSL instructors. It has been in place since 2014.

Course material provides a progression through genres and tasks related to the academic content. Tasks become gradually more complex and demanding as the course progresses. Teaching modalities include lecture-type classes, followed by tutorials with 20 students. Smaller structured discussion groups of six to seven students provide hands-on opportunities to perform tasks that involve interaction with peers and French-speaking monitors, engaging all four skills. Placement opportunities are co-organized by the centre and a community liaison agent. Student applicants must take part in an interview to assess their linguistic competence and their autonomy as learners. Efforts are made to match the host and type of job with the student's interests and area of specialization. Their language and content-related learning outcomes are evaluated via an oral presentation during an end-of-session round table with all students and teachers, their participation in the ensuing discussion, and their detailed written placement report, including their log book.

1.4.2. Teaching and Learning Approaches

The research team selected a pedagogical design based on the theoretical framework of French for academic purposes (FAP; see Chapter 4), as described extensively by Mangiante and Parpette (2004, 2011) and the action-based approach as a teaching framework (Puren, 2009), following the principles of the Common European Framework of Reference for Languages (CEFRL; Council of Europe, 2001). This approach defines the language learner as a social actor who has to perform a number of tasks in real situations and contexts of use.

Similar to English for academic purposes, FAP is considered a branch of French for specific objectives.[6] As mentioned by Delcambre and Lahanier-Reuter (2012), academic literacies are closely related to the cultural, geographical, and institutional contexts where a language is learned. FAP is particularly well suited for Glendon students since Glendon's language requirements are defined in terms of students' abilities to use their second language in an academic context, in their fields of specialization, and in related professional prospects. First, the language needs of university students are identified, then specific domains and contexts more directly related to particular learning situations are determined, which will serve as bases for the development of task-based content. Most Glendon students specialize in liberal arts. The cognitive skills needed to perform discipline- and field-related tasks in such academic contexts are somewhat similar across programs and favour the development of gradually complex learning content, thus providing students with adequate exposure to content-related discourse in French. Once they have become familiar with this type of discourse, they become more confident and competent when using it.

---

[6] FAP aims to prepare FSL students for subsequent study abroad in a French-speaking country. In order to develop their academic competence in French, FAP integrates diverse academic disciplines, and takes the FSL learners' limited time, needs, and motivation levels into account, in addition to overall efficiency.

1.5. Challenges

The new curriculum was implemented in 2012 and it reached the end of its first four-year cycle in 2016. Although the formal evaluation process planned in the initial project was not implemented, many changes have been made over the years, as it became obvious that the institutional response to a changing reality was not adequately addressing the many challenges:

Theoretical framework: In light of research conducted by the new team of instructors (Barysevich & Lebel, 2016; Lebel & Viswanathan, 2016; Lebel, Viswanathan, & Barysevich 2018; Viswanathan, Lebel, & Barysevich 2018), the initial FAP approach has been replaced with a new paradigm, sociodiscursive interactionism (Bronckart, 1997). This approach, which views texts and/or discourses as the only empirically verifiable manifestations of human communicative actions, offers a more solid foundation to address the challenges of bilingual education at Glendon.

Teaching modalities: Lectures for large groups followed by small group tutoring sessions have been replaced with two classes a week for groups of 25 students. These sessions are planned and coordinated by a new team of instructors and consist mainly of structured discussion groups comprising 6 to 7 students. Making oral interactions central to language teaching/learning is better suited to the implementation of an action-based approach fostering the development of a communicative competence within the academic context of lifelong bilingualism.

Course delivery: Listening, reading, and writing skills are now taught via online modules and hybrid courses, which were developed with the financial support of both York University's AIF (see York University, n.d.) and the provincial government's Ontario Online initiative (the program no longer exists, but some information is still available at OCUFA, n.d.). These courses have also been used as templates for the development of language support modules for non-Francophone students taking content courses in French. Hybrid courses promote learner autonomy, which is also at the core of the pedagogical approach.

Francophone monitors: These native speakers used to play a role in the language classrooms, but for administrative and logistical reasons they are now only involved in activities outside of the classroom, which are organized within the *Salon francophone*.

Community anchor: French-language activities beyond the classroom have been made mandatory for all levels of FSL courses in order to strengthen ties with Glendon's Francophone community and foster the development of sociolinguistic skills.

It should also be stressed that discipline program requirements continue to increase year over year, imposing an extra burden on students who have to invest more time and energy to accumulate more credits (for instance, in the case of double majors or international content programs), all within a four-year span. Huge second-language needs at the beginner level (many Glendon students are beginners in FSL in spite of French being taught in all Ontario high schools) may constitute a real obstacle to timely graduation for some students.

Conversely, students' commitment to learning French has proved to be critical to stimulate and improve learning (see Mougeon & Rehner, 2015). Making French a part of their everyday life is demanding in terms of time and energy, and it means taking risks. Whatever help they may get from the college in understanding their challenges and managing their learning path, FSL students still are the main actors in their learning experience. Individual strength and maturity certainly play a big role in achieving success, as the learning curve is steep. French is not very present overall in the everyday life of Ontario students, as is the case in several other Canadian provinces outside Quebec. It then becomes the responsibility of the college to create opportunities for authentic French language use, and, moreover, the responsibility of students to look for bilingual jobs or activities and opportunities for contact with Francophones.

In sum, the main challenge for Glendon is to reconcile its ideal bilingual mission, which some may consider too restrictive and outdated, with the reality of another bilingualism that does not necessarily include French but reflects the multilingual composition of the population, as well as, more generally, economy-driven pressures in our hemisphere.

2. CAMPUS SAINT-JEAN: FROM RELIGIOUS TO SECULAR, FROM FRANCOPHONES TO FRANCOPHILES

2.1. Historical Overview

Campus Saint-Jean (CSJ) has its origins in what was once called the Juniorat Saint-Jean, founded in 1908. This bilingual religious institution was set up to train Oblate missionaries, just as the settlement of Western Canada was accelerating. At that time, the teaching was done by priests from France from the Order of the Oblates of Mary Immaculate. It was therefore done in French, to further the mission of evangelization with Francophone settlers and Métis families, but also in English, so that the students trained there could return to the English-language school system if they later decided not to take holy orders. The French origin, initial practices of bilingual education, and vocation of binding together a community are factors that put the current mandate of the campus into perspective: to offer university training in French to Francophone minority students, to English-speaking students from immersion programs, as well as to international students attracted by the province's economic vitality. It also serves as an anchor for the local Francophone community.

Since the foundation of the Juniorat Saint-Jean, the institution has played a key role in the preservation or "survival" (Mahé, 2004, 183) of the Franco-Albertan community. Indeed, the Juniorat, a private institution, was a space for French education and the development of Francophone cultural life after the French language had been set aside by various provincial laws passed between 1892 and 1905 to establish and reaffirm the supremacy of English, notably as the sole language of instruction. Spurred by the closure of the Jesuit College in Edmonton, the Juniorat then evolved in the 1940s into a college not only for training priests and brothers but also for preparing lay people for liberal professions. In the 1960s, Collège Saint-Jean specialized in teacher training, affiliated first with Université Laval and then with the University of Alberta. To this day, education students form the majority of CSJ's student population.

Starting in the 1970s, the Oblates gradually withdrew, and in 1977, the college officially became a full-fledged faculty of the University of Alberta. Faculté Saint-Jean was then recognized to be French-speaking, any courses that its students may take in English (except ESL courses) being provided by the other faculties of the university. One of the particularities of the Faculté Saint-Jean is its multidisciplinary character, as it currently trains students in arts, education, science, business administration, nursing, and Canadian studies. The French language, used in class and by the administration, is the principal characteristic of the faculty, under the direction of the dean. In 2005, the faculty was renamed Campus Saint-Jean, emphasizing the Francophone micro-community that it constitutes, as well as recognizing its specific historical and geographical location, in the heart of the Bonnie Doon[7] French-language neighborhood, an enclave of French culture located four kilometers from the university's main campus.

2.2. Current Student Population

CSJ students have a variety of sociolinguistic and academic profiles that do not fit into clearly defined categories. According to internal statistics collected by the administration, 60% of students are from French immersion secondary schools. Most of these students report English as their first language. However, some students from "mixed" French–English families may actually come from immersion and yet identify French as their first language. This does not mean that they are Anglo- or Franco-dominant in practice. As for students from Francophone minority schools, they may in turn be part of the half of the CSJ student body who declare English as their mother tongue or who are Anglo-dominant.[8] It should also be noted that one out of 10 CSJ students comes from another Canadian province where French can be the majority or minority language, and one in 10 comes from abroad (Lemaire, 2014). It is therefore important to take into account this sociolinguistic and identity-based complexity in order to offer training that is respectful of students' French experiences and adapted to their specific needs.

---

[7] Bonnie Doon is the name of Edmonton's Francophone neighbourhood. Most French services are located there (for example, the headquarters of the Francophone school board, le Conseil scolaire Centre-Nord, a day-care centre, a bookstore, French-speaking medical practices, and various cultural associations). Bonnie Doon has a higher concentration of Francophones than anywhere else in the city.

[8] According to Chavez, Bouchard-Coulombe, and Lepage (2011), 54% of native Franco-Albertans say they use English as the main language of everyday communication (p. 40). Moreover, in Alberta, only 43% of Alberta children with at least one Francophone parent are enrolled in the Francophone elementary and secondary school system, and 18% of youth eligible to study in Francophone minority schools choose the French immersion school system instead (p. 43). Students with a Francophone parent may also go back and forth between the two systems, Francophone or French immersion, for a variety of reasons.

2.3. Administrative Context

On the administrative level, CSJ remains one of the 20 faculties of the University of Alberta, a unit that does not have formal departments, although, "sectors" and "divisions" have been set up internally to bring together university staff involved in the different programs. The faculty consists of about thirty professors and sixty sessional lecturers. Like the instructors, the administrative and technical personnel (about forty people), as well as the librarians, speak French as part of their professional practice.

The study environment is thus decidedly French-speaking and includes spaces for socializing, such as the university residence or the cafeteria. In fact, the language policy set out in the university calendar indicates that the "language of educational and social life is French." It also states that "all the members of the Campus Saint-Jean community are committed to respecting the immersive Francophone nature of the institution in the bilingual environment offered by the University of Alberta" (University of Alberta, n.d., "General information"). This policy (revised in 2016) is based on a new linguistic "vision," which is "to train bilingual citizens who, within a global environment, will contribute to the vitality of French." It also declares that "French, especially in a minority situation, depends on the communities that bring it to life." According to this document "CSJ supports a life in French for the members of its community, in a positive, inclusive environment open to linguistic experimentation."[9] A distinction is made between the mastery of the written standard, a so-called fundamental objective of CSJ, and the use of oral French, considered just as important but conditioned by context, and therefore more tolerant of linguistic variation. The vision, a framework document, brings nuance to the overall linguistic policy which is more normative, and reflects the diversity of language practices observed in a minority context (Villeneuve, 2018, p. 96). It allows a certain acceptance of errors, understood as part of the learning process, and champions the diversity of accents and linguistic variations, including code-switching and translanguaging. Cultural and community exchanges are encouraged in an environment described as "multicultural and multilingual" (p. 96). Several French-language student associations contribute to the development of student life in French. In addition, Edmonton's Francophone community regularly makes use of campus space in organizing cultural events such as film screenings. The community is also invited to join in the academic and cultural activities organized by the campus. Finally, various partnerships make it possible to integrate local community realities into certain courses. For example, courses taught using a community service format allow students to volunteer to work with Francophone associations in order to link theories explored in class and actual Francophone social life. It should be noted that activities aimed at recruiting future students do not simply consist of visits to schools, but also of significant involvement in the local and associative Francophone network.[10]

---

[9] All quotes are from a 2016 French-language poster (University of Alberta, 2016). Translations are the authors'.

[10] Examples include numerous collaborations between CSJ and the Francophone associations that welcome newcomers and immigrants to Edmonton, or the cultural or festive activities

Students wishing to attend CSJ must first meet the admission requirements of the University of Alberta (University of Alberta, n.d., [CSJ] "Règlements"). They must then demonstrate an adequate command of French by taking a placement test, which steers them toward the language courses adapted to their level of language skills, within the sequence of courses offered by CSJ, in preparation for the final French course. This test, created internally, focuses on French grammar. It is administered online and students must complete it independently to finalize their registration at CSJ.[11] Students whose results indicate a lower level of fluency in French are directed toward the appropriate courses. A diagnostic test, currently under development and in its pilot phase, should soon enhance the evaluation, taking into account reading, writing, and grammar skills. Finally, a bilingual writing centre, using peer tutoring, offers a free service for students to discuss and improve their assignments through collaborative learning with trained monitors (Lemaire & Wilson, 2014, 2018).

At CSJ, students from French-language schools have the opportunity to pursue studies entirely in French and to find a Francophone place of socialization and culture rooted in the history of Alberta's Francophone minority and in the fabric of the local community. Immersion students discover a comprehensive environment that goes beyond the classroom and emphasizes cultural and social dimensions. Finally, international students benefit from university training in French while having the opportunity to take courses in English on the main campus and to perfect their skills in both official languages. The Campus Saint-Jean, with its 700 students, is a privileged learning environment in that it constitutes a small community unto itself. The number of students per course remains reasonable for the university level, despite increases in recent years related to a higher demand for training, particularly in education. At present, enrolments do not exceed fifty students in non-language courses and 24 in French courses. Students wishing to broaden their horizons and enrich their training through an experience in a majority Francophone environment have the opportunity to go on an exchange and validate credits by participating in partner programs (exchanges at the universities of Tours or Avignon in France, and the *Explore* program in La Pocatière, Quebec).

Considering the varied sociolinguistic repertoires of students, CSJ is not only a place to learn French in the context of various disciplines, but also a place for intercultural education (University of Alberta, 2009, "Passport"). Although language learning occurs primarily through informal settings, some courses are formally recognized as part of students' education in intercultural matters and global citizenship.

---

co-hosted by the campus for children and teenagers, such as the "Forum of French for the future" (French for the future, n.d.).

[11] Students in the following categories are eligible to write the placement test:
- those who have completed the provincial high school requirements for French
- those who have completed a 4-year program (secondary or post-secondary) taught full-time in French
- those who have a first degree from an accredited university where French is the language of instruction

2.4. The Program

2.4.1. Organization

Campus Saint-Jean offers seven training programs in the following areas: arts, science, education, nursing, business administration, and Canadian studies.[12] In most cases, these programs allow students to obtain a bachelor's degree with 120 credits. Two 30-credit Master's degrees (in education and Canadian studies) are also offered. The main programs of CSJ, which attract the largest number of students, are delivered exclusively in French.[13]

The number of credits in French required to obtain a degree from CSJ varies according to the program, but the minimum is 60. The French courses, labeled FRANC, are taught by instructors from the arts sector, serving all programs. Some of these courses are French-language courses; others are courses in literature or linguistics. It should be noted that one French-language course is mandatory for all students, since they must pass it to obtain their diploma, regardless of their disciplinary orientation. This is a French course at level B2 of the CEFR (Gestion centrale DELF–DALF au Canada, n.d.) — the "strong" B2 level being required for students in education. In addition, with the exception of a few English courses, all (non-language) courses offered at the CSJ are taught and assessed in French. As is the case with SFU (see Section 3), CSJ does not differentiate between Francophone and Francophile students, nor between Alberta students, those from other Canadian provinces that are predominantly Francophone, and international students.

2.4.2. Teaching and Learning Approaches

The didactic approach adopted in French-language courses has been under frequent review since 2010. The course sequence was modified several times between 2010 and 2016. In addition to the final French course (a writing course with variations depending on the student's program), courses in linguistics, literature, and French language (basic or advanced) are proposed to meet students' needs. The French courses that students take in education are designed to allow them to pass the Diplôme d'études en langue française (DELF; see Chapter 10) at the B2 level, which they must obtain in order to have access to final-year internships and graduation.[14]

The didactic approach used in French courses is also largely influenced by the CEFRL. It is communicative, placing a strong emphasis on grammar teaching in context, in view of the weaknesses observed in students' French and in line with existing research (Lyster, 1987; MacFarlane & Wesche, 1995; Tedick, Christian, & Fortune, 2011). Oral

---

[12] The environment and engineering programs have been suspended in recent years, pending review and relaunch.

[13] The bachelor's degrees in nursing, business administration, environment, and engineering are obtained in bilingual programs offered jointly with the other (Anglophone) faculties of the University of Alberta.

[14] The passing mark set by CSJ for these students is an average of at least 72%, with a mark of at least 18 out of 25 for each of the four competencies assessed (reading and listening comprehension, written and oral expression).

and written language are studied together. Most teachers use a task-based approach (Gouiller, 2005), at minimum in the form of communication tasks to be performed, and sometimes in the form of projects leading to the completion of tasks in the local Francophone community. This approach is used especially in selected programs in which the language taught is French tailored to specific objectives (Français sur objectifs spécifiques or FOS), which can be academic (français sur objectifs universitaires, or FOU; see Chapter 4). This is currently the case for French courses taken by students in nursing, science, and business administration, which are aimed at developing language skills related to students' future professional practice.[15] Finally, linguistic development is supported through students' immersion in content courses taught in French, even if they are not centred on linguistic form.[16]

2.5. Challenges

For several years now, CSJ has been trying to reform its programs, and notably its French program, in order to meet the challenges of teaching a student body with such varied needs and profiles.

One of the first challenges is evaluating the students' level of French in order to offer them an appropriate course of study that will enable them to reach at least B2 level, if not a "strong" B2 level, given that the CEFRL was adopted because it is recognized internationally and by more and more Canadian universities. Additionally, Alberta school boards use it to assess students at the end of their secondary education. Currently, in-class assessments are conducted by instructors in the first week of classes to confirm the accuracy of the results of the online grammar test.[17]

Another difficulty lies in the evaluation of students at the end of the programs. Nothing is currently in place to assess students' language proficiency level at the end of their studies. Only education students have to write the DELF examination at the beginning of their last year of academic training. In 2016, the analysis of the results obtained by the students who wrote the DELF examination indicated an alarming failure rate. In fact, 70% of the first cohort of education students failed to reach the oral comprehension threshold and 48% did not meet the reading expectations (Lemaire, 2016). Given the extent of the failure rates, the administration decided, in December 2017, to temporarily lower the success threshold to 68% (with a score of 12.5/25 for each competency).

This raises the question of the relevance of an international test, prepared in France. Several researchers (Banon-Schirman & Makardidjian, 2006) have criticized the

---

[15] In addition to teaching specific vocabulary, the course prepares students for performing tasks in authentic situations, such as giving a thematic workshop to the elderly, a presentation on eating disorders to young adults, etc.

[16] It should be noted, however, that some content instructors strongly encourage the use of the CSJ's bilingual writing centre (CEB) and withdraw up to 10% of the final grade of the work if the quality of French is not considered sufficient.

[17] Students write a text that instructors evaluate, based on a list of grammatical elements for each level referenced in the CEFRL. In practice, the existing team of instructors is faced with the challenge of conducting systematic and focused assessments for all students in a time frame short enough to allow them to be redirected to another course without paying additional fees.

"francocentrism" ("gallocentrism" in Europe) of this tool and its lack of adaptation and relevance to the Canadian context. The main challenge here is how to best prepare students to pass the DELF without the French courses becoming fully dedicated to this exercise, therefore neglecting other content more relevant to the needs of students.

Additional support, in the form of DELF preparation workshops offered through the bilingual writing centre, has been proposed since the 2014–2015 academic year (Lemaire & Wilson, 2018).

Finally, while language skills development also takes place in non-language (content) courses, not all instructors are adequately trained in this domain, despite ongoing training workshops to develop an openness toward a field such as "Writing across the curriculum" (Andre & Graves, 2013; Graves, 2013) or to reinforce cooperation between content and language instructors. Such cooperation would not extend to the development of language support classes as in the adjunct model at the University of Ottawa (see Chapter 8), since this option was rejected during the recent reform of French courses, due to the lack of the financial and human resources required.

Another challenge in a faculty that so strongly asserts its Francophone identity is to ensure that students develop a bilingual literacy at the university level. In the case of the joint programs offered with other faculties, some of the courses are taught in English, but in other programs, such as the Bachelor of Education after Diploma, students take very few courses in English or none at all.[18]

In all cases, an improved evaluation of students at the end of their program would allow their language skills to be better recognized, and the issuing of commendations for excellence in French or of bilingual certificates could then be considered.

As for the challenges, it should also be noted that, as in the case of the FCP at Simon Fraser University (see below), the fact that Campus St-Jean is small, with a small pool of students, logically limits the number of options the institution can offer to keep programs economically viable, despite the desire to offer a diverse range of courses. To address this situation, CSJ now welcomes Francophiles and Francophones from a majority context, in addition to Francophone minorities, which sometimes creates tensions within the student population (Lemaire, 2013).

3. THE FCP: A PROGRAM IN FRENCH IN A MINORITY SETTING

3.1. Historical Overview

We will finally turn west, toward the youngest of the three programs described in this chapter. The Office of Francophone and Francophile Affairs (OFFA) at Simon Fraser University (SFU) was founded in 2003 in a very specific historic and linguistic context: to respond to a growing interest from high school students emerging out of the

---

[18] CSJ offers three main types of Bachelor of Education degrees: Bachelor of Education (B.Ed.), Bachelor of Education/Bachelor of Science (B.Ed./B.Sc.), and Bachelor of Education after Diploma (B.Ed.A.D.). Students who enrol in B.Ed.A.D. already have an undergraduate degree. Their training in education is then two years instead of four.

still young immersion system and the Francophone school system.[19] SFU as such was founded in 1965 and has approximately 37,000 students. OFFA's mission has remained the same over the years, related to the national and provincial government guidelines that define its funding: developing, coordinating, and promoting programs and courses offered in French to respond to the educational needs of the French minority communities in British Columbia. OFFA is working with two distinct faculties at SFU: Arts and Social Sciences (FASS) and Education.[20] The model presented here is part of the programs offered in FASS and is called the French Cohort Program (FCP) or, in its longer form, Program in Public and International Affairs. The inclusion of SFU in the Association des collèges et universités de la francophonie canadienne (ACUFC) since January 2012 has improved the perception of the university in Canada and impacted its programs.

3.2. Current Student Population

Every year, up to 25 students can be admitted into the French Cohort Program. The FCP welcomes a wide variety of students, most (80%) of whom come from local immersion schools in the lower BC mainland. Students may also come from the French school board (12%), from Core French program schools (8%), or other transfer or Canadian institutions. Very few international students have joined the program to date.

3.3. Administrative Context

OFFA is a purely administrative structure (not a department) that supports students who remain affiliated with their main departments (i.e., political science, French, and history, in the case of the FCP). Students who are seeking to be admitted to the FCP have to complete all general SFU admission requirements (SFU, n.d., "Student services"). Once admitted, students choose the FCP as their program, with a defined course list attached to it. As stated above, OFFA does not have its own students but supports the departments to which FCP students belong. A close partnership between the departments and OFFA is therefore essential to the success of the program and its students.

OFFA is located on SFU's Burnaby campus.[21] There, it can use the large and well-equipped offices and lounge rooms of the campus to hold university and community-oriented events, conferences, committee meetings, and so forth. OFFA's spaces do not serve as classrooms, however, even if the language support and summer grammar workshops for FCP students usually take place there. OFFA's offices create, inside of SFU, a Francophone space that is used by Francophone and Francophile students alike to study, work, rent films or books, and do group or individual work. OFFA's student lounge turns

---

[19] For an historical background about OFFA's creation, see Dudas and Chenard (2009). For a detailed presentation on the FCP model, see Cenerelli (2013), on which this present contribution is based.

[20] The federal government contribution for 2013–2018 has been valued at $10 million and confirms OFFA in its mission and vision (SFU, n.d., "Office of Francophone ... Affairs").

[21] Simon Fraser University has three campuses: Burnaby, Surrey, and Vancouver. Burnaby campus is the historic campus, founded in 1965, and housing most of the faculties and departments.

into a meeting or working spot where conversations are usually held in French and where computers and a small library facilitate their work. Events held at OFFA provide students and visitors with the opportunity to meet on common ground, open to Francophones and Francophiles. Of course, other French spaces do exist on campus, notably in and around the Department of French or the Faculty of Education.

The FCP is administered by a team of three: an associate director, an advisor, and a recruitment coordinator.[22] In addition, a marketing coordinator supports all promotional activities (publications, fairs, outreach, etc.) of the FCP.

OFFA's mandate includes the organization of cultural events, which are open to all French-speaking students at SFU, not to FCP students only. OFFA's location in an independent, rented office, non-affiliated with any department or faculty, underscores its mediation role between the university and different community and cultural networks. Given its strong community relations, OFFA can count on the support of numerous community partners who are also playing a more formal participatory role as members of its advisory committee, which also includes representatives from federal and provincial governments. The committee advises the director on all questions related to OFFA's development, program promotion, and activities.[23] Finally, OFFA works closely with other Francophone organizations or institutions in the province to support them in their work.

3.4. The Program

3.4.1. Organization

The FCP is a multi-disciplinary program with courses primarily taught in French. It leads to a Bachelor of Arts in four years, with a minimum of 120 credits, and a concentration

---

[22] OFFA usually recruits in all provincial French immersion schools, in schools of the French school board and in some selected local schools offering Core French programs. The recruitment staff will follow up with second visits to local feeder high schools. The number of schools visited will depend on the number of recruiting agents (between 50–80, with 150–200 presentations). OFFA's mandate limits recruitment activities mostly to British-Columbia.

[23] OFFA's advisory committee includes representatives from the following organizations:
- BC's French school board (Conseil scolaire francophone de la Colombie-Britannique)
- the Federation of Francophones in BC (Fédération des francophones de la C.-B.)
- the Federation of Francophone Parents in BC (Fédération des parents francophones de la C.-B.)
- Canadian Parents for French (British Columbia and Yukon)
- the Society of Economic Development in BC
- the Collège Éducacentre
- SFU's Faculties of Arts and Social Sciences and of Education
- SFU's Departments of French and of Political Science
- FCP student representatives of FCP and Education
- SFU's Continuing Education
- Heritage Canada
- BC's Ministry of Education

in political science and French. At least 75 of the 120 credits must be obtained for courses taught in French: courses given in the Department of French, but also at least eight courses in political science taught in French and two courses in history taught in French. Students have three options to choose from: a major in political science and an extended minor in French; a major in French and an extended minor in political science; or a double Major in French and political science (SFU, n.d., "OFFA: French Cohort Program"). The FCP therefore maintains the dual approach of having students specialize in French (since students need to obtain at least an extended minor in French) and allowing them to apply their knowledge of the French language to other disciplines such as political science or history, which are taught in French.

Linguistic support and clear and transparent evaluation models are key for the success of the FCP. Unlike Glendon College and Campus Saint-Jean, OFFA is currently not using the CEFRL to evaluate language knowledge at the start of their studies. A 30-minute in-house placement test is administered to any student applying to study in French at SFU; this test evaluates basic grammar notions as well as oral and written expression. Depending on their results, students will be placed in the appropriate language course levels. Since FCP students have the option of writing the test four months prior to the start of the school year in September, OFFA offers them targeted language training support over the summer, allowing them to catch up on possible gaps by September.

The program designation as a "cohort" program (the same 25 students are taking all the mandatory courses together[24]) and the designation of those courses as "cohort-specific or reserved for FCP students" (Simon Fraser University, 2019) clearly indicate the difference between a regular course and a cohort-specific course. Nevertheless, FCP courses have their equivalent courses in the regular system, to the extent that they have to respond to the same requirements and learning outcomes as the regular courses. But, contrary to other bilingual institutions where students may have the option of writing assignments in the official language of their choice, all course work in French is graded, there are no qualitative or passing grades, and all course work must be done in French (see Chapter 2). Further, FCP courses do not differentiate between Francophone and Francophile students: given the integration of all students in the same courses and given targeted linguistic support services, those with a weaker language knowledge are usually able to catch up in the first year of the program. The course sequence allows FCP students to learn French at the same time as applying their language knowledge in additional courses.

During their first year, FCP students are introduced to the study of political science in French; three language and writing courses from the Department of French quickly allow students to feel comfortable in writing and presenting in French at the university level. As of the second term, a course in history, given in French, is added to the list of mandatory courses. After the third year (spent in complete immersion in a Francophone institution in either Quebec or Europe), the focus shifts from language courses to content courses. Language learning takes place in its applied form through lectures,

---

[24] Depending on their placement test results, students may not have to take the first-term language courses.

oral expression (participation in classes and oral examinations), and written expression (written assignments).

Linguistic support is continuous but variable throughout the four program years. During the first year, language courses in French allow the students to work on their theoretical framework; this targeted and explicit language support is complemented during the following terms by more implicit language learning and by applying the knowledge in courses given in French. In addition, some of the courses in political science and history use a double correction system[25] for any written essays. Finally, consultation hours with a language instructor and grammar clinics[26] are offered.

Usually following the second year of full-time studies at SFU, students have to spend a mandatory study-abroad exchange in a Francophone partner institution in the province of Quebec or in Europe (France, Belgium, or Switzerland). This exchange is usually done with one of SFU's partner exchange institutions, which gives students an additional support system at SFU and at the partner institution.[27] During their exchange, students usually take the same courses as any Francophone students at the institution, depending on their academic interests (political science, literature, linguistics, etc.); they will often give preference to more European topics or topics covered less often in the FCP program. Credits earned during the exchange count toward their SFU degree.[28] This mandatory exchange is one of the main attractions of the program: students return transformed by their experience, armed with linguistic confidence as well as improved oral and written competencies. Finally, during the fourth year at SFU, language learning exclusively takes place implicitly through courses taught in French (in literature, linguistics, French culture, and political science). Courses taught in the Department of French at this level are not reserved for FCP students.

3.4.2. Teaching and Learning Approaches

In past years, the gap between students' expectations for a practical and future-oriented learning and a traditional academic approach to learning and teaching has become more evident. The FCP looks to respond to students' needs by supporting a model influenced

---

[25] A language instructor will have a first reading of the assignment and will point out mistakes and incorrect formulations to enhance the readability of the assignment. The content instructor receives the revised version that would include any language corrections.

[26] These are weekly non-credited meetings that focus on certain grammar questions. Led by research or teaching assistants, they usually take place for two hours per week; participation is voluntary.

[27] A cummulative grade point average (CGPA) of at least 2.67 is necessary to be eligible for an exchange program at SFU; FCP students who do not have the required CGPA may decide to study at a Quebec institution, for which they need a Letter of Permission.

[28] Current exchange institutions in Europe are: Science Po Paris/Reims, Institut d'études politiques (IEP) Strasbourg, IEP Bordeaux, Université Tours, Université libre de Bruxelles (Belgium, as of 2020; previously, students were also able to go to the Catholic University of Louvain), University of Lausanne (Switzerland). Additional regional campuses of Science Po are also open to the exchange students. In the province of Quebec, students have the choice between Université Laval and Université de Montréal.

by experiential learning (Balleux, 2000; Rogers, 1969) and community-oriented learning. Community engagement may take different forms, from informative meetings to full-blown research projects. As of their first term at SFU, FCP students establish direct contact with associations and organizations in the local Francophone and Francophile communities. One of the language courses in their first term has as its learning objective to connect students with community partners. These first connections are reinforced in the subsequent terms by regular meetings with community representatives organized by OFFA, in which FCP students are directly involved. Upper division political science courses deepen students' knowledge with research projects on community engagement. Experiential learning involves the above-mentioned mandatory study term abroad, an annual conference cycle (*Printemps de la Francophonie*), partnerships and projects with the local Francophone community, and research projects located in the community.[29]

In addition to experiential learning activities, there is a wide range of social activities, organized either for a particular cohort of FCP students (e.g., information sessions on co-op programs at SFU, on mandatory courses or language support, on graduate studies) or for all the cohorts at the same time. As for the formal program of study, it includes a total of 21 mandatory courses in history, political science, and French.[30]

3.5. Challenges

Since its beginnings, the FCP has been aiming to include all student populations, Francophone and Francophile alike, and the set-up as a cohort program was meant to integrate all students regardless of their linguistic background and previous education. Programs given in French are few, allowing for a very close follow-up with students and their learning process. The FCP focuses on the quality of the learning experience more than the number of students.

One of the main challenges remains the language level and knowledge with which students are entering the FCP and the university in general, similarly to what has been discussed for Glendon College and Campus Saint-Jean. Teaching in French immersion means less and less grammar and structural foundations and more and more oral expression. But the placement test imposed on all incoming candidates applying to study in French at SFU does not take this into account; rather, it confronts the students with questions about language forms that they may not have encountered in their high school education. At the same time, it is important that academic education maintain its language standards and expectations in order to produce fully bilingual and bi-literate graduates, with written and oral proficiency.

While some students appreciate the mandatory course schedule, others would prefer more flexibility in relation to course choices. As well, the small program size means that students often remain with the same instructors during the entire course of their

---

[29] FCP students are regularly accepted to conferences such as ACFAS (Association francophone pour le savoir) with political science research on governance in a minority setting or others.

[30] In addition to the FCP mandatory courses, students also need to adhere to the general university requirements in relation to writing, quantitative, and breadth courses (SFU, n.d., "Curriculum initiative").

studies. Some students would like to have more course choices, particularly in the upper course divisions in years three and four. Small changes and adaptations to students' demands are possible — and the recent curriculum change has responded to some of these requests. One of the main program goals remains to lead students to functional bilingualism, allowing them to integrate into the professional fields of their choice. In order to ensure a high level of language proficiency and quality in the program, it would be appropriate to introduce an exit examination. In the fall of 2013, a pilot project (overseen by Cenerelli, one of the authors of this chapter) allowed some fourth-year students to prepare for and pass the DALF at the C1 level.[31] However, as was the case with students at Campus Saint-Jean, the Eurocentric exam approach or the analytical tools that were not typical for Canadian institutions generated complaints. Finally, this kind of exam is directed mostly at second-language learners since first-language speakers are excluded from it.[32]

Despite those disadvantages, the DALF still provides students and administrators alike with the possibility of evaluating language knowledge at the end of the program, thus allowing them to adjust it, and to inform content and language instructors accordingly.

CONCLUSION

A changing student body and a diversifying Francophonie present new realities that institutions pursuing immersion programs must take into account. Institutions have to react to student needs. How to ensure that language acquisition and knowledge respond to academic standards if, in some cases, high school language courses may not prepare students adequately for the post-secondary level? Do we need to reduce the definition of immersion to teaching content in the French language?

Entrance tests imposed by the different institutions presented in this chapter show that today's reality may not always overlap with an historic mission. But does this change justify renouncing it completely? Interest in the French language continues to persist even if its use may be mostly seen as enhancing professional options. High school students who have succeeded in six to twelve years of immersion are used to learning in French. It is certainly of interest for tertiary institutions to continue providing those students with an option of post-secondary education in French, for the benefit of both the students and the country.

---

[31] A total of sixteen students in their fourth year (or higher) of the FCP participated in the DALF (C1) test; average result was 73.25/100. Best individual result was 85/100 (two students); worst individual result was 61/100 (one student). Students succeeded best in oral comprehension (average: 21.68/25) and oral production (19.62/25). Written production was the weakest, with an average result of 14.81/25. Two of the students, however, also showed a very promising result in written production with 92%. Written understanding produced an average result of 17.13/25. OFFA facilitated the DALF preparation by organizing orientation sessions and providing students with preparation manuals.

[32] In the case of this pilot project, one student (who self-identified as Francophone) was still able to pass the DALF; it is interesting to note that his oral comprehension was by far the weakest of the entire group (7/25).

REFERENCES

Alleyne, L., Chow, S., Famula, N., Rodrigues, J., & Thiang, K. (2010). Perceptions of and attitudes toward French L2 learning opportunities on- and off-campus among students not specializing in French at Glendon. Unpublished student research document. yorkspace.library. yorku.ca/xmlui/handle/10315/9861

Andre, J., & Graves, R. (2013). Writing requirements across nursing programs in Canada. *Journal of Nursing Education, 52*, 91–97.

Balleux, A. (2000). Évolution de la notion d'apprentissage expérientiel en éducation des adultes: vingt-cinq ans de recherche. *Revue des sciences de l'éducation, 26*, 263–286.

Banon-Schirman, P., & Makardidjian, C. (2006). Un outil controversé d'une standardisation européenne: le portfolio des langues. *Synergies Europe, 1*, 110–117.

Barysevich, A., & Lebel, M.-É. (2016). Action, genres et tâche: français à vocation universitaire. *Les langues modernes, 3*, 77–82.

Canada. Official Languages Act. (1969). Official Languages Act (1969) 1970, R.S.C. www.uottawa.ca/clmc/official-languages-act-1969

Cenerelli, B.B. (2013). Le modèle FCP de l'Université Simon Fraser: une immersion multidisciplinaire, expérientielle et communautaire. *OLBI Working Papers, 6*, 45–64.

Chavez, B., Bouchard-Coulombe, C., & Lepage, J.-F. (2011). *Portrait of official language minorities in Canada: Francophones in Alberta*. Cat. no.89-642-X no. 007. Ottawa: Statistics Canada. www.statcan.gc.ca/pub/89-642-x/89-642-x2011007-eng.pdf

Council of Europe. (2001). *Common European Framework of Reference for Languages: Learning, teaching, assessment*. Cambridge: Cambridge University Press. rm.coe.int/1680459f97

Delcambre, L., & Lahanier-Reuter, D. (Eds.). (2012). Littéracies universitaires: présentation. *Pratiques: linguistique, littérature, didactique* [thematic issue: *Littéracies universitaires: nouvelles perspectives*], *153–154*, 3–19.

Dudas, A., & Chenard, K. (2009). La création de la première structure administrative postsecondaire francophone de la Colombie-Britannique: une étude de cas dans le domaine de la francophonie. *Revue canadienne de science politique, 42*, 749–771.

French for the Future. (n.d.). Edmonton local forum of French for the future. www.french-future.org/programs/local-forums/edmonton-local-forum

Gestion centrale DELF–DALF au Canada. (n.d.). DELF DALF experts: The CEFRL. delf-dalf.ambafrance-ca.org/cefrl

Gouillier, F. (2005). *Les outils du Conseil de l'Europe en classe de langue*. Paris: Didier.

Graves, R. (2013). A rhetorical education in the arts. [originally appeared in *CASLL/Inkshed Newsletter*]. sites.ualberta.ca/~graves1/documents/ARhetoricalEducationintheArts.pdf

Laurendeau, A., & Dunton, A.D. (1967). *Commission royale d'enquête sur le bilinguisme et le biculturalisme: Vol. I. Les langues officielles*. Ottawa: Queen's Printer.

Lebel, M.-É., & Viswanathan, U. (2016). Une séquence didactique en français langue seconde: le groupe de discussion comme objet et comme dispositif authentique d'enseignement à l'université. In G.S. Cordeiro & D.Vrydaghs (Eds.), *Les genres dans l'enseignement du français: un objet ou/et un outil didactique?* (pp. 279–301). Namur, France: Presses universitaires de Namur and the Association internationale pour la recherche en didactique du français (AIRDF).

Lebel, M.-É, Viswanathan, U., & Barysevich, A. (2018). Le groupe de discussion et le suivi des pairs: un outil pour transposer le CECR à la cause de langue seconde. *La Revue canadienne des langues vivantes*, *74*, 650–670.

Lemaire, E. (2013). Étudier à l'université en français dans le contexte minoritaire ouest-canadien: ce que peut nous apprendre le dessin réflexif. *OLBI Working Papers*, *6*, 87–107.

Lemaire, E. (2014). Sortir de sa zone de confort, s'ouvrir, se replier: mise en scène de l'apprentissage du français dans le milieu universitaire francophone minoritaire ouest-canadien. *Glottopol: revue de sociolinguistique en ligne*, *24*, 38–63. liseo.ciep.fr/index.php?lvl=notice_display&id=36612

Lemaire, E. (2016, May). *Étudiants en éducation en contexte canadien francophone minoritaire: à l'épreuve du DELF*. Paper presented at the Canadian Association of Applied Linguistics' annual conference, Calgary.

Lemaire, E., & Wilson, S. (2014). Former à l'écriture dans le contexte de la francophonie minoritaire ouest-canadienne: impacts du centre universitaire de monitorat entre pairs. *Le Français aujourd'hui*, *184*, 1–8. www.afef.org/blog/espace.php?board=2&document=599

Lemaire, E., & Wilson, S. (2018). Le centre d'écriture bilingue: un espace alternatif de formation pour l'enseignement postsecondaire en milieu minoritaire. In S. Elatia (Ed.), *L'éducation supérieure et la dualité linguistique dans l'Ouest canadien* (pp. 180–210). Laval: Presses de l'Université Laval.

Lyster, R. (1987). Speaking immersion. *Canadian Modern Language Review*, *43*, 701–717.

MacFarlane, A., & Wesche, M.B. (1995). Immersion outcomes: Beyond language proficiency. *Canadian Modern Language Review*, *51*, 250–274.

Mahé, Y. (2004). "La survivance": Discourses and the curriculum in French-speaking communities in North America, 1840–1960. *Journal of Educational Thought*, *38*, 183–207.

Mangiante, J.-M., & Parpette, C. (2004). *Le français sur objectif spécifique: de l'analyse des besoins à l'élaboration d'un cours*. Paris: Hachette.

Mangiante, J.-M., & Parpette, C. (2011). *Le Français sur objectif universitaire*. Grenoble: Presses universitaires de Grenoble.

Mougeon, F., & Rehner, K. (2015). Engagement portraits and (socio)linguistic performance: A transversal and longitudinal study of advanced L2 learners. *Studies in Second Language Acquisition*, *37*, 425–456.

Ontario Confederation of University Faculty Associations (OCUFA). (n.d.). Ontario Online. ocufa.on.ca/?s=Ontario+Online

Puren, C. (2009). Conclusion-synthèse: variations sur la perspective de l'agir social en didactique des langues-cultures étrangères. *Le Français dans le Monde: Recherches et applications* [thematic issue: *La perspective actionnelle et l'approche par les tâches en classe de langue*], *45*, 154–167.

Rogers, C.R. (1969). *Freedom to learn: A view of what education might become*. Columbus, OH: Merrill.

Simon Fraser University. (n.d.). Curriculum initiative: Writing, quantitative, and breadth requirements. www.sfu.ca/ugcr/for_students/wqb_requirements.html

Simon Fraser University. (n.d.). Office of Francophone and Francophile Affairs (OFFA). www.sfu.ca/baff-offa/en.html

Simon Fraser Uninversity. (n.d.). OFFA: French Cohort Program in public and international affairs. www.sfu.ca/fassfr/en/frcohort.html

Simon Fraser University. (n.d.). Student services: Admission. sfu.ca/students/admission/admission-requirements.html

Simon Fraser University. (2019). Fall calendar: French Cohort Program in Public and International Affairs French Major with a Political Science Extended Minor. www.sfu.ca/students/calendar/2019/fall/programs/french-cohort-program-in-public-and-international-affairs-french-major-with-a-political-science-extended-minor/bachelor-of-arts.html

Stern, H.H. (1984). A quiet language revolution: Second language teaching in Canadian contexts — Achievements and new directions. *Canadian Modern Language Review*, 40, 506–524.

Tedick, D.J., Christian, D., & Fortune, T.W. (Eds.). (2011). *Immersion education: Practices, policies, possibilities*. Bristol: Multilingual Matters.

Toupin, L. (1986). Une terminologie en immersion propre à l'Association canadienne des professeurs d'immersion [ACPI]. *Les Nouvelles de l'ACPI*, 9 7. www.acpi.ca/journaux/V9N2.pdf

University of Alberta. (n.d.). General information: Linguistic policy. calendar.ualberta.ca/content.php?catoid=28&navoid=7076#linguistic-policy

University of Alberta. (n.d.). [Campus Saint-Jean]. Règlements de la faculté. www.registrar.ualberta.ca/calendar/Undergrad/Saint-Jean/Reglements/183.html#183.1

University of Alberta. (2009). *Passport: A "cours classique" for the 21st century*. Edmonton: University of Alberta, Campus Saint-Jean. www.youscribe.com/catalogue/documents/education/cours/passport-a-cours-classique-for-the-21st-century-360135

University of Alberta. (2016). [Campus Saint-Jean]. Le français, langue de vie au Campus Saint-Jean (CSJ). cloudfront.ualberta.ca/-/media/csj/nouvelles/2016/csjvisionlinguistique.pdf

Villeneuve, A.-J. (2018). L'acquisition de la compétence sociolinguistique en contexte minoritaire: l'apport potentiel de la communauté. In S. Elatia (Ed.), *L'éducation supérieure et la dualité linguistique dans l'Ouest Canadien* (pp. 85–108). Laval: Presses de l'Université Laval.

Viswanathan, U., Lebel, M.-É., & Barysevich, A. (2018). Un dispositif pour promouvoir et soutenir l'authenticité des interactions en classe de langues. *Nouvelle Revue Synergies Canada* [thematic issue: *La didactique des langues secondes: de la théorie à la pratique*], 11. journal.lib.uoguelph.ca/index.php/nrsc/article/view/3997

York University. (n.d.). Associate Vice-President Teaching and Learning: Academic Innovation Fund. avptl.info.yorku.ca/academic-innovation-fund/

CHAPTER 6

The Resources for French Immersion at the University of Ottawa

Hélène Knoerr

INTRODUCTION

IN CHAPTER 2, WE PRESENTED THE VISION and the political and ideological[1] background behind the *Régime d'immersion en français* (henceforth RIF), thereby introducing its key principles — philosophical, political, methodological, pedagogical. In this chapter, we will show how these guiding principles turned into specifications for the implementation of the program. We will then list the resources required for its delivery. We will conclude with an assessment of the RIF's strengths and weaknesses, and some recommendations to address the challenges associated with the implementation of such a program. Our analysis is based on information obtained through internal documents, the RIF's self-evaluation reports, and several conversations with the program director.

The RIF is the product of a political will, as expressed in uOttawa's *Vision 2010 Academic Strategic Plan* (2005b) to "play a leadership role in promoting Canada's official languages" (p. 1). The first step was to "create an immersion program and set up an intake structure that will enhance access for immersion students from across Canada" (p. 2). It must be noted that, at the time, although the highest proportion (about 15%) of Ontario high school immersion graduates enrolled in the province's universities had chosen uOttawa, only a fraction of them were taking courses in French, their second language (University of Ottawa, 2005a, p. 3).

1. THE RIF AS THE INCARNATION OF *VISION 2010*

The proposal to create the RIF was accepted by the Undergraduate Studies Committee on December 15, 2005 and by the Senate on January 16, 2006, with the mandate to allow immersion and Francophile students to study partially in French while earning their undergraduate degree (University of Ottawa, 2005a, p. 3). As defined by Vice-President Houle in Chapter 2, Francophiles are "a group of students from the Anglophone community who enjoy and value living in the French language and culture" (p. 46).

The University of Ottawa defines a *program of studies* as "[t]he set of courses that must be successfully completed in order to be conferred a degree, diploma or certificate from the University" (University of Ottawa, n.d., "Office of the Provost"). It consists of

---

[1] The term "ideology" is used as defined in the Cambridge Dictionary: a set of beliefs or principles, especially one on which a political system, party, or organization is based (Cambridge Dictionary, n.d., "Ideology").

at least one main studies module (or two, in some programs) and combines the courses required by the module, the optional courses, as well as fundamental courses (for the Faculties of Arts and Social Sciences) that are necessary to graduate from uOttawa. An *academic service*, on the other hand, is a complement to a program of studies, a structure that uses a variety of units and resources already available on campus, in order to offer a unique academic path combining courses and programs of studies delivered by academic units. Since students taking the RIF option are enrolled in 86 undergraduate programs,[2] the RIF is classified as a service: it does not run its own courses and modules but is available as an option. The RIF offers students the flexibility of a custom-tailored set of courses, taking into account the particular requirements of their programs. No language support is mandatory and students get to choose which content courses they want to take in French. The RIF does not hire its own instructors or create its own courses; rather, from among the courses taught in the 360 undergraduate programs offered in English at uOttawa, the RIF chooses the ones that are most suitable for immersion students to take in French.

Because it is not a program, the RIF does not evaluate students' progress in their discipline of study. Instead, it monitors the courses they select and makes sure that they take enough courses in French to meet the requirements. In a nutshell, here is how the RIF implements the mandate given by *Vision 2010* (University of Ottawa, 2014, p. 6; author's emphasis):

- Immersion courses to help students with transitioning to French-language content courses: students take a *content course* (taught in French by a Francophone content instructor) along with Francophone students, AND a *language support adjunct course* for immersion students only, taught by a language instructor, and specifically tailored to the content course, in order to assist with receptive (understanding assigned reading and lectures) and productive skills (participating in discussion groups, writing papers). The 90-minute adjunct course counts for three credits.
- *Pass/Fail* for up to 24 credits chosen by the students in the first two years of their program: these do not count towards the student's GPA (grade point average).
- *Scholarships* for French-language studies
- The option to write assignments and exams for the content courses in the official language of their choice, as per the University's *policy on bilingualism*

After this brief overview, we will examine in detail how the RIF fulfills its mandate — *to allow immersion students to study partially in French while earning their undergraduate degree* (University of Ottawa, 2005a, p. 3).

---

[2] This number (86) does not include the five programs in the Faculty of Sciences and the two programs in the Faculty of Engineering, which offer a variation of the RIF known as *Français enrichi*, whose requirements are different.

1.1. Immersion Students

The RIF targets high school students from French Immersion, Extended French, or Core French programs (see Chapter 4 for details), which means that Francophone students are not eligible. This sets the RIF apart from other initiatives implemented in post-secondary institutions in Canada, which allow Francophone and Anglophone students into their programs (see Chapter 5 for a complete description).

1.1.1. Recruiting

In 2005, Vice-President Houle[3] had established that there was a sufficient number of high school immersion graduates on campus to ensure that the RIF would be viable (see Chapter 2). The initial enrolment target was 1,000 students after five years[4] and 3,500 by 2020. To meet those targets, students have to be recruited while still in high school, before they select their post-secondary programs and universities. Consequently, recruiting activities have been front and centre in the RIF: As a fairly new initiative, the RIF must continue to make itself known and gain visibility from coast to coast, using a variety of tools and means to reach out to all members of the Francophone and Francophile communities.

1.1.1.1. University of Ottawa's students: The RIF has been trying to increase its visibility on campus in a variety of ways:

- Involvement in on-campus activities: whether participating in community events (in the *Carrefour francophone*'s programming, for instance; University of Ottawa, n.d., "Carrefour") or organizing its own social activities
- Immersion bracelets: These conspicuous purple rubber bracelets with the words *"Régime d'immersion en français"* are given to all students registered in the RIF, creating a visible community of users. How else could hundreds of RIF Francophiles registered in over 86 programs identify their peers among 43,000 students on a 42.5-hectare campus? A RIF student posted on her Facebook page: "On the bus now, on my way to the FRUNCH, our 'French immersion brunch,' to meet and greet! Can't wait to meet the other RIF students!! And I am wearing my Immersion bracelet!! ("Je parle 2017," September 4, 2013 [trans.])
- Publications: In 2005, the RIF published promotional pamphlets and in 2006, it launched the *Bulletin Immersion*, an e-newsletter for its current students. After a hiatus, the RIF started a monthly electronic *Bulletin d'information*, sent to all its students as of the 2018–2019 academic year.
- Internet and social media: The RIF has its own bilingual site within uOttawa (n.d., "French Immersion Stream") and is featured on the university's home page as well as on the main pages of several faculties; it also has its own Twitter account (University of Ottawa, n.d., "Immersion en français") and a Facebook page (University of Ottawa, n.d., "French immersion studies"). Students also post about

---

[3] Houle was Vice-President, Undergraduate Studies, at the time (2009).
[4] This target was reached and surpassed a year earlier than planned (2011).

their experience in the RIF on their own Facebook or YouTube accounts, indirectly helping with recruitment:

> Hi everyone, I am happy to say that I have received many email messages about University-level immersion. So I am sharing the link to uOttawa's Immersion Studies program in which I am registered ... Looking forward to seeing some familiar faces on campus next year! ("Je parle 2017," October 30, 2013 [trans.])

1.1.1.2. High school students: They are the RIF's prime target audience, and no effort is spared to attract them. The first *Bulletin immersion* was created for them as potential students. Over time, the newsletter has taken on a new mandate and the RIF is now using more active techniques:

- On-site presentations: The RIF's director and/or staff visit high schools all across Canada, talk to students about the *Régime*, and give them information brochures and promotional material (bookmarks, pens, pins, bus pass holders, etc.).
- Open House on the university campus: The RIF participates in these university-wide information sessions offered in the fall and in the spring via presentations to prospective students and their parents.
- Competitions and contests: The RIF either organizes or sponsors a variety of events targeting these students, such as the *Concours de français langue seconde Ottawa* for Core French, Extended French, and Immersion students in Grades 11 and 12 (OLBI, n.d., "Concours").
- Social media: Facebook posts by RIF students can reach high school students more effectively than many formal/institutional initiatives. For instance, the student behind the "Je parle 2017" Facebook account posted the following:

    > Étudiants chez Dr. John M. Denison Secondary School!! A lot of you probably remember me visiting your French classes this fall, when I talked about French immersion in University and all the exciting things you can do with French! I know the semester is just coming to an end! Please send me a message if you need help with your French classes before exams! ("Je parle 2017," December 13, 2013)

- Student bloggers: The RIF hires some of its students to write blogs about their experience and chat with high-school students:

    > What's my undergrad? History. Okay, sounds good. But that's not all. I'm taking it in french. Like français french. As in with a lecture hall full of francophone students. It's not that I've never spoken french before — I have. I was in french immersion for 12 years. But the french I've learned hasn't ever left the classroom. I don't know the idioms or expressions or even have the confidence to speak to francophones yet. I couldn't be more nervous or excited. If you want to see all my embarrassing moments and experiences of the next four years you've come to the right place. Wish me luck. It's going to be a bumpy ride :) (My nutty life ..., 2013, entry dated November 3)

1.1.1.3. High school teachers: The RIF is always represented during provincial and national events held by professional associations such as OMLTA, ACPI, ACPLS/CASLT annual conferences.[5] Direct access to the teachers is a very effective way to promote the program, distribute information and offer on-site presentations.

1.1.1.4. Parents: Offering scholarships that can total up to $4,000 over four years of RIF studies is a very strong incentive for parents, who typically finance their children's post-secondary education.

1.1.1.5. Francophone and Francophile associations: The RIF has established strong partnerships with several organizations such as Canadian Parents for French, *Le français pour l'avenir*, mainly by donating scholarships to be used as awards in the contests that they organize.

1.1.2. Assessing Language Proficiency

The RIF has been designed for students who have taken French as a second language (FSL) courses, which means that Francophone students are not eligible, just as they are not permitted to attend primary and secondary school immersion programs: "Immersion classes are therefore intended for children whose home language is English and who are willing to undergo a large part of their schooling through the medium of French" (Stern, 1984, p. 4).

Additionally, Anglophone students who have not taken FSL courses are not eligible either, since they do not have the language skills necessary to take a content course in French at the university level.[6] Admission officers therefore need to make sure that, among all the applicants, only students enrolled in FSL in an English-language schoolboard are accepted.[7]

The RIF requires a threshold level of linguistic competence to ensure that students are successful: in addition to a high school immersion/FSL diploma, students must take a proficiency test developed by uOttawa's Assessment and Evaluation Services (administered by the Official Languages and Bilingualism Institute, OLBI) and get a minimum mark of 60%, which is the threshold level for academic courses.[8] This is one of the characteristics that has set the RIF apart from initiatives such as CLIL or EMI in Europe, where students are admitted with no such linguistic requirements. The minimum

---

[5] OMLTA = Ontario Modern Language Teachers Association; ACPI = Association canadienne des professeurs d'immersion; ACPLS/CASLT = Association canadienne des professeurs de langue seconde/Canadian Association of Second Language Teachers.

[6] These students can register in regular FSL classes if they wish to do so.

[7] Typically, 85% of applicants are from Ontario (30% from Ottawa, 25% from the Greater Toronto area, and 30% from the rest of the province), 5% from Quebec, 5% from British Columbia, and 5% from the other Canadian provinces. A very small number of applicants were international students.

[8] For a number of years, students with a DELF score of B1 or B2 were exempt from the RIF admission test. As of September 2019, this option is no longer available.

level 7 (out of 9)[9] on the OLBI Proficiency Test means that RIF students can understand at least 65 to 70% of what they hear and read but that they may struggle with more complex or abstract language.

1.2. Getting Language Support

In the original 2005 plan published in *Vision 2010*, the RIF was built upon two pillars: adjunct language support classes and a qualitative system (see Chapter 2). The rationale was that many immersion students would feel that their level of proficiency in French was not sufficient to allow them to successfully take academic courses delivered in French and geared to an audience of native speakers. By offering them the option to enrol in language support classes entirely designed around their content classes, the RIF has built upon an experiment pioneered at uOttawa in the 1980s and 1990s known as the sheltered courses (see Chapter 8). These support classes allow immersion students to develop the language skills and the academic culture they need to not only survive but thrive in their content classes (see Chapter 8 for details). As demonstrated by their results on the admission test, most students face comprehension challenges (about 35% score at elementary level and more than 50% place at high intermediate).[10] Consequently, the language support courses make listening and reading comprehension a top priority: most courses are at the FLS 2581 level (Developing receptive skills), offered as adjunct courses for first-year content courses. At the FLS 3581 level (Developing productive skills), courses are mostly offered as adjunct courses for second-year content courses (University of Ottawa, 2014, p. 13). Later on, in addition to the original receptive/ productive model, a third level was offered, with advanced speaking and writing skills (FLS 4581 and FLS 4781, respectively) as adjunct courses for third- and fourth-year content courses.[11] But interestingly, students enrolled in these courses are not RIF students but students in the FSL major.[12]

Adding an extra course in a student's program (and timetable) can be problematic.[13] To minimize the challenge, language support classes are offered once a week for 90 minutes instead of the typical 3 hours for a credit course. However, students do receive the full three credits (see p. 124), since attending lectures, reading course materials, and writing assignments in a second language in the content course requires three or four times more work (and time) than in one's first language. They also need to complete assignments and homework for the language support classes.

To determine which content courses will be offered as immersion courses, the RIF scrutinizes enrolment trends in first and second years and selects those with the highest numbers of immersion students. Typically, there is one language support course associated with one content course, but when potential numbers warrant, an additional section at the same level (FLS 2581) or a section at a higher level (FLS 3581) can be offered.

---

[9] See Chapter 10 for a complete description of assessment procedures in the RIF.
[10] This is equivalent to B1 and B2 in the CEFRL (Council of Europe, 2001).
[11] Chapter 8 provides a full description of all the adjunct language support courses in the RIF.
[12] These courses are currently under review and will most likely be eliminated.
[13] Typically, students are not permitted to take more than five courses per term.

1.3. Studying Partially in French

In Houle's original plan, as presented in *Vision 2010*, the RIF required that students take 36 credits in French (whether FSL language courses or content courses delivered in French) between their second and fourth years. It also allowed for an academic path tailored to each student's level as determined by the proficiency test, with content courses matching their linguistic skills and language courses developing them.

However, these 36 credits excluded first-year content courses and first-level language support classes (FLS 2581, receptive skills), which turned the RIF into a real challenge for students with less advanced French skills.

Consequently, changes were made before the first group of students enrolled in September 2006: students still needed 36 credits in French (content and/or language), but they had all four years to take them, and first-year content courses were now eligible.

More changes were implemented in 2009, increasing the number of credits in French to 42 (about one third of a typical 120-credit undergraduate program), allowing first-year content courses and first-level language support classes up to a maximum of six credits, capping the number of language support classes (maximum of 12 credits), and requiring a minimum of six credits in advanced (3000- and 4000-level) content courses. These requirements are still in effect today.

The RIF's director makes a list of specific courses and courses sections that would be suitable for immersion, and sends it to the deans involved, for comments and approval. Typically, targeted content courses and sections have solid enrolment, are taught in two 90-minute blocks instead of one 3-hour block, and are daytime courses, in order to limit the cognitive demands placed on second-language students. Language support classes are carefully scheduled so that they do not immediately follow the associated content classes. Although the RIF cannot influence the selection of a content course's schedule, instructor, or teaching materials, there is a certain amount of control on which content courses will be offered as immersion courses (i.e., will have adjunct language support courses at the 2581 and/or 3581 level). Indeed, the selection has changed over the years, as experience showed that some content courses were not suitable for a RIF treatment for a number of reasons (University of Ottawa, 2014, p. 14):

- The course did not lend itself to language activities.[14]
- It already had a discussion group.
- Content, not language, was the main difficulty (chemistry, math, physics).

---

[14] These include:
    Anatomy: ANP 1506 — *Anatomie humaine et physiologie*
    Health Sciences: HSS 1500 — *Microbiologie et immunologie*
    Linguistics: LIN 1720 — *Introduction à la linguistique II: Les sons du langage*
    Political Science: POL 2556 — *Fondements de la recherche en science politique*
    Social Sciences: SCS 2550 — *Introduction à la méthodologie en sciences sociales*

- Enrolment was too low to ensure there would be enough immersion students in the adjunct language support course.[15]
- The instructor objected to the "Immersion" designation, either out of personal and/or linguistic insecurities[16] or because he or she would not accommodate the needs of immersion students.

RIF students also have several opportunities to take some courses outside uOttawa and still have them credited:

- In 2008, the RIF set up a 3-week study-abroad program in collaboration with the Université de Lyon (France). Under the supervision and guidance of a RIF language instructor, students took classes taught by Université de Lyon professors (counting as six credits) and participated in many cultural activities to experience real language in a real setting.[17]
- Many immersion students also take advantage of the university's International Office option to study at one of the 250 partner universities in 52 countries without being required to pay international student fees. About two-thirds of them select a Francophone university for their one- or two-term study-abroad exchanges.

1.4. . . . While Students Pursue Their Undergraduate Studies

The RIF is a service unit, not a program. Students interested in taking it first need to be admitted to uOttawa, which means that they need to meet the admission requirements of the specific program they want to register in. Typically, this is a fairly easy step for immersion students, whose average at admission consistently surpasses those of their Anglophone peers registering in English-language programs: there are twice as many immersion students registering with an average of 85% and above as there are Anglophones, and three times fewer immersion students with an average of 72% and below. Their profiles are similar to those of students admitted to the highest-ranking "U15" universities[18] (University of Ottawa, 2014, p. 23).

These high-achievers do not have any difficulty getting admission offers from their target programs. It is interesting to note that, although admission offers and registrations

---

[15] These include:
 Administration: ADM 2720 — *Marketing*
 Arts: ART 2560 — *Histoire de l'art*
 Canadian Studies: CDN 1500 — *Introduction aux études canadiennes*
 International Development: DVM 2505 — *Introduction au développement international: perspectives historiques*
 Music: MUS 2731 — *Formes et styles I : Moyen Âge et Renaissance*

[16] Not all uOttawa professors are native speakers of French or English and, with the globalization of education, an increasing number are Allophones.

[17] This study-abroad program was terminated in 2012 for financial reasons: the RIF had been paying for most expenses, so the program was quite expensive. The RIF is currently examining options to reinstate such a program.

[18] The designation "U15" refers to the fifteen most research-oriented universities in Canada.

rates remain stable from year to year, there has been a dramatic increase in the sheer numbers of admission offers and applications. This shows that young Canadian students are keenly interested in pursuing bilingual studies at uOttawa (University of Ottawa, 2014, p. 24).

Clearly, the RIF is not for everybody — students must have a minimal level of proficiency in French. It is also not for every program. As stated before, only programs offered in both French and English are eligible for the RIF. Furthermore, faculties must be able to offer most of their courses in French and agree to using the Pass/Fail system.

Immersion is only available in 4-year specialized programs[19] offering all their mandatory courses and at least 60% of their third- and fourth-year courses in French. Additionally, other programs are not eligible to be part of the RIF:

- programs *about* French (linguistics, translation, French as a second language, French literature) rather than *in* French are excluded
- programs offered only in French are not eligible (such as Nutrition) because students with an insufficient command of French could not be redirected in the English version of the same program.

The Pass/Fail system is structured as follows: students can designate up to 24 credits over the first two years under this system, which means that the grades they get in these courses will not count toward their GPA. But this is not an option in all faculties (for detailed background, see Chapter 2). In 2006–2007, the RIF was available in 55 programs in four of the six faculties offering undergraduate programs (Arts, Management, Social Sciences, Health Sciences). In 2012, it was available in 58 programs, and in 2017, that increased to 86 programs.[20]

Most RIF students register in a Faculty of Social Sciences program. This is the largest faculty at uOttawa and the one with the most bilingual programs, especially programs leading to a public service career. The Faculty of Sciences comes second (as of 2014 — the Faculty of Arts used to hold that position), followed by the Faculties of Management, Health Sciences, and Arts.

After completing their undergraduate program, students who meet the RIF requirements and pass the Second Language Proficiency Test (developed and validated by the Institute of Official Languages and Bilingualism; see Chapter 10 for RIF assessment procedures) get an "Immersion" designation on their degree. Figure 1 summarizes the RIF academic path.

---

[19] The number of required and optional credits depends on the type of specialization and is commensurate with the level of expertise: honours, honours with specialization, joint honours with a major or a minor. Some programs are available in more than one type of specialization (history, sociology, biochemistry) while others are only available in one (computer engineering, accounting, nutrition sciences).

[20] There is an alternate version of the RIF available for those faculties which do not allow the Pass/Fail system and/or cannot accommodate all of the RIF requirements — the *Français enrichi* — available in about 30 programs. Chapter 7 gives a complete description of this option and explain the differences with the regular RIF option.

1. Pass the Admission test for Immersion.
2. Complete the requirements of the program of study.
3. Complete at least 42 credits (14 courses) in courses taught in French, of which:
   - a maximum of 6 credits (2 courses) at the 1000 level;
   - a maximum of 12 credits (4 courses) for accompanying language courses (FLS 2581, 3581, 4581 and 4781), of which a maximum of 6 credits (2 courses) for FLS 2581; and
   - at least 6 credits (2 courses) taught in French at the 3000 or 4000 level, other than FLS courses.

   Note: Students in the Nursing program must complete 36 credits taught in French, and satisfy the other conditions.
4. Pass the Second Language Certification Test (FLS 3500).

Figure 1: *Régime d'immersion en français*
Faculties of Arts, Social Sciences, Health Sciences, and Management
(Source: University of Ottawa, 2014, p. 9)

Figure 1 shows that, although the RIF imposes a number of content courses at the first-, second-, third-, and fourth-year levels, it only requires about one third of courses be taken in French and it does not require students to take language support classes or French as a second language classes, whatever level they may be.

Clearly, the RIF is quite different from other university-level FSL studies options (see also the Preface and Chapter 5):

- Simon Fraser University (Burnaby, British Columbia), an English-language university designated as part of the Association des universités de la francophonie canadienne (AUFC, Association of Francophone Universities of Canada), has been offering a program in Public and International Affairs in French (*Administration publique et services communautaires*) since 2004 for bilingual students (admitting both Anglophones and Francophones into the same program). This program only accepts 25 students per year and imposes a fixed set of courses. Students take content courses in political science, governance, history, and research methodologies in French as well as a number of French-language courses. They have to spend at least one semester in a French-language university as part of the requirements of the program. At least 75 out of the required 120 credits (62.5%) must be in French.

- Glendon College, affiliated with York University in Toronto, allows both Anglophones and Francophones (also mixed in the same program) to take bilingual studies requiring six credits in second-language courses after their second year and six credits of content courses in French.

- At the Campus Saint-Jean of the University of Alberta in Edmonton, most students come from French immersion high school programs, which has put a heavy English trend on a once French-only environment (Chapter 5 provides an exhaustive account of these three programs).

- Laurentian University (Sudbury, Ontario) offers a certificate of bilingualism to Anglophone and Francophone students (again, mixed in the same program) who successfully complete 15 credits in their second language.
- The French-language Université de Moncton allows immersion students to take content courses in French if they successfully complete two to four French-language courses. There is no language support for the content courses (only the generic French language courses) but the environment is mainly French-speaking.

2. THE MEANS TO PURSUE ITS AMBITIONS

The RIF is an ambitious endeavour: it involves recruiting, assessing, and sheltering more than 1,100 students registered in 86 programs from four faculties, custom-tailoring an academic path for each one of them, offering them adjunct language support classes exclusive to them and to each content course they take, and providing generous scholarships as incentives to continue their studies in French. Such a project requires administrative, human, and financial resources

2.1. Administrative Structure

Administratively, the RIF is completely independent from departments and faculties: it is under the direct responsibility of the Vice-President, Undergraduate Studies, as designed by its initiator, François Houle. Its director answers to the university's central administration, not to department chairs or faculty deans.

The director supervises two employees: a receptionist and management assistant (a regular position shared between the RIF and the OLBI) and a special projects officer (a contract position whose description has changed over the years in order to meet the RIF's changing needs).

As a pan-university project, the RIF draws on instructors from the OLBI for language support adjunct courses, and from four faculties for content courses delivered in French.

The RIF functions as an interdepartmental unit, since its students are registered in programs from four home faculties. The director consults with the deans to select content courses suitable for immersion, to recommend content courses to RIF students, and to secure immersion seats in specific sections of content courses. Academic assistants from the faculties contact the RIF for matters such as admission requirements and course selection (whether content or adjunct).

2.1.1. The Director

The director was hired as the RIF was being implemented, in 2005. At that time, the position requirements were as follows:
- a relevant graduate degree or equivalent experience
- knowledge of project management principles and a vast experience in managing concurrent projects
- ability to set priorities and respond promptly to unforeseen situations
- theoretical and practical knowledge of strategic planning in order to establish short- and long-term operational plans

- experience in communication, to deliver strong strategies and effective messages
- knowledge of academic settings, programs, policies, and processes
- knowledge of high school FSL programs
- ability to analyze and manipulate data and statistics
- experience in preparing and supervising budgets
- possess team management skills as well as skills to motivate peers and subordinates
- very high level of bilingualism
- excellent written and oral communication skills
- ability to deliver effective presentations to large groups
- excellent interpersonal skills and ability to demonstrate courtesy to high school students as well as university professors and high-level administrators
- ability to develop personal networks inside and outside the university
- ability to motivate, convince, and unite

The director oversees overall recruitment strategies, student relations, supervision of student academic path, liaison with university stakeholders and external partners, budget management, and report writing (to document RIF activities).

2.1.2. Reception and Management Assistant

The reception and management assistant is a permanent, regular position—but not a full-time one, since it is divided between the RIF (60%) and the OLBI (40%, for the Academic Training Services).

This person is the first contact for RIF students who need assistance with course registration, language course selection, or available resources.

2.1.3. Communications/Special Projects Officer

In 2010, because of the growing enrolment numbers, a contract position was added to the RIF for a communications/special projects officer.

The communications officer supports RIF growth by designing, coordinating, and implementing recruitment strategies as well as by planning events and activities to reinforce its visibility and prestige. They are mainly in charge of communications: updating the RIF website, organizing contests, dealing with scholarship recipients, preparing handouts and posters.

In 2014, the position description was revised in order to meet a new challenge: student reception and retention.[21]

The student reception and retention officer presently deals with pressing issues such as checking eligibility to the RIF, tracking and analyzing enrolment trends, meeting with students, and setting up a cultural events program. In the longer term, once retention issues are addressed, the position will include the duties of communications officer.

---

[21] The current incumbent holds a master's degree in Education (Guidance counselling).

2.2. Human and Administrative Resources

The RIF team is presently composed of one director and two employees, for a student population of over 1,100. Extra staff are therefore necessary to address recruiting, registering,[22] assessing, teaching, and supervising those students. These human and administrative resources come from a variety of academic and service units.

2.2.1. Student Mentors

These students (see Chapter 9 for details) are hired through the university's Work–Study Program[23] to work within the Mentoring Programs offered in eight of the faculties. As described by the Student Academic Success Services, they are upper-year students who are trained to help students develop helpful, effective ways of approaching their studies. They support students by helping them to:

- develop effective learning strategies and study techniques
- strengthen their personal motivation
- maintain academic achievement
- set academic goals
- use effective time and stress management tools
- obtain a referral to professional resources if necessary

RIF student mentors also assist with some specific projects such as compiling resources, collecting and entering data, performing administrative duties, and helping with recruitment activities.

2.2.2. Liaison Officers

Part of the Strategic Enrollment Management (SEM) service, these individuals are in charge of recruiting undergraduate students across Canada. They travel the country to participate in educational fairs, meet with future students in their schools, introduce them to uOttawa, and discuss their plans with them. The RIF contributes financially to the SEM so that a number of their staff specialize in RIF presentations: in particular, they focus on Ontario high schools, visit over 200 FSL classes a year, and meet with Grade 11 and 12 students, first in the fall to introduce the RIF, then in winter to secure registrations.

2.2.3. Office of the Registrar

All applications are received and assessed by this unit, which is also responsible for registration procedures and online admission and registration systems. Adding the RIF as a

---

[22] Receiving applications and registering students is a combined effort: RIF, Office of the Registrar, Admissions, Strategic Enrollment Management, Liaison, Financial Assistance.

[23] The Work–Study program offers on-campus employment opportunities to lower-income students, which can be part-time (during the academic year, earning about $3,000) or full-time (during the summer, for about $6,000).

study option required entering a new codification procedure in the university's School Information System, with specific codes for programs offering the immersion option. A similar modification was required at the provincial level: the Ontario Universities' Application Centre (OUAC) had to add a RIF field to the English registration form used by high school students.[24]

2.2.4. Financial Aid and Awards Service

This unit sets the eligibility criteria and conditions for the French Studies Bursary, automatically awarded to all full-time students who are taking at least three courses (nine credits) each term, taught in French. However, RIF students receive preferred treatment: they only need to take two courses (six credits) taught in French, or in French as a second language.[25] This bursary can be renewed for the following three years.

2.2.5. Academic Assistants in Home Faculties

These individuals are a key contact for RIF students, who are registered in study programs and not directly in the RIF. It is crucial that they be aware of this fairly recent addition (2007) to the university.

2.2.6. OLBI Administrative Committees

Within the OLBI, the Undergraduate Studies Committee and the Advisory Committee set course objectives for the adjunct language support classes. In 2006, a Steering Committee had been set up to oversee the RIF formative assessment over its first five years, but it was not renewed after the initial phase. An Advisory Committee was set up on an ad hoc basis with a very restricted mandate and no directive powers (unlike the Undergraduate Studies Committee). It was only in existence for one year (2013–2014) and sporadic, informal meetings, called by the RIF director, have occasionally happened since, with no outcome. However, since 2018, the Advisory Committee has been revived, given a new mandate, and is meeting bi-weekly to review the RIF's strengths and weaknesses and to propose an improved version more in tune with its new vision.

2.2.7. Pedagogical Advisors

Pedagogical advisors are OLBI professors, appointed by the RIF director. They facilitate training sessions for instructors teaching language support classes. They are also responsible for reviewing syllabi and course outlines, making sure they are in line with immersion philosophy, pedagogical practices, and administrative requirements. Additionally, they develop new language activities for students and new resources for instructors.

---

[24] The OUAC is "a not-for-profit, centralized application service for applicants to Ontario universities. [It is] a division of the Council of Ontario Universities (COU) and facilitate[s] the process of applying to an Ontario university. [Its] activities are monitored by an Advisory Board, which includes representatives from all of the OUAC's various divisions" (OUAC, n.d., "About").

[25] Non-immersion students must take at least nine credits (three courses) per term to be eligible for the same bursary.

2.2.8. Content Instructors

Members of four different faculties (Arts, Management, Social Sciences, Health Sciences), they deliver over 40 courses a year for the RIF, on a full- or part-time basis. The director advises them via email, before the start of the term, that their course has been designated for immersion, and sends a four-page document summarizing the RIF, outlining its principles and objectives, and suggesting ways to support the students and collaborate with the language support course instructor.

2.2.9. Language Support Instructors

These full- or part-time OLBI members[26] are in charge of over 70 adjunct language courses each year. They can also teach one of the many regular FSL courses that may be recommended to students as part of their customized academic path.

2.2.10. OLBI Language Assessment Service

This service designs the entry and exit language assessments use for the RIF and for the Extended French Stream: the Immersion Admission Test and Productive Skills Test for entry, and the Second Language Certification Test, which students must pass in order to graduate from their program with the "Immersion" designation.

2.3. Financial Resources

As seen earlier, the RIF is a service, not a program. As such, it is not funded by student enrolment, unlike programs and faculties.

Implementing such an extensive operation requires a substantial budget. Funding for the RIF is provided by the Office of the Provost and Vice-President, Academic Affairs, with a budget of 1.1 million dollars a year, co-funded in equal parts by the university and an agreement between the federal government and Ontario (Ontario, Ministry of Education), via the Official Languages Support Programs (see Chapters 1 and 2). The annual budget is split three ways:

- 25% for operation (recruiting and advertising, cultural programming)
- 25% for human resources
- 50% for language support courses

Overall, this budget has remained stable over the RIF's first five years. As the student population grew, so did the operations budget, which stabilized in 2011 (University of Ottawa, 2014, p. 43), but then decreased in 2016. Still, funding obtained through the federal–provincial agreement has to be renegotiated every five years. Although it may be seen as a potential issue, the central administration is confident in the continued support of the federal government.

The RIF requires significant resources. But is it profitable, and is it viable? That is a difficult question to answer, as the returns on investment are sometimes of an intangible

---

[26] A special contract had to be devised for part-time RIF instructors, to take into account their having to also attend the content courses.

nature. The *Vision 2010 Strategic Plan* (University of Ottawa, 2005b) attempted to estimate the cost per student, but the university's financial analysts were unable to come up with a definitive figure due to the vast number of elements involved (such as buildings, faculty salaries, pension plans, as well as the additional cost of adjunct language classes). Furthermore, they were not able to determine how many of these immersion students would not have come to uOttawa if the RIF had not been offered. The final conclusion was that the RIF occupies a competitive market niche for uOttawa (Marc Gobeil, personal communication, May 2013):

- No other university can offer this option, on a comparable scale.
- The RIF brings in the best students (higher admission averages, higher GPAs, higher graduation rates).
- The RIF is a flagship program which positions the university as a leader in bilingualism.
- The RIF improves the linguistic balance within the student population.

The financial viability of the RIF may not be quantifiable, but it is quite profitable academically and politically.

3. STRENGTHS, WEAKNESSES, CHALLENGES AND OPTIONS

The RIF regularly surveys students on several issues, whether systematically with questionnaires, or informally with meetings and interpersonal exchanges. Two informal evaluations (2007, 2008), a self-evaluation report (2014), and a report on student retention and experience (2016) have highlighted the RIF's strengths and weaknesses.

3.1. A Positive Experience

An evaluation process was put in place from the very first days of the RIF in order to determine whether its objectives were being met (see Chapter 10 for a full account of these evaluations): Was it reaching its target audience? Was it delivered as intended? In the spring of 2007, the Program Evaluation Committee conducted a mixed methods study on the RIF's first year of operation. Its final report (Ryan, Courcelles, Hope, Buchanan, & Toews-Janzen, 2007) concluded that, overall, the students registered in the RIF were the students who had been targeted by the RIF, and that the RIF was being implemented as originally planned. However, the report outlined two pressing issues: first, only a fraction of the target population was registering in the RIF; second, the adjunct language courses were heavily criticized by students, because the nature of their content and the training of the instructors did not meet their expectations. Following the release of the report, the RIF quickly made adjustments by educating academic assistants, students, and language and content instructors about the objectives and methods of the immersion philosophy. A similar study conducted in 2008 (Ryan, Gobeil, Hope, & Toews-Janzen, 2008) revealed that, although progress had been made, these issues still remained; it recommended a series of measures regarding pedagogy, communication, recruitment, and marketing, most of which were implemented.

The 2014 self-evaluation report (University of Ottawa, 2014) showed that overall, RIF graduates viewed the experience as beneficial for their self-esteem, their problem-solving skills, and their personal networks. More than 85% stated that being bilingual had had a positive impact on their career, and 93% would recommend the RIF to other students (University of Ottawa, 2014, p. 37). They rated their uOttawa experience more positively than their non-immersion peers (79% rated it as Good or Excellent versus 68%) and more of them would choose the university again if they had the chance (8% answered Probably yes or Definitely yes, versus 64%) (p. 33). The RIF clearly was being viewed as a tremendous success in those respects.

3.2. Challenges Commensurate with the Successes

As successful as the RIF may be in some respects, it is still facing challenging issues in others.

3.2.1. Enrolment

The central administration has been pushing for more registrations, not only because the RIF has given the university a competitive edge but also because provincial funding is linked to the number of students. The *Destination 2020* strategic plan (University of Ottawa, 2013) set a new goal: "[to] raise the number of registrations in our French immersion programs to 3,500 (or 10% of our current undergraduate student population)" (p. 7), which is more than three times the initial target for 2010 (1,000 students). According to the RIF director, this push for growth would put the pressure on for more recruiting, but it might be detrimental to retention: the RIF may have to face a tough choice between attracting many new students and risking a higher dropout rate, or recruiting fewer but keeping them throughout the four years of their programs.

3.2.2. Retention

Indeed, the graduation rate of students who enrolled in French immersion upon entry has been very high. However, only 40% of them graduate with the "Immersion" designation on their degree (University of Ottawa, 2014, p. 1). Students dropped out of the RIF at different stages of their programs: some never even actually started, while others switched to the regular English program after a term or a year, feeling that their language proficiency was not high enough, the content too complex, or that they were not enjoying the immersion experience. At the beginning of the second year, about one quarter of the original cohort had left the RIF, and numbers continued to plummet in the third and fourth years: "34% fewer students are taking courses in French at the end of the third year, compared to the beginning of the first year" (Létourneau, quoted in University of Ottawa, 2014, p. 27).

3.2.3. Language Support Courses

Although available to all students regardless of their admission test results, this key feature of the RIF has not attracted as many students as it should. Too many students were misjudging their language ability and, as a result, were not seeking or receiving the support they needed (University of Ottawa, 2014, p. 5). It is worth noting that one third of these students had a score of F7 on the admission test, which means that they only understood about three quarters of what they were hearing or reading in French (p. 26).

3.2.4. Regular FLS Courses

The RIF has not required students with lower admission test scores to take remedial regular FSL courses to bring them to an adequate language proficiency level. As a result, many RIF students have not taken any advanced French courses over the course of their four years and have thus failed the exit test (Second Language Proficiency Test, FLS 3500), typically due to poor writing skills. If unaddressed, this issue may lead one to question the actual proficiency of immersion graduates.

3.2.5. Student-Determined Academic Path

The RIF gives students total control over their course selection and does not impose any courses beyond the very basic requirements. The director has admitted that students should be supervised more closely to make sure they give French a greater presence in their academic and extracurricular activities.

3.2.6. Funding

The discretionary budget has remained constant since 2006 while costs have been increasing. This financial strain has meant that the RIF has had to make difficult choices: What could be done within a shrinking budget? What should the priorities be?

3.2.7. No Pass/Fail System After the Second Year

Many RIF students said that they would like to be able to continue to use the Pass/Fail system in their third and fourth years, even if it was only for one course per year. Although their second language skills had definitely improved during the first two years, they still felt intimidated when it came to writing papers in French, especially at the level of complexity required in the latter years of their program (University of Ottawa, 2014, p. 32).

3.2.8. Language Support Classes

Unfortunately, some instructors were applying for adjunct courses even though they had not embraced the immersion philosophy and pedagogy (discussed further in Chapter 11). However, part-time instructors cannot be denied a course if they have enough seniority points.

3.3. Possible Solutions

The RIF compiled a list of measures to address these challenges (University of Ottawa, 2014, p. 19), some of which were then implemented, such as a speaking skills component for the admission test, to gain a more accurate picture of students' actual French proficiency. These measures fell under five main headings: assessment, academic path, sociocultural dimension, motivation, and administration (the most relevant and important are listed here).

3.3.1. Assessment
- The threshold level for admission to the RIF should be higher.
- Evaluation methods and schemes for the receptive skills adjunct courses (FLS 2581) should be revised so as to encourage students to use self-correction strategies and tools.
- Students should be required to take the Second Language Proficiency test (FLS 3500, mandatory exit test) at the end of their second year, which would allow them to take remedial FSL courses if they fail (if they wait until the end of their program to take the test and they fail it, they cannot graduate with the "Immersion" designation).
- RIF objectives could be aligned with CEFRL certifications, particularly the DELF.

3.3.2. Academic Path
- Create a required sequence of courses based on admission test scores. This would require weaker students to take regular FSL courses before taking content courses in French. These remedial courses would improve retention by allowing students to achieve an adequate level of proficiency for content courses in French. For example, students with an F7 score would be required to take receptive and productive skills courses, while students with an F8 score would have to take writing/grammar courses and students with an F9 score would be exempt.
- Require all immersion students to take one or more writing courses, whether regular FLS courses (such as FLS 2761, *Mieux écrire en FLS*) or adjunct courses (FLS 3581, *Expression*) to ensure that they are actually able to use spoken and written French in their field of expertise.
- Develop an automated tool to document students' course selections, in order to make it easier to supervise their academic path and recommend remedial measures before they drop out of the RIF.
- Collaborate more closely with faculties when it comes to students' course selection. Both the RIF and the academic programs should be involved in advising students on the courses they need to take in French.

3.3.3. Sociocultural Dimension
- Explore options for exchange and placement opportunities in French-speaking universities in Canada.
- Introduce a buddy system (see Chapter 9) in all immersion courses to improve students' experience and retention rates.

3.3.4. Motivation
- Create a Student Commitment Contract, which would explicitly state what is expected from students and what resources are available to help them meet these expectations.

- Offer a small financial incentive to students registering in an exchange or co-op program.

3.3.5. Administration

- Guarantee both content and language instructors that they will be working together on the same course for two or three years (see Chapter 9), which would allow them to build a rapport and work together developing activities (this would require collaboration from faculties).
- Rewrite the titles and descriptions of the adjunct courses in plain language to make them more accessible to English-speaking first-year students.
- Pair FLS 2581 (receptive skills) courses exclusively with first-year content courses and FLS 3581 (productive skills) exclusively with second-year courses.
- Require RIF students to write at least one paper in French in each academic term.
- Train immersion advocates in each faculty so that more academic assistants are aware of the RIF's rules and regulations.
- Credit co-op placements in French toward the requirements for the RIF.
- Change the English name of the RIF. "French Immersion Studies" can be misleading, since the term "studies" is typically used for a domain of specialization (such as "French Studies" or "Canadian Studies").[27]
- Use the single title *Régime d'immersion en français* for both the regular RIF option and the *Régime de français enrichi* offered in the Faculties of Science and Engineering.[28] Immersion is available with different configurations depending on the faculties involved, but it is still immersion (University of Ottawa, 2014, pp. 44–45).
- Add requirements and administrative constraints to improve teaching. Adjunct course instructors who consistently receive poor ratings in the University's official evaluations should no longer be eligible to apply for them, and any instructor considering teaching these courses should take a mandatory Immersion training workshop (University of Ottawa, 2014, p. 33).

4. REVIEW AND RECOMMENDATIONS

This chapter has explained how the RIF implemented the guiding principles stated in the university's long-term planning guide, *Vision 2010* (University of Ottawa, 2005b) in order to allow immersion students to continue studying in French in their undergraduate programs. The chapter has also established that the RIF was fulfilling its objectives, but that potentially serious challenges must be addressed; a series of remedial measures considered by the RIF have been presented. However, a thorough analysis of the situation has shown that these issues are not separate but systemic — they are being caused by the RIF itself in its present state. Consequently, if sustainable solutions are to be found, they must be systemic in nature.

---

[27] This has just been done (spring 2019): "French Immersion Stream" is the new name, in English, for the RIF.

[28] This change has been approved and should be in effect as of September 2019.

4.1. Review

The most daunting challenge faced by the RIF has undoubtedly been the retention issue: how is it that one third of the RIF students drop out after the first year, and only 40% graduate from their program with the "Immersion" designation? And this, in the face of such inducements as:

- a very high admission average
- $1000 in scholarship every year for four years
- Pass/Fail grades for 24 credits over the first two years
- adjunct language support classes tailored to their content courses and counting as three credits in spite of being only 1.5 hours a week
- a very flexible academic path when it comes to course selection

The 2014 self-evaluation report (University of Ottawa, 2014) pointed out what seems to have been (and continues to be) the culprit: the language proficiency of students admitted into the RIF (Daoust & Durepos, 2016, pp. 3–5) — a cause also mentioned by many of the immersion stakeholders, whether adjunct language course instructors, content course instructors, administrators, or the students themselves.

This should hardly have come as a surprise. Since the 1980s, research on primary and secondary school immersion has consistently shown that, although immersion students compare favourably with their Francophone peers with respect to reading and listening comprehension, they are severely behind when it comes to expressive skills, most notably writing (Harley, 1992; Lapkin, 1984; Lyster, 1987). This accounts for the feelings of insecurity voiced by RIF students in the self-assessment report: most students dropped out after they had used up their Pass/Fail credits. They realized they would not be able to obtain high enough grades to maintain their average and, consequently, their scholarships. As a result, they switched to the English version of their program of studies, from which they graduated with stellar grades.

Unfortunately, the RIF in its current configuration does not address this situation:

- First, the tests used to admit students to the RIF are not aligned with the language and the formats typically used in first-year university courses delivered in French.[29]
- Second, students who score at the lower limit have not been required to take French as a second language courses to improve their skills, particularly in grammar and writing.

---

[29] The first Admission Test, taken just after accepting an admission offer but prior to registering, is the generic test used by all students registering in a regular FSL course — it only assesses receptive skills. A second test, the Immersion Writing and Speaking Test, is taken separately, after the Immersion Admission Test; it assesses general everyday language. The admission procedure is currently under review and a new comprehensive test is being developed in order to better reflect the tasks expected from students taking first-year content courses in French.

- Third, adjunct language courses, and more specifically those focussing on productive skills, have not been mandatory, even though they are what distinguishes the RIF from "swim or sink" approaches, where students take content courses in a second/foreign language without any language support. University courses require good listening and reading skills in order to understand lectures and read academic texts in French. But they also require good writing and speaking skills in order to write summaries and assignments or to make oral presentations and participate in discussion groups.
- Finally, uOttawa's regulation on bilingualism has allowed all students to write their assignments and exams in all their content courses in the official language of their choice, which has meant that immersion students are not required to write in French.

This has, in turn, raised a problematic question: What is the actual level of French-language proficiency of RIF graduates?

Students are not required to take a single French language or adjunct language support course over the four years of their program. The only measure of their actual proficiency is the exit test, the Second Language Certification Test, required for the "Immersion" designation on their degrees.

Students are only required to take about one third of their program's courses in French — whether content, adjunct, or regular language courses. This is about the same as high school immersion, but it is substantially less than a program such as the one offered at Simon Fraser University, which requires more than half the courses in French (75 out of 120 credits) (see Chapter 5).

The system has not motivated students to improve their French proficiency — they don't need to. What *has* motivated them to register in the RIF have been the inducements listed earlier (see p. 143). Yet it is a well-known fact that extrinsic motivation — engaging in an activity for the benefits it might yield — is far less effective than intrinsic motivation — the enjoyment one gains from doing the task (Deci, cited in Pelletier & Vallerand, 1993). Additionally, there is a positive correlation between intrinsic motivation and academic performance in high school students (Fortier, Vallerand, & Guay, 1995; Grolnick, Ryan, & Deci, 1991).

How can the RIF strengthen and support student motivation? Introducing a contract might help. Studies show that contracts can be a powerful tool for intrinsic motivation, because it puts the learner in the driver's seat, in charge of the learning experience (Przesmycki, 1994). RIF students would commit to using French at every opportunity in their academic life, including amongst themselves; such a contact could go as far as committing to writing all their assignments and exams in French. Formative assessment practices have also been shown to improve intrinsic motivation (Tardif, 1992, p. 123). Finally, the RIF could reinstate a study-abroad component, another well-documented vehicle for motivation because it gives value to the learning task by turning it into a meaningful, socially and culturally situated act: students are more likely to engage into a task if they believe they will gain cognitive, affective, or social benefits from it (Vianin, 2006, p. 86).

Table 1: Student retention relative to language proficiency and language support classes
(Source: Daoust & Durepos, 2016, p. 4)

Test score	N^a (start)	after 1 yr (%)	N^b	after 2 yrs (%)	N^c	after 5 yrs (%)
F5–F6	133	57.1	88	38.6	37	13.5
F7	1,231	78.3	1,055	59.4	609	30.5
F8	1,317	77.4	1,127	63.5	703	38.8
F9	442	81.9	311	70.1	250	51.6
All	3,132	77.5	2,581	61.7	1,599	37.1
FSL courses	—	—	—	—	—	—
No FSL	1,107	55.2	878	35.3	489	13.1
Other FSL	469	72.1	383	56.9	218	29.4
FLS2581	1,169	82.1	934	66.4	546	35.5
FLS3581	196	89.9	178	78.1	131	58.0
FLS2581–3581	471	94.9	412	85.9	297	66.3
All	3,412	74.2	2,785	59.0	1,681	35.4

a = 2007–2014 cohort; retention after first year
b = 2007–2013 cohort; retention after second year
c = 2007–2011 cohort; retention after graduation

4.2. Recommendations

4.2.1. Student Retention

The two reports commissioned by the RIF (in 2014 and in 2016) established that the two most important predictors of student retention have been proficiency at admission and language support classes. Only 18% of students scoring F7 on the admission test graduate after four years, versus 26% of students scoring F8 and 27% of students scoring F9 (University of Ottawa, 2014, p. 23). A quantitative analysis done on RIF cohorts from 2007 to 2014 showed that students who scored high on the immersion admission test (i.e., students with a higher level of proficiency in their second language) were much more likely to stay in the RIF than those who scored low (even though retention rates dropped after the first year). It also showed that the more language support classes they took, the more likely they were to continue with the RIF option and graduate with it (Daoust & Durepos, 2016, p. 4; see Table 1).

It should be noted that these two elements were key components of the original RIF vision: designed for high school immersion students (as opposed to Extended, Intensive, or Core French students), and based on adjunct classes to alleviate students' feeling of inadequate linguistic competence (see Chapter 2).

We propose the following recommendations, organized under four main headings, in order to address the challenges facing the RIF.

4.2.1.1. Motivation

- Alleviate students' feelings of linguistic and affective insecurity and social isolation by increasing the (already important) role of immersion mentors and offer more opportunities of interactions with Francophone students — institutionalizing the Francophone/Francophile buddy system, for example.
- Track students with an at-risk profile (those with lower scores on the admission test) and offering them the resources and tools they need to improve their language skills.
- Use social media and networks (such as Facebook) to create immersion study groups.
- Offer social activities programming to foster a sense of belonging, a RIF identity, and create meaningful opportunities to use the language in a non-threatening way.

4.2.1.2. Assessment

- Raise the requirement to a score of F8 on the admission test.
- Redesign the admission test to better reflect the listening, reading, speaking, and writing tasks expected from first-year university students in academic language.[30]

4.2.1.3. Academic path

- Require students to take regular FSL courses to address weaknesses identified in the admission test.
- Bar students with lower admission test scores from taking content courses in French until they take remedial FSL courses (in their first year).
- Require students to take adjunct language support classes: currently, students can graduate with the "Immersion" designation without taking a single regular FSL course or a single language support class[31] if they take the required number of content courses in French.
- Require students to take advanced adjunct language support classes (FLS 3581) to promote the development of academic speaking and writing skills.

4.2.1.4. Administration

- Bar students from taking advanced adjunct language support classes (FLS 3581) from writing their content course assignments and exams in English. Students in the Second Language Teaching program are not eligible under the university's Regulation on Bilingualism,[32] so immersion students could be placed in that category as well.
- Allow 24 credits under the Pass/Fail system for the first three (not two) years of the program. There could be a limit on the number of courses under this system in third year: for example, one course per term.

---

[30] This recommendation is being implemented.
[31] Ironically, the adjunct language support courses are what makes the RIF unique.
[32] This would have to be approved by the university senate (Council of Deans).

4.2.2. Faculty

The second biggest challenge has been about the teaching staff. The RIF has virtually no control over who teaches immersion courses, whether the content part or the language part. As a result, some instructors have undermined the initiative because they do not adhere to the immersion philosophy (either because they do not share it or because they do not know it). Let us remember that, although university-level immersion was born at uOttawa in the 1980s (see Chapter 4): "[i]n the period since 2005, the faculty has been transformed through both generational change and the creation of over 250 new positions, with the result that newcomers now account for over 40% of all regular professors" (University of Ottawa, 2013, p. 1). The result is that many are not aware of the immersion culture and tradition within the university.

4.2.2.1. Content instructors
Content instructors may decline to teach an immersion course if they oppose the principle. However, if not yet tenured, such a move might be detrimental to their career, so they will take the course and treat it as a regular course, not acknowledging the particular needs of the Francophile students and not collaborating with the adjunct language course instructor. Part-time content instructors typically cannot afford to be too selective about immersion courses (assuming they know what they are). Furthermore, a simple form letter sent in a mass email does not foster a collaborative atmosphere around the immersion project. In order to secure content teachers' cooperation and active participation, the RIF needs to find successful ways to raise their awareness of and engagement with the initiative.

4.2.2.2. Language instructors
Language instructors have been, for the most part, immersion aficionados, especially among regular staff. Regrettably, some part-time instructors have only viewed adjunct language courses as a convenient way to make more money with less effort. They are paid 50% more because they are supposed to attend the content classes, but some of them do not always fulfill this requirement. Others have treated these language support classes as regular second language classes, teaching grammar and general vocabulary, or worse, turning them into a discussion group or a tutorial for the content course. But the RIF is helpless there: union regulations make it impossible to deny a course to a part-time instructor with enough seniority, since course allocation is based on seniority rather than, for example, on student evaluations (see Burger, Weinberg, Hall, Movassat, & Hope, 2011).

4.2.2.3. Recommendations
The following recommendations should help improve the quality of teaching:

- Introduce a new type of contract for the adjunct courses, thereby creating a new course category. This would allow immersion-specific clauses such as requiring instructors to attend content classes and to take an immersion training workshop before they can teach a language support course.[33]

---

[33] Mandatory attendance of content courses is now explicitly mentioned in all part-time contracts.

- Only assign adjunct courses to professors demonstrating their knowledge of and commitment to immersion principles (by attending immersion workshops and contributing language activities based on content courses).[34]
- Recognize the importance of content instructors, whose courses are designated as immersion. This could take the form of a reception hosted by the vice-president at the beginning of each term to welcome content and language instructors (and maybe immersion students), introduce the immersion principles and emphasize the importance of the RIF for the university (as outlined in *Destination 2020*). Such an event would be much more effective than a form letter sent via a mass mailing to make the content instructors feel like valuable members of a team.
- Encourage long-term collaboration between content and language instructors to promote teamwork and co-development of course material.[35]
- Create awards or scholarships to recognize collaborative projects by content/language course instructors' tandems, such as research on university immersion pedagogy or instructional material development.

CONCLUSION

The RIF has been a highly successful option among students, as consistently demonstrated by their responses to surveys and questionnaires over the years. It has also been a very effective recruiting tool for uOttawa. Immersion students register in courses in both English and French, bringing extra funding for French-language programs, freeing up space in English-language programs, and promoting intercultural exchanges between the two linguistic groups (University of Ottawa, 2014, p. 21).

With the RIF, the university has reached the first objective of *Vision 2010* (University of Ottawa, 2005b):

> play a leadership role in promoting Canada's official languages.... By 2010, we will have improved our linguistic balance and have become the standard among Canadian universities in the areas of acquisition, development, evaluation and promotion of the official languages. (p. 1)

It also plays a key role in achieving the goals set in *Destination 2020* (University of Ottawa, 2013, p. 7):

1. recruit more Francophone students and achieve a better linguistic balance in our student population
2. further our research efforts relating to the Francophonie
3. pool our areas of strength and enhance the visibility of the Francophonie on our campus
4. endow new chairs and support research and publication[s] in French
5. provide students with greater access to courses and programs of study in French and invigorate the campus's French-language social, cultural and scientific life

---

[34] Union regulations may not allow such measures to be implemented.
[35] Here again, union regulations may not allow such measures to be implemented.

The RIF offers an inspiring model to other Canadian universities and, potentially, to post-secondary institutions worldwide. It has departed from its original vision in certain respects, which has created a number of issues. Governance is key, and an Advisory Committee of experts in the field of post-secondary immersion will provide the academic, methodological, and pedagogical guidance that the administrative perspective is lacking. It is also important to focus resources on a small number of well-targeted initiatives likely to address the systemic challenges within the RIF, instead of scattering them on a wide array of unrelated measures that would address the symptoms but not the causes.

We hope that the recommendations put forth in this chapter will ensure the continuation of the RIF, a unique initiative in Canada, which gives uOttawa a leadership role in post-secondary immersion, and that it will serve as a framework for institutions contemplating implementing an immersion *dispositif.*

REFERENCES

Burger, S., Weinberg, A., Hall, C., Movassat, P., & Hope, A. (2011). French immersion studies at the University of Ottawa: Program evaluation and pedagogical challenges. In D. Tedick, D. Christian, & T. William Fortune (Eds.), *Immersion education: Practices, policies, possibilities* (pp. 123–142). Clevedon: Multilingual Matters.

Council of Europe. (2001). *Common European Framework of Reference for Languages: Learning, teaching, assessment.* Cambridge: Cambridge University Press. rm.coe.int/1680459f97

Daoust J.L., & Durepos, J. (2016). *Programme de mentorat/Mentoring program: Rétention et expérience étudiante.* Internal document, French Immersion Studies [Régime d'immersion en français], University of Ottawa.

Fortier, M.S., Vallerand, R.J., & Guay, F. (1995). Academic motivation and school performance: Toward a structural model. *Contemporary Educational Psychology, 20,* 257–274.

France. Ministère de l'éducation nationale et de la jeunesse. (n.d.). Centre international d'études pédagogiques (CIEP) [Home page]. www.ciep.fr/delf-dalf

Grolnick, W.S., Ryan, R.N., & Deci, E.L. (1991). The inner resources for school performance: Motivational mediators of children's perceptions of their parents. *Journal of Educational Psychology, 53,* 508–517.

Harley, B. (1992). Aspects of the oral second language proficiency of early immersion, late immersion and extended French students at Grade 10. In R.J. Courchesne, J.I. Glidden, J. St. John, & C. Thérien (Eds.), *Comprehension-based second language teaching* (pp. 317–388). Ottawa: University of Ottawa Press.

Ideology. (n.d.). Cambridge Dictionary. dictionary.cambridge.org/dictionary/english/ideology

Je parle 2017. (2013–2014). [Facebook account]. www.facebook.com/jeparle2017

Lapkin, S. (1984). How well do immersion students speak and write French? *Canadian Modern Language Review, 40,* 575–585.

Lyster, R. (1987). Speaking immersion. *Canadian Modern Language Review, 43,* 701–717.

My nutty life as a university student, woah. (2013, November 3). [Tumblr account]. laviebelleetfrancaise.tumblr.com

Official Languages and Bilingualism Institute (OLBI). (n.d.). Concours de français langue seconde Ottawa (CFL2). olbi.uottawa.ca/development/ottawa-school-boards

Ontario. Ministry of Education. (n.d.). French-language education in Ontario: The Canada–Ontario Agreement on Minority-Language Education and Second Official-Language Instruction 2013–2014 to 2017–2018. www.edu.gov.on.ca/eng/amenagement/ ententeAgreementEd.pdf

Ontario Universities' Application Centre (OUAC). (n.d.). About. www.ouac.on.ca/about

Pelletier, L.G., & Vallerand, R.J. (1993). Une perspective humaniste de la motivation : les théories de la compétence et de l'autodétermination. In R.J. Vallerand & E.E. Thill (Eds.), *Introduction à la psychologie de la motivation*, pp. 234–282. Montréal: Études Vivantes.

Przesmycki, H. (1994). *La pédagogie de contrat*. Paris: Hachette-Éducation.

Ryan, W., Courcelles, P., Hope, A., Buchanan, C., & Toews-Janzen, M. (2007). *Evaluation of the French immersion studies academic stream: Year 1*. Internal document. Ottawa: University of Ottawa, Centre for Research on Educational and Community Services (CRECS).

Ryan, W., Gobeil, M., Hope, A., & Toews-Janzen, M. (2008). *Evaluation of the French immersion studies academic stream: Year 2*. Internal document. Ottawa: University of Ottawa, Centre for Research on Educational and Community Services (CRECS).

Stern, H. (1984). The immersion phenomenon. *Language and Society*, *12*, 4–7.

Tardif, J. (1992). *Pour un enseignement stratégique*. Montréal: Logiques.

University of Ottawa. (n.d.). Carrefour francophone. www.uottawa.ca/communitylife/carrefourfrancophone

University of Ottawa. (n.d.). French Immersion Stream. immersion.uottawa.ca/en

University of Ottawa. (n.d.). French immersion studies at the University of Ottawa [Facebook page]. www.facebook.com/pages/French-Immersion-Studies-at-the-University-of-Ottawa/265179676863322

University of Ottawa. (n.d.). Immersion en français [Twitter account]. twitter.com/uOttawaFI

University of Ottawa. (n.d.). Office of the Provost and Vice-President, Academic Affairs. www.uottawa.ca/vice-president-academic/academic-regulations-explained/glossary?cat_1=P

University of Ottawa. (2005a). Proposition pour la création d'un Régime d'immersion en français langue seconde à l'Université d'Ottawa. Unpublished internal document: Proposal to the Senate of the University of Ottawa, May 2, 2005.

University of Ottawa. (2005b). *Vision 2010 — Academic strategic plan*. web5.uottawa.ca/vision2010/pdf/strategic_plan.pdf

University of Ottawa. (2013). *Destination 2020 — Discover the future*. The University of Ottawa's strategic plan. www.uottawa.ca/about/sites/www.uottawa.ca.about/files/destination-2020-strategic-plan.pdf

University of Ottawa. (2014). *Évaluation périodique. Régime d'immersion en français: Le rapport d'auto-évaluation*. Unpublished internal document. Printemps 2014. University of Ottawa.

Vianin, P. (2006). *La motivation scolaire: comment susciter le désir d'apprendre?* Bruxelles: De Boeck.

CHAPTER 7

Learning Modes and Situations in the *Régime d'immersion en français*: A Holistic Approach

Alysse Weinberg and Catherine Elena Buchanan

INTRODUCTION

IMMERSION IS NOT LIMITED TO LANGUAGE LEARNING; it may also be used for learning content in a variety of academic disciplines. Moreover it may be organized around other content learning situations and other language learning modalities. This chapter will discuss diversification within the *Régime d'immersion en français* (RIF) at the University of Ottawa (uOttawa) and expand on three learning modalities:

- formal learning (implemented and supervised by the institution)
- semi-formal learning (implemented by the students, but sustained or monitored by the institution)
- informal learning (implemented by students, outside any institutionalized framework)

The first section will define the underlying concepts — learning modalities and learning contexts. The second section will discuss the multiple and varied experiences of the many actors, situations, and models that form the basis of the holistic approach of the RIF. The limits and the contributions of this multifaceted approach to immersion learning at the university level will be outlined in the conclusion.

1. THEORETICAL FRAMEWORK

To better assist the reader in understanding its approach, some definitions that support the different concepts are presented in this section.

1.1. Definitions of Learning Modalities

The purpose of this section is to propose a classification of the many learning situations where an immersion approach can be implemented. These situations may involve different or complementary learning modalities. This classification was developed based on the work of the European Centre for the Development of Vocational Training (CEDEFOP, 2008):

- *Formal learning* is implemented and supervised by the institution. It is delivered in an organized and structured environment (in an educational or training institution or situation) and aims (in terms of objectives, duration, or resources) to teach language skills.

- *Semi-formal learning* is usually implemented by the institution but mainly depends on student engagement. Learning activities are planned by the administrative entities responsible for the programs, but they are not imposed.
- *Informal learning* is implemented exclusively by students outside of any institutional framework. It arises from the activities of daily living related to work, family, or leisure. It is neither organized nor structured in terms of objectives, time, or resources. In informal learning, the learner's main purpose is not acquiring language skills.

1.2. Notions of Place and Space in the Institution

The generally agreed-on definition of *place* is a concrete area, circumscribed and localized in time and space (Colleyn & Dozon, 2008). Augé (1992) attributes to place a notion of an identity, a relation, and a history. In the field of education, places can be classrooms, language laboratories, resource centres, or libraries. They therefore have specific functions defined by the institution, bringing together institutional players who also have a specific role, status and function. Some places may even have an official name designated by the institution: for example, the Immersion Mentoring Centre (University of Ottawa, n.d., "Service mentoring centres"), as part of the RIF at uOttawa, or the *Centre international d'études françaises* (CIEF) (International Centre of French Studies), at the Université Lumière Lyon 2 (n.d.).

On the other hand, the term "space" refers to a rather abstract design with fuzzy outlines. It encompasses places, actors, exchanges, learning modalities, language communication, and interactions between individuals. A space can be set up by the institution or built outside the established frameworks. It can be at the crossroads of an established place and a non-established space. A good example of such a place would be the Virtual Campus (University of Ottawa, n.d., "Virtual campus"), which is not only the product of pedagogical approaches proposed by the institution but also hosts student initiatives (for example, discussion forums). We can therefore speak of a virtual language space, but also of socialization in this language.

2. LEARNING MODALITIES AND LEARNING SPACES WITHIN THE RIF

This section proposes a typology of the learning modalities for an immersion program that will fit into different places, from circumscribed, enclosed and framed places (the classroom space) located in the immediate environment, limited to the academic circle (the university space), then moving outward to include Francophone associations and communities, which remain local (the community space), and ultimately opening up to the world through exchanges, mobility, and study-abroad trips (the international space). Finally, students leave face-to-face learning to get into the virtual spaces and social networks that are part of the everyday life of any twenty-first-century student. The virtual is becoming more and more a place and an essential mode of learning, integrated into the teaching of courses, and is naturally a part of the students' daily social life.

Table 1 illustrates in detail how the RIF puts the three learning modalities into practice. A holistic approach is necessary because RIF immersion goes beyond the acquisition of language skills and disciplinary knowledge — it is also organized around different learning modalities and their spaces. At uOttawa, the university and RIF sites are physically distinct from one another, one of the requirements under the definition of *learning modalities*.

The university offers a bilingual campus where both linguistic communities, English and French, can live and study in parallel streams, while the RIF is reserved for English-speaking students studying in French. The combinations of learning modalities, places, and situations are fluid, multiple, and mobile. Formal classroom learning can take place in either a content-area lecture or a once-per-semester workshop. This chapter limits its examples to the modalities actually experienced within the RIF; nevertheless, Table 1 can serve as a model and be applied to other immersion programs.

Table 1: Learning modalities and learning spaces at the RIF

Spaces	Learning modalities		
	Formal	Semi-formal	Informal
Classroom	Content courses Adjunct language courses Workshops (once a semester)	Voluntary student-to-student mentoring *Parrainage* (a buddy system)	Informal conversations between Francophone and Anglophone students
University	Compulsory information sessions provided by third- and fourth-year students	Immersion Club	Residence/social activities Debating society
Community			Work experiences Leisure experiences Movie nights Pot luck dinners Relations between friends
International	uOttawa-sponsored study-abroad trip to Lyon (France) Study exchanges in Francophone countries		Personal travel Graduate studies Volunteering
Virtual	Podcasts Wiki history website Blogs Virtual Campus	*Le portail francophile*	Social media Student blogs

2.1. Formal Learning Modalities

2.1.1. The Classroom Space

2.1.1.1. Courses: Courses offered by each immersion program are obviously the basis of classroom learning. These are French-language content courses offered in more than 80 programs by the Faculties of Arts, Social Sciences, Health Sciences, Education, Management, and Law. For example, in history, students can take HIS 1511, *Le monde au XXe siècle depuis 1945*. There are also French courses offered by the Official Languages and Bilingualism Institute (OLBI), such as adjunct language courses or advanced French as a second language (FSL) courses: for example, advanced grammar or pronunciation. Finally, students whose level of French is high enough can choose language or literature courses offered by the *Département de français*.

2.1.1.2. Workshops: Four educational workshops are offered each semester to RIF students. These focus on learning strategies essential to success in immersion courses:

- how to be a better reader by applying reading strategies
- how to take notes and better summarize and understand lectures
- how to successfully give an oral presentation
- how to use Antidote (Druide, 2018)[1]

All RIF students are strongly encouraged to participate in these workshops; however, since their introduction, fewer than 25% of first-year RIF students have enrolled in them.

2.1.2. The University Space

2.1.2.1. Mentorship: Student-to-student mentoring (see also Chapter 9) is an approach promoted by uOttawa and is implemented in each faculty. The RIF set up its own system to facilitate the integration of first-year students into university life. Mentors are third- and fourth-year RIF students, who are hired and paid by the RIF, and who already have immersion experience at the university. They can advise and guide new students in a friendly and reassuring manner. It is highly recommended that students contact their mentors as quickly as possible, even before they enter university. The RIF introduces them during university information days, usually six months before the registration period; new students also have access to the Immersion Mentoring Centre webpage, mentioned earlier. According to students, mentoring is one of the most popular support programs.

2.1.3. International Learning Space

More and more students are choosing to study abroad and away from their home university as part of their undergraduate university degree. Indeed, the more students are immersed in a language "bath," the more they will acquire new linguistic, social, and

---

[1] Software which helps with the correction of French language texts; it also includes many dictionaries and a grammar guide.

cultural knowledge. This immersion is even more important in the case of second- or foreign-language learning, because "the journey forces self-questioning by the change of personal benchmarks and through the confrontation to the Elsewhere, to the Other and to other cultural references" (Argod, 2013, para. 6 [trans.]). In her research, MacFarlane (2001) has argued that authentic contacts with native speakers, whether face-to-face or virtual, however limited, improve classroom learning and learners' self-confidence. Finally, the research by Mady and Arnott (2010) highlights the undeniable advantages that students derive from experiencing life in French outside the constraints of the classroom.

2.1.3.1. Study-abroad trip to Lyon—Immersion within immersion: Beginning in 2007, for five consecutive years, the RIF sent 20 students each spring to the Université Lumière Lyon 2 for a three-week study program centred on academic, linguistic, and cultural activities. The decision to offer this program was based on the results of research conducted on study-abroad programs in the United States, Canada, and Europe. This research highlighted the multiple benefits of these stays to reinforce the acquisition of varied skills such as linguistic and sociolinguistic competencies (Mougeon, Rehner, & Nadasdi, 2004; Regan, Howard, & Lemée, 2009; Thomas, 2002), both personal and intercultural (Meunier, 2013).

During their stay in Lyon, students attended lectures in class and events in the city, all tailored to their specific needs. Topics ranged from ancient to contemporary history, from social geography to different facets of culture (culinary, popular, and classical). Table 2 shows the students' schedule during the trip to Lyon in 2012. A language instructor from uOttawa accompanied the students, providing linguistic support, and facilitating their social and cultural integration. Thus, an immersion experience within immersion was created. Despite the success of this program and significant student interest, it was discontinued in 2013 for financial reasons.

2.1.3.2. International stay: The International Office (University of Ottawa, n.d., "International") organizes exchanges for full-time students to allow them to complete part of their degree at an institution abroad. After their experiences in Lyon, some second- and third-year students decided to pursue their studies abroad in French for a semester, for a year, and in some cases, even for several years. Since its creation, 60% of students enrolled in the RIF have gone to study abroad. They have travelled to continue their studies in various Francophone countries including Belgium, France, Luxembourg, Morocco, Senegal, and Tunisia.

2.1.4. The Virtual Space

2.1.4.1. Virtual learning platforms:[2] New technologies are now commonly used in university courses, and RIF instructors use them according to their techno-pedagogical skills. Some use the institution's recommended learning platform to share information with students, plan activities, provide resources, or offer them group work through

---

[2] These allow instructors to create dedicated course sites, to post information for students, and to provide discussion forums to help students network with one another.

Table 2: Student schedule in Lyon study-abroad trip (May 2012)

Week 2	Morning	Afternoon	Evening
Monday	9:00–11:00 History of Lyon 11:00–12:00 Adjunct language course	2:00–5:00 Field trip in Lyon	
Tuesday	Day excursion: Le Corbusier site in Firminy, Mount Pilat, Condrieu winery and wine tasting		
Wednesday	9:00–10:00 Adjunct language course 10:00–12:00 Visit to the Musée Lumière	2:00–4:00 History of Lyon	Play: *Petits chocs des civilisations*, by Fellag
Thursday	9:00–10:00 Course on theatre 10:00–12:00 History of social systems	2:00–4:00 History of gastronomy	
Friday	9:00–12:00 Field trip in Lyon	2:00–4:30 Adjunct language course	

the various discussion forums. This platform has evolved over the years, starting with Blackboard Learn,[3] and then moving to Brightspace.[4] Depending on the instructors' skills, other tools and supports are also used.

2.1.4.2. Wikis: Wikis are a non-institutionalized alternative to facilitate communication and information sharing. They are collaborative spaces for students to share knowledge on pages designed by the instructor so as not to intimidate the technophobic students. The files shared include diagrams, Powerpoint presentations, class notes, vocabulary exercises, and exam preparation sheets. Students are responsible and credited for the content they contribute to these templates.[5] Based on Vygotsky's notion of scaffolding (1978), and research on the use of wikis in language classes (Augar, Raitman, & Zhou 2004; Klobas 2006), wikis give students the opportunity to build their knowledge, alone or collectively, while fostering the creation of a learning community in an authentic context.

2.1.4.3. Podcasts: In 2009, a team of three professors from the OLBI developed a series of seven podcasts[6] to meet the special classroom learning challenges of RIF students (Weinberg, Knoerr, & Vandergrift, 2011). These podcasts were based on metacognition theory (Wenden, 1998) and included topics such as: listening comprehension (Goh,

---

[3] The virtual learning platform used at uOttawa until 2017.
[4] Brightspace is the new virtual learning platform set up by uOttawa to manage online pedagogy.
[5] There was an immersion history course wiki used by the students but it is no longer available.
[6] These podcast files are available in .mp3 or video format and can be downloaded and listened to on a computer or smartphone. They are also discussed in Chapter 9.

2008), preparing for lectures, note taking (Kiewra, 1987), the Cornell note-taking system, monitoring and problem solving, and new techonologies. These podcasts were designed to improve students' ability to listen, their note-taking skills during lectures, the development of lesson preparation strategies, and the ability to self-evaluate the strategies they use (Knoerr & Weinberg, 2013). These podcasts are public (available on YouTube; see University of Ottawa, n.d., "French immersion stream ... podcasts") and any student, anywhere, can view them and learn from them. At the beginning of each academic year, the director of the RIF and all the adjunct course instructors encourage the RIF students to view them and to use the strategies that suit their learning styles. In this way, they can better take charge of their own learning and be successful in their university career.

2.1.4.4. Content course sites — The case of a history course: The content and language instructors for a first-year uOttawa history immersion course (HIS 1520) developed an interdisciplinary website (Perrier, 2008; see also Chapter 9). The home site pointed to two complementary sites — one for the content course, and one for the adjunct language course — both illustrating the richness of the historical period under study with different links to maps, paintings, and artifacts (see Figure 1). The historical material and the language learning sections of the content course site are accessible to both Francophone and Anglophone students in the course. The same outline was followed to present the material on these two sites in a way that facilitates navigation between the two.

HIS 1520 -- Histoire de l'Europe (XVIe-XXe siècle)

Sylvie Perrier
HIS 1520 Page d'accueil

FLS 2581 -- Encadrement linguistique
Histoire de l'Europe (XVIe-XXe siècle)

Alysse Weinberg
FLS 2581 Page d'accueil

Ce site pluridisciplinaire a été élaboré pour intégrer l'apprentissage du français langue seconde dans le cadre d'un cours universitaire. Il s'agit d'une l'initiative d'une professeure oeuvrant dans le Régime d'immersion de l'Université d'Ottawa et d'une professeure du Département d'histoire.
Les deux volets de ce site sont accessibles à tous. Bonne navigation!

Figure 1: Interdisciplinary website pointing to the matching content and adjunct sites
(Source: Weinberg, 2008)

The adjunct course site, designed as a supplement to the language course, aims at teaching FSL, and offers oral and written comprehension activities. The site also offers game-type activities and songs to promote vocabulary learning and revision of key concepts taught in the history course (see Figure 2).

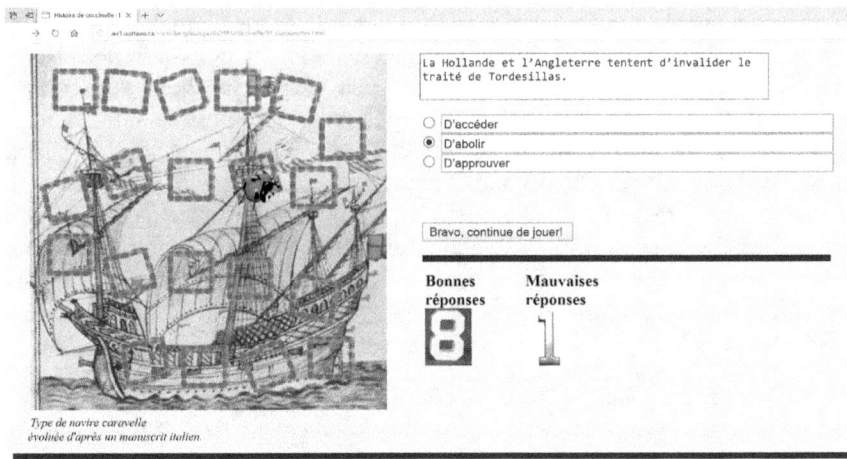

Figure 2: A game to review the academic vocabulary for FLS 2581
(Source: Weinberg, 2012)

The success of these first websites led to the creation of two more sites, based on the same model, for a second-year course in history (Weinberg, 2008). The site for the adjunct language course focuses on oral and written production activities related to the objectives of this level.

2.1.4.5. Blogs: According to Peters, Murphy-Judy, Laferrière, and Weinberg (2009):

> a blog, a combination of the English words web and log, is an online logbook. It consists of short entries, called posts, organized chronologically ... They usually contain text, but they can be embellished with images, videos, sounds, and hyperlinks. (p. 153)

Blogs were part of the course evaluation for the exchange experiences in Lyon. Like any good traveller, the RIF students were asked to record their impressions, reactions, and observations on three aspects of the experience: culture, civilization, and education. The entries could be written, recorded, or filmed, according to the technological skills of the students. The blog gave students the opportunity to take a fresh look at a new world for them, to keep memories of their trip, and to share them with family and friends, as illustrated in the following excerpt:

> [at restaurant *Le Canut et les Gones*, Lyon cuisine, May 18, 2010 [trans.]]
>
> *Student 1:* The evening of May 11 was not like the other nights of our stay in Lyon. An outing was organized to allow us to discover Lyon cuisine, a cuisine that has a history and a heritage. I heard that the city of Lyon was the "gastronomy capital of the world." I was expecting the planned cooking class to be based on the reputation that this city has inherited....
>
> Once the preparation was over, we all sat around a large table to taste what we had prepared. The brains of *Canut*, that is to say a white cheese beaten with cream and mixed with

fresh aromatic herbs, was served fresh in a hollow tomato, accompanied by bread and a good red wine. Despite the fact that this dish was not plentiful, I still appreciated it for its freshness and lightness, its beautiful presentation and its originality. The two pies, which were served later, were even more delicious. In the end, I think everything went well, both in the simplicity of the preparation and the quality of the meal. What a party!

2.2. Semi-formal learning modalities

2.2.1. The classroom

2.2.1.1. Voluntary buddy system (Parrainage): Francophone student to Francophile student[7] mentoring — *Parrainage* — was introduced in history classes under the joint leadership of the content and language instructors. It is anchored in a cooperative learning mode (see Chapter 9), where learning is done by peers and between peers. It is based on two main pedagogic principles: reciprocity and autonomy (Bandura, 1977; Brammerts, 2002). It has been referred to by various names: shared learning through the other, epistolary or linguistic exchange, traditional or virtual twinning, sponsorship, tandem work, and mentoring or e-mentoring. In the context of history courses, Francophone and Francophile students study and learn together to better succeed in their content courses. *Parrainage* helps Francophile students by improving their integration into French content courses; it transforms the competitive learning atmosphere into a more communal and collaborative experience. Since its implementation, the participation rate of Francophone students has been at 45% while the Francophile participation is close to 100% (Weinberg, 2013), thus developing students' self-confidence and encouraging them to continue their studies in French. As well, *Parrainage* has positively impacted their linguistic, academic, and social integration into the Francophone university community (Knoerr, forthcoming).

2.2.2. The University Space

2.2.2.1. Immersion Club: The Immersion Club was launched by the RIF director to create a sense of community among RIF students. This club is geared exclusively to RIF students and, like all clubs on campus, is funded partially by the university and partially by the club itself. The structure of the club is similar to that of other associations on campus. The executive committee organizes social and cultural activities every year to participate in Francophone events outside the classroom and to improve the club members' French through convivial exchanges: Francophone cinema evenings, *la semaine de la Francophonie*, a Montreal trip as part of White Nights (Wikipedia, n.d., "White Nights"), and a trip to the Quebec Carnaval.

---

[7] At uOttawa, any person whose mother tongue is not French but who has a positive attitude toward the French language and its culture and whose behaviour demonstrates a willingness to speak French, is officially defined as a Francophile student (University of Ottawa, n.d., "Le portail francophile").

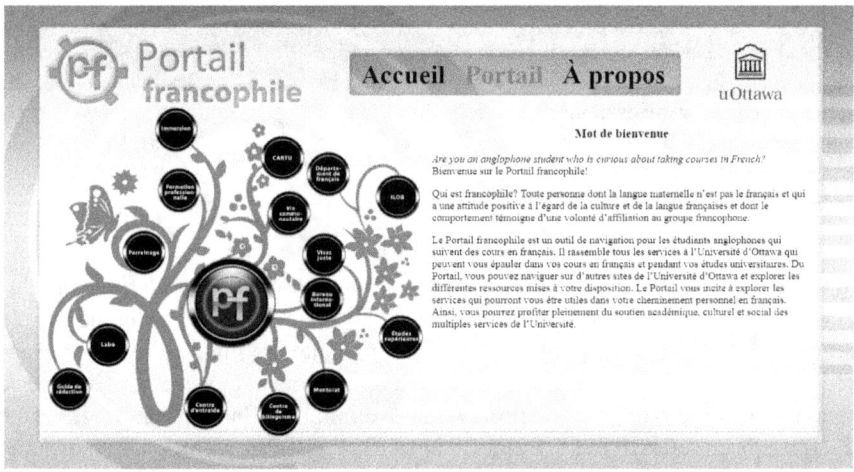

Figure 3: *Le portail francophile*
(Source: University of Ottawa, n.d., "Le portail francophile")

2.2.3. The Virtual Space

2.2.3.1. *Le portail francophile*: The *Portail francophile* project (Figure 3), launched in November 2010, was an initiative by two uOttawa professors, with the collaboration of four university units: the Student Academic Success Service, the RIF, the OLBI, and the Department of History. The purpose of the portal is to gather all uOttawa Francophone and Francophile resources on the same site, with a description and hyperlinks to access them.

2.3. Informal Learning Modalities

This section lists some of the more important places where the RIF students use their French. The information collected here is the result of spontaneous remarks from students who participated in an evaluation of the RIF through personal interviews or focus groups (Séror & Weinberg, 2013). These are informal learning modalities and are, as such, sometimes difficult to categorize. Since uOttawa is a bilingual institution, it offers a number of services intended primarily for Francophone students, such as a designated French-only residence and the *Société des débats français* (French Debating Club). RIF students use these places and situations for the opportunity to speak informally with Francophone students.

2.3.1. The University

RIF students certainly participate in various social activities with one another as well as with Francophone students. In those situations, they draw on the social opportunities offered on a bilingual campus.

2.3.1.1. Residence: At uOttawa, university residences reflect the bilingual nature of the university. Resident counselors must be bilingual to serve both populations. Anglophone and Francophone students can come together as roommates, or meet in common spaces and choose to integrate French into their daily lives. In addition, one residence is assigned only to students who wish to live in French (Francophones and Francophiles included). Many RIF students choose to live there and find themselves engaging in friendly and impromptu activities based on this affinity:

> *Julie:* It was very rewarding to see Anglophones and Francophones on the same floor in residence by sharing their culture and ... just very enriching.... there were concerts, the music was very enriching for everyone, we sang in the corridors all the Quebec songs [big smile]. It was really enriching for English speakers.

2.3.1.2. *Société des débats français*: The French Debating Club was founded at the university in 1887 to promote French. Since 1905, it has organized public debates with students. Meetings are modeled on parliamentary debates. The club participates in inter-university competitions, where students from uOttawa debate students from other French-speaking universities. Many RIF students attend these debates and sometimes even participate in playing decisive roles:

> *Sheila:* I was among the many Anglophones who participated in this club. We were debating in French and our mother tongue did not put us at a disadvantage in the debate tournaments.

2.3.2. In the Community

Students encounter many informal learning opportunities in the workplace and in leisure activities, as well as in their interpersonal relationships with members of the Francophone community.

2.3.2.1. The work environment: For financial reasons, students often have to both work and study. Ottawa has many opportunities to work in French. The uOttawa Work–Study Plan offers students the opportunity to obtain paid part-time employment on campus during the school year or full-time during the summer. Most of these jobs on campus require a certain level of bilingualism. Students may also find work in the National Capital Region, especially with the federal government. For example, some students find positions as pages with Members of Parliament. Other students will work in Quebec, the neighbouring province. This is informal learning and difficult to measure, but we know students take advantage of these bilingual positions, as language teachers in the RIF regularly receive requests for letters of recommendation from their students.

2.3.2.2. At leisure: Students benefit from movie nights, community meals, and other social activities between Francophone and Francophile communities, which strengthen the links between them. In some cases, interpersonal relationships can lead to a long-term romantic relationship with a member of the Francophone community, as this student points out:

> *Rachel:* Next year, I'm going to marry a Franco-Ontarian ... If you start in the classroom, it gives you the confidence of [living in French] in other circles.

2.3.3. International Travel

Some students want to deepen their knowledge of French language and culture outside of their formal studies. They undertake personal voyages to places which they had only read about in their content courses. Here is a quote from a RIF political science student, speaking about her experiences travelling in Europe:

> *Katerine:* [As] a student in the international development and globalization program ... [m]y biggest priority has been to go see the Palais des Nations Office [in Geneva]. The United Nations is a large organization, in principle, and this has been demonstrated by the grounds of the Office; it was absolutely beautiful. Before arriving, we decided to take a guided tour in French ... For me, this tour was an unforgettable experience. I had already visited the United Nations in New York, but I prefer the office in Geneva ... There were many things in the office of great artistic and symbolic significance. I learned much and particularly enjoyed the atmosphere and tranquility of the site. I cherished my time spent in Geneva at the Palais des Nations.

After obtaining their first degree, which included an enjoyable study abroad, some RIF students decide to enrol in graduate programs in France or Belgium. These are usually highly motivated students. One of them, Chris, said: "I returned to Paris this year because I wanted to do my MBA in French." Another student pushed his informal learning experience further by participating in a volunteer project abroad with a humanitarian aid association:

> *Tim:* I got the chance to get involved with a group of humanitarian volunteers working in the Dominican Republic. It was a whole group of Francophones. Thanks to this [immersion] program I was able to live and communicate at a level sufficient to do my work there. I found [the experience] quite excellent.

2.3.4. Virtual Space

2.3.4.1. Social media: Students are increasingly using social media to facilitate communication amongst themselves. Social media applications are evolving rapidly – email is being left behind and Facebook is losing ground to WhatsApp and Instagram. Most students have Twitter, LinkedIn, and Instagram accounts. On the other hand, study groups are created on Facebook. In short, personal communication and blogging preferences are rapidly changing. Students text constantly between themselves using Messenger. However, these are private informal exchanges and it is difficult to say how much they are used by students to expand their French studies and participate in the Francophone community.

Immersion, as it is experienced at uOttawa, illustrates a variety of modalities and spaces. Table 1 shows many of these formal, semi-formal, and informal learning modes through various means and supports. Many parts of this approach, such as websites and podcasts, have been the result of personal initiatives from a small number of instructors who wanted to support the RIF. Certainly, social media and web-based learning, with all its innovation and complexity, need to be a part of the design in a holistic pedagogy of immersion.

CONCLUSION

In this chapter, we have described different types of learning spaces which Gohard-Radenkovic (2013) called "the diversification of intra- and extra-mural experiences through multiple meeting places alternating between formal and informal modalities" (p. 147). The RIF has offered students spaces for meeting and social bonding, linked together through second language culture. This diversity is favoured by the location of the university at the boundaries of two provinces sharing the two official languages of the country. This linguistic coexistence flourishes on the bilingual campus of uOttawa, where Anglophones and Francophones from Canada and abroad come together. This has allowed students to come into "direct regular daily contact with the French and English languages" (Séror & Weinberg, 2013, p. 139). But this is not enough. The impact of natural immersion, as we have seen, can be best realized where effective programs are implemented to increase these learning places and modalities.

However, some elements are missing from this description. Why does the RIF not promote more community involvement? The university has introduced the concept of experiential learning (University of Ottawa, n.d., "CGCE"), where students engage voluntarily in the local or international community in projects related to their curriculum. Why has this pedagogical approach not been put into practice within the holistic approach of the RIF? An additional way, therefore, to strengthen the immersion experience for students would be to encourage them to get in touch with associations and businesses in the Francophone community, as is done at the Office of Francophone and Francophile Affairs at Simon Fraser University (see Chapter 5).

To conclude, we must point out the difference between the institutional discourse and the program put in place. Certainly, the political discourse of the institution proposes an ideal conception of the immersion program which sometimes clashes with its administration and economic constraints. For example, the study-abroad trip to Lyon, a proven success for five years, had to be cancelled because of budget cuts — practical considerations took precedence over the pedagogical principles. An exemplary collaboration between the history and language instructors was discontinued, for organizational reasons. In extreme cases, it is the very existence of the program that is at risk. To quote Gohard-Radenkovic (2013): "immersion programs often fluctuate between extension and extinction" (p. 16), depending on political issues, economic means, and qualified personnel.

REFERENCES

Argod, P. (2013). Le carnet de voyage reportage, outil de formation à la mobilité internationale. cdevoyage.hypotheses.org/685

Augar, N., Raitman, R., & Zhou, W. (2004). Teaching and learning online with wikis. In R. Atkinson, C. McBeath, D. Jonas-Dwyer, & R. Phillips (Eds.), *Beyond the comfort zone: Proceedings of the 21st ASCILITE Conference*, (pp. 95–104). Perth: Australasian Society for Computers in Learning in Tertiary Education (ASCILITE).

Augé, M. (1992). Non-lieux: introduction à une anthropologie de la surmodernité. Paris: Seuil.

Bandura, A. (1977). *Social learning theory*. Englewood Cliffs: Prentice Hall.

Brammerts, H. (2002). Apprendre en tandem: principes et objectifs. In B. Helmling (Ed.), *L'apprentissage autonome des langues en tandem* (pp. 19–24). Paris: Didier.

Centre européen pour le développement de la formation professionnelle (CEDEFOP). (2008). [VALID]ation de l'apprentissage non formel et informel en Europe: état des lieux en 2007 (pp. 45–46). Luxembourg: Office des publications officielles des Communautés européennes. www.cedefop.europa.eu/files/4073_fr.pdf

Colleyn, J.P., & Dozon, J.P. (2008). Lieux et non-lieux de Marc Augé. *L'Homme, 185–186*, 7–32.

Druide informatique. (2018). Antidote 10 (v.1.1) [Writing assistance software]. Montreal: Druide informatique, Inc. antidote.info/en/

Goh, C. (2008). Metacognitive instruction for second language listening development: Theory, practice and research implications. *RELC Journal, 39*, 188–213.

Gohard-Radenkovic, A. (2013). Radiographie de l'immersion dans l'enseignement supérieur en Suisse et à l'Université de Fribourg: les prérequis nécessaires. *OLBI Working Papers, 6*, 3–19.

Harrison, S., & Dourish, P. (1996). Re-placing the space. The roles of place and space in collaborative systems. In G.M. Olson, J.S. Olson, & M.S. Ackerman (Eds.), *Proceedings of the 1996 ACM Conference on Computer Supported Cooperative Work* (pp. 67–76). New York: Association for Computing Machinery Press.

Kiewra, K.A. (1987). Notetaking and review: The research and its implications. *Journal of Instructional Science, 16*, 233–249.

Klobas, J. (2006). *Wiki: Tools for information work and collaboration*. Oxford: Chandos.

Knoerr, H. (forthcoming). Le parrainage francophone/francophile comme outil d'intégration académique, sociale et linguistique. *Revue internationale de pédagogie de l'enseignement supérieur*.

Knoerr, H., & Weinberg, A. (2013). Balados sur les stratégies d'écoute et de prise de notes pour les étudiants d'immersion en français au niveau universitaire: de la conception à l'évaluation des impacts. *OLBI Working Papers, 5*, 71–83.

MacFarlane, A. (2001). Are brief contact experiences and classroom language learning complementary? *Canadian Modern Language Review, 58*, 63–83.

Mady, C., & Arnott, S. (2010). Exploring the "situation" of situational willingness to communicate: A volunteer youth exchange perspective. *Canadian Journal of Applied Linguistics, 13*(2), 1–26.

Meunier, D. (2013). Mobilité et apprentissage linguistique: des représentations contrastées. In E. Yasri-Labrique, P. Gardies, & K. Djordjevic Léonard (Eds.), *Didactique contrastive: questionnements et applications* (pp. 131–140). Montpellier: Cladole.

Mougeon, R., Rehner, K., & Nadasdi, T. (2004). The learning of spoken French variation by immersion students from Toronto, Canada. *Journal of Sociolinguistics, 8*, 408–432.

Perrier, S. (2008). HIS 1520—Histoire de l'Europe (XVIe au XXe siècle). aix1.uottawa.ca/~sperrier/europe

Peters, M., Murphy-Judy, K., Laferrière, T., & Weinberg, A. (2009). Développer les compétences à l'aide des TIC. In M. Peters (Ed.), *Les TIC au primaire: pour enseigner et apprendre* (pp. 147–165). Québec: Éditions CEC.

Regan, V., Howard, M., & Lemée, I. (2009). *The acquisition of sociolinguistic competence in a study abroad context*. Bristol: Multilingual Matters.

Séror, J., & Weinberg, A. (2013). Personal insights on a postsecondary immersion experience: Learning to step out of the comfort zone. *OLBI Working Papers*, *6*, 123–140.

Thomas, A. (2002). La variation phonétique en français langue seconde au niveau universitaire avancé. *AILE*, *17*, 101–121.

Université Lumière Lyon 2. (n.d.). Centre international d'études françaises (CIEF). cief.univ-lyon2.fr/

University of Ottawa. (n.d.). Centre for global and community engagement (CGCE). web5.uottawa.ca/els/index.php

University of Ottawa. (n.d.). French Immersion Stream: Resources — Podcasts. immersion.uottawa.ca/en/resources

University of Ottawa. (n.d.). International office. international.uottawa.ca/en

University of Ottawa. (n.d.). Le portail francophile. www.pf.uottawa.ca/portail.php

University of Ottawa. (n.d.). SASS — Service mentoring centres: French immersion studies. immersion.uottawa.ca/en/french-immersion-benefits#centre

University of Ottawa. (n.d.). TLSS — Teaching and Learning Support Service: Virtual campus. tlss.uottawa.ca/site/vc-home-page

Vygotsky, L.S. (1978). *Mind in society: The development of higher psychological processes*. Cambridge, MA: Harvard University Press.

Weinberg, A. (2008). Histoire de coccinelle: Les grandes découvertes. aix1.uottawa.ca/~weinberg/europe/fls2581/coccinelle/01_decouvertes.html

Weinberg, A. (2013). Parrainage francophiles–francophones à l'Université d'Ottawa dans le cadre du Régime d'immersion: pratique et perceptions. In E. Yasri-Labrique, P. Gardies, & K. Djordjevic (Eds.), *Didactique contrastive: questionnements et applications* (pp. 105–117). Montpellier: Cladole.

Weinberg, A., Knoerr, H., & Vandergrift, L. (2011). Creating podcasts for academic listening in French: Students' perceptions of enjoyment and usefulness. *CALICO Journal*, *28*, 588–605.

Weinberg, A., & Perrier, S. (2008). Histoire de l'Europe (XVIe au XXe siècle) [Homepage]. aix1.uottawa.ca/~weinberg/europe

Wenden, A. (1998). Metacognitive knowledge and language learning. *Applied Linguistics*, *19*, 515–537.

White Nights [*Nuits blanches*]. (n.d.). Wikipedia entry. en.wikipedia.org/wiki/White_Night_festivals#Montreal

CHAPTER 8

Content Learning and Language Support

Hélène Knoerr

INTRODUCTION

THE FIRST PART of this book explained the circumstances that paved the way for the arrival of immersion at the University of Ottawa, from the government's policies on official languages to the implementation of the *Régime d'immersion en français* (RIF) in 2005. The second part of the book has introduced the administrative structure of the RIF, as well as its places and modes of delivery. This chapter will look at the RIF from a pedagogical perspective. We will examine the possible articulations of content and language in an immersion context, with special attention to course levels, structure, objectives, and content. We will then consider the pedagogical implications of each option. Finally, we will assess these models and suggest recommendations to address the challenges they each face.

1. MODELS

Chapter 4 presented the theoretical models for immersion. This chapter will focus on their practical implementation at uOttawa in its programs and courses.

1.1. The Sheltered Model

When a team of researchers at uOttawa pioneered post-secondary immersion in a pilot experiment in the 1980s, they opted for the sheltered model. In this model, one section of a course with multiple sections is reserved for Allophone students and generally (but not necessarily) taught by a content instructor interested in or sensitive to language issues.[1] The sheltered model,[2] developed by Krashen (1982), was adapted to include an expert language instructor who attended content classes, did all the required readings, and spent some time at the beginning of each content class to prepare students to deal with the subject matter to be covered, in this case psychology (Burger, Chrétien, Gingras, Hauptman, & Migneron, 1984, p. 398).

1.2. The Adjunct Model

In this model, both Francophone and Francophile (= immersion) students attend the same sections of a content course, but an adjunct language support course for Anglophones only addresses potential difficulties due to language issues, such as vocabulary, cultural references in the lecture, or sentence structures in a reading.

---

[1] For a detailed description of this experiment, see Chapter 4. See also Burger et al., (1984).
[2] Although the label used at the time, "sheltered courses," reflects the fact that students were receiving language support, it is not the correct terminology.

In its RIF incarnation, the model combines a weekly content course (three hours) taught in French and a weekly language support course (one and a half hours). The language course instructor attends the content course and uses its lectures, textbooks, and readings to develop language activities that will "help you develop French skills directly relevant to your discipline" (University of Ottawa, n.d., "French Immersion Stream: Courses ..."). Both the content course and the language course are credited,[3] but separately, independently. In its initial edition in 1985, the immersion option was available for four introductory content courses: one in history (*Histoire générale du Canada depuis les découvertes*), one in sociology (*Sociologie de la famille*), one in linguistics (*Introduction au langage*), and one in political science (*Introduction aux sciences politiques*).[4] In 2018, it was available for first- and second-year content courses in the Faculties of Arts (16 programs), Social Sciences (16 programs), Science (17), Management (8 programs), and Health Sciences (4 programs), as well as in 13 bi-disciplinary programs (such as Communication and Political Science or Women's Studies and Sociology).

1.3. A Hybrid Model: The Régime de français enrichi (RFE)

In this model, implemented in the Faculty of Science and, more recently, in that of Engineering, Allophone students take biochemistry, chemistry, mathematics, or statistics courses in French along with French-speaking students, as is the case for the regular RIF model. However, because these content courses do not rely on natural (verbal) language to convey meaning, content, not language, is what makes them challenging: "[g]iven the similarity of the scientific terminology in English and French and the fact that many scientific problems can be resolved entirely by manipulating mathematical formulae or drawing and interpreting structures" (University of Ottawa, n.d., "Faculty of Science: Extended French Stream") support is offered not for French but for science, in the form of tutorial sessions facilitated by student mentors. This support distinguishes the RFE model from the "swim or sink," or submersion model (Chapter 4 provides a full review and description of the spectrum of immersion models). The RFE, created in 2011, is available in all honours degrees of the Faculty of Science (with the exception of the Ophthalmic Medical Technology program) and in six programs in the Faculty of Engineering.[5]

2. OBJECTIVES

The sheltered model implemented in Krashen's 1982 experiment had two objectives (Burger et al., 1984, p. 397):

- from a practical perspective, to allow the University of Ottawa's Anglophone students to transition from French as a Second Language courses to content courses given in French

---

[3] Although language courses are only offered for 90 minutes a week, or half a regular course, they count toward three credits.

[4] See Ready and Wesche (1992) for a complete review of these immersion courses.

[5] For an exhaustive list of these programs, see University of Ottawa, n.d., "French Immersion Stream: Programs."

- from a theoretical perspective, to test Krashen's hypotheses (1982) that sheltered courses offer students an effective and attractive way to improve their second language skills while learning a subject

The second language is the ultimate goal of the learning environment, content being the means to that end. This focus on language differentiates immersion from CLIL or EMI models where content is the focus and language is the medium (see Chapter 4 for a full review and description of immersion models): "CLIL is an approach in which a foreign language is used as a tool in the learning of a non-language subject in which both language and the subject have a joint role" (Marsh, 2002, p. 58). Furthermore, only students at an intermediate level (i.e., a score of 50–70% on the university's proficiency test),[6] or A2+ to B1−) were allowed to enrol in the sheltered courses since, as Krashen explained, "the beginning language student will not be able to participate since his language level will not be high enough to enable him to follow instruction" (1984, p. 63); CLIL/EMI programs do not generally have language requirements.

The models currently used in the RFE and the RIF have different objectives:

- In the RFE, the focus is on content, although there is a minimum language requirement: since there are no language support classes, support is offered for the content taught: "Extra support for your science courses in French to ensure your comprehension" (University of Ottawa, n.d., "Faculty of Science: Extended French Stream"). The same RIF webpage describes the option as "a unique opportunity for university students with a French immersion or extended French high school background to study Science in both French and English."
- In the RIF, the focus is on language: a language support course is available for each content course and custom-tailored to "develop French skills directly relevant to your discipline" (University of Ottawa, n.d., "French Immersion Stream: Courses..."). Boosting employability is a goal in both options (particularly in the government sector and international jobs) but the RIF wants first and foremost to develop a "Francophile" identity among its students, allowing them to experience the Francophones' social and cultural universe by sharing their language.

The RIF's page gives the following description:

> The uOttawa French Immersion Stream offers a unique experience. It gives students the opportunity to pursue part of their university studies in French while receiving individualized support in order to develop competencies in their field and in their second language (French). The program produces graduates who are functional in both official languages and are able to hold a bilingual position or pursue graduate studies in French. (University of Ottawa, n.d., "French Immersion Stream: About")

---

[6] This generic language test assesses listening and reading comprehension via multiple choice questions.

Both the RFE and the RIF models are different from content-based approaches in that students must demonstrate an intermediate level of proficiency (B1)[7] in order to be allowed to register (although the RFE is less language-oriented than the RIF).

2.1. Content Learning

2.1.1. The Sheltered Model

In the sheltered model, course material and student evaluation modes were identical in the sheltered and in the regular sections, but the content instructors knew that students in the sheltered section were non-native speakers. As a result, they altered the typical large lecture delivery mode, using more questions and imperative forms, repeating and reformulating, and checking comprehension more frequently. They would also change their usual sentence structures (shorter and less complex sentences) and use rephrasing and redundancy strategies to make themselves understood. They would use visuals and would write on the blackboard.[8] Finally, the content instructors had volunteered to teach the courses in the experiment. They were well aware that Anglophone students were in their classes, they knew them, and they worked in close collaboration with the language instructors to make sure that these students gained a good understanding of the course content. Some of these instructors actually authored publications on sheltered courses (Burger et al., 1984; Edwards, Wesche, Krashen, Clément, & Kruidenier, 1984).

2.1.2. The Adjunct Model

In the adjunct model, immersion students and Francophone students are in the same content course sections. They use the same course material, do the same assignments, write the same exams, and are evaluated with the same criteria. The language support course helps immersion students with language-related aspects of the content course. Content instructors do not change the way they teach or the way they speak, since it is a French-language course in a French-language program and most of the students registered in the course are Francophones. They do not know who the immersion students are and have no rapport with them. They do not volunteer to teach an immersion course, they are assigned one, and they are notified by email. If they are sympathetic to the immersion project, they seek out those students and look after them: they have them sit in the front in the lecture hall and check their comprehension, they put them together for discussion groups, they do not penalize language errors in assignments (as long as these errors do not obscure meaning), and they write complex vocabulary on the board and ask students if they understand. But they can also choose to treat all students in the same manner out of fairness, indifference, or worse, hostility (for more on these issues, see Chapters 14 and 16).

---

[7] "At level B1, the user becomes independent. He/she can maintain interaction: he/she can understand and maintain a discussion and give his/her opinion. He/she is capable of dealing with situations likely to arise in daily life" (DELF, n.d.).

[8] For more on classroom discourse with native and non-native speakers, see, for example, Long and Sato (1983).

2.1.3. The Enriched Model (RFE, *Régime de français enrichi*)

In this hybrid model, class sizes are much smaller than English-language classes, which facilitates comprehension and fosters a sense of linguistic confidence, even if immersion students and Francophone students are in the same content course section and in the same classroom. However, the small class sizes are not a result of careful planning but of demographics: first-year French-language courses attract two to three times fewer students than the same first-year courses in English — the ratio is 1 to 4 in third year. Content course instructors do not alter their pedagogy or their language. Support is provided in the form of optional tutorial sessions facilitated by bilingual mentors who usually conduct a review in English of the content taught in French.

2.2. Language Learning[9]

In a regular FSL course, instructors teach the grammar, vocabulary, communication, and culture of the target language. In an immersion context, the role of instructors is drastically redefined since, as Krashen (1982) posited, students acquire the target language through the medium of content, simply by practising the language without referring to grammatical notions (Burger et al., 1984, p. 398).

2.2.1. The Sheltered Model

In the initial experiment, language support was explicit, delivered at the beginning of each content class, first for about twenty minutes, and gradually for less, as students' linguistic competence increased. Only students at the intermediate level (A2+ or B1−) were allowed to register. Focus was on input comprehension, both in listening and reading. Because of the small scale of the experiment (one content course and thirty students in the first year, five courses in the final year), no particular infrastructure was required.

2.2.2. The Adjunct Model

With the adjunct model, language support is also explicit, but it is delivered separate from the content course, in its own weekly language course (90 minutes) available only to Anglophone students with a score of B1 or higher on the Immersion Admission Test.[10] These credit courses were designed specifically for the RIF, and their content is based exclusively on the content course they facilitate.

Accommodating hundreds of students taking content courses in over 80 programs requires a well-developed infrastructure. Language support is structured into three skill-based levels:

- FLS 2581: receptive skills
- FLS 3581: productive skills
- FLS 4581: advanced speaking or FLS 4781: advanced writing

---

[9] The RFE will not be discussed here, since it does not focus on language and does not offer language support (but RFE students must score B1 or higher on the Immersion Admission Test).

[10] The required level is higher than for sheltered courses because, in the adjunct system, content course instructors do not alter their teaching style or their language to accommodate a non-Francophone audience. Students need a higher proficiency in order to succeed in this context.

From a methodological point of view, this hierarchy reflects Krashen's theory that the input (i) a student receives should be one step above or more challenging than the student's current ability; the theory is expressed as $i + 1$(1982): comprehension precedes expression. From a language learning point of view, a first-year student's tasks consist in attending lectures (listening comprehension) and reading academic/scientific texts (reading comprehension). Introductory content courses typically have a very high enrolment (several hundreds of students), so content assessment is usually done in the form of multiple-choice questions (reading comprehension) or short answers. Later in their program, students are expected to do oral presentations, participate in discussion groups (speaking), write reading summaries, lab reports, and dissertations; assessment is done in the form of essay questions and term papers (writing).

The course structure also reflects the students' proficiency levels: "Based on your linguistic profile, you will receive course recommendations that will help you to continue develop your French skills" (University of Ottawa, n.d., "French Immersion Stream: Future students"). But there is no prescribed sequence of courses: students decide for themselves whether or not to register in a receptive or productive skills adjunct course. They are not required to do so based on their score on the Immersion Admission Tests: "[Y]ou select courses in French and build an immersion study plan" (University of Ottawa, n.d., "French Immersion Stream: Future students").

Most content courses only have an FLS 2581 adjunct language course, some have both FLS 2581 and FLS 3581 adjunct courses. FLS 4581 and FLS 4781 are different in their organization and objectives:

- they are not associated with a particular content course
- they are geared toward third- and fourth-year students working on their dissertation or on a research project
- they are very limited in number and enrolment is typically low
- in theory, they are associated with two content courses, but in reality they are not[11]
- they do not deal with course-specific content but with general academic formats: how to write an abstract or an essay, how to prepare for a debate or deliver an oral presentation
- focus is on form and accuracy, like a regular language course

3. OBJECTIVES OF LANGUAGE SUPPORT COURSES

3.1. General Objectives

In the 1980s experiment, language support classes had a fairly broad objective: improve students' second language proficiency and self-confidence, stimulate their interest, encourage their efforts and hopefully change their emotional attitude toward the language (Burger et al., 1984, p. 398). In today's RIF, each level of the language support system

---

[11] In fact, they are only linked to one content course, which will vary with the students. Furthermore, students enrolling in these courses are typically not Immersion students but students from the major in FSL.

is organized into general and specific objectives (University of Ottawa, n.d., "French Immersion Stream: Courses"):

- 2000-level: receptive skills (FLS 2581): "The goal of this course is to improve the students' French comprehension abilities (listening and reading) and ensure that the student will understand the material presented in the regular content course taught in French."
- 3000-level: productive skills (FLS 3581): "The goal of this course is to develop the students' writing and speaking skills, and give them the ability to express the concepts and ideas presented in the regular content course taught in French."
- 4000-level: advanced speaking/writing (FLS 4581/FLS 4781): "There are no corresponding content courses here: students must bring material from one of the level 3000 or 4000 content courses that they're taking in French (from the same semester as the one they are following [in] the FLS 4581 or FLS 4781 course)." The goal is "to help students make presentations and take part in debates or panel discussions in relation to their content course" and to "write research reports and scientific papers in relation to their content course."

Clearly, immersion courses are language-oriented more than content-oriented: these classes go beyond content review — they focus on improving the language skills needed to study in the discipline. Of course, language and content are closely linked, and distinguishing them can be a challenge (especially when it comes to testing), since content is taught and learned through language, and language is taught and learned in the context of content.

3.2. Specific Objectives

Specific objectives were developed by OLBI experts in order to meet the general objectives set forth by the RIF for each level of courses (Appendix 1).

These objectives were revised in 2014 by the RIF to reflect theories on action-based, strategic language learning (Appendix 2).

4. LANGUAGE CLASSROOM ACTIVITIES

As discussed earlier, in the sheltered model, language instructors would have about twenty minutes at the beginning of each content class, so there were no formalized or officially described language activities. Each class was:

> an exchange on content covered in class, with explanations of vocabulary or other language-related issues, ... occasionally there were exercises, games, discussions prompted by the content language or about content presented in class.... Reviewing vocabulary, technical terms, linking words and presenting useful strategies for asking questions gave students the tools they needed to monitor input, ask questions, clarify information with the content instructor. (Burger et al., 1984, p. 401)

In the adjunct model, however, classroom activities and assignments are prescribed by the course type (FLS 2581: receptive skills; FLS 3581: productive skills) and presented in detail in official documents.[12]

4.1. Language Activities for FLS 2581 Courses

As described on the RIF's website, "[t]he students will work on exercises to help them acquire vocabulary and strengthen grammar, recognize the structure of oral and written texts, extract the main ideas and better understand the arguments" (University of Ottawa, n.d., "French Immersion Stream: Courses").

Language learning activities focus mainly on assigned readings for the content course — students typically have to read up to fifty pages before each class. Activities include creating or completing reading notes, answering multiple-choice or short answer comprehension questions, identifying the best reformulation for a paragraph, the best interpretation for a table or a graph. Text and paragraph structure are presented and applied by asking students to identify main ideas, reformulations, and examples in selected paragraphs taken from required readings. Specialized vocabulary is learned using morphological activities (identifying roots and affixes and learning their meanings), semantic maps, matching exercises (to learn concepts and their definitions). General vocabulary is learned in the context of lectures and readings, with a particular focus on linking words (classifying them according to meaning) and pronouns and their referents. Listening skills are refined using video documents taken from the content course or from the Internet (on topics discussed in the content class), and used not only for listening comprehension but also to analyze the characteristics of spoken French in different registers. Listening strategies are also presented, taught, and applied in the classroom.

4.2. Language Activities for FLS 3581 Courses

As described on the RIF's website, "[t]he students will practise the different steps in writing an effective text, using specialized vocabulary, producing complex sentences and speaking easily and effectively about the subject matter of the course" (University of Ottawa, n.d., "French Immersion Stream: Courses").

Classroom activities focus on writing reading summaries, presenting concepts from the content class while paying attention to pronunciation, fluency, and engaging an audience. Activities for specialized vocabulary are similar to those used for FLS 2581; general vocabulary such as linking words is practised through writing activities. Commenting on graphs, figures, maps, or tables provides opportunities to review grammar elements such as numbers, percentages, dates, names (and grammatical gender) of countries and corresponding prepositions (crucial in history, geography, or political science, for example). The writing process is studied and each step is practised (researching, planning, drafting, editing) in the context of major academic writing formats (reading notes, summaries, critical reviews, dissertations). Collaborative/collective writing

---

[12] There are no similar official descriptors or detailed syllabi for FLS 4581 and FLS 4781, because they are not assigned to a particular content course.

activities are encouraged (for example, a wiki for lecture notes; see Chapter 7). Finally, students learn to use editing tools such as Antidote.

Strategies such as academic literacy and note-taking are also taught, to help students become competent linguistically and academically. Several reference tools have been developed by OLBI experts to that effect (see Chapter 7). Students are also encouraged to write a reflective learning journal to foster awareness of their language learning processes and strategies.

5. COURSE MATERIAL

Language support classes are based on the specific content course they accompany. As a result, course material cannot be a standard FSL textbook or grammar book. All course material comes from the content course: lectures, textbook (when applicable), assigned readings (coursepacks), Powerpoint presentations, audio or video documents used during lectures. Language instructors develop their own comprehension- or expression-based activities from these sources, which can be supplemented by other resources of their choice in the same field.

5.1. Course Material for Receptive Skills Courses (FLS 2581)

5.1.1. Listening Comprehension

In the political science content course, the concept of the State (*l'État*) was studied and its characteristics listed (see Figure 1). The language support class instructor found a video document online featuring an international aid worker talking about "rogue states" — that is, states which were no longer fulfilling their responsibilities. This document (no longer available online) reflected the course content in an indirect way (in the negative) and allowed students to review the vocabulary necessary to discuss the concept. Note that no previous knowledge was necessary in order to answer the comprehension questions — all the answers were in the video clip.

Qu'est ce qu'un État fragile?
1. Combien de types de missions un État est-il censé remplir?
2. Qu'est-ce que les missions régaliennes?
3. Quels services l'État fournit-il aux populations?
4. Quels services l'État fournit-il aux opérateurs économiques?
5. Comment définit-on un État fragile?
6. Quel pourcentage des pays dans lesquels l'Agence française de développement intervient concerne des États fragiles?
7. Quelles circonstances mettent un pays en situation de fragilité?
8. Les pays qui sont sortis d'un statut d'États fragiles sont-ils nombreux?
9. Où se trouvent ces pays?
10. Quels sont ces pays?

Figure 1: Listening comprehension-based activity for language support course FLS 2581 P1, associated with content course POL 1502 *Politique et mondialisation* (Knoerr, 2014)

5.1.2. Reading Comprehension

Language activities such as the ones shown in Figures 2 and 3 illustrate several ways to verify comprehension without requiring production.

5.1.3. Grammar in Context

Figure 4 demonstrates how to teach grammar in the context of the content course: French academic texts have their own particular style, including long, complex sentences with multiple verbs and pronouns. Students need to correctly identify verbs and subjects, pronouns and antecedents, in order to understand the texts. In this case, reading comprehension depends on grammatical knowledge. Key grammatical elements are pointed out but not explained, in order to verify comprehension.

5.1.4. Vocabulary Acquisition

The task in Figure 5 combines language and content: In a reading from the content course, students need to identify words related to the concept of the State, using definitions provided. After they transfer these words in the grid, they must then unscramble the letters in the circles in order to uncover a key definition (*monopole de la violence légitime*) which the content course instructor had emphasized a number of times. This task measures comprehension and vocabulary knowledge in the context of the content course.

Figure 6 shows a variety of vocabulary learning strategies through the use of different organizers, in the context of a personal dictionary task (a required component for the language support course).

5.1.5. Language Learning Strategies

Language support instructors increasingly teach listening, reading, and overall comprehension strategies, especially at the 2000 level. A resource (adapted from Knoerr & Weinberg, 2014, pp. 116–117) provided to students by one instructor as part of the course material suggests the following:

- *reading strategies*: do your content course readings before each class; look up unknown words
- *listening strategies*: prepare an advance mapping of each lecture based on the syllabus and the assigned readings; sit in front; focus on key elements, not details; ask questions; record the lectures
- *note-taking*: use a note-taking program or template (such as the Cornell system or mind-mapping); use abbreviations; review your notes; create a Wiki for note-sharing
- *study strategies*: read aloud your notes; work with a peer

A series of podcasts addressing these strategies is also provided on the RIF website (University of Ottawa, n.d., "French Immersion Stream: Resources").

Le texte compare les valeurs du libéralisme et du socialisme. Indiquez sur quelles valeurs les deux idéologies s'accordent ou se différencient en complétant le tableau.

	Libéralisme	Socialisme
Finalité de l'État		
Vision de l'Homme et du monde		
Place de l'économie dans la société		
Valeur (positive/négative) de l'économie		
Rôle de l'activité de production dans la liberté		
Finalité de l'humanité		
Vision de l'Histoire		

Figure 2: Reading comprehension-based activity (multiple choice) for language support course FLS 2581 P1, associated with content course POL 1501 *Introduction à la science politique* (Knoerr, 2014)

Lisez le texte p. 51–62 dans le recueil POL 1501 et complétez les activités/répondez aux questions.

1. Paragraphe 1 : surlignez l'idée principale, <u>soulignez</u> les reformulations, mettez les exemples [entre crochets].
2. Paragraphe 2 : quelles sont les 3 définitions de la citoyenneté et quels sont leurs auteurs?
   (a)
   (b)
   (c)
3. Quelles sont les trois dimensions de la citoyenneté selon l'auteur de ce texte?
4. La première dimension a un contenu _____ et fait référence à la notion de _____.
5. La possibilité de "concourir personnellement ou par leurs représentants à la formation de la loi" est un exemple de droit _____.
6. Tous les citoyens sont des nationaux (= ils possèdent la nationalité française), mais tous les nationaux ne sont pas citoyens. Donnez au moins deux exemples:
   _____, _____.
7. La deuxième dimension est surtout reliée au _____.
8. Deux facteurs causent des menaces pour les travailleurs sans qualifications professionnelles dans les pays développés : _____ et _____.
9. Cette menace se manifeste sous deux formes possibles:
   _____ ou _____.
10. Quel droit fondamental est enchâssé dans la Constitution française?
    _____

Figure 3: Reading comprehension-based activity (short answers copied from the text) for language support course FLS 2581 P1, associated with content course POL 1501 *Introduction à la science politique* (Knoerr, 2014)

Le chapitre dans lequel nous entrons de ce pas abordera successivement deux piliers déterminants légitimant l'ordre étatique moderne qui, quoique distincts, s'avèrent intimement liés : d'une part, la constitution, laquelle réside au cœur même de la définition et de la délimitation des divers organes d'autorité au sein de l'État; d'autre part, le système judiciaire, qui se pose en réalité, principalement par le truchement de ses institutions de dernier recours, à titre d'interprète et de gardien des dispositions constitutionnelles. La dynamique qui s'installe entre les deux prend une importance toute spéciale dans le cadre des régimes démocratiques libéraux en donnant consistance à la notion cruciale de constitutionnalisme, à savoir que les détenteurs de l'autorité, tout comme les citoyens, ne se situent pas au-dessus des normes légales en vigueur et ont l'obligation de s'y soumettre, a *fortiori* s'agissant de la loi constitutionnelle. Les gouvernants voient de la sorte leur marge de manœuvre balisée et limitée, ce qui protège du même coup les gouvernés contre les abus de pouvoir.

1. Combien de phrases y a-t-il dans ces 14 lignes?
2. Combien de verbes y a-t-il dans chaque phrase?
3. Repérez les pronoms relatifs et indiquez:
   (a) quel(s) mot(s) ils remplacent
   (b) quelle est leur fonction (sujet? objet? complément?) dans la phrase ou par rapport au verbe.

Figure 4: Grammar in context activity for language support course FLS 2581 P1, associated with content course POL 1501 *Introduction à la science politique* (Knoerr, 2014)

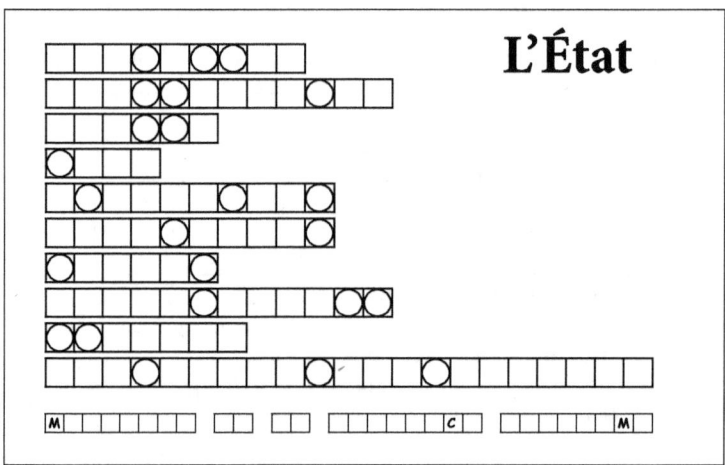

Figure 5: Specialized vocabulary acquisition activity for language support course FSL 2581 P1, associated with content course POL 1501 *Introduction à la science politique* (Knoerr, 2014)

Forme textuelle:
  Le **signe linguistique** (n.m.) a deux faces: le signifiant et le signifié
  Le **signifiant** (n.m.) est la forme sonore, les sons
  Le **signifié** (n.m.) est le concept associé à la suite de sons
  Le signe est **arbitraire**: il n'y a pas de lien a priori entre signifiant et signifié (convention)
  Le signe est **conventionnel**: les membres de la communauté sont d'accord sur le lien qui unit signifiant (Sa) et signifié (Sé)
  Le signe est **linéaire**: il se déroule dans le temps selon un ordre chronologique

Formes graphiques:

Définition	Caractéristiques
entité linguistique à deux faces : le signifiant (forme sonore) et le signifié (concept associé à la suite de sons)	arbitraire linéaire conventionnel
signe linguistique	
Exemple(s) CARRÉ □ [kaRe]	Contre-exemple(s) un mot une image

Référent (l'objet réel dans le monde)
Signe (sémantique)
Significant (sons) (phonétique, phonologie)
Signifié (concept)

Figure 6: Specialized vocabulary acquisition task for language support adjunct course FLS 2581 L1, associated with content course LIN 1701 *Introduction à la linguistique* (Knoerr, 2013)

5.2. Course Material for Productive Skills Courses (FLS 3581)

These courses allow students to focus on form in the context of the course materials from the content course. Figure 7 illustrates how to work on three different grammar elements, based on a table from the political science course:

- the grammatical gender (masculine or feminine) of country names and the different prepositions used in each case
- number forms used to express dates, percentages, and decimals
- the negative form

Games can also be used to integrate language and content. For example, one language support class instructor asked students to create a *Jeopardy!* game to be used both as a review of the key concepts from the political science content course and as a practice of specialized vocabulary, interrogative forms, and overall speaking skills.

Tableau 3 : Pourcentage de femmes parlementaires dans 24 législatures de pays différents entre 1945 et 1998

Systèmes	1945	1950	1960	1970	1980	1990	1998
Majoritaire uninominal	3,05	2,13	2,51	2,23	3,37	8,16	11,64
R. P. ou plurinominal	2,93	4,73	5,47	5,86	11,89	18,13	23,03

Pays à système majoritaire uninominal :
Australie, Canada, États-Unis d'Amérique, France (depuis 1960), Japon, Nouvelle Zélande (1945/1990), Royaume Uni.

Pays à représentation proportionnelle ou à scrutin plurinominal :
Allemagne (RFA* avant 1990), Autriche, Belgique, Danemark, Espagne*, Finlande, France (1945 et 1950), Grèce*, Irlande, Islande, Israël*, Italie, Luxembourg, Norvège, Nouvelle Zélande (1998), Pays Bas, Portugal*, Suède, Suisse.

* Israël n'existait pas et la RFA n'a pas organisé d'élection en 1945. Ces pays n'entrent donc dans les calculs que pour les années suivantes.
La Grèce, le Portugal et l'Espagne n'adoptèrent un système démocratique que dans les années 70 et n'entrent dans les calculs qu'à partir de 1980.

© International IDEA

Figure 7: Specialized vocabulary acquisition activity for language support course FSL 2581 P1, associated with content course POL 1501 *Introduction à la science politique* (reproduced by permission of International IDEA from *Les femmes au parlement: Au-delà du nombre* © International Institute for Democracy and Electoral Assistance, 2002, p. 72.)

6. IMPLICATIONS OF THE METHODOLOGICAL APPROACH

Selecting the adjunct model comes with a number of implications, which fall under two main categories, as outlined below.

6.1. Time

- Developing custom pedagogical activities is much more time-consuming than simply using ready-made activities from an FSL textbook or course.
- Each language support course is unique and, as a result, potentially short-lived. Should the content course no longer be included in the immersion offer, the pedagogical activities developed by the language instructor cannot be reused or transferred to another language course. Also, if the content course is assigned to a different content instructor, chances are that the assigned readings will also be different, which means that the language instructor will have to start from scratch again.
- The language instructor is completely dependent on the content instructor for the timely delivery of content course materials. A regular content instructor who has been teaching the same content course for some time will easily share their slides, course notes, and assigned readings with the language instructor well in advance.

But a part-time instructor hired at the very last minute, a few days before the first class, will certainly not be able to do so.
- The language instructor meets students only once a week while the content instructor meets them twice a week. As a result, the language instructor cannot cover all the material and needs to make a selection in the content to focus on during class. This frequently leads language instructors to assign some vocabulary building, reading comprehension, collaborative course notes sharing, or writing tasks as homework in order to save class time for interactions with the students.[13] Needless to say, these homework assignments will require some significant marking time from the instructor.

6.2. The Uniqueness of the Immersion Approach
- All the language activities developed by instructors must comply with the nature of the language support courses: comprehension-based tasks make up most of classroom activities at the 2581 level while 3581 courses mainly consist of production-based activities.
- Language instructors must be able to predict the language-related difficulties of the content course materials and develop activities in order to address them: In order to understand a sentence, students need not only to be familiar with the appropriate vocabulary but also to correctly identify the grammatical subject of a conjugated verb or the antecedent of a pronoun.
- Language support classes are there to facilitate the comprehension of the content courses they accompany, but they are not a tutorial or a discussion/study group for these courses. This is a subtle difference which some students fail to understand or accept: they complain that they have more work to do for the language course. Language instructors need to find meaningful, fun and engaging ways to integrate the language component to the content materials (addressed in Chapter 8).
- Assessment activities must assess language, not content. This is a very fine line, since content is transmitted through language and language is used in the context of content. Language instructors need to make sure that their assignments, tests, and exams measure their students' abilities to understand a document, reuse specialized vocabulary, or apply language conventions and genre-specific formats, as opposed to their students' knowledge of concepts or formulas.[14]

CONCLUSION: ASSETS, CHALLENGES, AND LIMITATIONS

Regardless of the model, several pedagogical challenges need to be acknowledged and addressed in order for immersion to be successful:

---

[13] This is the main reason why these weekly 90-minute courses count for three full credits: the amount of extra work to be completed outside of class is two to three times higher than for a regular language course.

[14] See Chapter 10 for a complete overview of assessment.

- *Teaching styles and pedagogical choices*: Content instructors who make their Powerpoint slides available to students before class make learning easier than those who do not provide any teaching aids and do not use any visuals during their lectures. Similarly, language instructors who are not flexible and who do not adapt their teaching to the immersion philosophy — teaching grammar and vocabulary as in a regular FSL class — do not equip their students with the tools they need to be successful in their content courses and to develop the language skills they need in their field of study.

- *A poor relationship between language and content instructors*: This can arise where one or the other (or both) exhibit a lack of belief in the immersion philosophy, of personal affinities, or of methodological understanding. Such a situation is regrettable in the adjunct model, in which language instructors and content instructors teach in parallel; but it is extremely detrimental to the sheltered model, in which both instructors are in a co-teaching context.

- *Dismissing the linguistic component*: Reducing the language support class to a tutoring session for the content course is a major risk, especially in the sheltered model, where students do not experience an authentic course for Francophone students but receive a simplified and potentially watered-down version. Would these students be able to successfully take a regular content course taught in French for a Francophone student population, with no special accommodations made for them and in which they would be in a minority context? Also, would they really improve their language skills? But the adjunct model is also at risk if the language support class becomes a tutoring session: Students often expect it to be exactly that and assume that the instructor will review the content course, not teach vocabulary or reading comprehension skills — indeed, some students complain when they are asked to do homework! Students should be made aware of the real nature and purpose of language support courses before and upon registering for one of them.

- *Assessment*: In a sheltered model, content instructors assess their students' knowledge of the discipline, but do they assess language? Studies have shown that students score better on the language proficiency test, which measures comprehension (Edwards et al., 1984), but there is no available measure of their productive skills. In an adjunct model, it is the responsibility of the language instructor to assess language skills, while making sure that what is being measured is language and not content. In other words, answers to all the questions asked in an FLS 2581 course examination must be present in an oral or written document — students must demonstrate their ability to understand what they are reading or hearing. Similarly, in FLS 3581 courses, tests should assess pronunciation, vocabulary, sentence structure, and paragraph organization, and not the memorization of definitions or formulas from the content course. Such an exercise can be tricky. Assessment in the content course can also be a challenge: if tests and assignments take the form of multiple-choice questions, they will be well suited to FLS 2581 courses; if they require summaries, essays, or reports, they will require productive skills and higher-order cognitive processes suitable for FLS 3581 students but not for their FLS 2581 peers.

These pedagogical challenges can be addressed, particularly by offering training workshops to language instructors and by fostering a positive relationship between language and content instructors.

Other challenges related to administration and/or policy can hinder the successful implementation of French immersion at the university level:

- The RIF does not require students to take FLS 3581 courses.[15] As a result, there is no available measure of immersion students' productive skills. Another side effect is low enrolment, leading to course cancellations. But most regrettably, this means that students can complete their program of study with the "Immersion" designation without any evidence of their ability to write or speak in French. An official uOttawa policy allowing students to write their assignments and exams in the official language of their choice in all their courses except language courses (University of Ottawa, 1974, part 6, art. 4.3) only compounds the problem. In order for the RIF to be consistent with its vision — to produce "graduates who are functional in both official languages and are able to hold a bilingual position or pursue graduate studies in French" (University of Ottawa, n.d., "French Immersion Stream: About") — immersion students should be required to take FLS 3581 courses and to write their assignments and exams in French, like their Francophone peers registered in the same programs.

- Some administrators have questioned the distribution of courses into receptive and productive skills. This continuum, based on theories backed and validated by decades of experimentation, is at the core of the RIF *dispositif*:

    (i) comprehension precedes expression
    (ii) comprehensible input is the necessary condition for second language acquisition.

    It should not be revisited without strong theoretical and methodological justifications.

Since uOttawa pioneered its sheltered course in 1982, French immersion has been implemented under different forms in order to meet the needs and constraints of each program. These constraints can be financial but also administrative (some programs, such as Engineering, do not allow optional or elective courses until the third year). But since they are external to the *dispositif* itself, they do not compromise its integrity — it still remains the reference in the field of French immersion in higher education.

---

[15] In its current form, the RIF does not require students to take any language support classes at all. This is currently (2019) under review.

REFERENCES

Burger, S., Chrétien, M., Gingras, M., Hauptman, P., & Migneron, M. (1984). Le rôle du professeur de langue dans un cours de matière académique en langue seconde. *Canadian Modern Language Review*, *41*, 397–402.

Diplôme d'Études en Langue Française (DELF). (n.d.). DELF B1. www.delfdalf.fr/delf-b1.html

Edwards, H., Wesche, M., Krashen, S., Clément, R., & Kruidenier, B. (1984). Second language acquisition through subject-matter learning: A study of sheltered psychology classes at the University of Ottawa. *Canadian Modern Language Review*, *41*, 268–282.

International IDEA. (2002). *Les Femmes au parlement: au-delà du nombre* (M.-J. Protais, Trans). Stockholm, Sweden: International IDEA (International Institute for Democracy and International Assistance). [Original work published 1998: *Women in parliament: Beyond numbers*]. www.elections-lebanon.org/docs_6_G_6_6a_12.pdf

Knoerr, H. (2013). Course material for FLS 2581 L1 [Language support course for LIN 1701 *Introduction à la linguistique*]. University of Ottawa.

Knoerr, H. (2014). Course material for FLS 2581 P1 [Language support course for POL 1501 *Introduction à la science politique*]. University of Ottawa.

Knoerr, H., & Weinberg, A. (2014). Stratégies d'écoute: les étudiants d'immersion en français au niveau universitaire ont la parole. *Dossiers des sciences de l'éducation*, *32*, 110–130.

Krashen, S.D. (1982). *Principles and practice in second language acquisition*. Englewood Cliffs, CA: Prentice Hall.

Krashen, S.D. (1984). Immersion: Why it works and what it has taught us. *Language and Society*, *12*, 61–64.

Long, M.H., & Sato, C.J. (1983). Classroom foreigner talk discourse: Forms and functions of teachers' questions. In H.W. Seliger & M.H. Long (Eds.), *Classroom-oriented research in second language acquisition* (pp. 268–285). Rowley, MA: Newbury House.

Marsh, D. (Ed.). (2002). CLIL/EMILE — The European dimension: Actions, trends and foresight potential. Strasbourg: European Commission. jyx.jyu.fi/handle/123456789/47616

Ready, D., & Wesche, M. (1992). An evaluation of the University of Ottawa sheltered program: Language teaching strategies that work. In R.J. Courchesne, J.I. Glidden, J. St. John, & C. Thérien (Eds.), *L'enseignement des langues secondes axé sur la compréhension* (pp. 389–405). Ottawa: University of Ottawa Press.

University of Ottawa. (n.d.). Faculty of Science: Extended French stream. science.uottawa.ca/en/programs-of-study/undergraduate-studies/extended-french-stream

University of Ottawa. (n.d.). French Immersion Stream. immersion.uottawa.ca/en

University of Ottawa. (n.d.). French Immersion Stream: About. immersion.uottawa.ca/en/about

University of Ottawa. (n.d.). French Immersion Stream: Courses: Immersion courses. immersion.uottawa.ca/en/courses#immersion

University of Ottawa. (n.d.). French Immersion Stream: Future students. immersion.uottawa.ca/en/future-students

University of Ottawa. (n.d.). French Immersion Stream: Programs. immersion.uottawa.ca/en/programs

University of Ottawa. (n.d.). French Immersion Stream: Resources. immersion.uottawa.ca/en/resources

University of Ottawa. (1974). Regulation on bilingualism at University of Ottawa 1974. www.uottawa.ca/administration-and-governance/policies-and-regulations/regulation-on-bilingualism

University of Ottawa. (2015). Cours d'immersion en français/French immersion courses. Automne 2015/Fall 2015, Hiver 2016/Winter 2016. olbi.uottawa.ca/sites/olbi.uottawa.ca/files/immersion_2016-2017_20160822.pdf

Appendix 1

Table 1: Specific objectives for language support classes (all levels)

	Oral language	Written language
FLS 2581	• Understand lectures in the content course • Identify the structure of an oral text • Identify the main and supporting ideas in an oral text • Identify vocabulary specific to the discipline • Recognize cohesion markers specific to oral discourse • Recognize and understand linking words • Understand a variety of accents in the content course	• Predict the topic of a text • Recognize the structure of a text and of a paragraph (main, reformulation, example) • Identify the main idea of a text • Recognize the point of a text (objective, thesis, intention) • Recognize and understand vocabulary (semantic fields, topic) • Identify vocabulary specific to the discipline • Recognize and understand linking words • Recognizing synonyms, antonyms, paraphrases/ reformulations • Understand graphs, figures, maps, tables • Identify pronouns and their antecedents
FLS 3581	• Talk fluently about discipline-related topics • Express the main and supporting ideas of an oral text • Speak after an oral presentation and participate in discussions • Use discipline-specific vocabulary • Comment on graphs, figures, maps, tables • Monitor one's own voice (tone, volume, pitch) to communicate expressively	• Apply the various steps of the writing process (planning, drafting, editing) • Draft an outline • Write a summary paragraph with the main and supporting ideas of a text • Use discipline-specific vocabulary • Use linking words to produce complex sentences • Use a variety of editing tools (including electronic ones) to produce accurate and error-free texts
FLS 4581 FLS 4781	• FLS 4581 Focus is placed on accuracy and correction of language as well as on analyzing selected models of academic- and discipline-related oral communication	• FLS 4781 Focus is placed on accuracy and correction of language as well as on analyzing selected models of academic- and discipline-related written communication

Appendix 2

Table 2a: FLS 2581 courses — revised in 2014

Communicative acts	Socio-cultural competences
• Understand the instructor during lectures • Understand written and oral texts from the content course • Understand interactions on content course-related topics • Demonstrate one's comprehension	• Examine academic culture (structure of a lecture, teaching and research tools, dissemination of knowledge, resources) • Identify the discipline's specific culture (accepted and valued sources, links between theory and practice) • Identify the instructor's theoretical positioning and teaching style
Learning strategies	
To gain comprehension: • Apply note-taking techniques • Identify text types • Predict the topic of a text • Recognize text structures • Identify the main ideas of a text • Identify supporting ideas of a text • Draw information from graphs, maps, and tables	To demonstrate one's comprehension: • Summarize the main points of a text • Paraphrase a statement or a definition • Compare and comment on data • Present the main ideas of a text, ask questions, discuss, and debate • Use editing and self-correcting strategies

Table 2b: FLS 3581 courses — revised in 2014

Communicative acts	Socio-cultural competences
• Make oral presentations based on the content course and topics • Speak after an oral presentation • Ask and answer questions • Participate in discussions • Express opinions • Comment on graphs, figures, maps, tables	• Examine academic culture (structure of a lecture, teaching and research tools, dissemination of knowledge, resources) • Identify the discipline's specific culture (accepted and valued sources, links between theory and practice) • Identify the instructor's theoretical positioning and teaching style
Learning strategies	
• Summarize and present the main and supporting ideas of written and oral texts (lectures, video recordings) • Paraphrase a statement or a definition • Compare and comment on data • Use discipline-specific vocabulary • Apply the various steps of the writing process (planning, drafting, editing) • Structure and organize a text (draft outlines for an essay, a reading summary, an oral presentation) • Use editing and self-correcting strategies	

CHAPTER 9

Collaborative Practices between Actors in Immersion:
Mentoring, *parrainage*, Tandem Work

Alysse Weinberg, Hélène Knoerr, and Aline Gohard-Radenkovic

INTRODUCTION

THE LEARNING OF A SECOND LANGUAGE generally springs from a desire to communicate or to acquire knowledge through that language. In immersion, the two goals are inseparable. With this in mind, the promoters of the *Régime d'immersion en français* (RIF) at the University of Ottawa sought to multiply the opportunities for exchanges among its many participants. Thus, different frameworks for collaboration were set up so that these exchanges would be as frequent and profitable as possible. This chapter focuses on the various types of collaboration planned and implemented to accompany, on the one hand, the students in their linguistic and academic acclimatization and, on the other hand, the language and content instructors who deal with the Allophone students.

First, different collaborative frameworks will be presented and linked to their respective methodological approaches. Next, examples of diverse forms of collaboration (for example, between students or instructors) will be described, with comments gathered from both students' reports of their collaboration with mentors and partners and from language-content instructors working together to put initiatives in place for RIF students. Finally, advantages and limitations of these collaborative frameworks will be summarized and recommendations for introducing collaborative practices into immersion programs will be made.

1. THEORETICAL FRAMEWORK: THE NOTION OF COLLABORATION

In this section the concept of collaboration and its various incarnations will be defined. The word "collaborate" comes from the Latin *collaborare*, which means "to work together." Yet, the concept of collaboration can be broken down into different facets, according to the intensity of the rapport between the people working together, the hierarchical relationship between the partners, as well as the places and times where these socialization phenomena are taking place. Regular teaching already presupposes a form of collaboration since it connects the instructor and the learners in constructing the learners' knowledge and skills.

Nevertheless, this chapter looks at other patterns of collaboration: those which operate between the RIF participants, in particular amongst the students and amongst the instructors. In this domain, there are numerous forms of collaboration, some of which are complementary. The terminology varies in this domain with activities such as exchanges, twinning, mentoring, *parrainage* (peer collaboration) (Gohard-Radenkovic, 2013; Weinberg, 2013), tutoring, or tandem work (Gohard-Radenkovic, 2004). Furthermore, thanks to new technology, collaborations can take many forms, such as cyber mentoring or social media exchanges.

1.1. Mentoring

The term "mentoring" can be traced to Homer's *The Odyssey*. When Odysseus, the king of Ithaca, left for the Trojan War, he asked his friend, Mentor, to serve as an advisor to his son, Telemachus. The traditional model of the apprentice who gains professional expertise or perfects his art at the feet of a master was followed in the industrial era by a model centred on career progression within hierarchies (Haney, 1997).

A mentoring collaboration puts two people of different levels together: an experienced person, the mentor, and a less experienced person, called a "neophyte" or a "mentee" (Haney, 1997, p. 211). The mentee benefits from the help of the mentor through the learning of skills and knowledge and improved chances of success in their work life. This term was the one adopted at uOttawa in order to avoid undervaluing the novice learner.

Mentoring fits into a constructivist vision of learning (Kerka, 1997), where experts can demonstrate problem-solving strategies and guide learners in their use. Thus, the mentor fulfils the role of guide, advisor, trainer, motivator, facilitator, and model in a situated context (Galbraith & Cohen, 1995; Haney, 1997; Kaye & Jacobson, 1996). In this relationship based on trust, the mentor gives his/her protegee the opportunity to test ideas, skills, and roles in complete security (Kaye & Jacobson, 1996). According to Houde (1995), for the mentee, the mentor embodies a figure of identification, transition, and foster parent.

1.2. Parrainage

Parrainage (peer collaboration) is a means of collaborative learning that is not directly supervised by an instructor: "It is done by peers and between peers" (Weinberg, 2013, p. 109). That is, students discover from one another the knowledge to be acquired and exchange knowledge they have identified as useful to their course. It is a relationship of mutual help and not of superiority, and it leads to a feeling of trust and friendship between the partners. Sometimes one of the partners is more knowledgeable than the other, but the development of the relationship is more important than the actual sharing of knowledge.

In academic contexts, the partnering relationship includes:

> a relationship of pupil to pupil, sometimes of the same age, sometimes of different ages. It is a supportive relationship of working together and not a relationship of authority. This relationship seeks the integration of the [weaker student] into the group, the class, or the school where the [more experienced] partner transmits the codes and rules of the school. It is a relationship which focuses on the success of the new student. (Floor, 2010, p. 5 [trans.])

1.3. Tandem

The concept of "tandem" is an approach that can be implemented in bilingual or plurilingual education contexts whose objectives, although mainly educational, may also be political.[1] It emerged in the 1970s in the milieu of language education. Tandem education became a *dispositif*, which has been extended to many types of education and academic situations.

The notion of tandem originates in the Franco-German Youth Office (FGYO),[2] which was set up in 1963. It used French–German meetings as a means of developing linguistic and cultural comprehension between young people from these two countries. Participants learn a second language through regular meetings, exchanges, internships, language courses, and intercultural training. They are supported by language monitors who themselves form French–German tandems.[3] The concept has been extended to other languages and to other forms thanks to policies on exchanges and mobility in the European Union. By relying on new technology, long-distance tandems, and the independent learning of languages in tandem have been developed (Berthoux, 2006; Helming, Branmmerts, Kleppin, & Cintrat, 2002; Macaire, 2004).

1.4. Tandems between Students

In the context of bi/plurilingualism, several universities in the European Union (Germany, Austria, and Switzerland in particular, and gradually also France) have developed the concept of tandems between students. Examples include the Ruhr-Universität Bochum (Germany) (n.d.) and the Université Lumière Lyon 2 (n.d.).

At the University of Freiburg (Switzerland), the Language Centre offered students from any faculty or discipline the option of a language tandem. Tandems could be used not only to improve their current knowledge but also to learn a language other than their usual language of study. This pairing of students became a tool that supported the development of personal plurilingualism beyond official and conventional bilingualism. In the Faculty of Law, tandem arrangements were offered to French and German students following the model of reciprocal immersion. Students in tandems worked on the same project chosen together, each writing in the language of the other and meeting regularly, both face-to-face or virtually.[4] Finally, this approach was mandatory for one semester for future language instructors who had worked though self-directed learning and self-evaluation, following a specific contract approved by the advisor who supervised the members of the tandem (Gohard-Radenkovic, 2004).

---

[1] The tandem is an integral part of the pluralistic approaches proposed in Beacco and Byram (2007).

[2] The creation of the FGYO and the idea of young people meeting together were introduced into the accord signed by German President Adenauer and French President de Gaulle in 1963.

[3] Monitors are trained in the implementation of this method and participate in linguistic and cultural tutoring at summer camps, intercultural workshops, and study-abroad programs.

[4] This type of tandem between students was abandoned in 2010. The immersion vision had moved from a co-constructivist and formative focus to a more measurable evaluation of students' competence skills, for certification purposes.

1.5. Tandems between Instructors

Collaboration between regular and specialized instructors is a common practice from primary right to the end of secondary school. It may be codified and quantified with well-defined roles for each partner.

Collaboration is "a style of direct interaction between at least two equal parties voluntarily engaged in shared decision-making as they work towards a common goal" (Friend & Cook, 2010, p. 7). For Sawyer (2007), it gives instructors the possibility of showing their creativity and innovativeness. Several researchers have highlighted the beneficial effects for instructors (Goddard, Goddard, & Tschannen-Moran, 2007; Moolenaar, Sleegers, & Daly, 2012; van Garderen, Stormont, & Goel, 2012; Vescio, Ross, & Adams, 2008).

According to Bunker (2008), a successful collaboration is characterized by the interrelation of six elements:

- mutual help, cooperation, and agreement on the educational values
- clearly established common objectives
- results-oriented focus
- a process of structured, permanent inquiry
- de-privatization of teaching methods
- reflective dialogue about teaching and learning

In the University of Freiburg's *Bilingue Plus* general program (refer to Chapter 4), meetings between language and content instructors took place to agree on the progression, content, types of examination, and evaluation at each stage of the program, following the reciprocal immersion model (Gohard-Radenkovic, 2013). But these occasional collaborations cannot be considered tandems, since they were informal and the participants met in the form of double or quadruple German–French tandems. In the *Bilingue Plus* program for future bilingual jurists, the language instructors formed official French–German tandems and from the beginning they worked closely together to implement the program and made adjustments to it (Gohard-Radenkovic, 2013).

2. MODES OF COLLABORATION WITHIN THE RIF

In this section, we will present two modes of collaboration. This analysis is based on data from different sources:

- interviews with graduates who spoke of their immersion experiences, in particular those with mentors
- informal interviews with RIF mentors
- the results of questionnaires and interviews with students who participated in the *Parrainage* project
- entries posted on the content course blog, and comments in the weekly learning journals of Anglophone students

These students also provided information in interview videos made at their end-of-term meeting. All this information has been collected since 2010, as part of a still on-going (2019) unpublished longitudinal study by Seror and Weinberg.

2.1. Modes of Collaboration between Students

2.1.1. Mentoring

The University of Ottawa has been successfully implementing mentoring since 2004. It is supported by the Student Academic Success Service (SASS) whose mission is "to be a catalyst for supportive and inclusive learning environments, by building connections, working in synergy with our students, our university partners and the community, as well as adopting and furthering academic support best practices" (University of Ottawa, n.d., "SASS"). SASS manages a pool of mentors in 19 centres, responding to the different needs of students. The centres are organized according to faculties — Arts, Social Sciences, etc. Mentor positions are offered under the Work–Study Program (WSP), which provides students paid employment on campus. In the Faculty of Arts, the Student Mentoring Centre employs ten student mentors during the fall and winter semesters and receives 3,000 visits a year. In addition to the provision of support and advice of all kinds, the role of the student mentors is to facilitate the transition to university life and to help students reach their personal, academic, and professional goals. The mentors also make sure first-year students develop effective study strategies and techniques for stress and time management. Depending on the experience of the mentors and the courses they have taken, the Centre can offer workshops on preparation for mid-term or final examinations for the courses they are familiar with.

2.1.1.1. *Dispositif:* In the Mentoring Centre affiliated with the RIF, four to five mentors work 10 hours per week for a whole semester. They provide advice to immersion students and help them to make the transition from secondary school to their first year at university. They are typically second-year students who have experience and training in working with other students. To become mentors, the students take the general training common to all mentors on the campus and given by SASS, and specialized training for immersion mentors, offered by the RIF director. Both obligatory training courses take place a week before the beginning of the semester and help students better understand the concept of mentor and the responsibilities associated with it:

> *Mentor 2*: [The director] showed me how to speak with students. And then I had technical training to learn how to use the computers and certain programs.[5]

2.1.1.2. Mentors: In practice, their intervention is limited to students newly arrived from secondary school, who come to see them especially at the beginning of their time at university:

> *Mentor 1*: I found that the first-year students come more than the others.

---

[5] Translations of quotes from mentors and mentees are by the authors.

Mentors contact students regularly, immediately upon their admission and again upon their arrival on campus, asking them to come and meet. After that initial visit, during which the mentors discuss the course choices of the students and their personalized academic path, they keep in touch with the students and make sure they follow their course of study:

Mentor 3: We convey the impression that we are there for them, nearby, ready to help them.

The main role of the mentors is to provide new students with judicious advice, based on their own university experience. But they also fulfil other functions:

Mentor 1: I helped a student who wanted to be president of the [student] association and he was one of my regulars. He came sometimes just to talk to me or the other mentors to practice his French, have a conversation, to feel at ease in French.

Mentor 2: As a mentor, I was also called upon as much to help students to negotiate their way through the university as to develop study plans or a progression of courses.

Mentor 4: You receive an e-mail [from a first-year student] "I want to see you because I don't know what courses to take." The student comes, and we find his file and you can see his file, you can check what he has already done. With this information you can find the best path for him to follow.

Mentor 5: You make requests for students [to come meet us] and in September, October, you are busy. In November, December the students come by choice to practice, to ask for help to correct their work.

The work of the mentor also includes an administrative component:

Mentor 5: It was an office environment where I had to write reports, intervene with students, and give workshops and presentations.

The mentors recognize that they have an influence on students. Through their personal example first-year students are motivated to be more involved in the university system, to become mentors themselves, and to allow another cohort to take advantage of the experiences they have had:

Mentor 6: In first year, when I was so nervous and I didn't know what to do, I had the opportunity to meet someone who had been through it. It was worth a lot to me I decided that if I could help students, if I could share my story, if I could transfer my experience to first-year students and help them, that would be wonderful.

2.1.1.3. Mentees: At the very beginning of the semester, the mentee contacts the Immersion Mentoring Centre or is contacted by them. The meetings which follow take place according to the needs of the mentee:

Mentee 1: It began with advice on the academic path. The mentors contacted me by email to ask me to come to see them to see the courses and the credits I had to take. I went to speak to them and that is how I discovered the Mentoring Centre. I went back to ask for help on my presentation. I took a speaking course and I was nervous about speaking because of my accent. I felt that I had an English accent. And then I went to practise after I had written my presentation. I practised with those mentors.

The advice put together by this group of experienced students proved to be a very valuable support, which the new students could count on when a question or a doubt came to mind. Thus, their help was appreciated by beginning students:

> *Mentee 2*: Yes, I went to see the mentors in the first weeks at university because I thought that ... I couldn't do the immersion program." ... I found it difficult at first. And they reassured me ... that I could do it ... it isn't easy for everybody: when you arrive at the university, it is a big change, so they reassured me that I could do it.

The mentees reported that the mentoring service responded to the needs of students newly arrived on the bilingual campus and they appreciated the personal help they had received from the centre:

> *Mentee 8*: In terms of actually getting information, the immersion mentors took the extra step. Rather than saying, "OK, well you need to call this person or that person," it was, "I'll call this person, I'll get back to you with the answer in a minute" or "Why don't you come in and we'll go over this?," as opposed to sending someone around to 50 million different stops to get the answer that they are looking for.

2.1.2. Parrainage

Parrainage refers to cooperation between student peers and aims to improve the learning experience of Anglophone students who are studying in French (Francophiles)[6] by facilitating their integration into content courses taught in French.

In the context of the RIF:

> *parrainage* is based on the concept of linguistic exchanges in which two people with different first languages work together and thus can learn the language of the other while discovering the other's personality and culture. It is founded on two main principles: reciprocity and autonomy. (Weinberg, 2013, p. 109 [trans.])

It permits the pairing of two linguistic groups of students who share the common objective of mastering the material in a content course. These disciplinary exchanges conducted in French also foster the development of Anglophone students' linguistic skills. This type of *parrainage* includes cooperative learning activities that use communication technologies: students communicate spontaneously by e-mail, in discussion groups, in forums, or through social media.

2.1.2.1. *Dispositif*:
Since uOttawa is a bilingual institution, it organizes its courses in French or English streams. Of course, there are always a few students taking courses in their second language, but the particular contribution of the RIF is to institutionalize this situation. The RIF is an official part of the French stream and has created a welcoming space for many Anglophone students who have decided to take their content courses in French.

---

[6] "Francophile" is the term used by uOttawa to designate students whose native language is not French but who have a strong interest in French in all its forms and in particular in studying in French (see the Introduction).

Nevertheless, this heterogeneity can present a difficulty for the teaching of the discipline in the absence of common references. *Parrainage* transforms this challenge into an asset.

The *Parrainage* project was put in place at uOttawa (Weinberg, 2013) as the result of cooperation between a history and a language instructor who promoted it as an essential element of their pedagogy. The initial project was put on paper and they began to recruit, select, and pair the participants. Since there were more Francophone than Anglophone students in the content course, some Anglophone students were paired up with more than one partner. The instructors formed teams and distributed e-mail addresses so that students could communicate with one another:

> History instructor: Out of the 70 students registered in the HIS 2736 course, only 50 completed the questionnaire and 22 of them (44%) agreed to participate in the experiment. Finally, the population studied consisted of 14 Francophones (one male) and eight Francophile students. We should note that three students were registered in third year while the others were in first year. (Weinberg, 2013, p. 110 [trans.])

During the semester, the students had face-to-face and virtual exchanges with their partners to discuss difficulties encountered in the history course, to prepare for exams, and to compare ideas about their assignments. Both instructors were responsible for the follow-up. The language instructor checked that the teams were meeting regularly while the content instructor posted questions or answered queries in her blog and organized face-to-face meetings.

2.1.2.2. *Parrains* and *parrainés*: The relationship between the two partners stems from the common ground that they share — the content course. It is not an institutionalized mentor/mentee relationship.

- The *parrainés* are Anglophone students who want to learn French. They are put in touch with Francophone students who volunteer to review the content course with them, thus bringing their individual points of view into play. The *parrainnés* may have several *parrains* who review their course notes and work with them. Their interactions are free-form and not supervised by the instructors.

- The *parrains* are French-speaking students registered in the same content course as the *parrainés*. These Francophones may be Quebeckers whose language is the language of the majority, students from other provinces, where French is a minority language, or international French-speaking students coming from France or Africa. Their contribution is voluntary and consists of working with Anglophone students outside of class time. They may share the notes that they have taken during their content course and discuss what they understood and retained from the course. They may also help them to do assignments to hand in to the content instructor and to prepare for exams. In addition to these activities suggested by the language instructor, some students initiate informal collaborations such as study groups, face-to-face meetings, or exchanges on Facebook (see Chapter 2).

2.2. Different Forms of Cooperation between Instructors

At uOttawa, the pairing of the content and language instructors is based on an administrative decision. As such, the cooperation between these two actors is imposed and not chosen. While the language instructors choose to teach immersion courses and select the ones they are interested in (at least for full-time instructors), such is not the case for the content instructors (see Chapter 4). Indeed, the decision regarding which courses are to be offered in the immersion format and, as a result, which content instructors will be involved, is made by the deans and the RIF director. If any of these instructors do not wish to participate, they must change their choice of course or course section. Consequently, many content instructors are neither prepared for nor included in these administrative decisions; most have never heard of the RIF nor the concept of university immersion. Neither content nor language instructors have received special training for this type of team teaching. Nevertheless, it must also be said that, parallel to this institutionalized pairing, a few content and language instructor tandems have developed excellent mutually supportive relationships. These relationships, however, are voluntary, informal, and not institutionalized.

2.2.1. Language and Content Instructor Tandems

The best example of such cooperation, *parrainage*, has been described above, in the context of a history course (HIS 1520 *Histoire de l'Europe*). In addition to working together to establish the pairing of Francophone and Francophile students, the two instructors developed different cooperative projects to provide pedagogical tools for their students. This cooperation emerged from the long friendship between the two instructors and their common enthusiasm for immersion. The language instructor contributed her web expertise while the content instructor brought her historical knowledge. This led to the development of a website with both an adjunct language and content stream to accompany and enrich a first-year immersion history course (see Figure 1).

In the content stream, for the history course, the content instructor would insert visual elements (maps, paintings, pictures, video segments, and texts) to illustrate the lecture component (Perrier, 2010a). This stream was useful to all students in the content course, immersion or not. In the immersion stream, students could familiarize themselves ahead of time with the vocabulary of upcoming lectures. They could also work on oral and written comprehension in different forms. Some were fun activities like songs and, for some units, an online game or a French variation of the Snakes and Ladders game (Weinberg, 2008). The native Francophone students could access these pages as well. Following this success, the two instructors created a similar site for a second-year history course, for which they were partnered as well (Perrier, 2010b).

The last project they co-developed in 2010 was *Le portail francophile* (see Figure 2). It consisted of an attractive home page pointing to all sites and resources supporting French language learning and culture on campus. These multiple initiatives were all aimed at facilitating the integration of Anglophone students into the Francophone milieu.

On a smaller scale, another language instructor brought RIF content instructors from five different disciplines (psychology, sociology, communication, political science, and second language teaching) on board to create comprehension activities for the students

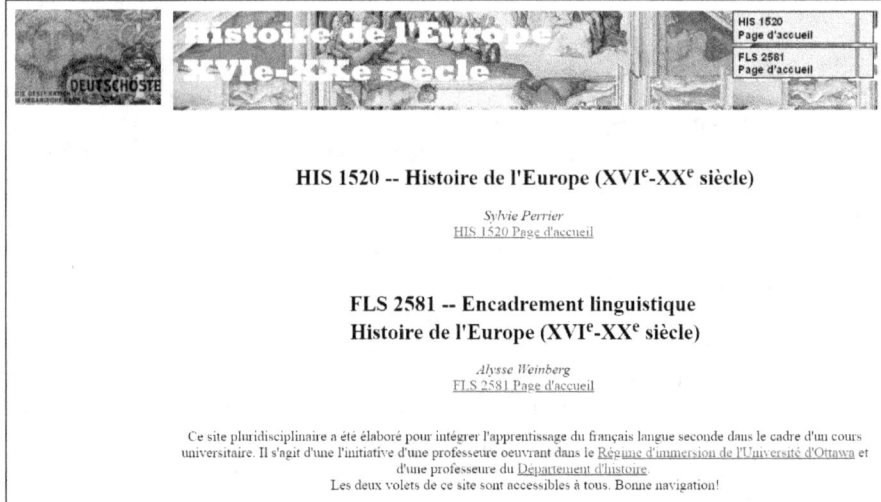

Figure 1: Home page common to the two sites, adjunct language and content
(Weinberg & Perrier, 2008)

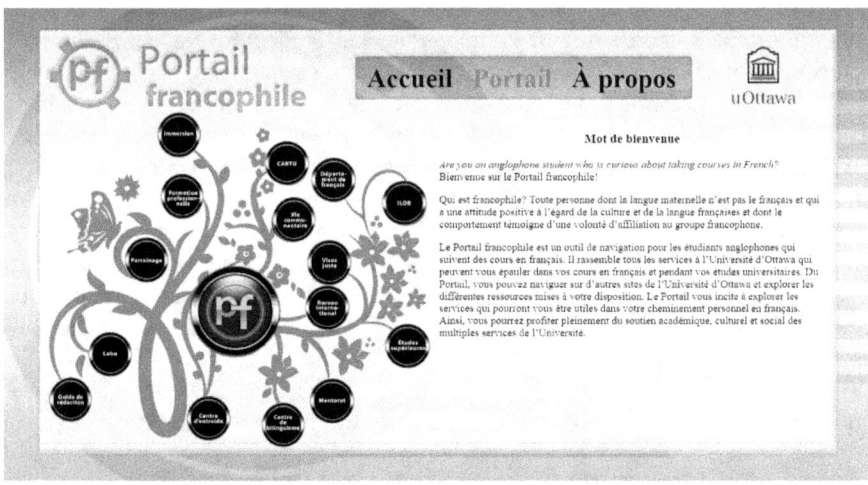

Figure 2: Home page of the *Portail francophile*
(University of Ottawa, n.d., "Le portail francophile")

taking adjunct courses. Instructors were filmed briefly presenting their training, their field, their course, and the main themes of the course. All recordings were authentic — that is, non-scripted and unedited. The five-to-six-minute clips were then cut into segments (according to the themes discussed) and uploaded onto an Internet platform. For each of these segments, the language instructor developed multimedia activities targeting comprehension and vocabulary of the discipline. The objective was to help immersion students become familiar with the courses that they were about to take and especially with the language to be used in the content course in French.

2.2.2. Research by and Collaborations between Language Instructors

Since the first pilot project of the 1980s (with the sheltered sections of the course *Introduction à la psychologie*), the community of immersion language instructors at uOttawa has developed its own culture with respect to immersion. The full-time instructors at the OLBI, who had been teaching the adjunct courses for many years, have often specialized in one discipline and channelled their enthusiasm for the immersion program through different forms of collaboration: on the one hand, research and dissemination of findings on immersion, and on the other, development of pedagogical materials.

With regard to research and dissemination of findings on immersion, several instructors have launched funded research projects in their adjunct courses (Weinberg, Boukacem, & Burger, 2012; Weinberg & Burger, 2010). Others have collected personal insights from immersion students (Séror & Weinberg, 2012; Weinberg, Séror, & Simonet, 2018) and from language instructors involved in the RIF program (see Chapter 13). As a result, they have published in specialized scientific journals (for example, Burger & Weinberg, 2014; Knoerr & Weinberg, 2013, 2014a; Weinberg, Knoerr, & Vandergrift, 2011) and given presentations at international university-level immersion conferences[7] to disseminate the results of their research.

Furthermore, in February 2012, instructors of the adjunct courses organised an international forum on *French immersion at the university level: Models, challenges and prospects*, which attracted Canadian and international researchers as well as practitioners (such as Wesche, Trépanier, Lemaire, Gohard-Radenkovic, and Räsänen), to catalogue the different implementations of French immersion. This forum led to the creation of an international inter-university research team coordinated by Professors Knoerr and Weinberg from the OLBI and the guest speaker, Professor Gohard-Radenkovic of the University of Freiburg. This collaboration resulted in a book outlining the major facets of a pedagogical approach for French immersion at the university level (Knoerr, Weinberg, & Gohard-Radenkovic, 2016). The English version of this book, updated and augmented, is what the reader is now holding in their hands.

There have been two thematic issues of the *OLBI Working Papers* on the subject of university-level immersion, guest-edited by Knoerr and Weinberg (eds., 2013) and just recently, by Knoerr, Weinberg, and Buchanan (eds., 2018).

In 2017, an international symposium, *Immersion in higher education: Where do we stand today?*, was held at uOttawa to mark the 10th anniversary of the RIF and 10 years

---

[7] Three conferences in particular: CARLA (Center for Advanced Research on Language Acquisition), ICLHE (Integrating Content and Language in Higher Education), and HEPCLIL (Higher Education Perspectives on Content and Language Integrated Learning).

Symposia comprising several presentations were organized at these conferences: Knoerr (2013, 2015); Knoerr and Weinberg (2014b); Knoerr, Weinberg, and Buchanan (2016); and Weinberg and Knoerr (2014).

of French immersion studies. The symposium looked at different aspects of university-level immersion programs in Europe, the United States, and Canada. The symposium presentations were compiled in a book, *Current issues in university immersion* (Knoerr, Weinberg, & Buchanan (eds., 2018).

Funded projects have been undertaken, leading to the successful production of educational or pedagogical tools. For example, in 2007, the OLBI's Weinberg and Knoerr made an inventory of the difficulties facing RIF students in their content courses. With the help of a specialist in oral comprehension, an OLBI colleague (Larry Vandergrift), they created a series of seven podcasts, to guide university immersion students in developing and implementing metacognitive, cognitive, and socio-affective strategies, to become good listeners (see Chapter 7). These resources are available on the RIF website (University of Ottawa, n.d., "French immersion stream ... Podcasts") and on YouTube.[8] The podcast project has been presented at conferences and in publications (Knoerr & Weinberg, 2014a; Weinberg, Knoerr, & Vandergrift, 2011).

3. CONTRIBUTIONS AND LIMITATIONS

This section presents students' perceptions of their participation in various collaborative projects. Some common themes, mentioned by the students themselves or by the instructors, emerged from these discussions. The effects of these collaboration projects on students' social interactions as well as their academic, linguistic, and professional values will be discussed.

3.1. Contributions

3.1.1. Academic Contributions

All the students reported better academic success thanks to the mentoring. Their administrative dealings with the university were eased because of their contacts with mentors, whose guidance facilitated their integration into their courses:

> *Mentee 1*: I received a lot of support from the mentors in the first year. It was my first course, in history. I came from Extended French[9] in secondary school. It was a different environment where everyone was speaking French, the professor was speaking French, the books were in French. I remember that I had problems. In my first year I often went to the Mentoring Centre. They helped me with my assignments. That experience with them really helped me to succeed in my course in first year.

As for *parrainage*, the *parrains* shared their knowledge of the discipline and thus helped their Francophile peers to succeed, particularly by sharing their course notes:

> *Parrainée 1*: It was a great opportunity to review my course notes and also ask questions.

> *Parrainée 2*: It was good practice for my comprehension of the discipline. To ensure that everyone has understood the same thing, because there may be different interpretations.

---

[8] See, for example, Podcast 7 (Weinberg, Knoerr, Vandergrift, 2011).
[9] Extended French: a language program in Canadian secondary schools. For an outline of the different FSL programs in Canada, see Chapter 1.

In addition, the students prepared for their exams together. Almost all the Francophiles recognized that the informal group meeting at the end of the term had better prepared them for the final exam:

> *Parrainée 4*: You had a chance to understand the content better. If you had problems, trouble with comprehension, you had a chance to ask the Francophones. Not only that, but you had the opportunity to be more comfortable with the course itself, with the instructor and also with the peers in our classes.
>
> *Parrainée 5*: With *parrainage*, I really liked the discussions that we had with other people to integrate other people's ideas and to discuss them.

The students recognized that this exchange helped them to master the course material. They were able to help one another and discuss linguistic aspects (vocabulary) as well as the subject matter of the content course. They became aware that the discipline could be taught from different points of view, according to the language of instruction. The perception of an event may be different, even contrary, depending on whether the course is taught in French or English. This is particularly striking in history courses:

> *Parrain 4*: It was interesting to hear the historical interpretations of other students.
>
> *Parrainée 5*: I appreciated the exchange of interpretations.

Furthermore, this sharing of knowledge is not unidirectional, since sometimes the Francophones were learning from the Francophiles:

> *Parrain 1*: [From Saskatchewan] This allowed new exchanges, getting to know new people. This allowed me to review the content, to be sure that I am understanding well because if I have to explain terms or concepts, I have to understand them well.

3.1.2. Linguistic Contributions

The work of the mentors at the Mentoring Centre allowed them to engage in language encounters which went beyond the academic context:

> *Mentor 1*: It gave me more confidence in myself, in my accent, my vocabulary in an academic and professional environment. I loved that experience! That's the best job I ever had.

The improvement in linguistic competence also affected the *parrainé*, as another student noted:

> *Parrainée 2*: [*Parrainage*] encouraged us to speak and to participate. It was much friendlier. I appreciate the fact that you can express yourself in your second language. That improved our confidence, not only with the course material but also in our ability to speak French. It helped my confidence a lot.

3.1.3. Professional contributions

The mentoring experience had long-term impacts. For one of the mentors, it helped her find a job:

> *Mentor 1*: It was an office environment where I had to write reports and interact with students; I had to give workshops. It gave me work experience in a language which is not my own ... I know that without these experiences I would not have found a job in the company where I am now.

3.1.4. Other Positive Repercussions

Mentors indicated that they felt a sense of pride in the usefulness of their work. They were conscious of the importance of their role and of the benefits that the different partners were getting out of it. They felt personal satisfaction in sharing their knowledge and their experience. The *parrains*, too, felt a sense of pride because they could share knowledge of their language as well as their general knowledge:

> *Parrain 2*: It is very enriching to work with students who speak another language. It allows you to share the love of the French language.

Finally, the students mentioned that the *parrainage* exchanges had surpassed the learning objectives of the course and had led to "better intercultural comprehension of the other language group" (*Parrainée 3*). *Parrainage* became a gateway to the other group, to understand it with its differences. These exchanges reinforced the new identity construction of immersion students (Séror & Weinberg, 2012, 2013):

> *Parrainée 3*: I have a better understanding of the differences and the problems between Anglophones and Francophones.

Table 1 summarizes the different advantages of *parrainage* for the two groups of students. It presents the distribution of the answers of the students organized around the four themes which underline the contributions of *parrainage*.

Table 1: The impacts of *parrainage* (Weinberg, 2013, p. 111 [trans.])

	Francophones $n = 13$		Francophiles $n = 7$	
	Yes	No	Yes	No
Better linguistic competence	9	4	5	2
Better understanding of the history course	11	0	6	1
Preparation for the final exam	1	11	7	0
Better understanding of the other linguistic group	8	5	4	3

This table shows the positive effects of *parrainage* on both types of participants. The Francophone students believed they better understood the course after they discussed it with Anglophones. This shows that there are many reciprocal advantages occurring here and not just a one-way transfer of knowledge.

One of the content instructors summarized the benefits of *parrainage* as follows:

History instructor: I was surprised how satisfied they were with the experience and to what degree the experience helped not only the course but served to create links between students of the two language communities. They all said that it was helpful to learn the course material, that it had a beneficial effect on their academic progress. But they were also pleased to have built friendships, to have had cultural exchanges. At that point, we understood that there was a need for cultural exchanges of this type within the groups.

3.2. Limitations

3.2.1. Parrainage

The infrastructure can sometimes be difficult to put in place and it rests on the shoulders of the instructors. This can jeopardize the continuity of the project. Although the RIF administration recognizes the importance of *parrainage*, the close collaboration between the two instructors needed to implement it remains rare — only two teams up to this point (2006–2019)! The administration has not been able to repeat this collaboration in other courses with other instructors. In order to succeed, collaborative projects should be a bottom-up process, starting with the instructors or with students themselves. If the language and content instructors develop trust and long-term continuity in their relationship, their opportunities for collaboration will be strengthened. This can improve the prospects for the development of collaborative projects for the students. Nevertheless, *parrainage* depends on the students' motivation and their willingness to participate in this exchange in spite of a busy schedule already full of different activities. One study (Weinberg, 2013) has already drawn attention to the minimal student participation in the *parrainage* project and the students' wish for greater involvement from other instructors.

3.2.2. Mentoring

The implementation of a mentoring program requires a substantial financial commitment in order to establish an office on campus with sufficient space for visiting students, to hire staff, and to advertise its different services. Another issue is the lack of continuity among the mentors who, as students, do not remain in those positions for long. It is therefore necessary to continually train new mentors. Finally, this system only works if the students who need it actually use it.

3.2.3. Collaboration between Content and Language Instructors

The relationship is *de-facto* asymmetric and hierarchical because most language instructors do not have a PhD, while all content instructors do.[10] The tandem concept presupposes not only reciprocity but also equal status in the conception and construction of this exchange. There should be prior preparation at different levels to legitimize the language instructors.[11]

---

[10] See Chapter 13 for more details on the relationships between language and content instructors.
[11] We will revisit this preoccupation of the administrators directly concerned with RIF management in Chapter 12.

3.2.4. Lack of Recognition

Finally, content instructors do not receive recognition for their time and energy in immersion collaborations since these projects usually do not relate to their discipline and therefore are not counted toward the advancement of their careers.

Equally important, all the work that language instructors put into custom-designing their courses on the spot week after week, organizing *parrainage* opportunities, and collaborating with content instructors is not recognized either. These instructors are not treated differently from regular FSL instructors who simply follow a textbook.

CONCLUSION

The procedures of collaboration that have been put in place at uOttawa, such as mentoring, *parrainage*, or instructor tandems, offer pedagogical approaches appropriate for RIF students. These *dispositifs* propose different modes of learning, teaching, and socializing with student participants from both language groups and instructors from different academic backgrounds. The students must go beyond individualistic competitive attitudes to take advantage of collaborative education and its benefits not only in the short term — academic success — but also in the long term — in the work place and in Canadian society.

Nevertheless, we must recognize that these *dispositifs*, like any project, do have limits. They require implicit involvement on the part of all participants, who need to develop collaborative practices in order to ensure the success of this two-way pedagogical intervention:

- For the institution, the involvement should translate into material and financial support, and the explicit recognition of these collaborations.
- Instructors should promote a new concept of teaching, centred on interdisciplinarity and collaboration rather than competition.
- Students need to become aware of the diversity of spaces and modes of learning, notably through collaborative practices, to excel in their *métier d'étudiant* (Coulon, 1988, 2005) — to learn to how to become adept university students.

To summarize, the reports of the various participants in these collaborative *dispositifs* teach us essentially one thing: collaborative practices cannot be imposed, but should develop naturally from a larger cooperative university culture.

REFERENCES

Beacco, J.-C., & Byram, M. (2007). *Guide pour l'élaboration de politiques linguistiques et éducatives en Europe: de la diversité linguistique à l'éducation plurilingue.* Strasbourg: Council of Europe.

Berthoux, C. (2006). Construction de compétences lexicales en e-tandem: une étude pour l'apprentissage de l'allemand. *Recherches en didactique des langues et des cultures: les Cahiers de l'Acedle, 2,* 1–6.

Bunker, V. J. (2008). *Professional Learning Communities, Teacher Collaboration, and Student Achievement in an Era of Standards-Based Reform.* Ann Arbor: ProQuest.

Burger, S., & Weinberg, A. (2014). Three factors in vocabulary acquisition in a university French immersion adjunct context. *Journal of Immersion and Content-Based Language Education*, 2, 23–52.

Coulon, A. (1988). Ethnométhodologie et éducation. *Revue française de pédagogie*, 82, 65–101.

Coulon, A. (2005). *Le métier d'étudiant: l'entrée dans la vie universitaire* (2nd ed.). Paris: Presses universitaires de France.

Floor, A. (2010). Le tutorat et le parrainage, de nouvelles manières d'apprendre pour une école de la réussite (Étude UFAPEC 2010 [Union des Fédérations des associations de parents de l'enseignement catholique], no. 20.10. www.ufapec.be/files/files/analyses/2010/2010-etude-tutorat-parrainage.pdf

Friend, M., & Cook, L. (2010). *Interactions: Collaboration skills for school professionals* (6th ed.). Upper Saddle River: Pearson Education.

Galbraith, N.W., & Cohen, N.H. (Eds.). (1995). *New directions for adult and continuing education* [thematic issue: *Mentoring: New strategies and challenges*], 66.

Goddard, Y.L., Goddard, R.D., & Tschannen-Moran, M. (2007). A theoretical and empirical investigation of teacher collaboration for school improvement and student achievement in public elementary schools. *Teachers College Record 109*, 877–896.

Gohard-Radenkovic, A. (2013). Radiographie de l'immersion dans l'enseignement supérieur en Suisse et à l'Université de Fribourg: les prérequis nécessaires, *OLBI Working Papers*, 6, 3–19.

Gohard-Radenkovic, A. (Ed.). (2004). *Communiquer en langue étrangère: de compétences culturelles vers des compétences linguistiques* (2nd ed.). Bern: Peter Lang.

Haney, A. (1997). The role of mentorship in the workplace. In M.C. Taylor (Ed.), *Workplace education* (pp. 211–228). Toronto: Culture Concepts.

Helming, B., Brammerts, H., Kleppin, K., & Cintrat, I. (2002). *L'apprentissage autonome des langues en tandem*. Paris: Didier.

Houde, R. (1995). *Des mentors pour la relève*. Paris: Méridien.

Kaye, B., & Jacobson, B. (1996). Reframing mentoring. *Training and Development*, 50(8), 44–47.

Kerka, S. (1997). Constructivism, workplace learning, and vocational education (ERIC Digest No. 181). Columbus, OH: ERIC Clearinghouse on Adult Career and Vocational Education. (ED407573 1997-00-00). www.ericdigests.org/1998-1/learning.htm

Knoerr H. (2013, March). *The impact of listening and note-taking strategies on the performance of immersion students*. Paper presented at the ICLHE Conference, Maastricht.

Knoerr H. (2015, September). *Investigating the ideologies of content professors in an adjunct immersion model*. Paper presented at the ICLHE Conference, Brussels, Belgium, The Netherlands.

Knoerr, H., Vandergrift, L., & Weinberg, A. (2010). Podcast #7: New technology for note-taking. Ottawa: University of Ottawa, Centre for university teaching. www.youtube.com/watch?v=KwviaGIQrdE

Knoerr, H., & Weinberg, A. (2013). L'immersion à l'Université d'Ottawa: une innovation héritée du passé. *Recherches en didactique des langues et des cultures: les Cahiers de l'Acedle*, 10(3), 15–35. (Association des Chercheurs et Enseignants Didacticiens des Langues Étrangères)

Knoerr, H., & Weinberg, A. (2014a). Stratégies d'écoute: les étudiants d'immersion en français au niveau universitaire ont la parole. *Les Dossiers des sciences de l'éducation*, *32*, 111–130.

Knoerr, H., & Weinberg, A. (2014b, March). *Designing pedagogical activities for language learning in an integrated language content approach*. Paper presented at the HepCLIL Conference, University of Vic, Spain.

Knoerr, H., & Weinberg, A. (Eds.). (2013). *OLBI Working Papers* [thematic issue: *French immersion at the university level*], *6*.

Knoerr, H., Weinberg, A., & Buchanan C. (2016, October). *University-level French immersion in Canada: Policies, pedagogy and practices, assessment and evaluation*. Paper presented at the CARLA Conference, Minneapolis, MI.

Knoerr, H., Weinberg, A., & Buchanan, C.E. (2018a). *Current issues in university immersion*. Ottawa: University of Ottawa, Groupe de recherche en immersion au niveau universitaire (GRINU).

Knoerr, H., Weinberg, A., & Buchanan, C.E. (Eds.). (2018b). *OLBI Working Papers* [thematic issue: *University-level immersion environments in Canada*], *9*.

Knoerr, H., Weinberg, A., Gohard-Radenkovic, A. (Eds.). (2016). *L'immersion française à l'université: politiques et pédagogies*. Ottawa: University of Ottawa Press.

Macaire, D. (2004). Du tandem au Télé-Tandem: nouveaux apprentissages, nouveaux outils, nouveaux rôles. www.tele-tandem.net/fr/wp-content/uploads/2010/02/Macaire-Du-tandem-au-Tele-Tandem.pdf

Moolenaar, N.M., Sleegers, P.J., & Daly, A.J. (2012). Teaming up: Linking collaboration networks, collective efficacy, and student achievement. *Teaching and Teacher Education*, *28*, 251–262.

Perrier, S. (2010a). Cours 12 — Napoléon et l'Europe. aix1.uottawa.ca/~sperrier/europe/cours12/cours12.html

Perrier, S. (2010b). L'Europe moderne (XVIe au XVIIIe siècle — HIS 2736). aix1.uottawa.ca/~sperrier/moderne/index2.html

Ruhr-Universität Bochum. (n.d.). University Language Centre (ZFA): Learning in tandem. www.zfa.ruhr-uni-bochum.de/ils/lernen/index.html.en

Sawyer, K. (2007). *Group genius: The creative power of collaboration*. New York: Basic Books.

Séror, J., & Weinberg, A. (2012). Construction identitaire et linguistique: le Régime d'immersion en français de l'Université d'Ottawa. *Synergies Europe*, *7*, 135–150.

Séror, J., & Weinberg, A. (2013). Personal insights on a postsecondary immersion experience. *OLBI Working Papers*, *6*, 123–140.

Université Lumière Lyon 2. (n.d.). Travaillez les langues en tandem: c'est possible à Lyon 2 !

University of Ottawa. (n.d.). French Immersion Stream: Resources Studies — Podcasts [Video]. immersion.uottawa.ca/en/resources

University of Ottawa. (n.d.). Le portail francophile. www.pf.uottawa.ca/portail.php

University of Ottawa. (n.d.). Student Academic Success Service (SASS) — About SASS. sass.uottawa.ca/en/about

Van Garderen, D., Stormont, M., & Goel, N. (2012). Collaboration between general and special educators and student outcomes: A need for more research. *Psychology in the Schools*, *49*, 483–497.

Vescio, V., Ross, D., & Adams, A. (2008). A review of research on the impact of professional learning communities on teaching practice and student learning. *Teaching and Teacher Education*, *24*, 80–91.

Weinberg, A. (2008). Histoire de coccinelle : Les grandes découvertes. aix1.uottawa.ca/~weinberg/europe/fls2581/coccinelle/01_decouvertes.html

Weinberg, A. (2013). Parrainage francophiles–francophones à l'Université d'Ottawa dans le cadre du Régime d'immersion : pratique et perceptions. In E. Yasri-Labrique, P. Gardies, & K. Djordjevic (Eds.), *Didactique contrastive: questionnements et applications* (pp. 105–117). Montpellier: Cladole.

Weinberg, A., Boukacem, D., &. Burger, S. (2012). Progrès lexicaux d'étudiants dans deux contextes d'immersion au niveau universitaire. *Canadian Modern Language Review*, *68*, 1–27.

Weinberg, A., & Burger, S. (2010). University level immersion: Students' perception of language activities. *OLBI Working Papers*, *1*, 111–142.

Weinberg, A., & Knoerr, H. (2014, March). *An after-graduation survey of university-level French immersion students*. Paper presented at the HepCLIL Conference, University of Vic, Spain.

Weinberg, A., Knoerr, H., & Vandergrift, L. (2011). Creating podcasts for academic listening in French: Student perceptions of enjoyment and usefulness. *CALICO Journal*, *28*, 588–605.

Weinberg, A., & Perrier, S. (2008). Histoire de l'Europe (XVIe au XXe siècle) [Homepage]. aix1.uottawa.ca/~weinberg/europe

Weinberg, A., Séror, J., & Simonet, T. (2018). Sur la piste des facteurs d'attrition et de rétention au sein du Régime d'immersion en français à l'Université d'Ottawa. *Canadian Modern Language Review*, *74*, 302–330. doi:10.3138/cmlr.2017-0059

CHAPTER 10

The Role of Testing in Immersion Programs

Alysse Weinberg and Amelia Hope

INTRODUCTION

EDUCATIONAL MEASUREMENT AND EVALUATION are integral to any educational system, not only for the assessment of student outcomes, but also for the evaluation of the teaching, the curriculum, the administration, and other aspects of a program. Measurement and evaluation can aid in decision-making for the full range of stakeholders, including students, teachers, program administrators, university administration, and funding centres. This chapter describes the assessment and evaluation practices in the *Régime d'immersion en français* (RIF, French Immersion Stream) at the University of Ottawa. Although these practices relate to the specific context of the RIF, they highlight the essential components of assessment and evaluation for any immersion program.

The chapter opens with a focus on the assessment of students which takes place at three critical junctures in the RIF: (i) before a student is admitted, (ii) in the classroom, and (iii) at the end of the program. The second part describes the evaluation of teaching and students' perceptions of the varied linguistic activities in their language courses. Finally, evaluation research concerning the program as a whole is presented. This research was done by the institution itself to measure the long-term impact of the program and includes surveys of former students who have since graduated from it and embarked on careers.

1. STUDENT ASSESSMENT

As Nagy (2000) has noted, one of the oldest functions of testing is to determine who possesses enough of a specific trait to gain a special privilege, such as admission to an institution or a profession. Testing in the context of immersion programs is no exception. This section considers the assessment of students in the program. It follows these assessments chronologically — in the same order as a RIF student would encounter them — from the admission test to the program-final certification test.

1.1. Immersion Admission Test

The RIF breaks down the walls between traditional second language courses and content courses. This novel approach can present RIF students with a considerable challenge, which can end in failure if the proficiency of the students is not at an adequate level. Thus, it is vital that the language skills of applicants be checked before they enrol. The admission process is designed to determine which applicants will be able to benefit from this type of pedagogy.

It is true that, in some cases, one can infer student language proficiency from a high school transcript. Many institutions, however, opt for a customized evaluation since there is no reliable common standard in Canada.[1] In this case, an institution can develop an admission test, which involves taking into consideration pedagogical, logistical, and financial factors.

1.1.1. Purchased or Developed?

Once it has been determined that certain admission criteria need to be met, one practical concern is whether to buy an off-the-shelf French test or to develop one. The market for French proficiency testing is not a large one compared to the number of English tests available, and so there are fewer commercial French proficiency tests available.[2] One option is to require potential applicants to take a standardized French test such as the DELF (*Diplôme d'études en langue française*), the TEF (*Test d'évaluation de français pour le Canada*),[3] or the TCF (*Test de connaissance du français tout public*). The first two are issued by the French Ministry of Education and are used to certify the French language skills of non-native speaking candidates. The DELF and the DALF (*Diplôme approfondi de langue française*, Alliance française, n.d., "DELF–DALF") consist of six tests, corresponding to the six levels of the Common European Framework of Reference for Languages (CEFR; Council of Europe, 2001). The university could ask all students to pass one of these already validated tests and open the RIF to those students who reach the appropriate level. One drawback to such a decision is that it may not be easy for all applicants to find a site that administers these tests. In addition, costs may be prohibitive for some applicants.[4] A further objection is that some language specialists have argued that these tests are too culturally specific or Eurocentric and, therefore, somewhat inappropriate for the Canadian context (Banon-Schirman & Makardidjian, 2006; Buchanan, 2014).

The option of creating an in-house test eliminates some of these disadvantages, but the development of an appropriate instrument requires time and effort, and is, therefore, expensive. When developing a language proficiency test for admission to a program, there are several important considerations:

- *Definition of the construct*: According to Laurier, Tousignant, and Morissette (2005), the test construct is a theoretical model that constitutes the "set of variables representing the network of skills, attitudes and knowledge that make up

---

[1] Moreover, it must be remembered that education is under provincial jurisdiction in Canada, and school boards establish their own standards.

[2] Note that the test market is not as developed in French as in English. There is a structural explanation for this difference: English tests were quickly privatized and funded, while French tests for a long time remained under the control of the public sector. They are now profitable.

[3] This test provides candidates with a linguistic snapshot of their level in French by placing them on a seven-point scale, with detailed descriptions for each skill at each level (Alliance française, n.d., "TEF Canada").

[4] The cost of the subtests can vary from $90 for the writing test to $460 for the complete four skills test.

a skill, as well as the interactions between these and other skills" (p. 66). The construct, therefore, corresponds to the performance that is to be measured.

- *Which skills should be measured*: Second language proficiency is generally taken to mean overall competence in a language, independent of a particular curriculum. The most widely used frameworks of language proficiency — for example, the Common European Framework of Reference (CEFR) and the proficiency guidelines of the American Council of Teachers of Foreign Languages (ACTFL, 2012) — stress the importance of language for communication over the acquisition of grammatical or lexical knowledge. Therefore, tests built according to such frameworks normally take a four-skills approach — that is, they consider reading, listening, speaking, and writing as the key components of proficiency.
- *Standard setting*: Standard setting allows for the calibration of the test scores to the desired competence level for a program or to the different language courses at the institution. At uOttawa, standard setting facilitates decisions about the score below which students are not admitted to the program, as well as the scores which permit admission into the first or second level of the adjunct courses (see Chapter 3).

For admission to the RIF, uOttawa chose to develop an in-house test. The Immersion Admission Test is an online language proficiency test. This test was developed and validated by the Official Languages and Bilingualism Institute (OLBI), which administers it.

1.1.2. Threshold Level

In order to be eligible for the RIF, students must obtain a score (60%) on the admission test which is equivalent to the Advanced Intermediate level of French courses offered by uOttawa. Students must also provide samples of both written and oral expression. These productive skills samples do not enter into the admission decision, but are used to assist in the placement of the students into the appropriate French as a Second Language course. They are also used in helping the RIF staff map out a personalized study plan for each student, adapted to their individual needs and academic program of study.

Students can be exempted from the Immersion Admission Test if they have a DELF certificate of level B1 or higher. Level B1, the third of the six levels specified in the CEFR taxonomy of proficiency in a second language, normally indicates that the learner is independent and can cope with many situations in everyday life. Currently, more and more new students arrive at the university with a DELF certificate, as a growing number of school boards in Canada are offering this test to their students at the end of their secondary education. However, the RIF will no longer be accepting the DELF certificate for logistical reasons: it takes a few months for results to be available, which means that students taking the DELF in their second semester of Grade 12 will not receive their results early enough to meet the deadlines associated with the registration process.

The Immersion Admission Test (or the DELF/DALF) can indicate with some certainty which students will likely succeed in taking content courses in French. That being said, tests results cannot guarantee future academic success. For one thing, although speech and writing samples are collected from the students, they do not figure into the admission decision. This has meant that a few students have been ill-equipped for those French content courses with heavy writing or speaking demands. It is also true that there are students who pass the admission tests but have difficulty in French content courses for a variety of other reasons, such as the instructor's accent, the pace of instruction, poorly organized lectures, or the intrinsic complexity of the discipline (University of Ottawa, 2014, p. 25).

1.2. Assessment of Academic Performance in Courses

As in the majority of academic settings, students in the RIF are assessed on their success in meeting course objectives. However, assessing student success in the adjunct courses is somewhat complicated: the borderlines between the material in the content course and the teaching of the language are blurry. Also, unlike the admissions and certification tests, which are standardized instruments developed by the Measurement and Evaluation Sector of the OLBI, student assessment in the adjunct courses is left up to the instructors who teach them.

1.2.1. Assessment of Language or Content?

When evaluating student performance in the adjunct classes, it must be determined whether the tests should address the student's mastery of the disciplinary content, of the language, or of both areas. The answers to this question depend largely on the immersion model adopted. Brinton, Snow, and Wesche (2003) argue that it is not possible for content-based language instructors to evaluate language alone. They justify this position by noting that "content mastery is ... the essential facilitator of the language learning process" (p. 182). They further point out that the objectives of the language instruction are performance-based; that is, the skill of interest is the ability of students to use the second language to accomplish an academic task in the content area.

The content versus language question has preoccupied the language instructors of the immersion courses since the inception of the program. The suggestion by Brinton et al. (2003) — that the same test could be used to evaluate both language and content — is theoretically defensible, but administratively impossible at the university. As described above, the university's immersion courses have two components taught by two different instructors. Students receive three credits in the content course and three in the language course; university guidelines do not allow for the same assignments or exams to be submitted in both courses. The content course must have its own assignments and exams, prepared and evaluated by the content instructor. This means that evaluating the students' mastery of the content material lies squarely with the content instructor; the language instructor cannot tread onto that turf. Only achievement in language skills can be evaluated in the adjunct course. It must be recognized, however, that the "boundary between content evaluation and language assessment is sometimes fuzzy" (Knoerr, 2010, p. 104).

For example, in a content test (e.g., in history), students may be asked to:

Identify the following individuals or groups in two or three sentences:
1.1. Mao Tse-Tung
1.2. Chiang Kai-shek
1.3. Kuomintang

These items clearly measure mastery of the discipline; students must recall and produce information acquired from their textbooks or lectures. These types of test items are thus "out of bounds" for the language instructor teaching the adjunct course because they tap content rather than language skills.

In a language test, the language instructor could find a different text which covers similar content and thus assess the students' ability to apply their reading or listening abilities to new content about these people and groups (Hope, 2006, section XII, slide 4, p. 2).

While arguing that the language must be evaluated in the context of the content, Brinton et al. (2003) note that language instructors must carefully choose the material and the task which will serve as a basis for language assessment. The goal is to make sure that a student's mastery of the content does not unduly affect the evaluation of the student's language skills.

Figure 1 illustrates the distribution of the evaluative tasks of the different instructors.

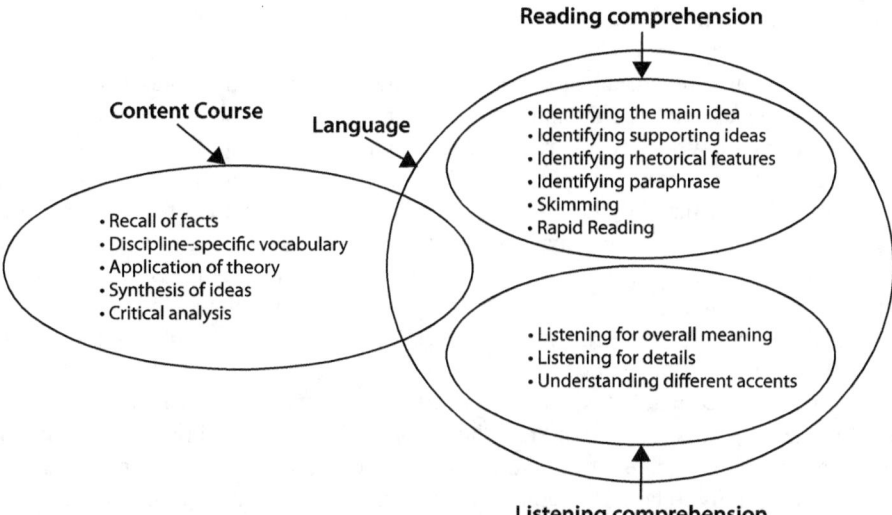

Figure 1: Testing content, language, and content-based language (adapted from Hope, 2006, section XII, slide 5, p.2)

During her training sessions with language instructors, Hope (2006) stressed that testing factual recall, application of a theory, the synthesis of ideas from the lectures and readings, and critical thinking about the concepts are the responsibility of the content instructor. The language instructor can assess a student's ability to identify main or supporting ideas when reading a text related to a discipline, to identify and summarize ideas in a text, to demonstrate the ability to guess word meanings from the context, and to demonstrate understanding of different accents. Hope (2006) subsequently presented models of tests to characterize the difference between *disciplinary tests*, which assess the knowledge coming from the content course, and the *language tests*, which evaluate the language skills.

1.2.2. Evaluating Receptive Skills or Productive Skills

In addition to the distinction between evaluation of content knowledge and language skills, a distinction is made in the RIF between *receptive skills* and *productive skills*.

The first level of the adjunct courses is focused on the improvement of reading and listening. The language instructors must ensure that their evaluation measures only receptive skills. Knoerr (2010, p. 105) lists evaluation tasks that instructors can use in this context. Ideally, instructors of the first level adjunct courses should develop test items that require the students to answer with a minimum of productive skills. If the students must use their productive skills to demonstrate their reading or listening comprehension, then care should be taken not to mark the students on their productive skills. Item formats that require little production include multiple-choice questions, matching exercises, true/false questions, and cloze tests. Examples of these item types are displayed in Figure 2.

The second level of the adjunct courses focuses on productive skills (see Chapter 3 for complete descriptions). These courses are designed to improve skills in written and oral expression in French, and to enable students to express the ideas and concepts presented in the associated content course in French. In these courses, students are expected to be able to write a well-structured text using the discipline-specific vocabulary, to produce complex sentences, and to speak with some ease and accuracy about the subject taught. Test formats in the second level adjunct courses include written texts such as summaries, descriptions, comparisons, or persuasive essays, oral presentations, and discussions. This work can be done individually or in small groups. Students use the material in the content course as a basis for their work; during the exams, they can use the content documents to search for the information needed to complete the language task (Figure 3).

It should be noted that RIF students, like all students at uOttawa, can submit assignments and tests in the language of their choice, according to the bilingualism regulation put in place in 1974 (University of Ottawa, 1974, part. 6, art. 4.3). This regulation does not, of course, apply to language courses, but many RIF students take advantage of this option in the content course they are taking in French. They must be able to handle the lectures and readings in French but they can do their homework and tests in English.

1.3. The Second Language Certification Test

As a bilingual institution, uOttawa has a long history of testing and evaluating the bilingualism of its students. Indeed, until 1994, all students in the Faculty of Arts and Social Sciences had to pass a second language proficiency test in order to graduate. Students from other faculties were required to pass a six-credit course in their second official

Nom: _____ Note: _____ 34 pts / _____ 10 %

FLS 2581 H3
Examen de fin de session
Compréhension de l'oral

Écoutez l'enregistrement suivant sur la Crise de 1929 et répondez aux questions par un énoncé complet, en complétant les phrases ou en encerclant la bonne réponse. Vous entendrez cet enregistrement à deux reprises. Commencez par lire les questions pour vous familiariser avec le sujet. Les questions sont mentionnées selon l'ordre chronologique de l'enregistrement. Vous ne serez pas évalué pour la correction orthographique de vos réponses.

1. Le ___ octobre _____, dès le début de l'ouverture de la _____ de New York. _____ millions d'_____ étaient jetées sur le marché et perdaient en quelques minutes plus de _____ de leur valeur.   6 pts

2. Nommez trois conséquences de cette crise.
   a)
   b)
   c)   3 pts

3. Les contemporains de la Crise de 1929 ont compris immédiatement l'étendue de la crise.
      Faux   Vrai   1 pt

4. Quelle est l'attitude du journaliste américain Forbes après le jeudi noir?
   a) alarmiste
   b) confiant
   c) étonné   1 pt

Figure 2: Excerpt of a final exam for a receptive skills adjunct course
(Weinberg, 2012)

Nom: _____ Note: _____ 20 pts/ _____ 10 %

FLS 3581 H3
Examen de mi-session
Expression écrite

1. Àprès avoir consulté la carte de l'Europe et le texte sur les traités de Paris et leurs conséquences, rédigez un texte pour répondre à la question suivante :
   Que pensez-vous des conséquences de ce traité pour l'Europe ?
   Vous avez 45 minutes pour rédiger un texte de 300 mots. Nous vous suggérons de prendre au moins 5 minutes pour **dresser** le plan de votre réponse et de réserver 5 minutes pour vous relire à la fin de la rédaction.

Figure 3: Excerpt of a mid-term exam for a productive skills adjunct course
(Weinberg, 2013)

language. These requirements were abandoned in 1994, although some academic departments maintained bilingualism standards for their students.[5] In 2003, university administrators, wanting to reaffirm the linguistic duality of the university, introduced a new test, the Second Language Certification Test (SLCT). For most students, the test is an option if they want to graduate and enter the job market with proof of their proficiency in their second language. For students in the RIF, however, passing this test is an exit requirement.

If students pass the SLCT, they receive a certificate attesting to their level of bilingualism. This certification can be an asset when RIF students enter the labour market. Although it is not officially sanctioned by government agencies as a substitute for their own bilingualism tests, it is recognized as credible proof of bilingualism, which can facilitate access to jobs where proficiency in the second language is a required or desirable qualification.

The OLBI offers this test in either French or English for students who register for a self-study language refresher course at any time during their program. However, RIF students are strongly advised to take this test before the end of their third year of study, so as to have time to take the test again if they do not pass it on their first attempt. They may take a practice test online (OLBI, n.d., "Test") and will receive a feedback report if they take the test within eight weeks into the term.

The SLCT is made up of four subtests, in listening, reading, writing, and speaking. Test item topics are academic in nature but accessible to students in any program of study. The official description of the four components of the test is shown in Figure 4.

The SLCT provides its results in terms of levels of difficulty and competence, on a scale of one to four. The first level indicates that the student experiences difficulty understanding or communicating while Level 4 indicates that comprehension and communication skills are considered superior. In order to pass the test, students must obtain at least a Level 2 in each of the four components of the test. Figure 5 shows the official descriptors of these four levels.

2. EVALUATION OF TEACHING

In Canada, universities and colleges conduct official course evaluations at the end of each semester. These evaluations serve several purposes:

- They provide an opportunity for students to describe their experiences in courses.
- They produce information on teaching and courses for institutional decision-makers.
- They give feedback to instructors on their teaching which can help them make useful changes to their teaching practice.

The RIF administrators and researchers, however, do not have access to this data to understand the level of student satisfaction with RIF courses. Therefore, they needed to conduct their own studies to better understand the student experience and to assess

---

[5] This exit requirement discouraged more and more students from choosing uOttawa, so the central administration decided to abolish it in 1994.

Listening Component
- The listening component consists of four to six recorded listening passages which is heard twice. The test questions are all multiple-choice and are printed in the test booklet. Students mark their answers on a computer-readable "bubble" sheet. This component includes between 30 and 40 questions and lasts approximately 60–90 minutes.

Reading Component
- The reading component has two parts: a reading comprehension section and a Cloze passage. The reading comprehension section consists of four to six reading passages, which may vary in length from approximately 400 to 800 words. This section includes approximately 30 to 40 multiple-choice questions. The cloze passage consists of a passage with blanks where words have been deleted from the text. Students must choose, from multiple-choice options, the word that best fits the blank. All answers must be marked on a computer-readable "bubble" sheet. The entire Reading Component lasts approximately 60 to 90 minutes.

Writing Component
- The writing component is a written composition. Students have 50 minutes to write approximately 300 to 400 words on a specified topic of general interest. The topic is presented in such a way so as to elicit a written response relating factual information and providing opinions and/or recommendations about this information.

Speaking Component
- The speaking component is an oral interview. After an informal conversation with the interviewer, students are given a short reading passage, and are asked to discuss some of the issues raised in the passage. The interview, which is recorded, lasts between 15 and 20 minutes.

Figure 4: Description of the Second Language Certification Test
(OLBI, n.d., "Second Language ... Description")

Listening Comprehension (L) and Reading Comprehension (R) Skill Levels

L1, R1 Incomplete global comprehension.
L2, R2 Almost complete global comprehension; understands many explicit details.
L3, R3 Complete global comprehension; understands almost all explicit details.
L4, R4 Complete global comprehension; understands all explicit and implicit details.

Speaking (S) and Writing (W) Skill Levels

S1, W1 Communicates with difficulty.
S2, W2 Communicates somewhat effectively, with some imprecision.
S3, W3 Communicates effectively, with ease and minor imprecision.
S4, W4 Communicates very effectively, with ease and precision.

Figure 5: Level descriptions of the Second Language Certification Test
(OLBI, n.d., "Second Language ... Results")

the level of their students' satisfaction with this novel course format. These studies took place in 2006 (Burger, Weinberg, Hall, Movassat, & Hope, 2011) and in 2009 (Weinberg & Burger, 2010; Weinberg, Burger, & Boukacem, 2012). They analyzed the perceptions of students registered in the two levels of the adjunct courses, FLS 2581 and FLS 3581, with respect to the effectiveness of the language activities designed to improve their language skills and their learning in the content course. These studies looked at many aspects of teaching: listening, reading, speaking, writing, grammar, vocabulary acquisition, integration of new technologies, the teaching material, time spent by students in studying for these courses, assessment practices, language skills improvement, as well as global judgments of the RIF program.

The first survey instrument (Weinberg, Burger, & Hope, 2008) was adapted from a questionnaire developed by Ready and Wesche (1992) for research conducted during the 1980s on sheltered and adjunct courses (see Chapters 4 and 8). This study showed that students' reactions were generally positive and that there were no significant differences between the responses of students enrolled in the two different levels of the adjunct courses.

The student responses in this first study echoed some well-accepted educational principles; for example, that smaller class sizes were perceived as better for learning. Students also indicated that they enjoyed and learned more from activities, such as vocabulary tasks, when they saw a clear relationship between the language learning activity and the objectives of the content course. The study revealed that some students did not understand the objectives of the RIF program and considered the adjunct course attached to the content course as a tutoring session rather than as a complementary language course. Students projected this dissatisfaction onto the language instructors and criticized them for their lack of expertise in the content course.

The second study, in 2009, yielded two research publications. The first (Weinberg & Burger, 2010) was based on a qualitative methodology that surveyed 22 students enrolled in four adjunct classes, two for psychology and two for political science. These classes had very different teaching styles. The psychology class was extremely structured and included a great deal of repetition and review of the same material. Exams were multiple-choice questions. The political science class, on the other hand, was less structured and based on lectures. There was less repetition and students had to write short or long essays for course work. In focus group discussions, students in both of these courses described the different language activities in the adjunct course and provided their perceptions on how useful the activities were for mastering both the material in the content course and new language skills. The students in the four classes reported that they had been engaged in the adjunct classes in the same types of language activities based on reading, listening, writing, speaking, and vocabulary building. In general, the students enrolled in the lower-level adjunct course tended to be slightly more positive about their activities than those in the second-level adjunct courses.

Through repeated evaluations we were able to observe how the students' perception of the RIF program evolved. In the second publication on the 2009 study, Weinberg, Burger, and Boukacem (2012), further research was done, using statistical analysis. T-tests indicated that there was no significant difference over time with regard to student satisfaction about teaching vocabulary. However, results showed that FLS 3581 second-level students tended to be slightly more positive about their language courses than the FLS 2581 lower-level students—the opposite of the earlier study.

Satisfaction levels for many FLS 2581 activities were different in 2009 from those of 2006. Researchers attempted to understand whether these variations were a result of evolution in the pedagogy of the program or simply due to changes in the sampling. Student responses concerning two activities—the teaching of reading and the use of multimedia activities—differed significantly ($p = .05$) between the two periods. While there were certainly positive or negative variations in the level of satisfaction for the other activities, there were no statistically significant differences in student satisfaction between 2006 and 2009. These variations might have been due to chance.

The responses from the FLS 3581 students showed that these students were generally more satisfied with all activities than those enrolled in the lower-level adjunct course. There was no drop in the level of satisfaction for these students from one survey to the other. The teaching of reading was the most important and popular activity, followed by that of vocabulary. The responses for two components—the course in general and the teaching of reading—differed significantly between 2006 and 2009 (see Weinberg et al., 2012, for more information).

These studies helped us draw some general conclusions. We saw an overall increase in student satisfaction with adjunct courses since their introduction in 2006. However, the satisfaction of FLS 2581 students did not reach that of FLS 3581 students. This difference in attitude could be explained by various factors: the higher number of students in the FLS 2581 groups, which made these groups more heterogeneous, or simply the difficulties experienced by first-year students during their transition to university (see Chapter 6). Ready and Wesche (1992) cite other factors that may have had an impact on student satisfaction, such as the difficulty inherent in certain subjects or the perceived dysfunction of the content–language pair. Students in 2014 confirmed that these issues related to their experiences as well.

3. PROGRAM EVALUATIONS

When new programs are launched, just as it is customary to elicit student course evaluations, it is also a best practice to conduct evaluations to ensure that its goals are being met. Through the systematic collection and analysis of data, decision-makers and stakeholders can gain a better understanding of the effectiveness of the program. The RIF has been the focus of three evaluations since its creation in 2006. The first two internal studies were carried out in 2007 and 2008, at the request of the university itself. The third took place in the spring of 2014.

3.1. Internal Evaluations

In 2006, the Centre for Research on Educational and Community Services at uOttawa set up a committee to conduct a formative institutional evaluation of the RIF. This committee consisted of the RIF director, instructors from the OLBI, and a specialist in program evaluation from the Faculty of Education. The committee's mandate was to establish whether the RIF was meeting student expectations as well as fulfilling its mandate as established by the university.

In 2007, the first evaluation (Ryan, Courcelles, Hope, Buchanan, & Toews-Janzen, 2007) concluded, among other things, that the program had successfully targeted and recruited the desired population for the RIF. The records from the Registrar's Office revealed that 65% of RIF students chose to study at uOttawa specifically to take advantage of the opportunity to pursue French immersion. Furthermore, these students had higher academic qualifications (84.3% average high school marks) than students not in the RIF (81.5%). However, the evaluation report concluded that the RIF program lacked visibility and attractiveness among students already at the university. It also indicated that the program administration and implementation were satisfactory. With regards to the RIF adjunct courses, the evaluation reported that students felt these could be better. Students responded that the teaching of the adjunct courses could be improved and that the language instructors needed more training with the material in the content course. This misunderstanding among students about the role of the adjunct instructors spurred the RIF administrators to clarify program objectives and methods for students, language instructors, and faculty in the participating disciplines.

The second evaluation (Ryan, Gobeil, Hope, & Toews-Janzen, 2008), conducted the following year, focussed on the same issues. It revealed that, after changes had been made in accordance with the first report, there were improvements in student perceptions of the RIF. The report nevertheless proposed further changes to the pedagogy of the adjunct courses and suggested modifications to the communication and marketing strategies for the RIF in an effort to expand student recruitment.

3.2. External Evaluation

3.2.1. Purpose of the External Evaluation

In Canadian universities, mandated program evaluations are conducted periodically in order to verify that the objectives of programs are being met. The heads of departments are responsible for the preparation of evaluation documents which describe the strengths and weaknesses of the programs and serve as the basis for a further, objective analysis by external evaluators from other Canadian universities. The external evaluators complete their analysis with a report followed by recommendations.

These program evaluations are meant to assess the degree to which university programs succeed in the following goals (University of Ottawa, 2014, p. 3):

- achieving desired program objectives and learning outcomes
- meeting the needs of students and providing them with a university experience that lives up to their expectations
- contributing to the achievement of the mission and academic plans of the University
- providing access to human, financial, and material resources that students need, in terms of both quantity and quality
- meeting standards of viability and appropriateness

The RIF administrators began this evaluation exercise in May 2013. Various university services, such as the Student Academic Success Service (SASS) and the Registrar's Office, helped in collecting and analysing data as part of this evaluation. The evaluation also relied on data collected in 2013 and 2014 in surveys and interviews with students and immersion graduates (University of Ottawa, 2013, 2014).

3.2.2. Results

Among the results of the external evaluation was the fact that immersion students completed their university studies with greater success than Anglophone students not enrolled in RIF. Among RIF students, 72.9% had a cumulative grade point average (GPA)[6] higher than 6.0, while only 52.8% of the non-RIF English-speaking students obtained that level of academic achievement. As Table 1 makes clear, 30.3% of the RIF students had GPAs between 8.0 and 10.0, while 42.6% were between 6.0 and 7.9.

Table 1: Grade point averages for RIF and Anglophone students (University of Ottawa, 2014, p. 30)

			2012–2013	
			Immersion students	Anglophone cohort
	GPA obtained		%	%
A+	10.0	90%–100%	0.3%	0.4%
A−, A	8.0–9.0	80–84, 85–89	30.0	16.8
B, B+	6.0–7.0	70–74, 75–79	42.6	35.6
C, C+	4.0–5.0	60–64, 65–69	20.7	33.1
D, D+	2.0–3.0	50–54, 55–59	5.3	8.0
E	1.0	40–49	0.7	1.0
F	0.0	0–39	0.3	1.1

The evaluation also revealed that, six years after beginning university, three quarters of immersion students had graduated; however, only 40% of them had met the overall requirements of the RIF. In other words, they had obtained their university degree but did not graduate with the "Immersion" designation on their diploma. Students abandoned the RIF at different points during their academic careers, some even before they actually started their first year of university. Undertaking university studies is, of course, stressful, and adding the stress of studying in their second language proved to be too much for some students. Others left the RIF after a semester or a year, because they believed that their French proficiency was too low or the program too difficult. Some simply found that they didn't like the immersion experience. About one quarter of the original cohort dropped out at the beginning of their second year. Enrolment continued to decline in their third and fourth year.

---

[6] For more information on the weighted score, please consult Academic Regulation (University of Ottawa, n.d.).

Not only did students leave the program; they also took fewer courses in French as their studies progressed. The percentage of RIF students taking at least one course in French decreased, from 80% in the first year to 71% in the second year and 59% in the third year. In other words, a significant proportion of students stopped taking French courses by their third year of studies (34% fewer students) compared to the number taking a French course at the beginning of their first year (University of Ottawa, 2014, p. 30).

When students drop out of the RIF, they often do not communicate with the RIF administration. It is up to the staff to contact them and try to understand their reasons for leaving. Some students appreciated these efforts at follow-up contact, but others perceived them as annoying. Indeed, "some students admitted to having blocked the email address of the RIF to stop receiving messages from us" (University of Ottawa, 2014, p. 27). In order to understand the reasons for this phenomenon, SASS organized focus groups with immersion students. Students cited many different reasons for abandoning the RIF, but two reasons were repeated more often than others: they found the experience too difficult or demanding and they were dissatisfied with the adjunct courses. In fact, since the first evaluation of the RIF in 2007, the satisfaction rate in these adjunct courses remained low, between 60% and 70%. Students gave various explanations for their dissatisfaction (University of Ottawa, 2014, p. 35):

- The course focusses too much on grammar and not enough on the discipline, or, to the contrary, the course focusses too much on the discipline and not enough on grammar.
- There is more work in the adjunct course than in the content course.
- The professor does not want to talk about the discipline and looks only at the language elements encountered in the readings.
- The adjunct course is boring because the activities are repetitive or too easy.
- The activities and materials used in the adjunct course do not come from the content course.
- The adjunct course is unstructured or poorly organized.
- The discipline instructor is not receptive to difficulties second language students face.

Another reason why students left the RIF was the concern that they could no longer use the Pass/Fail option for French content courses in their third year (see Chapter 6). They were afraid of lowering their GPA and thus compromising their opportunities to pursue graduate studies.

The SASS undertook a study (Daoust & Durepos, 2016) to measure the impact of adjunct courses on student success by comparing outcomes of Anglophone students enrolled in adjunct courses to those of Anglophone students enrolled only in the content course. The study showed that students taking the adjunct course with the content course earned higher marks in the content course than those who had not. In addition, students enrolled in the RIF had higher university graduation rates than other

Anglophone students. Six years after entering university (spanning the cohort years from 2007 till 2014), 81% of RIF students had graduated, compared to 69% for the English cohort.

Even though many students abandoned the RIF, not all of them abandoned their efforts to improve their French language. Nearly 20% of the students who left the RIF demonstrated their interest in learning or maintaining their knowledge of French by enrolling in FSL classes or even in content courses taught in French during the rest of their studies. Those students who graduated with the "Immersion" designation on their diplomas were positive about their RIF experiences. When asked about the impact that immersion had or continued to have on them, the students responded that the RIF helped develop their self-esteem, strengthen problem-solving skills, and create new personal contacts. More than 85% of them acknowledged that their bilingualism had had a positive effect on their career, whereas only 50% of the non-RIF graduates made the same assertion. Finally, 93% of RIF graduates said that they would recommend immersion studies, and even 69% of those who did not graduate with the "Immersion" designation said they would recommend it. Figure 6 summarizes the positive responses[7] students made about the impact of the RIF in their lives.

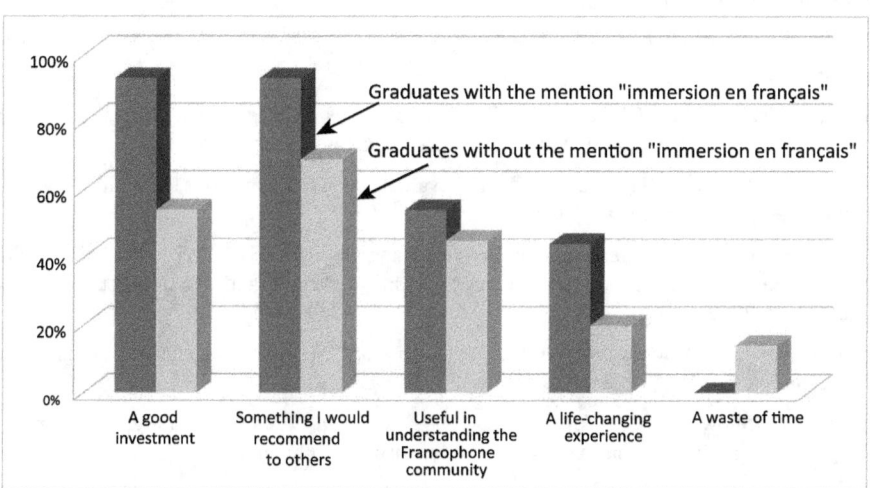

Figure 6: Comparison of the impact of immersion on graduates with and without the "Immersion" designation on their diplomas (University of Ottawa, 2014, p. 30)

CONCLUSION

This chapter has discussed the various ways in which assessment and evaluation have been used in the *Régime d'immersion en français*. We began by explaining how student assessment is handled in the RIF. Such assessments are a normal aspect of university courses but, because the RIF lies at the intersection of content and language, the task is

---

[7] A positive response is defined as choosing a value of either 4 or 5 on a 5-point Likert-type scale.

more complex. The complexity arises mainly because the content and language instructors take responsibility for different parts of test domains — specifically, the language instructor must take care to avoid testing knowledge of the content. Furthermore, the content instructors must accept that the language level of the non-French students is weaker than the language level of Francophone students — although this is not a severe problem since students have the option of submitting all their assignments and tests in English.

Collecting information from students about their experiences in immersion courses has been another way in which evaluation is used in the RIF. Student surveys and interviews organized by program administrators have allowed the RIF staff to better understand teaching practices, with the view to improving course design and quality of teaching.

Finally, university administrators have collected evaluation data to assess the degree to which the RIF is meeting program and university objectives. The information gathered can also help the university to promote one of its flagship programs and recruit students.

This model of how assessment and evaluation is approached in the RIF at uOttawa can help to raise issues and serve as a framework for other institutions wishing to implement an immersion program.

REFERENCES

Alliance française. (n.d.). DELF-DALF: Diplôme d'études en langue française et Diplôme approfondi de langue française. www.af.ca/ottawa/tests_et_examens/delf-dalf/

Alliance française. (n.d.). TEF Canada: Test d'Évaluation de Français pour le Canada. www.af.ca/ottawa/tests_et_examens/tef-canada/

American Council on the Teaching of Foreign Languages (ACTFL). (2012). ACTFL Proficiency Guidelines 2012. www.actfl.org/publications/guidelines-and-manuals/actfl-proficiency-guidelines-2012

Banon-Schirman, P., & Makardidjian, C. (2006). Un outil controversé d'une standardisation européenne: le portfolio des langues. *Synergies Europe, 1*, 110–117.

Brinton, D.M., Snow, M.A., & Wesche, M.B. (2003). *Content-based second language instruction.* Michigan Classics Edition. Ann Arbor: University of Michigan Press.

Buchanan, C. (2014). *The influence of the Common European Framework of Reference (CEFR) on French as a Second Language (FSL) teaching methodologies in primary and secondary schools in British Columbia and on the preparation for the Diplôme d'études en langue française (DELF).* Internal report. Ottawa: University of Ottawa, Official Languages and Bilingualism Institute (OLBI).

Burger, S., Weinberg, A., Hall, C., Movassat, P., & Hope, A. (2011). French immersion studies at the University of Ottawa: Program evaluation and pedagogical challenges. In T. Fortune, D. Tedick, & D. Christian (Eds.), *Immersion education: Pathways to bilingualism and beyond* (123–142). Clevedon: Multilingual Matters.

Council of Europe. (2001). Common European Framework of Reference for Languages: Learning, teaching, assessment (CEFR). www.coe.int/en/web/common-european-framework-reference-languages

Daoust J.L., & Durepos, J. (2016). *Programme de mentorat/Mentoring program: Rétention et expérience étudiante*. Internal document, French Immersion Studies [Régime d'immersion en français], University of Ottawa.

Hall C., Movassat, P., & Hope, A. (2008, October). *Testing receptive language in immersion courses*. Paper presented at the meeting *Tailoring language support to university content courses*, at the CARLA–CAL symposium, St. Paul, MN. [CARLA = Center for Advanced Research on Language Acquisition, CAL = Center for Applied Linguistics]

Hope, A. (2006). Testing receptive skills in immersion courses — Slides 4 and 5. In A. Weinberg & S. Burger (Eds.), *Guide à l'intention des professeurs de langue — cours d'immersion*. Internal document. University of Ottawa: Official Languages and Bilingualism Institute (OLBI).

Knoerr, H. (2010). L'immersion au niveau universitaire: nouveaux modèles, nouveaux défis, pratiques et stratégies. *OLBI Working Papers, 1*, 89–110.

Laurier, M., Tousignant, R., & Morissette, D. (2005). *Les principes de la mesure et de l'évaluation des apprentissages*. Montréal: Gaëtan Morin.

Nagy, P. (2000). The three roles of assessment: Gatekeeping, accountability, and instructional diagnosis. *Revue canadienne de l'éducation, 25*, 262–279.

Official Languages and Bilingualism Institute (OLBI). (n.d.). Second Language Certification: Final Exam: Description. olbi.uottawa.ca/programs/register-credit-course/second-language-credit-courses

Official Languages and Bilingualism Institute (OLBI). (n.d.). Second Language Certification: Final Exam: Results. olbi.uottawa.ca/programs/register-credit-course/second-language-credit-courses

Official Languages and Bilingualism Institute (OLBI). (n.d.). Test de pratique. Ottawa: University of Ottawa, Service d'évaluation linguistique à L2 test. fsl3500.wordpress.com/test-de-pratique

Ready, D., & Wesche, M. (1992). An evaluation of the University of Ottawa sheltered program: Language teaching strategies that work. In R.J. Courchesne, J.I. Glidden, J. St. John, & C. Thérien (Eds.), *L'enseignement des langues secondes axé sur la compréhension* (pp. 389–405). Ottawa: University of Ottawa Press.

Ryan, W., Courcelles, P., Hope, A., Buchanan, C., & Toews-Janzen, M. (2007). *Evaluation of the French immersion studies academic stream: Year 1*. Internal document. Ottawa: University of Ottawa, Centre for Research on Educational and Community Services (CRECS).

Ryan, W., Gobeil, M., Hope, A., & Toews-Janzen, M. (2008). *Evaluation of the French immersion studies academic stream: Year 2*. Internal document. Ottawa: University of Ottawa, Centre for Research on Educational and Community Services (CRECS).

University of Ottawa. (n.d.). Administration and Governance: Academic regulation I-10 — Grading system. www.uottawa.ca/administration-and-governance/academic-regulation-10-grading-system

University of Ottawa. (1974). Regulation on Bilingualism at University of Ottawa 1974. www.uottawa.ca/administration-and-governance/policies-and-regulations/regulation-on-bilingualism

University of Ottawa. (2013). *Régime d'immersion: sondage des diplômés*. Internal document. Ottawa: University of Ottawa.

University of Ottawa. (2014). *Évaulation périodique. Régime d'immersion en français: Le rapport d'auto-évaluation*. Unpublished internal document. Printemps 2014. University of Ottawa.

Weinberg, A. (2012). Examen de fin de session. FLS 2581 H3.

Weinberg, A. (2013). Examen de fin de session. FLS 3581 H3.

Weinberg, A., & Burger, S. (2010). University level immersion: Students' perceptions of language activities. *OLBI Working Papers*, *1*, 111–142.

Weinberg, A., Burger, S., & Boukacem, D. (2012). Trois ans plus tard: comment les étudiants évaluent-ils le Régime d'immersion en français de l'Université d'Ottawa? *OLBI Working Papers*, *4*, 55–77.

Weinberg, A., Burger, S., & Hope, A. (2008). Evaluating the effectiveness of content-based language teaching. *TESL Ontario: Contact Research Symposium Issue*, *34*(2), 68–80. www.teslontario.org/uploads/publications/researchsymposium/ResearchSymposium2008.pdf

CHAPTER 11

Training Modalities for Immersion Stakeholders

Catherine Elena Buchanan, Hélène Knoerr, and Sandra Burger

INTRODUCTION

THE PREVIOUS CHAPTERS have outlined the administrative, didactic, and pedagogical characteristics of the *Régime d'immersion en français* (RIF) of the University of Ottawa (uOttawa), highlighting its many innovative and unprecedented features. Any new initiative, by definition, requires appropriate training to guarantee that the approach and means of implementing it will be understood by participants and will therefore succeed. In this chapter, the elements of training within the framework of the RIF will be described for each of its players: administrators, language and content instructors, and students. The initial training model implemented by the RIF will be presented through its evolution, including the challenges it has faced. Other institutions' training for the immersion approach will also be examined and options will be proposed for the RIF. Finally, a series of recommendations will be put forth for effective training for French immersion at the university level.

The immersion approach at uOttawa is described in detail in Chapter 8 of the present book. It can be summarized as follows: a content course which Anglophone students take in French with Francophone students is paired with an adjunct language course (ALC) reserved for those Anglophones students and taught by a language instructor. It is designed to help students understand the subject matter and to improve their second language skills in oral and written comprehension and production. The language instructor creates pedagogical activities based on the material of the content course with the help of different aids: audio and video recordings, Powerpoint slides, graphs and tables, research articles, or course textbooks. Written and oral expression activities are those typical of an academic context: paragraph structure, specialized vocabulary, reading notes, summaries, paper or essay preparation, as well as presentations and debates based either on topics covered in a moderated discussion group or on extracts from the readings assigned by the content instructor. The ALC only deals with grammar in context and only in order to address difficulties encountered in the content course documents. For the ALC, assessment is based on language in context and not on the subject matter of the content course (see Chapter 10).

Immersion teaching, therefore, requires a particular methodology, different from that of traditional foreign language teaching. Instructors must be flexible, open-minded, and creative, capable of adapting quickly and prepared to address the particular vocabulary of a discipline and the linguistic issues arising from a written or oral document, so they can create original pedagogical material tailored to the discipline and the course. However, the typical training of language instructors does not teach this approach or prepare them to respond to the particular requirements of an ALC.

But language instructors are not the only ones in need of training for this novel approach — all the other stakeholders in immersion also require it:

- Although the RIF is offered in over eighty programs at uOttawa, *administrators* are rarely aware of its existence, let alone of its characteristics. They are therefore not in a position to advise students appropriately. Furthermore, as the former Provost and Vice-President, Academic Affairs (see Chapter 2) pointed out, the deans of faculties do not value the importance of the RIF for uOttawa and do not necessarily make an effort to include or to accommodate immersion in their programs.
- As for the *content instructors*, unless they have been in direct contact with language instructors, they have not had the chance to hear about the RIF. Although most of them are permanent professors, native speakers, with extensive teaching experience, more and more are part-time, doctoral students, or research assistants teaching a course for the first time that has been designated as "Immersion." They are not always used to having Anglophone students, let alone a peer instructor, in their classroom.
- And finally, the *students* are accustomed to traditional second language courses or to French immersion where the subject is taught in the second language by a single instructor. Thus, they do not necessarily understand the specific purpose of the ALCs: some consider it a tutorial for the content course. They do not necessarily see the ALC for what it is: a language course, in and of itself, linked to a particular content course.

The structure of the RIF was envisioned by François Houle, based on university immersion models previously in place at uOttawa. However, its current incarnation is new and no training model for this immersion approach was planned when the RIF was first launched (see Chapter 2). This was built *ipso facto* in the field, tapping into the expertise of different sectors of the Official Languages and Bilingualism Institute (OLBI).[1]

1. INITIAL TRAINING OF THE DIFFERENT RIF STAKEHOLDERS

1.1. Administrators

The RIF director[2] is responsible for all aspects of the implementation of the RIF: communications, coordination, and promotion of the RIF to an audience that ranges from content instructors and various faculties of uOttawa, language instructors, and students, to schools both across the country and abroad. Because his position is that of an administrator, the director delegates the responsibility for pedagogical coordination to regular full-time language instructors from the OLBI.

---

[1] The OLBI has been in existence for 10 years (since 2008), successor to the Second Language Institute (SLI), in operation for 40 years before that.
[2] This position is not attached to the OLBI or the Faculty of Arts, but is directly linked to the central administration, through the vice-president (see Chapter 2).

1.2. Content Instructors

All content instructors in tenure-track positions hold a doctorate and have a strong research record. Excellence in teaching is usually optional. Bilingualism (at least passive) is a condition for obtaining tenure. A sampling of current (2019) position descriptions reflects these points (University of Ottawa, n.d., "Office of the Provost").

These are, for example, the requirements for a position in the Department of Mathematics and Statistics:

> Science — Tenure-track position in Mathematics
> **Skills requirements:**
> **Education:** PhD or equivalent in Mathematics.
> **Work experience:** We are seeking candidates with a proven record of research excellence, who can teach at undergraduate and graduate levels, and who have the desire and ability to supervise graduate students. The position is open to all research areas of Mathematics.

Similarly, for the Faculty of Education:

> Faculty of Education — Tenure-track position — Indigenous Education
> **Education:** PhD in Education or equivalent in a field related to the position.
> **Work experience:** A demonstrated excellent track record of research in Indigenous Education in collaboration with Indigenous communities in Canada. A demonstrated ability to teach at the undergraduate and/or graduate levels in a context of interdisciplinary collaboration. Ability to teach hybrid and on-line courses. Passive knowledge of the other official language in Canada is a requirement for tenure. Active knowledge of both official languages is an asset.

Only in the Telfer School of Management is the quality of teaching highlighted:

> Telfer — Tenure-track Assistant or Associate position with Telfer School of Management
> **Skills requirements:**
> **Education:** PhD (or ABD) in Finance or Economics.
> **Work experience:**
> - Commensurate with rank and experience, a high-potential program of research in Finance; for candidates applying at the Associate rank, the quality of the research program must be demonstrated by articles published in high quality peer-reviewed journals; Members of the finance faculty have recently published in premier finance and accounting journals including Contemporary Accounting Research, Journal of Financial Economics, Journal of Financial and Quantitative Analysis, Management Science, Review of Accounting Studies, and Journal of Business venturing.
> - Strong teaching competency at the undergraduate, professional (MBA/EMBA) and Masters and/or PhD levels as demonstrated by past teaching evaluations and a presentation given to faculty members and students if invited for an interview;

- Applicants appointed at the Associate Professor level with experience in graduate student supervision are preferred;
- Ability to define, lead, manage and attract funds for internationally recognized excellent research.

For part-time instructors, the only requirements are the diploma (typically a master's degree or equivalent) or teaching experience — but what matters most is seniority, as defined by the union of the part-time instructors at uOttawa.

1.3. Language Instructors

All ALCs are taught by OLBI instructors with either academic or language teacher status:

- Academic rank instructors (at the adjunct and associate levels) have the same requirements for hiring as content instructors. That is, they hold a doctorate in second language teaching (SLT), in applied linguistics, or in a related discipline; a solid research record; and at least two years' teaching experience in a post-secondary institution.
- The status of language instructor is deemed "non-academic". At the time of their hiring at the OLBI, instructors in tenure-track positions hold at least a master's degree in SLT,[3] in applied linguistics, or in a related discipline, and have at least two years' teaching experience in a post-secondary institution.

These two types of instructors are generally trained to teach traditional FSL (French as a second language) courses but are not familiar with the particular characteristics of the approach adopted by the RIF.

Since there are not enough tenured faculty to teach all the ALCs, the OLBI calls upon part-time instructors who hold at least a master's (preferably in SLT). However, the urgency of the need sometimes forces the administration to relax its hiring criteria and accept either a specialized diploma in a different discipline (translation, or the discipline to which the ALC will be matched), or professional experience judged to be equivalent to a master's. But here again, it is the seniority criterion that prevails. These instructors, therefore, do not necessarily have training in SLT and if they do, that training does not include the particular features of the RIF's approach of immersion.

Finally, some part-time instructors may come from secondary or elementary school immersion programs in which the disciplinary content is taught in French following the sheltered model approach (see Chapter 4). Again, if they are trained in this type of immersion, it is quite different from the adjunct model implemented in the RIF.

1.4. Students

As seen, Canadian students have all taken FSL, to a varying extent, during their primary or secondary education.[4] But that approach is different since instructors teach the

---

[3] Language instructors [level] III hold a master's degree; language instructors [level] IV hold a doctorate.

[4] For a detailed description of the various immersion pathways in Canada, see Chapter 1.

content in French. Also, because of the shortage of qualified native speakers of French among FLS instructors, there is no guarantee that instructors will be Francophones, especially in Western Canada. Additionally, the quantity and quality of French used in the classes may vary. Thus, students are used to studying in French but not necessarily French in and of itself. In contrast, the RIF approach differentiates the linguistic aspect from the disciplinary aspect, and explicitly emphasizes the forms of language as an object of study — at least in the advanced levels of ALCs. This, therefore, constitutes a completely new experience, for which the students may not be prepared.

2. MODELS AND ELEMENTS OF TRAINING

In 1985, twenty years after the beginning of immersion in Saint-Lambert, the founder of the Canadian Association of Immersion Professionals (CAIP), André Obadia, deplored the absence of proper immersion training in teacher programs in Canada:

> The situation is quite sad. Like school boards in their early days, the faculties of education tried to respond hastily to the needs and the growing number of immersion teachers. Improvisation and anomalous programs are inevitable (Coulombe, 1983; Obadia, 1984). Sixteen faculties out of 47 propose some training in immersion and the majority of them generally offer a course in addition to the traditional teacher training. In other words, in the vast majority of cases, particularly in most Eastern [Canadian] universities, the training of immersion teachers is considered to be additional specialized training. It is placed on the same footing as training for children with special needs or teaching music, for example. In short, it is one or two courses — often given in the summer, and sometimes leading to a certificate — that constitute the immersion teacher's training. The temporary solutions seem to have been permanent. We don't yet seem to have succeeded in giving immersion a life of its own or on a conceptual and philosophical level in identifying the Canadian pedagogical phenomenon. (1985, p. 416 [trans.])

Obadia then proposed a model for immersion-specific training (Figure 1). Twenty years later, CAIP published a review of teacher education programs in Canada (Karsenti & Dumouchel, 2006). Only 20 of the 58 universities offered some kind of option in FSL or in immersion, always as "additional specialized training" that consisted of "one or two courses," as mentioned by Obadia, above (1985, p. 416 [trans.]).

Today, the offerings are hardly better — they typically never go beyond one or two courses in the entire training of a future instructor at the primary or secondary level. The B.Ed. — *Français langue seconde* at the University of Prince Edward Island is the only one with two mandatory courses on immersion:

- ED 4800 *L'enseignement dans les contextes de l'immersion en français, du français de base et du français langue première en milieu minoritaire* (but not exclusively in immersion contexts, since it also deals with Core French and minority language contexts)
- ED 4900 *L'intégration de la langue au contenu*, the only course dealing with integrating language and content (University of Prince Edward Island, n.d.).

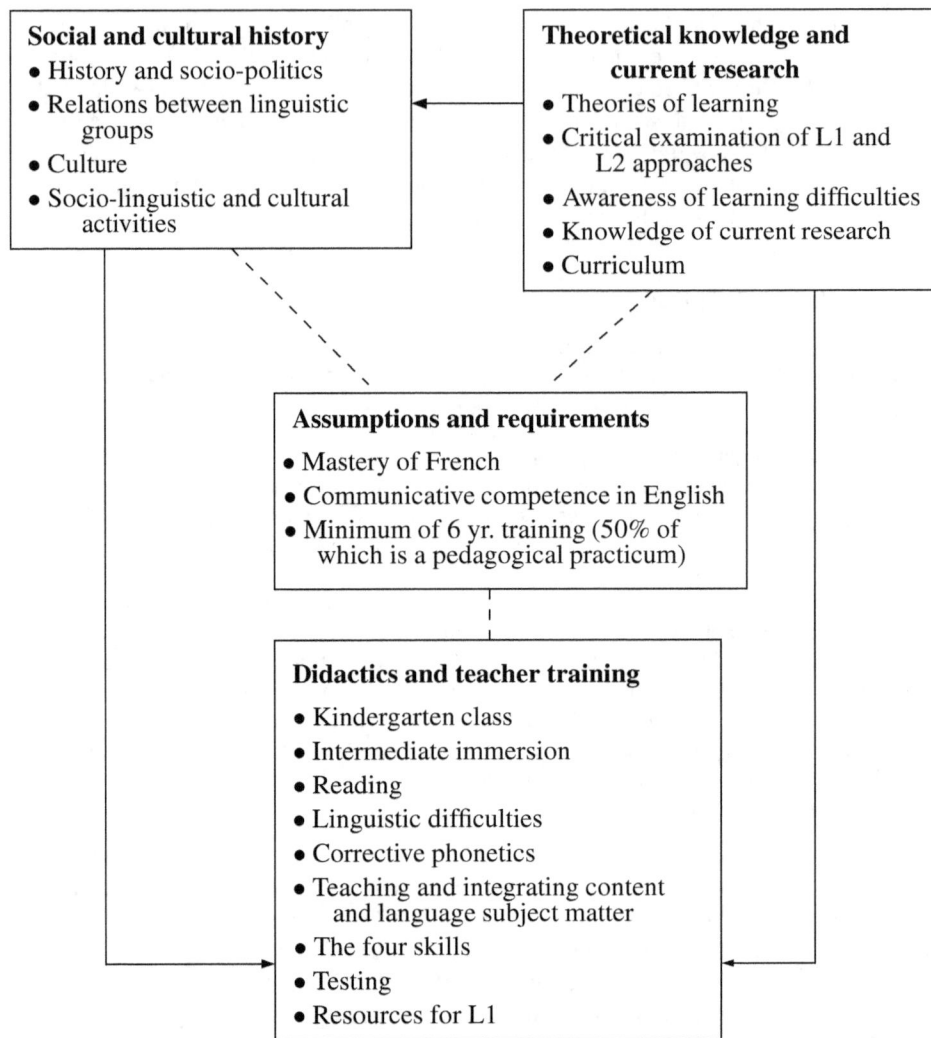

Figure 1: Schematic representation of the main components of immersion instructor training program (Obadia, 1985, p. 422 [trans.])

For other B.Ed. programs, language training is optional. Some courses on language acquisition and on immersion school settings are offered. Student teachers also have the option to do their practicum in immersion schools:

- At uOttawa, the course DLS 3502 *Immersion française* consists of the following elements: History of the implementation of French immersion. Study of different types of French immersion programs, the principal research findings, the methodology, pedagogical material, and testing techniques [trans.].

- The Université du Québec à Montréal (UQAM) offers DDL 1251 *Didactique du français langue seconde : immersion française*, an introduction to the guiding principles of immersion and to the objectives and content of immersion classes in primary schools (UQAM, n.d.).
- At the Université de Saint-Boniface (Manitoba), the former course EDUB 3261 *L'acquisition et l'apprentissage du français en contexte d'immersion*, described as a "[t]heoretical course. Familiarization with second language acquisition and learning theories and its pedagogical approaches" (Karsenti & Dumouchel, 2006, p. 50 [trans.]), has been replaced by a more general course, EDUA 3993 *Éducation française en contextes minoritaire et d'immersion*, again bundling immersion with minority language education (Université de Saint-Boniface, n.d. [trans.]).
- At the Université Sainte-Anne (Nova Scotia), the course PEDA 3303 *Immersion en français langue seconde — approche pédagogique et didactique* is a

    > course based on the needs of teachers who must implement and successfully manage French immersion in a public school. The course introduces teachers to the main variations of French immersion. The course explores contributions of psychology and linguistics to the teaching of French as a second language. (Karsenti & Dumouchel, 2006, p. 56 [trans.])

- In Quebec, the Université Laval offers DID-3961 *Didactique du français (accueil et immersion)*, which presents the fundamental principles of immersion and the integration of language and content, as well as the basics of teaching in pluriethnic contexts (*classes d'accueil*, bridging classes for newcomers to Canada) (Université Laval, n.d.).
- McGill University used to offer Teaching French as a Second Language (TFSL), a joint program with the Université de Montréal (120 credits), with an optional 3-credit course on immersion teaching (EDSL 345). This program is no longer available, but students may enrol in a 15-credit *Certificat d'études supérieures en pédagogie de l'immersion française (Cert. ed. sup.) pédagogie de l'immersion française* [Certificate in Immersion Pedagogy] (McGill University, n.d.).

Still, as incomplete as these training programs for primary and secondary immersion teaching may be, at least they do exist. In contrast, there is simply no training available for post-secondary immersion teaching.

2.1. Language Instructors

2.1.1. Pedagogical Advisors

The first two pedagogical advisors had already participated actively in immersion experiments conducted by what was then the Second Language Institute (SLI) and thus had both theoretical and practical knowledge in this field. From the outset of the RIF, they were able to set up training in the form of both collective and individual pedagogical interventions. Their functions can be summarized as follows (Weinberg & Burger, 2007, p. 41):

- provide initial training
- facilitate collaboration between instructors (ALC and content)
- advise ALC instructors during the term
- organize an end-of-term meeting
- visit each ALC and all content courses once
- propose the selection of immersion courses for the following years
- tape content and language courses

For the first terms of the RIF, toward the end of August, the pedagogical advisors organized workshops. This training consisted of several aspects, particularly the adjunct teaching model, communication with the content instructor, assessment in ALC, and resource materials. These sessions began with a general briefing on the unique model of immersion teaching and the learning of FSL, followed by practical workshops on a particular theme.

Although optional, these training sessions were extremely popular initially. All instructors who had to teach ALCs, including part-timers, attended.[5] Certain instructors with a strong background teaching previous immersion courses led the round table discussions. The training sessions provided practical advice for the classroom as well as a wide range of tools for the term to come.

Over time, participation in these meetings dwindled. At the moment, the remaining sessions are part of the pre-term meetings set up for all language instructors of FSL and ESL courses at the OLBI. They are more oriented toward administrative matters than pedagogical or methodological issues: the Virtual Campus,[6] course outlines, workshops for students (using the Antidote software,[7] note-taking), and the resources available on campus (Academic Writing Help Centre, immersion mentors, etc.). With respect to the RIF language instructors, all information that used to be provided by the pedagogical advisors is now on the Virtual Campus:

- the Toolkit for language instructors (the information comes from the *Guide à l'intention des professeurs de langue*; see next section)
- templates of ALC course syllabi (including objectives, resources and assessment)
- descriptors of the four levels of adjunct language courses
- a summary of the pedagogical approach
- examples of term planning and diagnostic tests
- a list of computerized and paper resources available at the Julien Couture Resource Centre (University of Ottawa, n.d., "OLBI")

Only new instructors are invited to individual training meetings before and during the term.

---

[5] They were paid $50 in compensation.
[6] The Learning Management System used at uOttawa.
[7] Antidote 10 is a one-stop, multi-resource platform that is useful to anyone writing in French or English (Druide, 2018).

2.1.1.1. Guides for language instructors: The first *Guide à l'intention des professeurs de langue — Cours d'immersion* (Weinberg & Burger, 2006) was prepared by the pedagogical advisors, and appeared at the launching of the RIF in the fall of 2006. The first page listed the names of the advisors, their contact information, and a general outline of their duties. A second page gave instructors general administrative information (definition of functions, important dates, services available at the university). Then the guide presented:

- a chart showing the four levels of ALCs (see Chapter 8), allowing language instructors to situate themselves within the model and to understand the linguistic path of the learner
- the characteristics of content courses and ALCs
- template and examples of course outlines
- examples of pedagogical activities and assessment grids for receptive and productive skills
- two publications about assessment and reinforcing receptive skills in the context of ALC
- on-line resources
- a bibliography
- seven articles about different components of university immersion methodology

This guide offered language instructors valuable information and an overview of current and past best practices in the RIF. It included research on previous immersion models at uOttawa, with the intent to give language instructors the theoretical and methodological foundations underlying the pedagogical practices of the program. A second edition was developed the following fall (Weinberg & Burger, 2007). It was quite similar to the first, but new sections were added on resources for students and two publications by language instructors (one on understanding a content course for FSL students, the other on teaching and evaluating reading in a content course). These guides were intended to ease the burden of getting on-the-job training through classroom teaching and consultations with colleagues from various backgrounds.

In 2010, a new pedagogical advisor published a third *Guide du professeur de langue* (Dansereau, 2010). This guide was quite similar to the first two; however, the research and methodological parts were eliminated and there were no publications describing the theoretical foundations of the immersion approach employed by the RIF. It took a purely practical approach — the RIF, the actors, the organizational chart, the descriptors of ALC levels, the pedagogical approach, assessment, samples of course outlines, and practical information such as virtual resources — but it did not give language instructors the rationale for the adjunct approach[8] they were being asked to put into place.

All language instructors received this guide — a paper copy was distributed to new language instructors and an electronic version was available on the Virtual Campus.

---

[8] Only a bibliographical list was included.

> Teaching FSL in the context of the RIF at uOttawa: What you should keep in mind...
> 1. ALCs are different from regular FSL courses.
> 2. The role of the language instructor is to encourage the development of second language skills which will facilitate the comprehension of the content course (FLS 2581) or allow students to express themselves with ease about the material in a discipline course (FLS 3581, FLS 4581 and FLS 4781).
> 3. The language instructor will not provide any explanation or information on the content of the discipline course.
> 4. All activities in the ALC will take place in the context of the course content.
> 5. The language instructor will be required to develop their own material to meet the objectives of the course.
> 6. The language instructor will propose activities in which the context and tasks will be meaningful for students.
> 7. The language instructor will prioritize the documents (textbooks, collections of readings, videos, etc.) used in the content course.
> 8. The teaching of grammar is not a specific objective of ALCs.
> 9. The instructor will assess language and not content (of the discipline course).
> 10. Good collaboration between the content and the language instructors will contribute to the success of the immersion program.

Figure 2: Language instructor guide (Dansereau, 2010, p. 1 [trans.])

Currently, the pedagogical training for language instructors depends entirely on their own initiative. Figure 2 presents an overview of the teaching principles.

2.1.1.2. Classroom observations: When the RIF began, the pedagogical advisors acted as mentors for language instructors. They had experience teaching ALCs and were familiar with the particular learning context of a given discipline since they had already taught the first immersion courses offered before the creation of the RIF (see Chapter 8). For the first three years of the RIF, their mandate was to visit each content course and each ALC at least once each term. The goal of these observations was to offer tailored training, pedagogical feedback, and in-depth dialogue with the language instructors. Thus, pedagogical advisors were able to establish an atmosphere of trust with the language instructors and explore the best pedagogical practices for a specific ALC. These observations were suspended when a complaint was lodged by a part-time instructor with their union; they have not resumed since (unless instructors request them). Today, although meetings with the pedagogical advisors are still possible, they are not obligatory and are rarely requested by the language instructors.

It should be noted, however, that there was never any intervention with the content instructors.

2.1.1.3. Follow-up meetings: During the first years of the RIF, meetings organized by the pedagogical advisors took place during the term. The director of the RIF, the head of language assessment, and full-time and part-time language instructors were invited. The theme of these meetings varied, according to the pedagogical needs identified by the actors: for example, assessment of aural and reading comprehension skills, sharing of audiovisual resources dealing with listening comprehension, or the use of the Antidote software.

These workshops were great training opportunities because all instructors could speak freely of their pedagogical successes as well as the challenges they faced. The outcome of these exchanges allowed everyone to feel confident and proud of their teaching, because they could, in this safe place, interact with colleagues who were experiencing the same issues in the classroom.

This careful administrative follow-up guaranteed not only that everyone was on the same page, but that all language instructors received training. Nevertheless, the rhythm of these meetings has not been maintained over the years and professional follow-up of new instructors has unfortunately disappeared.

2.1.1.4. Training DVD: A first DVD, *L'immersion, une solution miracle* (Burger & Weinberg, 2006), was created by the pedagogical advisors of the time. It includes four sections:

- an overview: a brief summary of the structure of immersion courses, with a clear description of the courses and their syllabi. The theoretical foundation, in particular Krashen's main contribution,[9] is also explained.
- the content course and its ideal instructor: the course planning must be transparent, the instructor should reformulate concepts in several ways, use different aids, and be a good language model, providing rich and varied input. The ideal instructor should have strong pedagogical training and be attentive to the needs of students while remaining flexible.
- the ALC and its language instructors: these same characteristics are expected from language instructors, in addition to their ability to adapt to the framework of a given discipline.
- student and instructor testimonials

This DVD was filmed in an authentic classroom situation where language instructors teach and students work on the language. It features activities on different skills and oral presentations by some students.

2.1.1.5. Handbooks of pedagogical activities: Unlike a traditional second language class, in an ALC language instructors cannot rely on a French-language textbook. They must create all activities and assessment schemes based on the material in the content course to foster language development. All classroom activities have to be developed on the spot.

The pedagogical advisors launched an initiative to compile collections of pedagogical activities for the first two levels of ALCs, namely receptive and expressive skills.

---

[9] For a description of Krashen's theory, in particular the theoretical foundations which form the basis of the RIF approach, see Chapter 3.

A call was made to experienced colleagues to bring together their best ALC activities paired to their respective disciplines and content courses. Two handbooks (*recueils d'activités*) were produced: two editions of *Comprendre un cours de discipline suivi en langue seconde* (Dansereau & Buchanan, 2009, 2011) and *S'exprimer en langue seconde dans le contexte d'un cours de discipline universitaire* (Dansereau, 2011). The featured activities, which had proven their worth in the classroom, still serve to this day as a model to be followed or adapted for a given content course. Language instructors receive a copy of these handbooks at the beginning of each academic year.

2.1.2. Language Assessment at the OLBI

Assessment in the context of an ALC presented many challenges for language instructors in the first years of the RIF. In the absence of models to follow, the pedagogical advisors called on the expertise of the director of the OLBI's language assessment sector. She proposed a variety of model activities that assessed targeted language objectives as part of disciplinary content. Indeed, one of the main challenges of ALCs is to evaluate language as linguistic content, not as the disciplinary knowledge conveyed by it. Designing assessment activities is like walking a tightrope, since the boundaries between language and content are blurred. Fortunately, the language assessment director has guided a large number of language instructors through this exercise. In addition, the sector archived all the evaluations that had been developed in the ALCs. A bank of exams has been built up over the years, and new and experienced instructors can consult them on site and use them as inspiration for their courses. Finally, the director provided consulting services to all instructors to ensure that their assessments measure language knowledge rather than the disciplinary content.

Another DVD, *Testing receptive skills in immersion courses* (University of Ottawa, n.d.), was also created, based on a presentation given by OLBI's director for language assessment. She developed training on the assessment of receptive skills in the context of an ALC in which the language instructors were asked to distinguish between assessing language and assessing disciplinary content. The director demonstrated the nuances of these exercises through diverse hands-on activities.

Then, still in the early years of the RIF, a collection of thirteen DVDs was produced by the pedagogical advisors for training purposes for RIF learners and instructors (Burger, 2006). Thirteen content instructors who personified the "ideal" instructor for an immersion course were filmed: as good instructors and communicators, in addition to taking into account their audience, they reformulated key concepts.

These practical training tools aimed, among other things, to facilitate the understanding of the content course while encouraging learners to gain confidence in their language skills. Unfortunately, these DVDs are not known to current staff and instructors, since they are tucked away in a corner of the Julien Couture Resource Centre.

2.1.3. The Julien Couture Resource Centre

The Julien Couture Resource Centre (JCRC) is an integral part of the OLBI. Situated on the ground floor, it comprises two sections, one for students and one for instructors. It is attended by undergraduate and graduate students and faculty in general. The centre has a rich and varied collection composed of a range of methods for French as a second/foreign language and English as a second/foreign language; scientific journals and books on various aspects of language didactics; foreign language acquisition; linguistics and education.

The Julien Couture Resource Centre has devoted a section to the different components of university immersion. This designated collection has grown over the years and continues to expand. It includes:

- content course textbooks and related material[10]
- research articles on the different elements of university immersion approaches
- syllabi from previous sessions (ALC and content courses)
- the collection of thirteen DVDs of lectures from various disciplines: sociology, geography, management, history, etc.
- audio recordings of lectures made by language instructors
- the DVDs described earlier, regarding immersion and the testing of receptive skills
- the three editions of the *Guide à l'intention des professeurs de langue* (Dansereau, 2010; Weinberg & Burger, 2006, 2007)
- all handbooks (Dansereau, 2011; Dansereau & Buchanan, 2009, 2011)

In addition, the large front window of the JCRC, which looks out onto a busy hallway, displays the latest research publications of the teaching staff of OLBI, some of which concern the RIF and its current endeavours (Knoerr, Weinberg, & Gohard-Radenkovic, 2016; Knoerr, Weinberg, & Buchanan, 2018a).

2.1.4. Conferences

In 2011–2012, the RIF celebrated its fifth anniversary by organizing two events. The first, a roundtable entitled *Plein feux sur l'immersion!*, organized by Alysse Weinberg, highlighted the successes and challenges of former and current students of the RIF (uOttawaImmersion, 2011). The second, a research forum entitled *Immersion at the university level: Models, challenges and prospects*, organized by Hélène Knoerr and Alysse Weinberg, focused on research undertaken on post-secondary immersion models in North America and in Europe (CCERBAL, 2012). It was composed of four main sessions: i) Immersion models, ii) Stakeholders in FIS at uOttawa, iii) Issues and research, and iv) Perspectives. These sessions were chaired by experts and stakeholders, all working in a university immersion model. A special issue of the *OLBI Working Papers* was devoted to it (Knoerr & Weinberg, 2013).

In 2017, an international symposium was held, marking the 10th anniversary of the RIF and ten years of French immersion studies at uOttawa. The event looked at different aspects of university-level immersion programs in Europe, the United States, and

---

[10] These can be used to create materials or exams, as their content is directly related to the content of the discipline course.

Canada. The plenary presentations and the thematic roundtables were published as full papers in Knoerr, Weinberg, and Buchanan (2018a), and the individual papers appear in a thematic issue of the *OLBI Working Papers* (Knoerr, Weinberg, & Buchanan, 2018b).

2.2. Content Instructors

When a content course is identified as an immersion course, the RIF management team sends a form letter to the content instructor explaining briefly the sequence of immersion courses and their role, as well as giving the name of the ALC instructor associated with their course, advising them that they will be contacted in order to request essential information about their course. This standard letter is accompanied by a document entitled Immersion Courses: Some useful information. In two pages, the document summarizes the rationale behind the RIF and its implementation, the objectives of ALCs, and the role of the content instructor. A list of contacts (the RIF website, contact information for the secretariat, the director, and the pedagogical advisor) is also provided. It also emphasizes what is expected of the content instructor (see Appendix for details).

However, the presence of the language instructor is only mentioned at the end of the first page, in a short sentence: "The language instructor will attend your [content] course in order to offer students linguistic support adapted to what they are studying" (p. 247), and their role is not explicitly defined. But what is clearly stated is that "Consultation and collaboration of content and language instructors will greatly facilitate the success of this approach" (p. 248). Thus, this is more an information piece than instructor training.

It should be noted that content instructors were invited to the sessional meetings at the beginning of the RIF, but as they did not attend, the invitations were discontinued.

2.3. Students

Future immersion students receive information on the RIF in high school in the context of school visits conducted by liaison officers from the university (see Chapter 15 for details on their duties). These officers give presentations on the RIF and distribute informative and promotional material. They also recruit many students at the Ontario Universities Fair (www.ouf.ca). And, of course, the RIF website (University of Ottawa, n.d., "French Immersion Stream") addresses students and their parents directly to help them discover the RIF through texts, photos, and video documents.

This institutional information is complemented by peer information available on both social media and YouTube. That is, former and current students of the RIF post blogs and videos to explain the concept and share their experiences. For example, a fourth-year student (under the pseudonym "Frenchie Freshman") published several videos describing her life as an immersion student (May 4, 2013, "I survived first year") from the worst moments of doubt to the most successful episodes (Mar. 7, 2013, "Midterms and beavertails"). Another student created a Facebook page entitled "Je parle 2017" (2013–2014), where she posted testimonies, comments, and advice on the RIF, with posts on discouraging times, successful moments, as well as key events.

The RIF's website also features testimonials from students, an easily relatable source of information for prospective and current students can easily relate. These informative pieces come as video clips (see, for example, uOttawa Future, 2019) and written quotes (University of Ottawa, n.d., "French Immersion ... Testimonials").

Once enrolled in the RIF, students have direct access to immersion mentors, themselves students of the RIF, in the third or fourth year of their program. Mentors guide, inform, and support new students (see Chapter 9). They are not only an extremely valuable source of information, they are also models with whom new students can identify.

Finally, to help the student population more directly, a team of OLBI instructors developed a series of seven podcasts on second language listening strategies that are based on metacognitive theory (Weinberg, Knoerr, & Vandergrift, 2011). These short videoclips, featuring RIF students interacting with instructors, provide immersion students with tools addressing elements such as listening strategies, preparing for the content course, solving comprehension problems, note-taking, and integrating new technologies (see Chapter 9). The podcasts are available via the RIF website (University of Ottawa, n.d., "French Immersion ... Podcasts"), where links lead to their YouTube locations. These give newly enrolled students the opportunity to learn their "trade" (to use Alain Coulon's expression, 1997) as immersion students. They are also highly recommended to ALC instructors as teaching tools.

Thus, there are many resources available to help students familiarize themselves with the concept, but always in a relatively informal and fragmented way.

2.4. Administrators

2.4.1. Deans

Deans are key players in the implementation of the RIF because they are the ones who decide whether their faculty or programs will participate in the RIF or not. The director of the RIF must therefore ensure that they know and understand the concept by meeting them individually. These personal interactions, which took place at the beginning of the RIF, have ceased, even though the main reason the position of RIF director had been created at such a high administrative level was to have the legitimacy to discuss issues with the deans on an equal footing (see Chapter 2):

> Within the institution he must meet at least the vice-deans of studies every year, try to meet as many instructors as possible and educate them, that's why he's 13 [administrative level 13]. So that he has legitimacy. This is an important position at the executive level. My logic of fighting for a 13 was because institutionally it matters. (Houle, 2012 [trans.])

But it is not enough to make the case for pedagogical legitimacy. Deans must also be aware of the importance of the RIF for uOttawa in several respects:

- *academically*, since it is the only university in the world to offer such an option in French, which gives it excellent visibility
- *strategically*, since the RIF positions the institution among the world leaders in the field
- *financially*, since the RIF is an important recruiting tool and therefore a key means of accessing government funding (uOttawa is targeting 3,000 RIF registrations over the coming years)

Finally, it is necessary to go beyond today's prevailing culture — which devotes an unfailing cult to marks, associating a numerical value with academic excellence — and to make deans aware of the issues inherent in the RIF. Thus, as former Provost and Vice-President, Academic Affairs, Houle pointed out, "we must minimize the importance of passing marks" (2012 [trans.]) which, for some deans, is not acceptable and therefore constitutes the main obstacle to their faculties' participation in the RIF. This is particularly the case in the Faculties of Science and of Engineering, where qualitative grades are seen as favouring English-speaking immersion students by giving them the opportunity to receive a simple Satisfactory/Unsatisfactory rating, and thus maintain their average even if they do poorly in the course, while their peers in the corresponding English-language programs do not have this option. Nevertheless, the concept of qualitative marks is in effect in numerous universities, both Canadian (McGill, Simon Fraser, etc.) and American (Johns Hopkins, to name just one).

2.4.2. Support Staff

While the liaison officers are well aware of the RIF, since some are paid by it to visit high schools to promote it to Grade 11 and 12 students, the support staff in uOttawa's host faculties are too often poorly aware of this relatively new addition to the campus. Although all faculties are offered a meeting with the RIF director, only half (Arts, Administration, Health Sciences) have taken advantage of the opportunity. The others simply pass on the information sent to them by the RIF. However, support staff are an important point of contact for RIF students, who are primarily enrolled in a faculty program. Therefore, it is essential to inform them about the RIF. In this regard, some staff have specialized in immersion, which they have championed within their units, and the RIF is considering promoting and supporting this type of initiative thanks to which these champions will bring their colleagues on board.

3. CONTRIBUTIONS AND LIMITATIONS OF THE RIF TRAINING

3.1. Contributions

A wide range of training resources is now available to language instructors. These resources, which are original, rich, and varied, have been developed internally by specialists and are therefore appropriate to the specific needs of the RIF. They take into account all aspects of immersion at the university level. They offer personalized coaching as well as collective training opportunities. Their accessibility is facilitated thanks to the Julien Couture Resource Centre and the Virtual Campus.

Furthermore, the RIF has put numerous resources into place to help immersion students understand the challenges they will have to face and the characteristics of the RIF approach. In particular, the presence of mentors, who themselves are immersion students, constitutes a considerable advantage for new recruits to the program. New students benefit from their mentors' shared experiences on academic, linguistic, identity, social, and affective levels.

Finally, the series of seven podcasts previously mentioned makes academic success strategies accessible to all, beyond the RIF.

3.2. Limits

Unfortunately, even though resources exist, they are not used much for institutional training. First of all, the training of ALC instructors is not compulsory. As a result, instructors who have never taught in the RIF are not required to attend training workshops, meet with the pedagogical advisors, or become familiar with the approach. This means that such training will only be taken by those who have an intrinsic motivation to do so and a well-developed professional sense of ethics, since their participation is neither remunerated nor recognized by the RIF management.[11]

The interactions between pedagogical advisors and the teaching staff have decreased significantly, as have teacher training initiatives. In particular, the dimension of individualized follow-up no longer exists. Pedagogical advisors no longer observe ALC instructors in the classroom, which prevents them from playing a mentoring role and ensuring that educational activities are in line with the RIF philosophy. In fact, as reported by students, certain instructors treat these courses as regular FSL courses and teach grammar instead of focusing on the material in the content course, while others repeat the content course instead of focusing on the language difficulties. In the past, it was also reported that certain instructors were not attending the content classes. Furthermore, no pedagogical support exists for the final two levels of ALC courses.

Content instructors do not have access to training on the philosophy of immersion and the pedagogical approach used by the RIF. The first contact with the RIF and the ALC instructors is made by the administration, in a cold and impersonal manner. Any follow-up is left to the goodwill of language instructors.

Certain academic development and service coordinators are poorly or even ill-informed about the RIF, so they do not always advise students about their best interests, sometimes even encouraging them to drop out of immersion.

3.3. Recommendations

Training in the pedagogical approach of immersion in the context of the RIF should be made mandatory by drawing up a contract specific to ALCs. The *Guide du professeur de langue* and both handbooks (the *recueils d'activités*) should be given to all language instructors, along with a list of the resources available at the Julien Couture Resource Centre and the two DVDs (*L'immersion* ... and *Testing receptive skills* ...). A paper copy of the *Guide* should be made available at the resource centre.

Training should also be provided to all immersion actors. One of the mandates of an Immersion Advisory Committee could consist of exploring the possibility of creating a module or a hybrid course, based on the principle of mandatory training for certain categories of staff at uOttawa (University of Ottawa, n.d., "Human resources: Mandatory").

An annual meeting should be held between the RIF director and faculties offering the RIF, in order to give them a presentation about the RIF and its characteristics, and to suggest ways to properly welcome and advise students.

---

[11] Although article 5.1.2 of their collective agreement states that staying informed about current pedagogical developments is part of their teaching responsibilities (University of Ottawa, n.d., "Human resources: Association").

In addition, the Provost and Vice-President, Academic Affairs should organize, at the beginning of each term (or school year, if all immersion courses are assigned in September), an official reception that would bring together the key actors in immersion: the RIF administration, the deans of the faculties offering the RIF, the content instructors who teach courses designated as immersion, the RIF's pedagogical advisors, ALC instructors, and immersion mentors. The Provost and Vice-President, Academic Affairs would highlight the key role of the RIF in uOttawa's mission and the importance of faculty collaboration for its success. This would be followed by a series of short presentations in which its director would describe the RIF and how it enhances uOttawa as a national and international leader in official languages; the pedagogical advisors would present the roles of ALC and content instructors; the mentors would describe their experiences as immersion students and their role with new recruits. The rest of the reception would give all players the opportunity to meet and mingle, thus providing a personal contact opportunity between each paired content and language instructors. In this way, participation in the RIF would be recognized and valued.

CONCLUSION

The immersive approach in the RIF requires a tailored methodology, different not only from that of traditional second or foreign language teaching, but also from that of French immersion in primary and secondary schools. It also involves actors who are aware of the issues at stake, whether they are language or content instructors, administrators, or students. However, the typical teacher training program does not address this very particular approach and thus does not prepare them for their mission. As for the other actors, they have yet to receive training in/about the RIF. It is therefore essential to set up a complete training system to ensure that the concept is understood, shared, and implemented by all participants, which would guarantee its success and sustainability.

REFERENCES

Burger, S. (Comp.). 2006. [Video recordings of English-language university lextures. In-house training videos]. Ottawa: University of Ottawa, Second Language Institute.

Burger, S., & Weinberg, A. (2006). *L'immersion, une solution miracle?* [DVD]. Ottawa: University of Ottawa, Second Language Institute.

Canadian Centre for Studies and Research on Bilingualism and Language Planning (CCERBAL). (2012, February). International forum: "Immersion at the university level: Models, challenges and prospects." University of Ottawa. ccerbal.uottawa.ca/en/immersion-2012

Coulon, A. (1997). *Le métier d'étudiant: l'entrée dans la vie universitaire*. Paris: Presses universitaires de France.

Dansereau, M.-C. (2010). *Guide du professeur de langue*. Ottawa: University of Ottawa, Official Languages and Bilingualism Institute (OLBI).

Dansereau, M.-C. (Ed.). (2011). *S'exprimer en langue seconde dans le contexte d'un cours de discipline universitaire: recueil d'activités à l'intention des professeurs de langue en immersion postsecondaire* [Handbook]. Ottawa: University of Ottawa, Official Languages and Bilingualism Institute (OLBI).

Dansereau, M.-C., & Buchanan, C.E. (Eds.). (2009). *Recueil d'activités: compréhension écrite et orale d'un cours de discipline suivi en langue seconde* [Handbook]. Ottawa: University of Ottawa, Official Languages and Bilingualism Institute (OLBI).

Dansereau, M.-C., & Buchanan, C.E. (Eds.). (2011). *Comprendre un cours de discipline suivi en langue seconde: recueil d'activités à l'intention des professeurs de langue en immersion postsecondaire* [Handbook], 2nd ed. Ottawa: University of Ottawa, Official Languages and Bilingualism Institute (OLBI).

Druide informatique. (2018). Antidote 10 (v.1.1) [Writing assistance software]. Montreal: Druide informatique, Inc. antidote.info/en/

Frenchie Freshman. (2013, May 4). I survived first year [Video file]. www.youtube.com/watch?v=kW3KxFYZ3cw

Frenchie Freshman. (2013, Mar 7). Midterms and beavertails [Video file]. www.youtube.com/watch?v=YtWZP2AyuoM

Houle, F. (2012, Nov. 6). [Personal interview; translated from French].

Je parle 2017. (2013–2014). [Facebook account]. www.facebook.com/jeparle2017

Karsenti, T., & Dumouchel, G. (2006). Les programmes de formation des maîtres en français langue seconde (FLS) ou en immersion au Canada. Ottawa: Association canadienne des professeurs en immersion. www.acpi.ca/documents/programmes-fls.pdf

Knoerr, H., & Weinberg, A. (Eds.). (2013). *OLBI Working Papers* [thematic issue: *L'immersion en français au niveau universitaire/French immersion at the university level*], 6.

Knoerr, H., Weinberg, A., & Buchanan, E.C. (Eds.). (2018a). *Current issues in university immersion*. Ottawa: University of Ottawa, Groupe de recherche en immersion au niveau universitaire (GRINU).

Knoerr, H., Weinberg, A., & Buchanan, C.E. (Eds.). (2018b). *OLBI Working Papers* [thematic issue: *University-level immersion environments in Canada*], 9.

Knoerr, H., Weinberg, A., Gohard-Radenkovic, A. (Eds.). (2016). *L'immersion française à l'université: politiques et pédagogies*. Ottawa: University of Ottawa Press.

McGill University. (n.d.). Certificat d'études supérieures en pédagogie de l'immersion française (Cert. ed. sup.) pédagogie de l'immersion française (15 crs). mcgill.ca/study/2019-2020/faculties/education/graduate/programs/certificat-detudes-superieures-en-pedagogie-de-limmersion-francaise-certedsup-pedagogie-de

Obadia, A. (1985). La formation du professeur d'immersion française au Canada: une conception philosophique et pédagogique en devenir ou à la recherche d'une troisième voie. *Canadian Journal of Education, 10*, 415–426. doi:10.2307/1494841

Université de Saint-Boniface. (n.d.). Baccalauréat en éducation, niveau élémentaire. ustboniface.ca/en/sslpage.aspx?pid=10255

Université du Québec à Montréal (UQAM). (n.d.). DDL1251 — *Didactique du français langue seconde: immersion*. etudier.uqam.ca/cours?sigle=DDL1251

Université Laval. (n.d.). DID-3961 Didactique du français (accueil et immersion). www.ulaval.ca/les-etudes/cours/repertoire/detailsCours/did-3961-didactique-du-francais-accueil-et-immersion.html

University of Ottawa. (n.d.). French Immersion Stream: Resources — Podcasts. immersion.uottawa.ca/en/resources

University of Ottawa. (n.d.). French Immersion Stream: Testimonials. immersion.uottawa.ca/en/testimonials

University of Ottawa. (n.d.). Human resources: Association of part-time professors of the University of Ottawa. hrdocrh.uottawa.ca/info/en-ca/aptpuo/concepts/collective-agreements/aptpuo/dita/article-5.html

University of Ottawa. (n.d.). Human resources: Mandatory training sessions. www.uottawa.ca/human-resources/mandatory-training-sessions

University of Ottawa. (n.d.). French Immersion Stream. immersion.uottawa.ca/en

University of Ottawa. (n.d.). Office of the Provost and Vice-President, Academic Affairs — Faculty relations — Faculty Recruitment — Openings. www.uottawa.ca/vice-president-academic/faculty-relations/faculty-recruitment/openings

University of Ottawa. (n.d.). OLBI: Julien Couture Resource Centre. olbi.uottawa.ca/about/julien-couture-resource-centre

University of Ottawa. (n.d.). Programs and courses: Second-language teaching (DLS). catalogue.uottawa.ca/en/courses/dls/

University of Ottawa. (n.d.). *Testing receptive skills in immersion courses* [DVD]. Ottawa: University of Ottawa, Official Languages and Bilingualism Institute (OLBI).

University of Ottawa. (1974). Regulation on bilingualism at University of Ottawa 1974. www.uottawa.ca/administration-and-governance/policies-and-regulations/regulation-on-bilingualism

University of Prince Edward Island. (n.d.). Bachelor of Education — Français Langue Seconde. www.upei.ca/programsandcourses/baccalaureat-en-education-francais-langue-seconde

University of Prince Edward Island (2011). Minutes of the Eighth Senate Meeting, held Friday, March 11, 2011. home.upei.ca/files/home/senateminutesmarch11-2011.pdf

uOttawaImmersion. (2011, Oct. 13). Plein feux sur l'immersion! [Video file]. Symposium held at the University of Ottawa. www.youtube.com/watch?v=DeozpQydcz4

uOttawa Future. (2019, Apr. 1). French immersion with Madison. [Video file]. www.youtube.com/watch?v=HiGm16yPlU0&t=6s

Weinberg, A., & Burger, S. (2006). *Guide à l'intention des professeurs de langue: cours d'immersion*. Ottawa: University of Ottawa, Institut des langues secondes.

Weinberg, A., & Burger, S. (2007). *Guide à l'intention des professeurs de langue: cours d'encadrement linguistique*, Version 1a. Ottawa: University of Ottawa, Institut des langues secondes.

Weinberg, A., Knoerr, H., & Vandergrift, L. (2011). Creating podcasts for academic listening in French: Students' perceptions of enjoyment and usefulness. *CALICO Journal, 28*, 588–605.

Appendix
Information sent by the RIF to content instructors [trans.]

Immersion courses

Some useful information

RIF at uOttawa

Rationale

uOttawa plays a leadership role on the national scene with respect to official languages. The RIF is one of the initiatives put in place to enable Anglophone students coming out of French as a second language programs at the secondary school level to develop their language potential and thrive in a milieu where the two cultures co-exist.

In a few words, the RIF is:

- a bilingual path which accompanies a specialized program (offered in 86 programs)
- more than 1800 students in 2018–19
- linguistic sheltering in more than 80 courses a year
- the right to receive qualitative grades S/NS (Satisfactory or Not Satisfactory) — except for students in the Faculties of Science and Engineering
- receive the "Immersion" designation on their diploma
- access to bursaries for students in French
- a mentoring centre for immersion
- social and cultural activities, thanks to the Immersion Club
- immersion and adjunct language courses (ALC)

Students enrol in certain disciplinary courses (history, sociology, economics, etc.); according to their level of competence, they register in one to the following ALCs:

- FLS 2581: This course develops second language comprehension abilities and thus, helps the student to assimilate the content subject matter.
- FLS 3581: This course develops second language oral and written production abilities and thus, gives students the confidence necessary to express ideas in French.

Each section of these courses (FLS 2581 and FLS 3581) is associated with only one particular content course. The ALC is 90 minutes long.

The language instructor will attend your classes in order to offer the students linguistic support adapted to what they are studying. Thus, the majority of the course activities will stem from the content of the discipline course.

The role of the content instructor

You can contribute to the success of the students by sharing certain documents with the ALC instructor and by encouraging the students to prepare their assignments in French.

Before the beginning of term:

- Submit your course outline to the language instructor as soon as possible.
- Send your course pack and/or textbook as soon as possible.
- Register the language instructor as an auditor on Virtual Campus.
- If possible, meet with the language instructor before the beginning of term or during the first week of classes.

During the term:

- Send course notes or additional material in advance to allow the language instructor to prepare support material that will be offered to the students.
- If necessary, answer the language instructor's questions.
- Occasionally allow the language instructor to tape your class (solely for the students' benefit).
- Authorize, at the request of the language instructor, that your assistants (if you have any) meet the immersion students in an ALC.

> *Consultation and collaboration between the content and language instructors will greatly facilitate the success of the approach.*

Language of Assignments

In the ALC, all assignments must be done in French.

In your content course, ALC instructors actively encourage their students to write in French for short assignments. As for essays and final papers, students have a choice. If they decide to write in French, you could choose not to penalize them (or to penalize less severely) for their mistakes in grammar, spelling, or other language errors.

Except in language courses, all students have the right to write their assignments and answer examination questions in the official language of their choice. (*Regulation on bilingualism at the University of Ottawa 1974, Part Six, line 20(3).*)

For more details

Visit the website:

http://www.immersion.uottawa.ca

Or contact:

The Secretariat of the French Immersion Stream: 613 562-5747

CHAPTER 12

Biographical Interviews with the RIF Administrators:
Potential Mediators of a Linguistic and Cultural "In-Between"

Aline Gohard-Radenkovic

INTRODUCTION

THIS CHAPTER IS WRITTEN from the point of view of the administrators who have managed the *Régime d'immersion en français* (RIF) at the University of Ottawa since it began (academic year 2006–2007). It deals with the analysis of the representations of the immersion experience, using a qualitative interpretative approach in language didactics (Second Language Acquisition Theory), based on transverse concepts of representations and strategies. Its objectives complement the other chapters: to investigate the itineraries, perceptions, and logic of the actors and co-actors[1] in an institutional French immersion environment.

More specifically, the chapter aims to identify various cultural, social, linguistic, mobility capitals, and so forth (discussed in Chapter 16), by analyzing biographical interviews with its two administrators. These observations will give an insight into the reasons why they made a number of choices — or non-choices — as well as how they conceived of their duties and positions, how they perceived the issues of the academic institution and the various RIF actors, as well as the decisions, actions, and propositions they implemented to develop the institutional environment.

---

[1] Definition of "mobility actors" and "co-actors" used in this chapter:

They are all those who actually move, i.e. pupils, students, interns, teachers, researchers, education and administration officers, corporate or international organization executives, expatriates, cooperants (young people working abroad in lieu of military service), war refugees, immigrants, exiles, etc. But "mobile" actors are not the only ones who played a key role in the mobility process, in the process of their mobility and their integration. Mobility actors are also all those who, in one way or another, are sought by individuals or groups in situation of mobility, either because they work in education or language training (teachers, instructors, interpreters), or because they have other functions in the sphere of education, vocational training, social and medical services, administration, international affairs, non-profit sectors, the judiciary, etc. They are the co-actors of these mobilities. (Gohard-Radenkovic & Rachédi, 2009, pp. 6–7)

1. THEORETICAL AND METHODOLOGICAL CHOICES

1.1. Immersion Actors are also Mobility Actors

European researchers in cultural anthropology, sociolinguistics, and anthropology of communication (Agulhon & Xavier de Brito, 2009; Anquetil, 2006; Dervin & Byram, 2008; Gerber, 2012; Gerber & Gohard-Radenkovic, 2011; Gohard-Radenkovic, 2013a; Gohard-Radenkovic & Rachédi, 2009; Murphy-Lejeune, 2001, 2002, 2003; Papatsiba, 2003; Pungier, 2009, 2012; Robin, 2013a, 2013b) have been addressing the issue of mobility by imagining diversified reasons and, thus, complex individual itineraries. These itineraries are no longer organized between the here and there in a bipolar mode; they now feature multiple trajectories, an initial mobility (familial, interregional, touristic, or migratory) possibly leading to others (linguistic, academic, professional, marital), in a multipolar mode. The main point is that, among these different types of mobility, people can endorse a language, role, identity, and status, which are different not only from one country or region to another but also within the same place of social integration, all while acquiring a great deal of experience in learning and mobility.

As a result, the course of these moving actors eludes any attempt at ordinary or unilateral categorization. Therefore, researchers, whatever their scientific anchorage, are compelled to adopt a dynamic and kinesic vision of the movement phenomena rather than a static and unique one.

1.2. Favouring the Autobiographical Approach

Accordingly, it is more and more common to resort to a qualitative interpretative approach to study the individual moves in depth,[2] in terms of social micro-processes. The autobiographical approach is a preferred way to analyze these singular itineraries and the various processes going on, particularly in cases of mobility and integration. Qualitative researchers are trying to understand the logics specific to social actors at a given time and in a given context. They are also interested in the reciprocal effects of the political contexts and their developments (macro), and of the institutional relays (meso) and their issues, on the trajectories and logics of the various actors (here, from the academic institution), and particularly, on their linguistic and "imaginary identity" as well as on their strategies (micro) (Gohard-Radenkovic, 2006, 2007).

These multiple past and present experiences are, according to Bourdieu (1980), "a biographical capital," in particular through mobility, and a "mobility capital," according to Murphy-Lejeune (2001, 2002). They include previous linguistic, social, and cultural capitals, as well as those acquired through mobilities. Since then, the reflective approach has also served as a qualitative research tool and method *per se* (Gohard-Radenkovic, Pouliot, & Stalder, 2012), in addition to playing an active role in learning and training.

Indeed, there are two quite separate usage levels in the autobiographical approach:

- *For mobility actors*, it serves as a means of observing and investigating themselves in relation to others, in order to develop a reflective and retrospective approach to their immersion experience in a foreign language and to their integration into a new context.

---

[2] The *thick description*, according to Geertz (1986); see Chapter 16.

- *For researchers* (who have already compiled or collected biographies, biographical interviews, journals, etc. for research purposes), it serves as a means of observing and analyzing mobility actors who have been asked about their language and mobility trajectories, and about their immersion experience in a language or a discipline and/or their integration within a new context.

The autobiographical approach should therefore be considered as a narrative paradigm in all disciplines:

> In the last decades, stories have become prominent again and are at the forefront of Social Studies. Consequently, at a more local level, one can only think of the powerful comeback of biographies, not only within the anthropological genre of testimonials but also as sociological and psycho-sociological tools of inquiry and/or intervention. (Sohet, 2007, p. 49 [trans.])

Biographies are based on self-analysis, self-expression, self-reflection, psychosocial, socio-anthropological introspection (Gohard-Radenkovic, 2004, 2013b) and, on a broader level, on reflectivity, according to Ricœur (1991, cited in Bachelart & Pineau, 2009), who expressed the triple process as follows: subjects relate their own stories within the stories they tell themselves about themselves.

In the present case, the biographical interview approach was chosen to learn about the experiences of both Marc, the current RIF director, and Patrick, his predecessor, who had set up the administrative structure, and whose testimonial excerpts are used in counterpoint.[3]

2. EARLY EXPOSURE TO BOTH LANGUAGES

2.1. *Proactive French Immersion: Home Language, Language of Instruction*

Marc, born and raised in Manitoba, came from Francophone families on both sides in a "predominantly Anglophone province"; from the start, he pointed out his very early exposure to English:

> We lived in the country, outside Winnipeg, and we were the only Francophone family in the area. The closest Francophones we knew lived twelve kilometres away. We were in the country. I was exposed to English at a very early age.

However, Marc mentioned that French and the minority French speakers survived among the majority of English speakers, through a proactive family policy:

> My mother taught in the French system in Manitoba. My father had belonged to ... what do you call it? Some organization ... I'm not sure whether it was the Knights of Columbus or Manitoba's Francophone Community Sector, but they were both very much involved in developing the Francophone community, education, or business.

Speaking French at home, which became the rule, was reinforced by doing his schooling in French in a Francophone school which, luckily, was in the next village.

---

[3] [All interviews were conducted in French; they appear here in the author's translations.]

This proactivity was not always flawless, especially during family gatherings when everyone spoke French, even though some of the aunts' Anglophone husbands did not necessarily speak it. Each "side" stuck to their position or rather, to their own language:

> I have several maternal aunts, and everything was done in French even though some of my aunts were married to Anglophones. So, that's when things started to change at home. My uncle Ed and my uncle Pete. Ed understood French; Peter, not a word. His family was Dutch. He used to say: "I'll learn French when you learn Dutch." So, in short, neither side budged.

It is important to note here that, when interviewing informants from a bilingual context they did not choose, the matter of "mixed families" very rarely came up, as if this mixed majority–minority family combination could contaminate the rest of the family and undermine the preservation of French. In that respect, Marc's testimonial shows that these diversities, at the very core of the fragile family cohesion, were really felt as a threat. The fact that he brushed it aside, at least in his testimonial, by saying: "So, in short, neither side budged," suggests it was an extremely sensitive topic.

It is hardly surprising to learn that Patrick, also of Manitoban origin, came from the Francophone minority and was raised in a family who was equally eager to preserve French, and, therefore, sent their children to a Francophone primary school. But, it was difficult to maintain French in a predominantly Anglophone environment, and, in Patrick's case, the breaches of domestic rules came from within, not from outside. His sister was the one who decided to switch to English and gradually led the family to its sole use at home.

2.2. Constant Exposure to English, Language of Socialization, Language of Information

From Marc's testimonial, it appears that all his friends, schoolmates, and later, his girl-friends (with a few exceptions) came from the English-speaking world:

> I remember telling the girl next door, who was babysitting me one evening or one day: "*je veux* player *dans le* sandbox," and she had understood. My mother had found it funny. There was only one little boy in the street. So, he was my friend but he only spoke English so I spoke broken English, but he managed to understand me. But, then, at that age, there is no need to talk a lot. We rode our bikes, we jumped, we squashed frogs. That's what kids do. So, that was my first contact with the English language.

When the family moved to Ottawa, Marc was still exposed to both languages:

> In this new neighbourhood, [...] I had] a few Franco friends, but there were other children in the street, a few Anglophones. So, I also played with them. I continued to improve my English skills with these other children. And I was always listening to English TV programs, English music, Michael Jackson, stuff like that.

Another way of being constantly exposed to English came from media culture, which greatly influenced Marc's itinerary: it enabled him to build predominant Anglophone cultural references. And in Manitoba, his parents "consumed Anglophone TV channels" because of their omnipresence and the lack of French programs:

We used to listen to these programs on Radio-Canada, but we only had three or four radio stations, and mostly in English. So, there was *Sesame Street*, *Mister Dressup*, *Friendly Giant*. Children's programs, in English. So, I learnt to speak English very early.

But watching the news in English was also linked to the fact they did not relate at all to Quebec, which they found too inward-looking and, as Marc said, too ethnocentric:

> The news, my parents used to almost always listen to the news in English because the Francophone network was "Quebecocentric" ... I recall that they talked about county and village issues and we didn't care because it wasn't our world, it wasn't our community. Whereas on the English network, they talked about the whole country.

A recurrent theme arises here, one which is strongly expressed later in the interview: while Quebec Francophones are indeed a minority compared to Anglophones, they nevertheless represent the majority in relation to other Francophone minorities, which are scattered and often isolated in various regions of French Canada. Identity boundaries exist, not only between Francophone and Anglophone areas, but even more so between Quebec Francophones and Francophones outside Quebec: the latter feel themselves to be a minority group, not only toward their Anglophone neighbours, but also toward Quebecers, to whom they relate neither culturally nor linguistically, as we will see later.

3. INTRANATIONAL MOBILITIES AND LINGUISTIC IDENTITY SHIFTS

3.1. Speaking Both Languages Alternately According to the Social Circles

As previously seen, Marc started primary school at a French-speaking school. When he moved to Ottawa (he was then eight or nine years old), he continued attending a Francophone primary school, where he took his first English lessons, which were easy for him: "I had no problems there because I was more advanced than most in my new neighbourhood." His language of instruction remained French all through his schooling, although he was constantly immersed in an Anglophone context:

> When I was a teenager, I was here, in Ottawa, always in Francophone schools. But the context being what it was, mainly Anglophone, with a few friends in primary school, I spoke English because it was in fashion and I never questioned it. At eleven or twelve, you don't raise serious identity issues. So, always in a French school, but I had a few friends with whom I spoke English. Media consumption in English. But I was still fluent in French because we spoke it at home. Speaking English at home wasn't an option. Of course, we used certain expressions. We listened to hockey in English.

If English was the language of socialization, it also led to building and sharing a common "youth culture" (music, sports, leisure activities, news, etc.), dominated by Anglophone references that are part of Canadian culture.

Marc insisted on the daily alternating identity shifts[4] between French and English, especially in his menial jobs:

---

[4] This notion of "identity shifts" (*bricolages*) must be understood in its ethnological sense. The term (originally *bricolage*) is borrowed from Lévi-Strauss (1962), who attributed it to the combination of cultural facts. It is used in cultural anthropology, sociolinguistics, anthropology/ethnography of communication.

> I was a paper boy. It was the Anglophone newspaper. The customers were all, almost all, Anglophones. I worked at the grocery store. Everything was done almost exclusively in English, although we had Francophone workmates, Francophone customers.

3.2. Linguistic Remediation Strategies According to "Romantic" Circles

Within the socialization groups, falling in love contributed to the alternating use of French and English since, according to Marc, he had "mainly Anglophone but also Francophone girlfriends." Being able to speak both languages, he sometimes played the role of language mediator,[5] and sometimes, of linguistic intermediary:

> I dated girls from exogamous families, so the language they really favoured or used to communicate was essentially English. And me, as I was perfectly bilingual, using one or the other didn't bother me.

> So, it was mostly English. Actually, it wasn't until I went to university that I dated a girl who could hardly speak English. And, then, it was really hard work for me to develop a way of expressing myself in French.

What a strange coincidence in their itineraries! Patrick also moved to Ottawa, but later than Marc. His account provides the same socialization and acculturation experiences (media, school, sports, friends, girlfriends) through the use of English, which prompted him to say that, actually, he had never really either learned English or inherited French, but that, from the start, he had two mother tongues which he used indifferently, depending on the circumstances and interlocutors. As for Marc, he described his bilingual teenage experience like this: "I sailed through it in French with an increasing presence of English in my life."

What emerges from these statements is indeed a deliberate immersion in French but limited to school and family, whereas it is clear that English prevailed daily in all spheres of life, i.e. relationships, culture, media, or love.

4. OTTAWA: A BILINGUAL UNIVERSITY ENVIRONMENT OF DIFFERENCES

4.1. Awareness of Cultural References Specific to Linguistic Groups

When he started university, Marc was in Ottawa and quite naturally, without a second thought, decided to attend uOttawa: "Since I was already there, why not stay?" He chose French as his obvious language of instruction and therefore, took most (eight) of his courses in French and only two in English. He explained that he organized his program not in relation to the language or subjects, but in relation to the days and the instructors:

> And so, for the next four years, I chose courses in English, in French. I didn't care. What was important, was the class schedule. I did not want to take classes on Tuesdays during the day because I went skiing on Tuesdays ... So, I chose my classes based on the course schedule; in my third and fourth year, in relation to the instructor. If a Francophone

---

[5] The notion of linguistic and cultural (re)mediation has been developed in cultural anthropology, sociolinguistics, anthropology/ethnography of communication.

instructor was more interesting, I would maybe take his class. If he or she was less interesting, I would switch to English classes.

After drifting about for one or two years in various disciplines, he finally found what he liked — communication, which made him realize not only what he was interested in, but also who he was:

> Perhaps because what had always interested me as a teenager were the phenomena of movement and people ... Acculturation in Sweden, in Finland. Why do these young people speak English so well? Advertising phenomena ... So, I studied stuff like that and it was part of the curriculum, it dealt a lot with cultural contacts. The sharing of ideas, and, in several courses, we talked of language and identity.

Through his communication studies, he also realized that, depending on the context in which one lived or grew up, one could speak the other official language very well without necessarily sharing its implicit cultural references, especially if one had not been initiated into the other possible world that the other group's language had built:

> And at one point, in third year, it was a political communication class and the instructor asked us: "Which journalists do you admire?" They all mentioned Bernard Derome and great Francophone journalists, and, me, I only had Anglophone journalists in mind.

Given this discrepancy, Marc tried to fill the gaps by almost frantically acquiring this media culture whose knowledge was essential to study communication within the Francophone sphere:

> I was a volunteer radio host at the University of Ottawa ... So, I kept working and, in addition, I also discovered French music, because we had to play it on the community radio ... So, I discovered lots of artists, the music got to me. I had never heard such things before. I loved it! So, I started listening to French music, and, in short, I started to take an interest in all French cultural representations, from cinema to TV, music, literature.

Like Marc, Patrick never had very many identity issues until his teenage days in high school. Then, the Manitoban social environment (the Council of Francophone Students, active Francophone networks, community activities, etc.) made him become aware of his Francophone affiliation. He said: "I then rediscovered the importance of French in my life." To follow up on that awareness, both in terms of language and identity, he enrolled at uOttawa to study political science in French.

4.2. From Linguistic Flexibility to Linguistic Insecurity

As well as sharing ideas with other students, the communication course struck at the very heart of Marc's belief that he was "perfectly bilingual." He was well aware that he was not "from there," but he discovered that his accent (different from Quebecer or Franco-Ontarian) and his language ("full of anglicisms") stigmatized him from every side: Francophones and Anglophones or other Francophone minorities:

> I spoke with a different accent from the others and, at the baccalaureate, for the first time, I met a lot of Quebecers, who sometimes thought I was an Anglophone, sometimes made fun of my accent, the expressions I used. Plus, we had specific turns of phrase, anglicisms. I didn't know they were anglicisms. Nobody had ever told me.

Marc also recalled that his first experiences as a volunteer host at the radio station (which only broadcast in French) were painful, for he could feel that his accent and his expressions were not "adequate." The words he used reflected the actual discomfort he experienced, not only socially and linguistically but also almost physically:

> So, here I was, with my tongue stuck and heavy in my mouth, my lips which didn't move the way they should have ... but I was on the air, with my accent, and the station manager urged me to listen to myself, and, I found that very difficult, to listen to myself on the radio, to hear my accent, words which didn't make sense, turns of phrase that didn't hold water. It was another blow to my ego.

If spoken language was hard to bear — as it is immediately audible and, therefore, quite a stigma — writing also brought its share of pitfalls and bad surprises:

> Once, when I handed in an essay, the instructor came to see me, and she told me: "Marc, I can see that you got the gist of the subject and your ideas are interesting. However, your written French is very weak." It shocked me because no one had ever told me. Yet, I wrote essays in French for my other classes. I felt it. It was sometimes a bit hard to find the right expressions. But here was someone who told me about it and I was a bit hurt.

On the other hand, Patrick did not mention any such discriminating experiences when he arrived at uOttawa. Is it perhaps because he had never experienced them or, perhaps, because he had simply forgotten them (or forgot to mention them in the interview)? Or perhaps it was because he was too eager to talk about his experience as an administrator of the newly created RIF, which was one of the major objectives of the interview.

After the euphoria of moving freely from one language to another, from one culture to another, without giving it a second thought (like a game), he experienced the difficult task of being a "hybrid speaker," stuck in-between, who believed he was bicultural but was not, who used both languages indifferently, though, in a tense bilingual context where people lived together and, at the same time, kept each other at bay.

5. STRATEGIES TO RECLAIM FRANCOPHONE LANGUAGE AND IDENTITY

5.1. (Re)gaining Control over Poorly Mastered French Language

On his own ("Then, I took steps to remedy that"), Marc, along with his Quebecer girlfriend, enrolled in a French grammar class (which he had been avoiding for years) in order to fill in the gaps. This is when his life took a major turn: he became aware of how "precarious" his Francophone language and identity were:

> From that time on, I think I realized to what extent my language, my commitment to my culture were precarious. Like many Francophones, I told myself and admitted that I was a proud Francophone but then I didn't do anything to experience that culture or understand it. I was just a Francophone — that was it.

He then sought every means and opportunity to improve his spoken and written language skills:

> During my third and fourth year, I did my best to speak French more often, do my homework in French, seek opportunities to work in that language. So, when I graduated I got a job in a small town — it was a government program supporting community organizations

looking for young employees, and I got a job in the Penetanguishene [Ontario's Georgian Bay area] region.

The impact of that experience on his itinerary will be discussed later.

5.2. Montreal: Dealing with an Undermined Sense of Belonging

When Marc moved to Montreal in 1997 to work full-time, his reactions fit in with the existing discrimination, already mentioned above, between Quebecers and other Francophone groups. He finally discovered that his Franco-minoritarian universe and the Francophone complicity within the Anglophone world had protected him:

> It was different there, because I had always lived in a Franco-minoritarian environment and, when we ran into someone, when we heard French in the street, I always had a surge of brotherly feeling for that person. Hey, Francophone! We met in this Anglophone world, so, we felt something really special ... But in Montreal, oh la la! It made me so uncomfortable, for several months, to hear French everywhere. To see French on billboards, shop names, metro stations. I was really confused.

However, not only did he feel exposed in Montreal but he also relived the same demeaning experiences regarding his language and his accent as in Ottawa, which still haunt him today:

> Again, I worked really hard on my oral and written skills. And the young people I met were from Quebec, Montreal. So, I learned to speak like them. I never managed to speak like them, because they would often tell me: "Hey, you're not from here! Your accent is different! You're an Anglophone!" Which really hurt me. "Hold on! Some Francophones live elsewhere in Canada and they've got different accents."

Once again, there arises the issue of the Francophones outside Quebec, who are a minority in their Anglophone region and then minoritized again by Quebecers within the Canadian Francophonie, an issue which often stirs debates and fuels tensions among Canadian Francophones (Martel, 2007). Marc's testimonial provides a more subdued vision of this dichotomy, very common in Canada, and especially in Quebec.

6. PROFESSIONAL ITINERARIES SUPPORTING FRANCOPHONIE: EMERGENCE OF AN IDENTITY AWARENESS

6.1. An Experience in Penetanguishene

Let us recall Marc's first professional experience in Penetanguishene, where he discovered the history of the existential struggles of isolated Francophone minorities, from their fight against English and English education to the anglicization of their family names. It is the non-physical violence specific to any colonization: un-naming others or ensuring that they be self-named (for the sake of religious, political, or economic expediency), particularly by relinquishing their surnames, which are their most precious possession, since the aim is to obliterate their family identities and histories:

> Penetanguishene ... It's a native name. It's an old Francophone community, but isolated. North of Toronto. Some people have lived there for two hundred years but there had been enormous tension within the community. In Ontario, in the 70s, French secondary schools

were declared illegal by order of the council. Schooling had to be carried out in an English school. And in that community, they set up underground schools. They held demonstrations. In short, when I was there, I heard a lot about Francophone struggles. People who wanted the right to educate their children in French, to manage their own system. And, here I was, in the building where the first underground school had been organized.

So, it was interesting to see families called Roy, but on the headstones, it said King. The priest had urged the families to become anglicized, as it was to their economic advantage. I was really shocked!

This experience marked a turning point for Marc in terms of his emerging Francophone awareness, which was being built on his historical awareness of the struggles of minorities, and which society — mainly schools, the perfect place for the construction of a collective identity — omitted from history textbooks. Moreover, Marc found it meaningful to work as a radio host[6] and community liaison officer, where, as an intermediary, he could pass along the French language as well as knowledge of Francophone culture:

And I met families whose children didn't speak French at all, but who attended a French school, and, 10-, 12-, or 15-year-old children who said: "Je aime le," which was taken word for word from the English "I like it," but they said that, "Je aime le," and, perhaps, my French wasn't very good but it really bothered me to hear that. So, I was there for a few months, I worked at the radio station, but I was also a community liaison coordinator, so I worked with school children on behalf of the organization which broadcast, I forgot what it was called; I think it was the Francophone Centre of Huronia or something like that. So, I brought cultural programs to schools. Then, in the schools ... I found it interesting to encourage the kids to ask questions in French. It really helped them with their lessons at school.

Furthermore, he became a staunch defender of correct French and a champion of Francophonie by telling the students about his own experience and his own problems as a Francophone.

6.2. Ottawa: Learning How to Promote Canadian Heritage

The two years Marc spent in Montreal, although painful at times, were crucial for his professional — and personal — itinerary, as he found a bilingual position in a prestigious institution in Ottawa, in the Office of the Governor General, which came as a kind of consecration for his efforts to (re)conquer both his (correct) French and his Francophonie:

So, in that respect, the two years I spent in Montreal were quite rewarding for me. And through the connections I made at work, I managed to find a job in a Crown corporation in Ottawa, and it was a bilingual job ... And there, it was interesting because these people, here, Mrs. [Adrienne] Clarkson and Mr. Saul: Francophiles. They loved French and wherever they went in Canada, they made sure they engaged in activities in French. Even if we were in the Northwest Territories, they always insisted on visiting a French school, meeting the Francophone community, and, Mr. Saul, especially, spoke constantly of French as

---

[6] Marc stated: "I could do it because I had been a volunteer radio host when I was at the University of Ottawa."

a second language. He pushed these young people to learn French to better understand their country, its history, and fellow citizens.

Yet another element appears in Marc's testimonial: it is impossible to be or become a good Francophone without knowing the cultures involved. The knowledge of one's own cultural references involves knowing those of the other:

> Both knew what was going on in both cultural communities in Canada and I found it remarkable. And I learnt a great deal with them. With John Saul and his French as a second language projects, I gave further consideration to what was happening in Canada in terms of learning French as a second language. I became acquainted with the work groups and, and at some point, when I was told about this position at the university, I checked the job description and I thought: "I know this and that, I can do this, I can do that, this job was designed for me!"

It is worth noting how Marc reorganized his story to legitimize his position as RIF director: "I know this and that, I can do this, I can do that, this job was designed for me!" It was the same with Patrick: he talked at length about the various jobs he had held at uOttawa, as a bilingual employee. Despite his lack of training in immersion — but thanks to his position as head of the liaison office, which helped him develop numerous contacts with various university departments and Francophone networks outside Quebec — Patrick concluded by stating his legitimacy when he was approached by François Houle (see Chapter 2), at the start of the project: "I fit the profile for the position of RIF administrator."

7. MANAGING THE RIF: DRAWING FROM THE LINGUISTIC AND CULTURAL "IN-BETWEEN"

7.1. Understanding the Needs of Some and the Logic of Others

Appointed in late December 2007, one year after the RIF had begun, Marc specified right away that he was privileged, since his own experience allowed him to understand the perspectives and rationales of the various stakeholders:

> I should say that it is something innate but also learned, with what I have studied, this transmitter–receiver issue ... and all the filters which are required between the transmitter and the receiver, I could understand what these young people were going through, the difficulties they might have in communicating what they really meant, but I could also understand what others said.

At first, Marc found that the educational structure and linguistic support for the students were coherent: "Since I didn't know the institution, I thought it was adequate, but I started to change things to reflect my own views."

Trained in communication and experienced in the field of media, Marc focused on the external as well as internal image and promotion of the RIF as it grew, although still barely known within the university:

> I tried to personalize it a little, rejuvenate the way communications looked. But it was all there, I refined communications, some of the structures and because it was still rather small and I was alone, I was lucky enough to meet a lot of students and better understand their

motivations, their anxieties and achievements ... So, we worked hard to make people, the various actors, more aware, and to meet again with faculties, ... instructors, whenever possible.

According to Marc, Patrick was almost the same age, with the same looks as the students when he became director. Since he took part in all activities, he had gotten to know them all personally. But when Marc was then appointed, he was not free to do the same, being slightly older than Patrick, and having a young family.

In his detailed account on the implementation of the institutional environment, Patrick agreed with Marc's point of view. When he started, he had concentrated his efforts on inserting the administrative structures of the institutional environment into the various departments (including the Registrar's Office): he found a way to link content courses and language courses, and which types of exams the students should take entering or leaving the RIF program.

Because the RIF was still taking shape, it was vital to attract Anglophone students and to create meeting places for them to relate to. Patrick created the *Club d'immersion* with sociocultural activities, and the Immersion Mentoring Centre to welcome and guide students. His idea of a study-abroad component (see Chapters 4 and 7) was also one of the RIF's founding principles.[7] Patrick insisted on his idea of immersion within immersion:

> I definitely wanted it to be abroad. Most of them had already been to Quebec. I wanted something more flashy to attract students ... especially when recruiting high school students. We had money, scholarships for the trip.

While building on the experience of the former Second Language Institute[8] and using his internal networks, Patrick took on the role of founder and mediator, by putting the various actors of the academic institution — the RIF's friends and foes[9] — in touch.

> Working on campus with all the actors was the key to success ... They didn't all agree with the RIF ... changing something in the information system was *enormous* ... being an insider was crucial. If I had been an outsider, it wouldn't have worked.

7.2. Identifying Difficulties and Increasing Awareness

At the beginning, Patrick became personally involved with the content instructors whose courses had been "elected" as immersion courses by the administration, and he told them what comprehension difficulties Anglophone students were encountering:

> How can we increase awareness amongst content instructors? Not only did we have to inform them that immersion students were attending their classes, but also to try and explain to them the challenges the students faced. So, in my first year here, I tried to meet up with some instructors to tell them that those students read more slowly, didn't understand everything that was said, were a bit dazed by the speed and the language level, and, therefore, they could easily spend two or three minutes trying to figure out what had just been

---

[7] Patrick said that he had received a ten-page document with a number of strategies and principles to set up the immersion program.

[8] The predecessor to the Official Languages and Bilingualism Institute (OLBI), founded in 2008.

[9] Specifically, the Faculty of Science, which refused to join the project (see Chapter 2).

said. And once they had figured it out, they would realize they had missed the last two or three minutes and so, they would be totally lost. So, that was what I tried to explain.

Very quickly, however, these personal connections, which Patrick had initially prioritized, had to be left behind, as the RIF grew and became more complex — its profitability became a new priority. Marc agreed, adding: "But it was a special job because I had to do everything, and when you do everything, you can't do anything right because you're all over the place." As well, it appeared that the means "to inform the content instructors that their course had been elected and to make them aware beforehand of the students' difficulties" were insufficient — even inefficient — compared to the challenges the content instructors faced with the linguistic and cultural integration of Anglophone students into Francophone courses:

> So, I had to repeat this exercise at each session and I had no time, so, we wrote a letter ... Two pages long, I think, to explain to the instructors what students were going through and what we were trying to do for them ... Here are the letter and the document sent to the discipline instructors.[10] We don't know if that document had a real impact on the instructors, as its primary goal was to raise their awareness, but some instructors reacted to the letter and the document, fearing that additional tasks would be forced upon them. The university didn't inform them that they would be teaching immersion classes, so, sometimes, this letter came as a surprise for some of them.

In other words, these instructors were faced with a *fait accompli* and it is easy to understand their response to this institutional "symbolic violence" (Bourdieu, 1980) which touched two sore points: their status as instructors within the university and their status as Francophones within Ontario society. Marc described their response by calling them "French language purists":

> So, it frustrated and offended them to have students who couldn't write, couldn't speak in their course. So, they didn't seek to communicate with these students, they didn't seek to accommodate them, and they could be very unpleasant. In some cases, these people were defenders of the French language and they felt threatened, and others, were, as they say, "dyed-in-the-wool," looking for a homogeneous society, and here came from elsewhere others with different accents and it upset them. They told them: "You don't belong here!" There were people like that, students, as well as instructors and administrators.

In their defence, it should be said that these content instructors' rejection of Anglophone students, regarded as outsiders, matched the institutional "violence" they experienced.[11] The difficulties Marc mentioned were also echoed in Patrick's testimonial, indicating that he was already aware of the tensions between the groups involved:

- the non-OLBI French language instructors, who were hardly or not at all prepared for the challenge, had to become immersion instructors in no time

---

[10] The document, called "Immersion courses: Some useful information," can be found in the Appendix to Chapter 11 (p. 247).

[11] Perhaps the itineraries of content instructors could also be explored, to see how their relationships with languages and their language biographies affected and keep affecting the way they behave toward Anglophones in the immersion courses.

- the content instructors, even those who agreed, were not always willing to share their course material, and made working in tandem difficult — and in some cases, impossible

Finally, another point made during the interviews was that the more students who joined the RIF, the less manageable it became (both Marc and Patrick commented on this). If at first, candidates were quite proficient in French, later, quantity outweighed quality which was, however, a RIF hallmark. As a result, students with a lower level of French were recruited, which inevitably generated intake, management, and training issues, in administration as well as in teaching.

This issue, which started with the creation of the institutional environment itself, recurred like a leitmotif amongst all the actors interviewed for the purposes of this chapter. It would appear that no remediation strategies had been thought of to end these by-now chronic tensions.

8. MOVING TOWARD REMEDIATION STRATEGIES TO SUPPORT THE RIF?

8.1. Rethinking Alliances and Including the "Majority"

Marc recalled what has been noted throughout the interviews: that is, both he and his predecessor, Patrick, had had the same itinerary and profile. Indeed, both came from Manitoba's Francophone minority and both had protected French and Francophonie without rejecting the majority:

> What is interesting in this position, in fact, for who we are, myself and my predecessor, is that we both come from Manitoba. He was from the Francophone minority, so both of us have been exposed to English a lot, but, we are both very proud to be Francophones. But the one thing lacking is being suspicious of Anglophones.

Unlike Francophones, Marc suggested including, not excluding, Anglophones:

> We often hear in speeches, that us Francophones, "we have to stick together, we have to work harder, we must fear the Anglicization of our communities," which is true. I agree with that. But at the same time, we could do it with the Anglophones' help, and, we do understand it in the West, in our world, because with three or four per cent of the population, we can't do it alone.

Marc went even further, when he mentioned the strategies developed among Manitoba's minorities, strategies of dominated versus dominant, which certainly called for useful alliances:

> We needed allies and in French Manitoba, our allies were often natives and Jews. Because the Jews were despised as much as the Francophones, so the largest hospital in Winnipeg was founded by the Jews who had the money and the Francophones who had the people, but who couldn't go to the Winnipeg General Hospital because they weren't part of high society.

Marc applied the same alliance strategies to his current position, which was reminiscent of the interlinking and networking strategies recommended by Patrick.

8.2. The Legitimacy of "Bilingual Francophones": Renegotiating Asymmetrical Relationships

Both itineraries, Marc's and, in counterpoint, Patrick's, sound unique but they have many similarities: both administrators, serving as managers of a French immersion program, have had to juggle two languages[12] all their lives, while keeping French as the common thread in their life trajectories and life stories. Both languages, used alternately, could change status according to the context, self-revelations as and when academic and discipline choices were made, as well as linguistic and interregional mobilities, jobs, and so forth. Their linguistic experiences in natural immersion could have brought out new affiliations along the way or the impression of reconquering a neglected language, a lost identity. This linguistic and cultural in-between has obviously influenced their conception of the RIF, its management and growth. At the outset, Patrick had been more focused on the viability and attractiveness of this brand new institutional environment to the students. In turn, Marc has been more concerned with promoting the RIF's image and dissemination in Canada and abroad. Both men, being bilingual, have felt entitled to their administrative position: Patrick, because the university very quickly appointed him liaison officer within the educational institution; Marc, since he had previously held a prestigious post and been taught French as a second language by Francophiles. Indeed, Marc mentioned this clearly at the end of his interview:

> So, all my jobs focused on Canadian culture and identity, and, here I am, in this position, where I have the opportunity to play a specific role in the development or enhancement of bilingualism. A major factor in terms of Canadian identity.

In addition, both men have shown and demonstrated, again and again, that one had to deserve this kind of post, which means being aware of one's bilingualism and what it represents in terms of social and identity issues — in fact, being a good Francophone within that bilingualism. Both believe their itineraries are all the more commendable and legitimate as they belong to a twice minorized minority within Francophonie itself. Therefore, they had to work much harder to be accepted by Anglophones — as well as by other Francophones.

However, based on their own stories of linguistic and international student mobilities, the two narrators have spoken about a skill, often forgotten (or discarded) within the utilitarian approach used today in language learning for academic or professional purposes. In short, it is impossible to progress or work in a bilingual environment without knowing the cultural references and, therefore, one's interlocutors' symbolic world, issues, and logics, whatever they may be, in order to carry out a project in the other language. That is why they both[13] supported the idea of a study-abroad component because it allows the students to grasp a cultural depth they must learn to decode; it also

---

[12] It is interesting to point out that they only mentioned learning other languages and other student mobility experiences at the very end of the interview — and only in passing (Marc learned Russian and even lived in Russia, where he acted as "an improvised mediator"). This omission suggests that, for them, it all comes down to the two languages of Canada's bilingualism.

[13] For Marc, at least at the beginning.

forces them to question the obvious and self-evident, and take a necessary step back, which cannot be achieved without experiencing disorientation — that is, a disorentation in the immersion language.

But let there be no mistake! Theirs has been a story of initiation, with good guys, who accepted and included them in the larger French community, and bad guys, who made fun and excluded them. This story, with its obstacles and hardships, failures and successes, led inevitably to the implementation of the RIF program, which has sanctified an itinerary, at once erratic, exhilarating, and painful, aimed at one and only one goal: acknowledging the experience of a linguistic and cultural in-between at all levels of the educational institution and society.

Let Marc have the final word (shared with Patrick), when both of them seem to have shifted the issue of a *de facto* asymmetric bilingualism in favour of Francophone minorities and have turned it into a powerful tool, thanks to their newly acquired skills as potential mediators:

> So, this is the way we feel, Patrick and I, that we want to develop this Francophilie to include that pool of Anglophones, who not only understand our language but also our own world, and who will be able to support us.

CONCLUSION: THE ROLE OF MEDIATOR CANNOT BE IMPROVISED

On account of their itineraries, the two administrators have acknowledged the importance of immersion and, for all the above-mentioned reasons, have been able to identify the issues specific to the RIF. However, they each have had a totally different, even opposite, way of managing this program. Let us now attempt to understand its specificities as well as its consequences.

From the start, Patrick created the necessary social ties to generate an environment of trust among potential candidates. He also put the various actors involved in touch with one another, in one way or another, to implement the *dispositif*. However, Marc could not take the same approach, as he was not always available to oversee a then rapidly growing enrolment: "I couldn't afford to be off every Tuesday night to go the movies and every Friday night to go out for a drink with the students."

Moreover, Patrick, who was there at the very beginning of the project's implementation, was fully committed to linking the institutional and the pedagogical dimensions of the project. Marc actually acknowledged that difference and explained:

> So, how do I picture this job? There was the program, that specific process for Anglophone students, with the guidance you probably know, and things were going well. I found that everything there was coherent. Since I didn't know the institution, I found it adequate, but I started to change things and add my personal touch. I tried to rejuvenate the image of the program. Even though Patrick was younger than me, communications were marketed almost corporately, so I tried to personalize it a bit, update the look of communications ... But it was all there, I just refined communications and some of the structures, because it was still rather small and I was alone.

Thus, while Marc very quickly prioritized marketing aspects for the purpose of dissemination, considering the RIF as a finished product to be launched on the Canadian, and more widely, the North American, university market, he has done so for two implicit reasons linked to the technocratic approach of his management:

- He was trained and well experienced in communications; as a result, he has been expected by the administration to reinvest his expertise as a communicator to serve the image of the university. Why should he challenge the mission entrusted to him? In order to be recognized and integrated, each individual co-opted by the educational institution, expresses the *doxa*—the dominating discourse (*discours d'autorité*, Bourdieu, 1980).
- He did not have an in-depth knowledge of the pedagogical side of the institutional environment and believed that "everything was in place... it was all there"; since he had not specialized in (immersion) pedagogy, he has not wanted to interfere. He therefore has embraced a static vision of the immersion institutional environment as if it were a "nice model," immutable in its promotion. He has not seen the holistic approach inherent in any institutional environment, that is, seen as a complex work in progress, whose actors and co-actors (who could change along the way) were all stakeholders. A single and unilateral change—and, even more, a series of changes—would automatically endanger this fragile structure.

It is clear that being experienced in mobilities is not sufficient for becoming a "professional mediator," aware of the challenges faced by the educational institution's various actors. As Morin (1991) said, "Experiencing something doesn't make you *experienced*. Each experience has to be constantly renegotiated and re-meditated" (p. 10 [trans.; emphasis in original]). Experiencing the in-between, even in a variety of forms, does not, under any circumstances, mean becoming automatically experienced unless retroactive and reflexive work has been done.

A necessary "decapitalization of experience" (Maillard, 1998) should therefore be carried out, not only with students but also with all RIF actors and co-actors; that is, a "socio-anthropological introspection" (Gohard-Radenkovic, 2004, 2013b). Going from experience to awareness is one step, but going from awareness to action remains a major issue, since it is not about "individual goodwill," but about a complex process of conscientization, awareness-raising, both collective and individual, which is at stake within the educational institution itself.

REFERENCES

Agulhon, C., & Xavier de Brito, A. (Eds.). (2009). *Les étudiants étrangers à Paris: entre affiliation et repli*. Paris: L'Harmattan.

Anquetil, M. (2006). *Mobilité Erasmus et communication interculturelle: une recherche-action pour un parcours de formation*. Bern: Peter Lang.

Bachelart, D., & Pineau, G. (2009). *Le biographique, la réflexivité et les temporalités: articuler langues, cultures et formation*. Paris: L'Harmattan.

Bourdieu, P. (1980). *Le sens pratique*. Paris: Minuit.

Dervin, F., & Byram, M. (2008). *Échanges et mobilités académiques: quel bilan?* Paris: L'Harmattan.

Geertz, C. (1986). *Savoir global, savoir local: les lieux du savoir*. Paris: Presses universitaires de France.

Gerber, A. (2012). La "Gazette": un journal collectif "performatif", lieu de transformation d'une identité sociale. De l'étranger–visiteur à l'étudiant–observateur. In A. Gohard-Radenkovic, S. Pouliot, & P. Stalder (Eds.), *Journal de bord, journal d'observation: un récit en soi ou les traces d'un cheminement* (pp. 317–338). Bern: Peter Lang.

Gerber, A., & Gohard-Radenkovic, A. (2011). Étudiants africains à l'Université de Fribourg: un "étranger d'un certain type"?, ou Le récit de vie, révélateur du rôle de médiateur. *Canadian Diversity*, *8*(5), 89–92.

Gohard-Radenkovic, A. (2006). *La relation à l'altérité en situation de mobilité dans une perspective anthropologique de la communication*. Post-doctoral degree in communications, Université Lumière-Lyon II.

Gohard-Radenkovic, A. (2007). Comment analyser les rapports identitaires entre groupes et entre individus en situation de mobilité? *Igitur [Rivista annuale di lingue, letterature e culture moderne]*, *8*, 43–56.

Gohard-Radenkovic, A. (2013a). Politiques de rétention au Canada: écarts entre logiques des acteurs de l'institution et logiques des étudiants étrangers en situation de transition. In C. Hauser, P. Milani, M. Pâquet, & S. Skenderovic (Eds.), *Sociétés de migrations en débat. Québec–Canada–Suisse: approches comparées* (pp. 97-112). Porrentruy: Presses de l'Université Laval and Société jurassienne d'émulation.

Gohard-Radenkovic, A. (2013). Vers une "introspection socio-anthropologique" de l'intime et de l'apprendre: contre-point. In M. Berchoud, B. Rui, & C. Maillet (Eds.), *L'intime et l'apprendre: la question des langues vivantes* (pp. 181–190). Bern: Peter Lang.

Gohard-Radenkovic, A. (Ed.). (2004). *Communiquer en langue étrangère: de compétences culturelles vers des compétences linguistiques* (2nd ed.). Bern: Peter Lang.

Gohard-Radenkovic, A., Pouliot, S., & Stalder, P. (Eds.). (2012). *Journal de bord, journal d'observation: un récit de vie en soi ou les traces d'un cheminement*. Bern: Peter Lang.

Gohard-Radenkovic, A., & Rachédi, L. (Eds.). (2009). *Récits de vie, récits de langues et mobilités: nouveaux territoires intimes, nouveaux passages vers l'altérité*. Paris: L'Harmattan.

Lévi-Strauss, C. (1962). *La pensée éloignée*. Paris: Plon.

Maillard, P.-Y. (1998). *L'approche biographique: un outil pertinent pour la démarche spécifique du volontariat?* (Unpublished qualification thesis). Sciences de l'éducation, University of Freibourg.

Martel, J. (2007). Estates General of French Canada. In *The Canadian Encyclopedia*. www.thecanadianencyclopedia.ca/en/article/estates-general-of-french-canada

Morin, E. (1991). *Autocritique*. Paris: Seuil.

Murphy-Lejeune, E. (2001). Le capital de mobilité: genèse d'un étudiant–voyageur. *Mélanges Crapel*, *26*, 137–161.

Murphy-Lejeune, E. (2002). *Student mobility and narrative in Europe: The new strangers*. London: Routledge.

Papatsiba, V. (2003). *Des étudiants européens "Erasmus" ou l'aventure de l'altérité*. Bern: Peter Lang.

Pungier, M.-F. (2009). Traces d'expérience de la langue dans des journaux d'étudiants japonais en mobilité ou le récit d'une métamorphose. In A. Gohard-Radenkovic & L. Rachédi (Eds.), *Récits de vie, récits de langues et mobilités: nouveaux territoires intimes, nouveaux passages vers l'altérité* (pp. 51–74). Paris: L'Harmattan.

Pungier, M.-F. (2012). Croquer l'expérience ou la capitaliser? À propos d'un séjour de mobilité en France dans des journaux de bord de deux étudiants japonais. In A. Gohard-Radenkovic, S. Pouliot & P. Stalder (Eds.), *Journal de bord: un récit en soi ou les traces d'un cheminement* (pp. 287–316). Bern: Peter Lang.

Robin, J. (2013a). "Français? Où est le col?" Quand les étudiants suisses germanophones futurs enseignants du primaire doivent apprendre le français et effectuer un séjour de mobilité en région francophone. In M. Vatz-Laaroussi, E.-M. Riard, C. Gelinas, & E. Jovelin (Eds.), *Les défis de la diversité: enjeux épistémologiques, méthodologiques et pratiques* (pp. 119–128). Paris: L'Harmattan.

Robin, J. (2013b). Séjour de mobilité linguistique obligatoire dans la formation des enseignants: oui, mais comment? Le cas de la PHBern. *Babylonia, 1*, 94–98.

Sohet, P. (2007). *Images du récit*. Montréal: Presses de l'Université du Québec. citeseerx.ist.psu.edu/viewdoc/download?doi=10.1.1.132.7681&rep=rep1&type=pdf

CHAPTER 13
Language Ideologies of Immersion Stakeholders: The Case of Language Instructors

Jérémie Séror and Alysse Weinberg

INTRODUCTION

AS WE HAVE SEEN IN THE PREVIOUS CHAPTERS, the RIF (*Régime d'immersion en français* / French Immersion Stream) at the University of Ottawa is centred on bringing together both language and content instructors as a collaborative team. Despite the importance of this collaboration, the relationship has often been overlooked in research except for a few rare studies (e.g., Creese, 2002; Davison, 2006). Indeed, research on the integration of content and language has focused more often on other issues, particularly the interaction between students and their instructors (Blanc, Carol, Griggs, & Lyster, 2012; Smit, 2010), linguistic and content objectives (Hellekjaer, 2010; Nikula, 2012), and the challenges encountered by instructors teaching in a second or foreign language (Milne & Nuñez-Perucha, 2010; Stoller, 2004).

This chapter addresses this research gap by investigating the point of view of language instructors on the process of working with content instructors. Drawing on interviews with language instructors, the analysis focuses on the language ideologies suggested by the discourse of these instructors and how they reflect both the tensions and underlying power relationships that shape the collaborative and educational processes (Baquedano-Lopez & Kattan, 2008; Guardado, 2014; McGroarty, 2010; Moore and Py, 2011) associated with the RIF.

1. THEORETICAL FRAMEWORK

Language ideologies are defined as judgments, values, and beliefs about language and their use by members of a linguistic community (Baquedano-Lopez & Kattan, 2008). They represent a central question in linguistic anthropology because they are seen as working at all times as frames of interpretation for the daily activities of a community, thereby laying the foundations for various core beliefs and stances associated with that community's culture (Verschueren, 2011). As McGroarty (2010) argues, language ideologies are abstract and often operate in implicit ways. However, they contribute to conveying specific world views that determine the choices and possible interpretations for the actors involved in a communicative interaction. Taking into account the ideologies that underlie a communicative act is therefore closely linked to the goal of seeking to better understand the relationship between language and human activity (Schieffelin, 2007).

A great deal of research has focused on language ideologies and their impact on education and the socialization processes. This work has analyzed the language ideologies that underlie language practices within educational communities and their impact on learner experiences (Duff, 2010; Guardado, 2013; Talmy, 2004, 2008). Guardado shows, for example, the value given to the ideology of cosmopolitanism by young immigrants enrolled in scouting programs offered in Spanish, their mother tongue. For his part, Talmy analyzes the impact of school (and language course) practices that reinforce the stereotyped and negative conception of the "fresh-off-the-boat" second language learner as a marginalized identity in ESL classrooms.

These studies highlight the mechanisms inherent in ideological judgments as well as the importance of bias-inducing innuendoes (Quenot, 2012; Trimaille & Eloy, 2013). Evaluating a language, its form, and uses, also entails an evaluation of the individuals who accept or reject these same norms and values (McGroarty, 2010). In other words, investigating language ideologies offers a critical means of exploring the relationships, hierarchies, and balances of power that link the various actors associated with any language-mediated activity.

2. METHOLOGY

In the spring of 2013, extensive data collection was undertaken by Séror and Weinberg, drawing on interviews conducted with various actors associated with the RIF, including content instructors, language instructors, students, and administrators. This chapter focuses on data stemming from the interviews with language instructors. It reports on what language ideologies were revealed as these individuals spoke about their work and how they perceived the strengths and weaknesses of the RIF (see also Chapters 14, 15, and 16). Data analysis reveals these ideologies as powerful frames for the manner in which language instructors position themselves and are positioned by other actors in the RIF.

This study is based on the analysis of semi-structured interviews (Merriam, 1998) with ten language instructors. The interviews lasted about one hour each and were conducted at the researchers' offices. The topics covered included the experiences of language instructors, their experiences with the RIF program, and their contacts and relationships with the content instructors. Each interview ended with recommendations from language instructors based on their experiences and perceptions of the immersion *dispositif*.[1]

Four of the participants were full-time tenured instructors. The other six were part-time non-tenured instructors. All of them had more than 10 years of experience and had already been teaching adjunct courses at uOttawa. All the instructors agreed to participate in this study and responded positively to the invitation issued by the authors of this chapter to discuss their RIF experiences.

Drawing on traditional qualitative techniques (Denzin & Lincoln, 2017), each interview was recorded and transcribed so that ideas and themes could be coded and organized into relevant categories. The following questions guided the data analysis:

- What language ideologies can be found in the interviews with the language instructors teaching adjunct classes at uOttawa?

---

[1] A *dispositif* refers to a complete teaching and learning system, including stakeholders, programs, and resources (Gohard-Radenkovic, Knoerr, & Weinberg, 2014, p. 9 [trans.]).

- How do these language ideologies affect the relationship and interactions between the language and the content instructors associated with the RIF?

3. RESULTS AND RECOMMENDATIONS

Three fundamental themes/ideologies emerged from the interviews with language instructors regarding their accounts of their role within the RIF and their relationship with content instructors:

- the importance of the process for selecting and matching language and content instructors
- the benefits of a stable, long-term relationship between language and content instructors
- the prestige assigned to content courses and the impact on the value assigned to the work of language instructors

A discussion of each theme will be made in the sections that follow and will include the problems identified by the instructors, an analysis of the ideologies underlying these problems, and proposed solutions. These solutions will be used to start a discussion on the importance of ideological alignment among key actors for the optimal implementation of a university immersion program.

3.1. The Process for Selecting and Matching Language and Content Instructors

During their interviews, language instructors often discussed the difficulties arising from the current process used to assigning them to a content course and instructor. This matching process involves decisions made jointly by the RIF director and each relevant academic department, which are then shared with the instructors. Language instructors emphasized how strange it was that the two individuals most directly involved, and who should be working closely together, were not in fact part of the decision-making process that establishes teaching pairs for the RIF.[2]

Equally problematic, according to language instructors, is that the content course that will be associated with their language support class will not necessarily be identified as an immersion course when it is added to the teaching load of a content instructor. Moreover, content instructors will only be officially notified that their course has been designated as an immersion course two weeks before the beginning of a session, when they will receive an email from the RIF director notifying them that their course will include immersion students and providing a brief overview of the rationale and intent of the RIF (see Appendix in Chapter 11).

This selection process and management approach is driven by administrative considerations. Such a perspective has been criticized by educational researchers for its impersonal and unidirectional nature, as it presents instructors with a *fait accompli* decision made without consulting them. Brooke (2013) refers to policies of this type as representative of an ideology that favours top-down governance and establishes a division of

---

[2] Language instructors choose to teach in the RIF—they can identify the courses they want to teach; however, the content instructor they will be working with is always imposed on them.

labour where decisions are centralized with minimal attention paid to the preferences, expectations, and interests of the actors directly involved in these programs.

Language instructors lament the dangers of this protocol which, in the worst cases, matches them with content instructors for whom their compulsory participation with the RIF is an unpleasant surprise. It is frequently perceived as an additional poorly understood burden to their work load, thrown at them at the last minute:

> P1: Exactly, for her [the content instructor], it came as a surprise, too. She was given her teaching load at the last minute and I think she did not even have any information [about the program] ... It was a surprise ... So already we started on the wrong foot.[3]

The situation is even more complex for the many part-time content instructors who, by the nature of their contractual commitment, have only a limited knowledge of the RIF and the pedagogical benefits of this university-sponsored approach. In addition to having to prepare for a new course, they now have to deal with an extra level of complexity, including the potentially delicate situation of having to deal with the presence of a language instructor (who can be a full-time tenured instructor) in their class during the whole semester.

According to language instructors, under the current circumstances, their presence is too often seen as an intrusion and a bother. At worst, content instructors see them as unwelcome strangers who can observe and thus report on any teaching weaknesses they might witness in class. Indeed, being observed by a colleague opens the door to a possible questioning of their teaching practices and, in the case of non-Francophone instructors, their language skills. This sentiment is exacerbated by the administrative situation described above, which allows little time for a content instructor to learn and understand the nature of the collaboration that is desired in the immersion approach. Consequently, the seemingly arbitrary matching of instructors undermines the chances to establish a genuine trusting relationship between the two parties based on a shared goal. During their interviews, P1 and P2 noted this source of tension:

> P1: The instructor, he arrives and he finds himself with another faculty member, another instructor ... and one can easily misinterpret that ... "Oh, he is here to judge my French."
>
> ...
>
> We can imagine ... you do not speak well and a language instructor is put in front of you, in your face, for all your classes and he will or can speak about your language skills in his classes with your students during the whole term.
>
> P2: The full-time content instructor, I could not even approach him. He became tense. He said to me, "What do you want here?" He felt threatened or judged. When I approached him, he treated it like a criticism so I stopped approaching him.

Language instructors also pointed out that some content instructors did not, in fact, agree with the idea that English-speaking students should be able to attend a course originally designed for Francophones. In their eyes, Anglophone students were unwanted

---

[3] All interviews were conducted in French. The translations are the authors'. Participants were coded as P1 to 10.

intruders, perceived as hindering the class and adding to the burden of teaching since they might need extra help and be potentially disruptive, compared to teaching a homogeneous monolingual and monocultural class of Francophones (Séror & Lamoureux, 2014).

> P2: Instructors do not know how to teach a course where there are people who speak French as a second language. I imagine they are not supposed to [know how to teach these students]. It is not their job. They are impatient with English-speaking students.

Some content instructors were reported to have gone as far as to question the right of Anglophones to access a content course for Francophones with linguistic support that exceeded the level of support offered to Francophone students at the university. For them, immersion was thus an unfair program that favoured Anglophones at the expense of Francophones. Some even felt that they were betraying their own community by participating in the RIF: Why help majority Anglophone students when no similar services were offered to the minority population of Francophones? Indeed, the situation of the RIF students is unique. Anglophone RIF students constitute a minority in the predominantly Francophone content classroom while in the larger social context of the campus and of Canada, the situation is reversed, the Francophones being the minority in an English-dominated continent.

> P2: Yes, I remember that he [the content instructor] told me: "English students, why are they bothering us, they just have to take the course in English."
> ...
> Another instructor asked me: Why would I help Anglophone students if I do not help Francophone students in difficulty? The content instructor thought it was a blatant injustice to give course materials in advance to immersion students when he was not doing the same for Franco-Ontarians.

The process used by the administration to match content and language instructors neglected to take into account the attitudes and perceptions of the content instructors toward the immersion program. This oversight could result in a situation that forced people to work together, people who did not agree on the fundamental principles and ideologies at the heart of an immersion-based pedagogy. Immersion promotes the integration of second-language learners with native speakers and the establishment of language support for these learners. However, some content instructors hold a political ideology that promotes the separation of Francophones and Anglophones, and would rather see support provided to Francophones while excluding Anglophones.

To summarize, according to the language instructors, recruiting content instructors with an understanding of and acceptance for the objectives and issues of the RIF program would improve the collaboration between language and content instructors:

> P10: The more the content instructors are aware [about immersion], the more informed they are about immersion, the more help [the language instructors] will receive.

The language instructors strongly recommended that the selection and pairing should involve the participation of both sides of the teaching team at the heart of the immersion approach. The pairing decision would thus be made with the input of the educational actors rather than being a centralized decision imposed by the administration on instructors. This process would ensure that both instructors have a chance to discuss and confirm their understanding of the RIF and that participating faculty members are more engaged and more convinced of the benefits of the program. In other words, content instructors should be able to decide whether or not to participate in the *dispositif* according to their personal interests and ideological and pedagogical convictions. With such a system, some content instructors may refuse to participate in the RIF, and this is a possibility that should not be overlooked. However, as suggested by one participant, this is a decision that should be respected:

> P1: I think that, at first glance, it is the question of respect [toward the content instructor teaching] in this program. First of all, [the administrators have] to approach the content instructors asking them: "Do you want [your course] to be an immersion course ... or would that bother you?"

This sense of consent on the part of the instructors involved is currently lacking, yet our findings suggest that it is an essential foundation for creating a strong and lasting relationship between the language and content instructors. Without an agreement of shared goals and ideologies, not only will the collaboration have a contentious start, but there is also a strong risk of hurting all the participants in the RIF program, especially the students:

> P7: It is the students who will suffer if there is no easy flowing communication between the two instructors.

3.2. The Benefits of a Stable, Long-Term Relationship Between Two Instructors

The language instructors' concerns highlighted the importance of establishing a stable and lasting relationship with the content instructors. This principle was recommended by all language instructors interviewed. However, sadly, these same instructors also reported that this type of long-term relationship was in fact nothing more than wishful thinking since the current university hiring process does not guarantee that a language instructor will work with the same content instructor from one year to the next.

This instability can be explained in part by institutional forces linked to the distribution of teaching assignments and to term-to-term scheduling. From one year to the next, departments must manage a constantly changing roster of instructors due to sabbaticals, course releases, and incompatibilities arising from new timetables and course schedules. Other factors aggravate this situation, especially for part-time instructors, who teach the majority of language courses for the immersion program. In particular, their union seniority, or lack of it, affects their hiring from semester to semester: it is the most important factor used to determine which part-time content or language instructor will have priority in their choice of courses. Consequently, even if a part-time instructor has taught an immersion course for a year, he or she may be bumped the following year by a colleague with more seniority points, thereby taking the course away from them. This results in constant uncertainty regarding the stability of a partnership between content and language instructors.

The language instructors expressed the disillusionment they felt whenever they learned that they would have to work with a brand-new content instructor, meaning that the effort they had invested in familiarizing themselves with the content and work methods of the prior instructor could not be taken advantage of:

> P1: The ideal is that there would be continuity, because then we can build together and become more at ease with one another. We could have projects and collaborate. But if you lose continuity, from one side or the other, everything is lost ... Everything has to start from scratch every time — negotiating the relationship and learning the content.

This constant risk of having to set up a new relationship with a new instructor is a significant source of stress, and represented a demotivating factor for language instructors. Indeed, in their view, the lack of stable long-term partnerships hindered their efforts and led to a reduction in the number of hours they were willing to spend developing the specialized teaching materials needed to effectively support their students. In the worst cases, some language instructors admitted that they would even hesitate to teach an adjunct course because of this lack of continuity:

> P8: Only if I were sure that I could work with Mr. X, only then would I accept to teach this course again.

Interestingly, the interviews revealed that the content instructors also suffered from this lack of continuity. A language instructor told us about the case of a content instructor who also refused to continue, for much the same reason:

> P4: This content instructor, I know he refused to teach [in the immersion program] again this year. I understand. For the insecure instructor teaching in his second language, why open oneself up to criticism every semester, to feel nervous every time one works with a different professor?

Conversely, the interviews underscored the value stemming from stable and lasting relationships between language and content instructors. Language instructors noted that compatible tandem partnerships reinforced the teamwork approach necessary for the RIF, by fostering the conditions and time needed to ensure a deeper understanding of each instructor's learning objectives and pedagogy:

> P4: The more we work together, the further we go beyond our initial expectations ... We start working together as a team, rather than independently.

In another example, the rare case of a five-year, uninterrupted collaboration between a language instructor and an instructor in the history department (both full-time faculty) was cited on several occasions to illustrate the benefits that are only possible through long-term partnerships between the language and content instructors. This collaboration led to the creation of a series of tools to facilitate student learning in several history classes (see Chapter 9). Research on the impact of these tools clearly showed that the stability of a sustained relationship between the instructors had been a critical factor in student success.

The testimonies reported in this section have emphasized the importance of building a close, stable relationship between language and content instructors. Here again we see the weaknesses of a bureaucratic, instrumental approach to staffing that does not take into account the personal and interpersonal work that is gradually being built in any collaboration between language and content instructors. The institutional predilection for top-down control of hiring unfortunately removes the human and relational dimension, which is at the heart of the immersion pedagogy at uOttawa, from the equation.

One is left wondering whether, instead, a more bottom-up approach would be better suited for this educational system (Tochon, 2011). Such a system would prioritize the stability of the language and content instructor partnerships, and could actively seek to identify and retain teams that have demonstrated an affinity and ability to work together effectively. Conversely, deliberate efforts would be made to limit partnerships marked by difficulties and tensions. Moreover, rather than using the traditional assignment of courses based on seniority alone, mechanisms should be put in place to protect the most cohesive teams by giving instructors (including part-time ones) the assurance of being able to give the same course several times for a minimum period—for example, three years. The stability of these collaborations would thus take precedence over the exclusive use of seniority points when allocating courses.

3.3. Inequality of Status in the Hierarchical Structure of the University

The last theme that emerged from the language instructors' comments was associated with the forces and ideologies that positioned them and their perceived contributions within the university. Indeed, several language instructors indicated that they felt relegated to a second-class status by the content instructors, who were inclined to denigrate them and not consider them as university instructors in their own right:

> P3: The relationship with the language instructor is badly established .... We are not seen as a peer, only as a language teacher.
>
> ...
>
> P10: This instructor is well known [in his field]. He is a high-ranking instructor and thinks highly of himself. He has some contempt for language instructors.

Other instructors indicated that they were sometimes even questioned about their status as instructors by content instructors who sought to lower their role to that of a teaching assistant or tutor:

> P9: In some cases, I felt a professional distance between the content and the language instructor. An instructor even asked me if I was an instructor like him—an instructor in his own right. I could have been his teaching assistant. Indeed, sitting in the lecture hall, one is assimilated into being a student.
>
> ...
>
> P1: The content instructor thought I was doing tutoring.

This lack of understanding of their role even pushed one language instructor to develop a particular strategy to counteract the perverse effect of these perceptions. Starting from her first contact, she explicitly presented her rank and status within the university by offering her business card to the content instructor:

P1: The content instructor thought I was an assistant teaching languages ... So, I had to go to his office with my business card to introduce myself, to say that I, too, was full-time and tenured and ... that we were associated with each other equally.

The difficulties experienced by language instructors echo the lack of prestige accorded to language teaching elsewhere in the world (Benesch, 2001; Johns, 1990; Swales, 1989). This ideological positioning was emphasized in both Johns and Benesch, who pointed out the imbalance between the status of the language instructor and that of the content instructor: the language instructor is most often positioned as a subordinate who must gain the approval of the content instructor, who is perceived to have a greater right to identify him or herself as an expert. Even when instructors share the same ranks, there is an inequality in terms of prestige. Instructors who teach language are considered second-class instructors — unless they teach literature and linguistics.

This relationship of subordination between the two instructors is often used as a justification to limit the access of the language instructor to the course content and support material. Indeed, the interviews revealed that the content instructors controlled their course and, indirectly, the language instructor's course:

- They could refuse access to content course notes and teaching materials used in the classroom.
- They could also reject the recommendations proposed by the language instructor to help immersion students overcome language difficulties encountered in the course or during the completion of assignments.
- Some language instructors told us of the blunt refusal of some content instructors to penalize less severely the language aspects of assignments completed in French by RIF students.[4] The content instructor who clearly announces in class that he or she will not make any accommodation for language learners ends up discouraging students risking to submit their work in French.

This unequal division of power separates the two categories of instructors and reinforces the content instructor's supremacy and status. This not only aggravates the lack of understanding and collaboration identified by language instructors, but also undermines the effectiveness of their teaching. One can see the frustration of the language instructors who, after working on written skills with their students, realized that the immersion students submitted their content course assignment in English because the content instructor had refused to acknowledge and make accomodations for them.

Other cases illustrated the marginalization perceived by language instructors. One pointed out, for example, that only language instructors are contractually obliged to attend the content course — contract documents clearly state this obligation. Content instructors do not have this requirement:

---

[4] This recommendation is often made by language instructors because, at uOttawa, students have the option of submitting their work in either of the two official languages (University of Ottawa, 1974, "Bilingualism," Part 6, line 20 (3)).

> P7: The language instructor attends the content class, but the opposite has never been done. Only once did a history instructor come to the language class and he gave some advice there at the end.

This representation of the discipline of languages as inferior to the more noble and prestigious academic disciplines has also affected how content instructors perceive language instructors:

> P1: It was very clear that, in his mind, he was clearly superior as a business administration instructor ... than any language instructor could ever be ...

Another language instructor reported how a content instructor had categorically refused to communicate with him or recognize him, due to his lack of a doctorate degree:

> P2: An instructor told me "What is your training? Do you have a doctorate?" I answered, "No." He replied, "Oh, I do not need to talk to you then."

The situation is worse for part-time language instructors who have neither academic recognition nor job security. One such instructor even declined to elaborate on the rejection he had experienced from a content instructor, as he had been so alienated and scarred by that painful experience:

> P7: There was some tension with a [content] instructor ... a rather unpleasant attitude ... It is a problem which I'd rather not return to. She did not even look at me. I have nothing to add.

3.4. Enhancing the Status of Language Instructors

The cases illustrated above highlight the dangers of a perceived hierarchy that would place language instructors below content instructors. The immersion approach is an inclusive one, which not only seeks to integrate language and content but also values both content and language instructors and their collaboration as equal and essential facets of students' learning experience. However, for language instructors, this ideal vision of integration and collaboration between language and content experts is clearly not being achieved. The essential contribution of language instructors is to help language learners and content experts integrate language and disciplinary knowledge (Lyster & Ballinger, 2011).

Some of the language instructors stipulated that institutions had a role to play in helping to change these attitudes. They suggested, for instance, that events such as a reception or an immersion teaching award offered during a ceremony would help publicly acknowledge and reward the value and contributions of language instructors. They also suggested that an award designed to recognize the language and content instructor team of the year would also encourage a closer, more equal, and more harmonious relationship between these two key immersion stakeholders. Most importantly, this type of institutional undertaking would have the effect of counteracting prejudices and stigmatized representations of language instructors on campus:

> P2: If the administration gave recognition to these instructors ... [through] a formal social recognition [ceremony organized] by the administration ... I think this would help more than just to receive an email or two letters.

In the absence of such official recognition, three additional recommendations were made by language instructors:

- First, the RIF, in consultation with the different departments involved, should organize mandatory information sessions at the beginning of the semester for both the language and content instructors involved in the immersion program. The purpose would be to present the RIF objectives, the pedagogy specific to immersion, the rights and obligations of each partner, and finally, the relationship between the two instructors and the mutual benefits it can generate. Currently, annual information sessions as well as training workshops are organized by the RIF for language instructors; content instructors do not attend them.[5]

- Second, the RIF pedagogical advisors should visit each department to answer and address any questions or concerns from content instructors about immersion pedagogy. These opportunities to communicate directly with content instructors and their department heads are essential for the optimal implementation of the RIF, a program whose success depends on a shared vision of the objectives and the work to be done by all actors, in a relationship where everyone is seen as equal partners.

- Finally, language instructors emphasized the need to select only content instructors who are truly committed to an immersion pedagogy. Faced by what, at times, is a complete lack of interest in immersion pedagogy and thus in collaborating with a language instructor, language instructors underscored the need to track and document which instructors seem to be willing to invest the time and effort needed to truly engage in collaborative forms of teaching. This would lead to establishing a pool of collaborative content instructors who could be counted on from semester to semester, based on demonstrated pedagogical skills and ideological commitment to the RIF pedagogy and tandem teaching.

In her interview, P1 described the ideal instructor as follows:

P1: It should be the best [instructors]. Take the example of Mr. X. He sees me as an equal.... He works with the language.... He values bilingualism.... He is a journalist.... So, for him, the fact that someone wants to become bilingual and to improve the quality of their French is something.... He was sold on the idea, the idea of improving the second language [of his students].

Even if attitudes and ideologies differ from one content instructor to another, the goal would be to identify those instructors whose personal background and training have allowed them to acquire a greater awareness of the mission, values, objectives, and approaches of the RIF (see Chapter 14).

CONCLUSION

In this chapter, we have analyzed language instructors' perceptions in order to identify the different ideologies that influence their relationship with other key stakeholders at

---

[5] These sessions are not mandatory, and few language instructors attend them. To our knowledge, since 2006, only one content instructor has attended these sessions.

the heart of the RIF. The language instructors spoke primarily about their relationships and interactions with their content counterparts. Our results confirm the complexity of these relationships. Specifically, tensions associated with status and ideological positioning emerged as key themes. The following themes were highlighted:

- arbitrary recruitment practices, both for language and content instructors, which work against the establishment of long-term stable collaborations
- a lack of stability and continuity year over year that reduces the effectiveness of collaborations between language and content instructors
- the presence of ideologies that reduce the perceived value and status of language instructors and give higher importance to the work of content instructors. These often-tacit ideologies reinforce feelings of inferiority among language instructors, creating tensions and frustrations which negatively affect tandem teaching and collaborations

Since the introduction of university-level immersion programs (Navés, 2009), several researchers have stressed the crucial role of the collaboration between language and content instructors (Knoerr, 2018; Stewart & Perry, 2005; Stewart, Sagliano, & Sagliano, 2002; Stoller, 2004). This is particularly the case in the adjunct model, where the implementation of a true immersion pedagogy requires a genuine culture of cooperation between the language expert and the discipline expert. The tensions identified above can be interpreted as symbolic of language instructors' displeasure with a lack of ideological recognition and understanding of the full complexity and value of their work, and the way in which this ultimately creates obstacles that prevent a culture of cooperation to flourish.

In conclusion, according to its stakeholders, fundamentally different visions[6] of the RIF coexist at uOttawa. It is clear that, without rapprochement, we will find ourselves with parallel ideologies that represent immersion in contradictory and sometimes even confrontational manners for the the key stakeholders involved. The establishment of a harmonious relationship between language and content instructors need not be a utopian dream. It does require, however, that the ideological perceptions governing these relationships be taken seriously and that work be undertaken to ensure a shared vision of the roles and obligations of the actors involved. This vision may well need to be accompanied with institutional forms of recognition and more explicit communication of the common goals, roles, and responsabilities that unite both language and content experts. It is this holistic and more deliberately integrated vision that must be advocated, defended, and introduced at every level by any institution considering the implementation of university immersion.

---

[6] One could also speak of divisions of the world (Bourdieu, 1987) due to different paths and especially different statuses.

REFERENCES

Baquedano-Lopez, P., & Kattan, S. (2008). Language socialization in schools: An historical overview. In P. Duff & N. Hornberger (dir.), *Encyclopedia of language and education: Language socialization* (vol. 8, pp. 161–173). Philadelphia: Springer.

Benesch, S. (2001). *Critical English for academic purposes: Theory, politics, and practice.* Mahwah: Erlbaum.

Blanc, N., Carol, R., Griggs, P., & Lyster, R. (2012). Lexical scaffolding in immersion classroom discourse. In E. Alcón Soler & M.P. Safont-Jordà (Eds.), *Discourse and language learning across L2 instructional settings* (pp. 31–51). Amsterdam: Rodopi.

Bourdieu, P. (1987). What makes a social class? On the theoretical and practical existence of groups. *Berkeley Journal of Sociology, 32*, 1–17.

Brooke, M. (2013). A critical analysis of selected policy making decisions in the US and the UK with regard to the implementation of information and communication technology (ICT) in national state primary and secondary school education systems. *Open Journal of Modern Linguistics, 3*, 94–99.

Creese, A. (2002). The discursive construction of power in teacher partnerships: Language and subject specialists in mainstream schools. *TESOL Quarterly, 36*, 597–616.

Davison, C. (2006). Collaboration between ESL and content teachers: How do we know when we are doing it right? *International Journal of Bilingual Education and Bilingualism, 9*, 454–475.

Denzin, N.K., & Lincoln, Y.S. (2017). *The SAGE handbook of qualitative research* (5th ed.). Thousand Oaks, CA: Sage.

Duff, P.A. (2010). Language socialization. In N. Hornberger (Ed.), *Sociolinguistics and language education* (pp. 427–454). New York: Multilingual Matters.

Gohard-Radenkovic, A., Knoerr, H., & Weinberg, A. (2014). Introduction. In H. Knoerr, A. Weinberg, & A. Gohard-Radenkovic (Eds.), *L'immersion française à l'université: politiques et pédagogies* (pp. 1–20). Ottawa: University of Ottawa Press.

Guardado, M. (2013). Toward a critical multilingualism in Canadian classrooms: Making local inroads into a cosmopolitan identity. *TESL Canada Journal, 30*, 151–165.

Guardado, M. (2014). The discourses of heritage language maintenance: Engaging ideologies in Canadian Hispanic communities. *Heritage Language Journal, 11*, 1–28.

Hellekjaer, G.O. (2010). Language matters: Assessing lecture comprehension in Norwegian English-medium higher education. In C. Dalton-Puffer, T. Nikula, & U. Smit (Eds.), *Language use and language learning in CLIL classrooms* (pp. 233–258). Amsterdam: John Benjamins.

Johns, M.A. (1990). L1 composition theories: Implications for developing theories of L2 composition. In B. Kroll (Ed.), *Second language writing* (pp. 24–36). Cambridge: Cambridge University Press.

Knoerr, H. (2018). Collaboration between language and content instructors: keystone and weak link of content and language integration environments. In H. Knoerr, A. Weinberg, & C.E. Buchanan (Eds.), *Current issues in university immersion* (pp. 175–204). Ottawa: Groupe de recherche en immersion au niveau universitaire (GRINU).

Lyster, R., & Ballinger, S. (2011). Content-based language teaching: Convergent concerns across divergent contexts. *Language Teaching Research, 15*, 279–288.

McGroarty, M. (2010). Language and ideologies. In N.H. Hornberger & S.L. McKay (Eds.), *Sociolinguistics and language education* (pp. 3–39). Clevedon: Multilingual Matters.

Merriam, S.B. (1998). *Qualitative research and case study applications in education.* San Francisco: Jossey-Bass.

Milne, E.D., & Nuñez-Perucha, B. (2010). Metadiscursive devices in university lectures: A contrastive analysis of L1 and L2 teacher performance. In C. Dalton-Puffer, T. Nikula, & U. Smit (Eds.), *Language use and language learning in CLIL classrooms* (pp. 213–231). Amsterdam: John Benjamins.

Moore, D., & Py, B. (2011). Introduction: Discourse on languages and social representations. In G. Zarate, D. Levy, & C. Kramsch (Eds.), *Handbook of multilingualism and multiculturalism* (pp. 263–270). Paris: Éditions des archives contemporaines. (Original work published 2008)

Navés, T. (2009). Effective content and language integrated learning (CLIL) programmes. In Y. Ruiz de Zarobe & R.M. Jiménez Catalán (Eds.), *Content and language integrated learning: Evidence from research in Europe* (pp. 22–40). Bristol: Multilingual Matters.

Nikula, T. (2012). On the role of peer discussion in the learning of subject-specific language use in CLIL. In E. Alcón Soler & M.-P. Safont-Jordà (Eds.), *Discourse and language learning across L2 instructional settings* (pp. 133–153). Amsterdam: Rodopi.

Quenot, S. (2012). Orientation, interculturalité et équité dans l'enseignement bilingue français-corse. In J.-M. Eloy & C. Trimaille (Eds.), *Idéologies linguistiques et discriminations* (pp. 85–108). Paris: L'Harmattan.

Schepens, P. (2011). Le concept d'idéologie analysé depuis une position phénoménologique. *Semen, 30*, 17–41. journals.openedition.org/semen/8951#article-8951

Schieffelin, B.B. (2007). Langue et lieu dans l'univers de l'enfance. *Anthropologie et Sociétés, 31*, 15–37.

Séror, J., & Lamoureux, S. (2014). Intégrer les étudiants anglophones dans le cadre d'un programme d'immersion universitaire au Canada. *Dossiers des sciences de l'éducation* [thematic issue: *Les langues étrangères à la fac*], *32*, 95–110.

Smit, U. (2010). CLIL in an English as a lingua franca (ELF) classroom: On explaining terms and expressions interactively. In C. Dalton-Puffer, T. Nikula, & U. Smit (Eds.), *Language Use and Language Learning in CLIL Classrooms* (pp. 259–277). Amsterdam: John Benjamins.

Stewart, T., & Perry, B. (2005). Interdisciplinary team teaching as a model for teacher development. *TESL-EJ, 9*(2), 1–17.

Stewart, T., Sagliano, M., & Sagliano, J. (2002). An alternative team-teaching model for content-based instruction. In Y.C. Cheng, K.T. Tsui, K.W. Chow & M.M.C. Magdalena (Eds.), *Subject teaching and teacher education in the new century: research and innovation* (pp. 457–488). Hong Kong: Hong Kong Institute of Education, Kluwer Academic.

Stoller, F.L. (2004). Content-based instruction: Perspectives on curriculum planning. *Annual Review of Applied Linguistics, 24*, 261–283.

Swales, J. (1989). Service English program design and opportunity cost. In R.K. Johnson (Ed.), *The second language curriculum* (pp. 79–90). Cambridge: Cambridge University Press.

Talmy, S. (2004). Forever FOB: The cultural production of ESL in a high school. *Pragmatics, 14*, 149–172.

Talmy, S. (2008). Forever FOB? In A. Reyes & A. Lo (Eds.), *Beyond Yellow English: Toward a linguistic anthropology of Asian Pacific America* (pp. 347–366). Oxford: Oxford University Press.

Tochon, F.V. (2011). Reflecting on the paradoxes of foreign language teacher education: A critical system analysis. *Porta Linguarum, 15*, 7–24.

Trimaille, C., & Eloy, J.-M. (Eds.). (2013). *Idéologies linguistiques et discriminations*. Paris: L'Harmattan.

University of Ottawa. (1974). Regulation on bilingualism at University of Ottawa 1974. www.uottawa.ca/administration-and-governance/policies-and-regulations/regulation-on-bilingualism

Verschueren, J. (2011). *Ideology in language use: Pragmatic guidelines for empirical research*. New York: Cambridge University Press.

CHAPTER 14

Experiences of Immersion Stakeholders at the University of Ottawa:
Content Instructors

Hélène Knoerr

INTRODUCTION

CHAPTERS 12 TO 16 IN THIS BOOK take an insider's look at immersion, as it is experienced on a daily basis by its various stakeholders — students, instructors, administrators — at the micro level: How does immersion impact their personal and professional/academic paths? This particular chapter looks at the experience of content instructors.

Among the stakeholders, content instructors are, in many ways, the least involved in the *Régime d'immersion en français* (henceforth RIF) at the University of Ottawa, simply because they do not have a say regarding their involvement — if the course they are teaching is designated by their faculty as an immersion course, then they are teaching an immersion course, whether they like it or not. Moreover, they are experts in their fields, not in language pedagogy or methodology, and most of them have never heard about the RIF and its philosophy — indeed, some of them do not understand why they should accommodate Anglophone students in their French courses, when these students can take the same courses in English. But as Perrenoud (2000) has pointed out, understanding a specialized text goes beyond understanding its vocabulary or technical jargon — it requires an understanding of its community, its culture, its explicit codes and implicit rules, its practices, in order to be able to situate it in its semantic and conceptual contexts. Some content instructors also feel uncomfortable having a language instructor in attendance, out of a sense of insecurity (they think they will be judged by their peers) or of superiority (they think language instructors have a lower status; see Chapter 13).

But content instructors are key stakeholders in the *dispositif* implemented by the RIF: the pedagogical team can only work if the triple bind — between content and language, between content instructor and immersion students, and between content instructor and language instructor — works. In this chapter we will analyze the life stories of six content instructors in order to identify their language ideologies and their beliefs. In turn, this will allow us to highlight the winning conditions for the pedagogical partnership at the core of the adjunct model implemented in the RIF.

1. CONCEPTUAL/THEORETICAL FRAMEWORK

1.1. Rationale for the Theoretical Positioning

Our analyses are based on the concept of ideologies, which include beliefs, values, and behaviours, as they are translated into representations or perceptions in discourse.

These ideologies and beliefs have a powerful influence on teachers' methods, actions, and behaviours—indeed, they are an excellent predictor of teachers' behaviours (Pajares, 1992). They are therefore extremely relevant in order to understand not only how they may influence content instructors in the RIF but also how the RIF experience may influence these ideologies and beliefs: there is a constant interaction between beliefs, experience and practice (Woods, 1996; Woods & Knoerr, 2014), one informing and being informed by the others. Research has shown that teachers' most deeply-ingrained beliefs can be changed by experiences, even short-term ones (Wong, 2013). Exploring whether the immersion experience has changed content instructors' beliefs regarding the immersion philosophy and their own pedagogical practices gives us an insight into the "ideal" content instructor—what are the characteristics most conducive to a successful pedagogical partnership such as the one at the core of the adjunct immersion model.

1.2. State of the Art: Theoretical Framework

Among these ideologies, we will focus on language ideologies, a concept exposing the relationships between language acts and metalinguistic discourses on the one hand and cultural, social, and political structures and processes on the other (Irvine & Gal, 2000; Jaffe, 1999). Language ideologies materialize in metalinguistic discourses and practices, such as:

- beliefs (mostly unconscious) regarding the basic criteria of what constitutes a language
- collective notions of good/bad usage in oral and written language, as evidenced in culture-specific genres and registers
- ideas and convictions on the language criteria associated with social, individual or collective attributes such as legitimacy, authority, authenticity, citizenship—in other words, the link between good/bad usage and good/bad behaviour
- convictions or certainties regarding the (cultural or political) connections between language and identity in all its aspects, from personal to national to supranational. (Jaffe, 2008, pp. 517–518)

In analyzing the representations and ideologies as materialized in the discourse of six content instructors involved in the RIF, we will ask the following questions:

- What types of ideologies, and more specifically, language ideologies, have emerged from these content instructors' past experiences with language(s), education/training, and mobility, and how do these ideologies impact on their relationships with language instructors and with immersion students?
- Were these content instructors' pedagogical practices and beliefs and ideologies about the concept of university-level immersion changed by their RIF experience?
- Is there a typical profile, a set of characteristics most desirable in content instructors for the success of the RIF *dispositif* — or any *dispositif* based on the adjunct model?

2. METHODOLOGY

2.1. Corpus

Upon approval of uOttawa's Research Ethics Committee, the RIF director, Marc Gobeil, sent an email message at the end of October 2012 to the twelve content instructors who had taught at least one course for the RIF in the past three years, asking if they would agree to a one-hour interview.[1] Six responded favourably: four male and two female instructors, aged 40 to 60 (five regular instructors and one contract instructor), from six disciplines: political science, sociology, history, communication, psychology, and second language teaching. The interviews were conducted in November 2012. Table 1 summarizes the characteristics of the respondents.

Table 1: Characteristics of the six content instructors

Instructor	Origin	First language	Other languages	Mobility
Communication	Quebec	French	English	Ottawa
History	Quebec	French	English, Spanish	Cuba, Spain
Second language teaching	Guadeloupe	French creole	French, English	France, United States, Canada
Psychology	Bolivia	Quechua, Spanish	French, English, German	Switzerland, Canada
Political science	Quebec	French	English	Bolivia and around the world
Sociology	Quebec	French	English	Sudbury (Ontario)

2.2. Data Collection and Inquiry Methods

Upon confirmation of each interview, participants were sent two documents: a table collecting biodata regarding personal, linguistic, educational, and academic/professional backgrounds, and a set of topics to guide the interview:
- past experiences with languages, domestic and international mobility
- past experiences in education/training in their field of expertise as well as in language and/or content teaching
- current experiences in the RIF, including their perceptions of the RIF stakeholders
- overall assessment of their RIF experience: benefits, assets, limitations, and challenges

---

[1] Text of that request:
   The RIF has commissioned a report on the representations of its stakeholders on their experience with the program. Would you agree to share your experiences in a one-hour interview? Interviews will take place November 5–16 [2012]. Please indicate your preferences by November 2. Thank you for your collaboration.

All interviews were about forty minutes long and were recorded digitally, then transcribed and analyzed thematically. Participants signed a consent form detailing the research and explaining how the data collected would be used.

2.3. Methodological Choices and Rationale

The life histories approach[2] was used to explore participants' individual experiences at the micro level in the macro level context of their time, of history: Which elements did they select? How did they interpret their own experiences, actions, and thoughts? Atkinson (1998) defines life history (or life story) as "a fairly complete narrating of one's entire experience of life as a whole, highlighting the most important aspects" (p. 8). There are many forms of life histories/stories, but the common denominator is that, although the researcher guides the interview, the participants tell their narratives in their own words (for an overview of the various forms, see Denzin, 1989). This approach is particularly relevant in helping us answer our three research questions since they are situated in time and space, and aim at highlighting participants' experiences.

2.4. Methods and Tools for Analysis

The six life histories collected were analyzed using a combination of three methods: thematic analysis (Braun & Clarke, 2006), life course analysis (Elder, 1998), and comparative analysis (Kalleberg, 1966; Lijphart, 1971). First, we identified the themes emerging from each life history; then we compared how each theme is narrated in each story. We also created biographical categories, such as "key moments." Finally, by comparing narratives using these combined guidelines as a framework, we were able to highlight some common paths or elements, which we then categorized into types.

3. ANALYSES

3.1. Identifying Recurring Themes

After transcribing all six interviews we were able to identify perceptions and representations pertaining to five recurring themes:

- *Previous beliefs and ideologies related to immersion and language learning*:

    Because of their previous experiences as language learners and scholars, all six instructors had thought through the concepts of language, language learning/teaching methods, relationships between language and culture, and the cognitive and affective implications of language learning.

- *Previous language learning experiences*:

    All six instructors had learned at least one other language, with more or less success and ease, but always by choice, which may make them feel a kinship to immersion students, who also choose to study in their second language.

---

[2] This qualitative approach originates in ethnosociology and was later used widely in urban sociology by the Chicago School as of the 1920s.

- *Experience with majority/minority status situations*:

    The four instructors from Quebec went from majority Francophone status to minority Francophone status when they left their native province, a shift that is also experienced by immersion students who go from majority Anglophone status in Canada to minority status in the content courses they take in French at uOttawa.

- *Impact on pedagogical practice*:

    Five out of six instructors explicitly stated that teaching in the RIF, and more specifically knowing that there were immersion students in their classes, caused them to change the way they teach in general.

- *Impact on beliefs*:

    Most content instructors stated that their immersion experience caused them to revisit their beliefs about language, culture, and the majority vs minority dynamics.

3.2. Defining Moments in Life Courses

Analysis of the life histories revealed key moments which acted as triggers for the participants. Interestingly, these defining moments were always positive, always chosen or initiated, and never related to an encounter. In all six cases, it was a trip, for school or for holiday, which happened in early adult life, when they were about to embark on post-secondary education. The Guadalupian-born professor left home to pursue his post-secondary education in Bordeaux, France, before moving to the United States, where he taught French as a second language. His Bolivian-born colleague left for Switzerland on a scholarship to learn French, upon graduating from high school. The four Quebec-born professors also seized opportunities to travel after high school: the history professor left to study in Europe in 1986, and in 1991 she moved to Paris, where she did her doctorate; the communications professor moved to Ottawa in the mid-1980s in order to learn English at the Second Language Institute (now the OLBI); the sociology professor moved to Sudbury to take a teaching position at Laurentian University in Northern Ontario; the political science professor travelled all around the world and lived in Bolivia for two years before and during her years of post-secondary education.

3.3. Common Characteristics

Analysis of the narratives also showed that all six content instructors share a number of characteristics:

- *An interest in languages*:

    Each content instructor had had a life experience that triggered an interest, love, or even passion for other languages. In some cases, it was a language learned in early childhood (Creole or Quechua) or on the job (Italian); in others, it was a second or foreign language (French or English) learned as a *lingua academica*; in still other cases, it was the subject/object of study (second language teaching, communication, sociology). Whatever the case, the experience left an indelible mark in the lives of the participants:

Psychology instructor: Since childhood I have always been interested in English. It had nothing to do with school, I loved English simply because it was another language, that's all.... I was lucky enough to be awarded a scholarship to study in Switzerland. They asked, "Can you speak French?" And I replied, "No, not at all." They asked, "Do you have a problem with learning another language?" And I replied, "No, not at all."

- *Mobility by choice*:

All six instructors willingly left their birth places to seek out other destinations, whether the move was geographic (from Quebec to Ontario, from an island to the mainland, from Canada or South America to the US or Europe), linguistic (from one language to one or more others), sociocultural/sociolinguistic (from majority to minority status), or professional (the same career in different locations or different careers in the same location). This experience of mobility opened their minds to other languages and cultures:

Communication instructor: I am from Quebec City, where you only get to speak English twice a year to tell tourists where the Château Frontenac is. I used to spend my summers in the United States, a very exotic locale for me because people spoke another language. The best two summers of my life were spent here in Ottawa learning English at the Second Language Institute.

Psychology instructor: I studied and worked for nine years, first in Geneva, then in Fribourg.... I had the opportunity to live in the United States for a while....In 2008 we arrived here.... We chose Ottawa because it was Canada's most bilingual city with 20% Francophones and 80% Anglophones and, of course, bilingual people. And it has Canada's only bilingual university.

The history instructor took a group trip to Cuba when it first opened to tourism, then she went to Spain to practice her school Spanish (she learned Castilian in high school), and in 1991 she went to Paris to do her doctorate. She also visited a friend in Italy, where she learned the language informally.

- *Awareness of the minority/majority dynamics between linguistic groups*:

This tension is very present in Canada between Anglophones and Francophones, between Francophones from Quebec and Francophones outside Quebec, but it also exists around the French-speaking world: Creole versus French, dialect varieties versus standard French, school French versus real-life French, indigenous/colonized languages versus colonial power languages:

Sociology instructor: Getting a teaching job in Sudbury changed my life. As a Quebecer, I never considered moving to Ontario but I chose to become a Franco-Ontarian. I taught at Laurentian University for two years. I went from Quebec City, a majority Francophone environment, where 97% of the population speaks French and jabbers in English, to the exact opposite.... My experience in Sudbury was an eye-opener on the degrees of French in Canadian culture. I left behind the typical Quebec representation, where there is Quebec and then there is Canada — it is all black and white.

The history instructor emphasized the dynamic positioning of the Franco-Ontarian community, when it comes to protecting and promoting French: the government has embraced a more inclusive definition of "Francophone," whereby French is one of the languages used in everyday life, unlike the more restrictive, exclusive Quebec definition. She confessed that when she first arrived at uOttawa, she had never heard the term "Franco-Ontarian."

3.4. Impact of these Characteristics on Students and Pedagogical Practices

The set of characteristics shared by these six instructors seem to have two types of consequences on their relationships with their students and on their pedagogical practices, and beyond — in their professional lives in general:

- *A deeply rooted respect and admiration for immersion students, who give themselves a challenge they are not required to face*:

  All six instructors mentioned this element, almost like a leitmotif. In their eyes, these students, who are already struggling with the transition from high school to university, take on the additional challenge of studying in their second language, and potentially running the risk of getting lower grades than they would probably get in their first language; they leave the comfort of their majority status (Anglophones in Canada outside Quebec) to willingly place themselves in a minority situation, in classrooms filled with Francophones, in a social and academic culture that is foreign to them; faced with the risk of failing, they work twice as hard as their Francophone peers.

  > *Communication instructor*: I think it is amazing that an Anglophone should choose to do this, because the cultural dimension, the examples, the intuitions, the realities, the culture are foreign. I have a lot of respect for Anglophones who have access to all the disciplinary knowledge in their own language and culture and books but who choose to jump into the unknown, to expose themselves and be exposed to the other culture. I have a lot of respect for these people, I say, "Hats off." And I always publicly congratulate immersion students in class.... They do all the required readings, which the Francophone students don't do.

  > *Political science instructor*: I have a lot of admiration for those who take the risk, because it is a risk, to pursue their post-secondary education in a language other than theirs. I think it is a challenge, a handicap they choose to take on, and it is important that we support them.... They are often more serious than the average non-immersion students.

  > *Psychology instructor*: I have an awful lot of admiration for immersion students.

- *The ability to revisit, rethink, and change their beliefs and pedagogical practices*:

  Because these instructors had to demonstrate flexibility in their past experiences as language learners and in their life choices, they seem amenable to change, to embracing other ideas and practices that are better suited to their new experiences. They also seem more able to see things from somebody else's perspective:

> *Political science instructor*: Teaching immersion courses helped me to learn that I had to talk at a more reasonable pace, which is better for me in general.

This instructor actually modified the quiz on required readings for her course in order to allow students to use their reading notes during the quiz, after the language instructor suggested it: "If the students wrote reading notes, it means they did the assigned readings; allowing reading notes for the quiz might encourage more students to do the readings and make reading notes" (personal communication, Jan. 6, 2015):

> *Psychology instructor*: There are things I didn't question before. It forced me to talk more slowly, more clearly, with more volume.... It encouraged me to be more accessible and more intelligible for all my students.

> *Communication instructor*: It encouraged me to improve the way I communicate, to look for examples from all around the world instead of repeating the same models within the same cultural boundaries.

The history instructor added that teaching an immersion course forced her to think more about her vocabulary choices, to write less common or more challenging words on the blackboard.

> *Second language teaching instructor*: What really changed was the relationship I developed with the language instructor.

> *Political science instructor*: It forces you to keep in mind that different people think according to different frameworks.... It is particularly true from a legal perspective. For example, the Common Law tradition[3] and the Civil Law tradition are completely different, and so the way things are codified and analyzed are completely different, depending on which tradition you come from. Having students from both languages and therefore both traditions forces us to keep in mind that there is this dual tradition in our disciplines.

> *Sociology instructor*: What was transformative for me was the RIF's inclusive approach, considering Francophiles as full members of the *francophonie*. The University of Ottawa, because of its dual nature, is the only bilingual university in the area. If it wants to grow, it needs to open up. I experienced *francophilie* with immersion students in my classes; they became bilingual and they are now bilingual for life, Francophiles forever. It works! Whoever started this idea had a fantastic intuition. Now it needs to extend to the graduate and postgraduate levels. Franco-Ontarie [Francophone Ontario] is getting old, it needs new blood, and this is it. I was skeptical at first, but now I am more of a believer!

---

[3] Originating in the courts of the English kings in the centuries following the Norman Conquest, *Common Law* is a body of law derived from judicial decisions of courts and similar tribunals (case law) — that is, it arises as precedent. It is the system used in Canada, both federally and provincially, with the exception of Quebec, where French-heritage *Civil Law* is also used to regulate private matters. For more information on this, see Canada (2017).

4. INTERPRETATIONS

4.1. Open Minds, Open Journeys

As shown in our analyses, previous experiences with languages and mobility have a major impact on the relationships between content instructors and immersion students. All six instructors know first-hand what it means to leave a linguistic majority context for a linguistic minority context, which makes them empathetic to the immersion students, who are experiencing the same situation.

All six content instructors have also been language learners, discovering in the process the structuring role of language in the construction of knowledge and the close relationship between language and culture (including academic and disciplinary culture). This is precisely what immersion students are discovering: they are not familiar with the references, they cannot understand humour in the second language, they have trouble understanding what their Francophone peers are saying, and they have to learn the academic norms and conventions of the other language. The fact that all content instructors expressed respect toward immersion students indicates that they will establish a good rapport with them.

All content instructors have experienced geographical mobility for academic and professional reasons, leaving their language environment to study and then teach in another province or another country, just as immersion students leave their English-speaking families to come to uOttawa and study in French.

Previous language learning experiences have brought an awareness of the concept of language, of the challenges of language learning, and of the best practices in language teaching, creating positive and open attitudes toward the RIF language instructors. These social predispositions (Bourdieu, 1980; Murphy-Lejeune & Zarate, 2003) play a significant role in the life paths of these content instructors, transforming their beliefs and ideologies, their rapport to the language and culture of the "other" linguistic group, and increasing their ability to adapt to their new professional environment.

4.2. From Content Expert to Teaching Expert

Teaching in the RIF changed these content instructors' beliefs toward the concept of university-level immersion: at first skeptical, they became sold on the concept of *francophilie*, an inclusive approach infusing new blood into the Francophone community and producing individuals who "became bilingual and they are now bilingual for life, Francophiles forever," as the sociology instructor put it. Their immersion teaching experience led them to revisit not only their beliefs but also their pedagogical practices, becoming better teachers in the process — teachers who are attuned to the challenges that their students face.

In the end, analyzing the life histories of these six instructors allows us to paint a picture of the ideal content instructor for the RIF:

- an individual whose past language experiences have led them to identify with the second language learners in their immersion courses
- someone whose past mobility experiences have opened them up to other languages and other cultures

- a person with an awareness of the majority language/minority language dynamics and an ability to question and change their beliefs and pedagogical practices

In short, ideal content instructors have lived through the same initiation experiences as their students and have become facilitators rather than conductors in disciplinary knowledge and skills.

CONCLUSION

Limitations of this Study

The main limitation of our study is that only those instructors who believed in the concept of French immersion in higher education participated. Some instructors do not share this view and others actively oppose it (see Chapter 13). Although they did receive an invitation to participate, they declined. Their experiences and beliefs would probably have shed a different light on the RIF.

For example, one of the content instructors who refused to participate to an interview cited the negative impact of the RIF on the Franco-Ontarian minority:

> The Franco-Ontarian community is fragile and adding fifty Anglophones to a class of 120 Francophone students does little to help.... I don't think that the RIF helps Franco-Ontarians.... The university is anglicizing our French environment, with no consideration for the consequences. As a Franco-Ontarian, I deeply resent the lack of respect towards my community. (personal communication, May 25, 2014)

Recommendations from the Content Instructors

The content instructors interviewed had a positive experience of the RIF, but they also expressed concerns about some of its aspects and suggested some avenues to address them:

- *A lack of consideration from the RIF*:

    Content instructors are told in a mass email from the RIF director that their course has been designated as an immersion course, without any consultation. This is the most cited issue. They would appreciate a more personal approach, including the opportunity to meet with the various stakeholders and to express their concerns[4] via "discussion spaces":

    > *History instructor*: I received a letter: my course had been designated but I was never consulted.... I think all email or mail communications should also be accompanied with personal contact.

    > *Psychology instructor*: I think it would be great to go beyond the written messages and to create discussion spaces where we could talk to the language instructors about the concerns we may have, and also possibly meet with some present or past immersion students — that would be very interesting.

---

[4] This criticism is shared by other content instructors, such as François Houle, a political science instructor, who became vice-president and created the RIF. See both his interview in Chapter 2, and further comments in Chapters 12 and 13.

- *The proficiency level of immersion students*:

  Students with a low score on the admission tests can take a content course in French without having to take a language support class or a regular FSL class (see Chapter 10, on evaluation and assessment). However, these tests are only assessing a student's ability to understand general interest written or oral documents, not discipline-specific, academic level texts. This can become a major issue in content courses requiring written assignments, oral presentations, or discussion groups, or if the content instructors speak very fast, with an unfamiliar accent, or have a limited command of French:

  > *Political science instructor*: Students who are not taking the language support classes in first year should be required to demonstrate their ability to really understand academic texts in French.

- *A number of administrative/political irritants*:

  First, language support classes are not mandatory, and after the second year they are no longer linked to a specific content course. Since qualitative grades are no longer available after the second year, students tend to drop out of the RIF in alarming numbers at that point, posing a real retention challenge (see Chapter 12).

  Second, the university's Regulation on Bilingualism (University of Ottawa, 1974, "Bilingualism," Part 6, line 20 (3)) allows all students to write their assignments, tests, and exams in the official language of their choice[5] (except in language courses), which does not encourage students with weaker writing skills to do their course work in French, especially since most instructors subtract marks for language errors.[6]

  > *Communication instructor*: The only problem is when these students don't play the immersion game, when they write their assignments in English, since it is their right.

  Finally, some content instructors may well be experts in their fields, but their command of French is not enough for them to be comprehensible by non-Francophone students:

  > *Political science instructor*: It is good that first-year courses are designated as immersion courses, but it would be great if that support was also available later in the course of the program.... When they graduate, can they really say, "I would now be able to do a degree in French"?

  > *History instructor*: The pressure for research excellence from the university goes against the message on bilingualism:[7] science faculty are hired to do research, not to teach, and their command of the language is quite weak.

---

[5] Other RIF stakeholders share this view; see Chapter 6, for example.

[6] Instructors may allocate up to 20% of a mark to language quality. Still, many content instructors make an exception for immersion students.

[7] This refers to *Vision 2010*, uOttawa's Mission Statement (2005), and its number one objective — to play a leadership role in promoting Canada's official languages:

- *Self-confidence*:

  Some instructors, whether junior or senior,[8] are not comfortable with the RIF's adjunct model/dual teaching approach and with having a peer attending their classes. Every effort should be made to ensure that all RIF instructors are confident in their pedagogical skills:

  > *History instructor*: I don't feel this way at all, but some of my colleagues resent having another instructor attending their lectures — they feel they are being judged and evaluated.
  >
  > *Sociology instructor*: Some instructors find it hard to have another instructor watch them teach. For me, the language instructor is a collaborator, not an enemy or a judge. I am sure that language instructors can feel that.

Our research has provided a number of key elements that can be used by administrators to make the RIF successful in the long term:

- first, a typification (categorization) of the ideal content instructor[9]
- second, a series of recommendations to ensure that students persist in the RIF and graduate from their programs with the "Immersion" designation
- third, a number of amendments to existing administrative practices which, although they are justified in the general context of a bilingual university, are detrimental to the specific context of the RIF and its students.

It has also uncovered the conflicting forces and processes between official discourses on the promotion of bilingualism and actual measures and means to achieve a balanced bilingualism. The accounts provided by the six content instructors also show that all the stakeholders who are favourable to the RIF are keenly aware of these contradictions and are willing and able to find individual solutions to institutional challenges.

> Recruiting bilingual professors: Through a central fund designed to allow hirings at the associate and full professor levels, recruit top-calibre professors who are bilingual or are determined to contribute to this specific goal of the University. The first hirings will take place in 2006–2007. (p. 3)

[8] This concern is shared by a substantial number of language instructors (see Chapter 8).

[9] These characteristics of the ideal content instructor were already listed in the RIF language instructors' guide (Weinberg & Burger, 2007, p. 20 [trans.]): Content instructors should:
- be knowledgeable about the founding principles of the immersion approach and courses
- be willing to collaborate with language instructors
- be experienced instructors trained in pedagogy
- speak clearly
- be attentive to the specific needs of second language students
- be able to create a comfortable, non-threatening environment for immersion students

REFERENCES

Atkinson, R. (1998). *The life story interview*. Thousand Oaks, CA: Sage.

Bourdieu, P. (1980). *Questions de sociologie*. Paris: Minuit.

Braun, V., & Clarke, V. (2006). Using thematic analysis in psychology. *Qualitative Research in Psychology, 3*, 77–101. doi.org/10.1191/1478088706qp063oa

Canada. Department of Justice. (2017). Where our legal system comes from. www.justice.gc.ca/eng/csj-sjc/just/03.html

Denzin, N.K. (1989). *Interpretative biography*. London: Sage.

Elder, G.H., Jr. (1998). The life course and human development. In W. Damon (Series Ed.) & R.M. Lerner (Vol. Ed.), *Handbook of child psychology* (Vol. 1, pp. 939–991). New York: Wiley.

Irvine, J., & Gal, S. (2000). Language ideology and linguistic differentiation. In Paul V. Kroskrity (Ed.), *Regimes of Language* (pp. 350–383). Santa Fe, NM: Santa Fe School of American Research Press.

Jaffe, A. (1999). *Ideologies in action: Language politics on Corsica*. Berlin: Mouton de Gruyter.

Jaffe, A. (2008). Parlers et idéologies langagières. *Ethnologie française, 38*, 517–526.

Kalleberg, A. (1966). The logic of comparison: A methodological note on the comparative study of political systems. *World Politics, 19*, 69–82. doi:10.2307/2009843

Lijphart, A. (1971). Comparative politics and the comparative method. *The American Political Science Review, 65*, 682–693.

Murphy-Lejeune, E., & Zarate, G. (2003). L'acteur social pluriculturel: évolution politique, positions didactiques. *Le français dans le monde: Recherches et applications* [thematic issue: *Vers une compétence plurilingue*], juillet, 32–46.

Pajares, F. (1992). Teachers' beliefs and educational research: Cleaning up a messy construct. *Review of Educational Research, 62*, 307–332.

Perrenoud, P. (2000). Le rôle de la formation à l'enseignement dans la construction des disciplines scolaires. *Éducation et francophonie, 28*. www.acelf.ca/c/revue/revuehtml/28-2/05-Perrenoud.html

University of Ottawa. (1974). Regulation on bilingualism at University of Ottawa 1974. www.uottawa.ca/administration-and-governance/policies-and-regulations/regulation-on-bilingualism

University of Ottawa. (2005). *Vision 2010—Academic Strategic Plan*. web5.uottawa.ca/vision2010/pdf/strategic_plan.pdf

Weinberg, A., & Burger, S. (2007). *Guide à l'intention des professeurs de langues: cours d'encadrement linguistique*. Ottawa: University of Ottawa, Institut des langues secondes.

Wong, R.M.H. (2013). A change in teaching philosophy: The effects of short-term teaching immersion on English teaching beliefs and practice. *Teacher Education and Practice, 26*, 43–62.

Woods, D. (1996). *Teacher cognition in language teaching*. Cambridge: Cambridge University Press.

Woods, D., & Knoerr, H. (2014). Repenser la pensée enseignante. *Le français dans le monde—Recherches et applications, 56*, 16–32.

CHAPTER 15

The Student Experience in the *Régime d'immersion en français* at the University of Ottawa:
From Spaces of Tensions to "In-Between" Spaces?

Sylvie A. Lamoureux

INTRODUCTION

"THE STUDENT EXPERIENCE" has been a buzzword phrase in post-secondary environments for the past decade. A simple overview of the strategic plans of various Canadian post-secondary institutions since 2005 reveals its important status through the various goals that have been set in order to optimize it. In a context marked by global competition for student recruitment and the decline in student populations in North America, the student experience — as it is reported in various university rankings — can influence students in their choice of a post-secondary institution.

Furthermore, the student experience represents a burgeoning field of research in North America, particularly with regard to access to university studies and academic perseverance, in an era marked by a rise in student populations and increasingly diverse student profiles. Once the exclusive territory of psychology, the research field surrounding the student experience is now interdisciplinary, subscribing to the broader field of studies on higher education. Since the turn of the century, there has been an increase in qualitative research in this field, which has brought to light the perspectives and voices of students in order to better understand the complexity and diversity of this experience, notably for particular groups (Hernandez & Lopez, 2004; Kanno & Harklau, 2012; Lamoureux, 2007; Montgomery, 2010; Watson et al., 2002). Thus, studies have gone beyond the portraits of cohorts of students presented as homogeneous, in order to emphasize the divergences and similarities between the various subgroups that comprise them. While a growing number of studies have focused on the student experience of young Francophones in minority settings in Canada since 2007 (Desabrais, 2013; Lamoureux, 2007, 2011, 2012; Pilote & Magnan, 2012), one group of students has gone relatively unnoticed: those participating in post-secondary level French immersion programs. The paucity of studies on this topic can be explained in part by:

- the small number of these programs in Canada[1]
- the relative newness of these initiatives, especially the leading one, the *Régime d'immersion en français* (French Immersion Stream, henceforth RIF) program at the University of Ottawa

---

[1] For more details on the Canadian programs dedicated to French immersion students in post-secondary studies, see Knoerr (2018) and Lamoureux (2018).

- the fact that the students who participate in these types of programs are somewhat invisible or in an "in-between" situation[2]

However, researchers have begun to take these groups into consideration. Studies on the commitment to French by students participating in French immersion programs, whether during compulsory education (Mandin, 2010; Roy, 2010, 2012; Roy & Galiev, 2011; Schafer, 2013) or at the post-secondary level (Byrd Clark, 2009, 2010, 2012; Byrd Clark & Labrie, 2010; Byrd Clark, Lamoureux, & Stratilaki, 2013), are multiplying, particularly since the late 1990s. Furthermore, since 2006 and even more so since 2011, there has been an emergence of studies that focus explicitly on the experience of university students who participate in French immersion programs (Cenerelli, 2013; Durepos, 2014; Lamoureux, 2013; Lemaire, 2013; Séror & Lamoureux, 2014; Séror & Weinberg, 2012, 2013; Skogen, 2006).

In 2010, a study was launched at uOttawa to gain insight into the RIF student experience. After briefly situating the context of the RIF, this chapter will present the theoretical framework and methodology of the study from which these data were gathered. The analysis will focus on two aspects of the student experience:

- the expected and lived experience of the students' post-secondary choices
- the students' impressions of the supporting resources of the RIF

The chapter will end with concluding remarks.

1. CONTEXT

RIF students, like those in other similar programs offered in some Canadian universities, are graduates of English-language secondary schools, where they have studied French as a second language with other "Anglophones."[3] The majority of them were registered in French immersion or enriched French programs (see Chapter 1) and took content courses in French, exclusively with other Anglophones. By registering in the RIF, they find themselves in a bilingual academic and social environment for the first time, where they take content courses created for Francophones, taught in French, with other Francophone students.[4] Thus, in French content courses, RIF students find themselves in a minority linguistic situation within the "group" of Francophone students, which is a new

---

[2] Along with their English-language courses, they must take a certain number of classes in French; that is, content courses created for Francophone students following a French-language curriculum. Thus, if they are not identified explicitly in the recruitment forms of participants in studies on the student experience, these populations are grouped with students registered either in English-language programs or French-language programs.

[3] We recognize that not all English-language high school students speak English as their mother tongue. However, in the context of this article, we reduce the possible linguistic identity representations to the binary context of Canada's official languages: students in French-language high schools are considered Francophone and students in English-language high schools are considered Anglophone. We fully acknowledge, however, the complexity of the overlapping linguistic identities of young Canadians.

[4] For more information on the detailed profiles of RIF students in 2010, see Lamoureux (2013).

reality for almost all RIF students. The experience of being a linguistic minority within a linguistic minority can impact their perception of their linguistic or cultural capital, and perhaps even of their student identity.

2. THEORETICAL FRAMEWORK[5]

This study called upon numerous concepts to structure the project and guide the analyses. The notions of *habitus* and *capital* (Bourdieu, 1991) as well as that of *historicity* (Foucault, 1969) allowed for a better understanding of the way in which RIF students had taken up their *métier d'étudiant* (occupation of being a student; Coulon, 2005) — that is, their entry into university networks and discourse. The transition from secondary school to university is a moment when students attempt to integrate into new academic and social environments. They quickly notice that their way of "doing school," their expectations in terms of "normal" social and academic processes, do not produce the desired effects or expected results. They are forced to recognize that they are evolving in a new environment and that, as a result, they will need to adapt to new realities, which will imply *habitus* transformations.

The student experience is a comprehensive concept that goes beyond the confines of their occupation of being a student, to consider not only what the students experience in academic and social spaces once they have begun their university studies, but also the way in which they imagined this experience before arriving at university (Cashmore, Green, & Scott, 2010; Lamoureux, 2007). This study placed importance on the impressions the students had of their social, academic, linguistic, and sometimes geographical transition.

Building on Dubet's sociology of experience (1994) and Dubar's socialization (2002), the study aimed to situate the reality of RIF students within the body of work on access to post-secondary studies (Astin, 1993; Braxton, Sullivan, & Johnson, 1998; Labrie, Lamoureux, & Wilson, 2009; Seidman, 2005; Tinto, 1987, 2006) and their integration into student life (Cabrera & La Nasa, 2005; Leclercq & Parmentier, 2011; Nils, 2011; Upcraft, Gardner, & Barefoot, 2005). In the context of this research, the focus was to capture the RIF students' lived experience of academic and social spaces, of their linguistic choices, and of their evolution over the course of their years of study at uOttawa.

The analysis presented in this chapter is based on the "in-between" concept. This notion may resemble or parallel the "betwixt spaces" that Palmer, O'Kane, and Owens (2009) view as part of life's transitions, which include the transition to post-secondary studies. It may also evoke Bhabha's "third space" concept (1994), taken up by Roy (2010). Yet, the issue here is not hybrid identity or transculturalism, nor of a lack of acknowledgement of an identity. The space in-between represents an area of tensions, or even potential contradictions, gathered from participants' testimonies regarding their post-secondary experience, whether real or imagined.

Data analysis revealed different iterations of this in-between space. It could be identified in the words of a single student discussing their impressions, between what they

---

[5] This section has been adapted from Lamoureux (2013). We wish to extend our thanks to the *OLBI Working Papers* editor for authorizing our use of this excerpt.

said they had hoped or expected to live as a student experience in the RIF and what they chose to live, once in a university environment. The space in-between could also be identified in the statements of broader groups of participants, when two very different perspectives on the same experience emerged, which could not be explained by the single variables or characteristics of students participating in the study (e.g., sex, prerequisite program—immersion or basic French, university program, cohort). This in-between concept did not guide the conceptualization of the study, but rather emerged following the analysis.

This study highlighted moments of the RIF students' experience where they were situated between two linguistic representations or perceptions, or the in-between space that encompassed the tensions between their personal expectations of RIF and the reality of their school and social choices.

3. METHODOLOGY

The data on which this chapter was built was collected in 2010. It is therefore representative of a specific moment in the development of a program that itself continues to evolve. The results have already been used in other studies that present the impact of the RIF's supporting resources on the student experience (Lamoureux, 2013), and that bring to the fore certain challenges related to the integration of Anglophone students into courses intended for Francophones (Séror and Lamoureux, 2014).

The qualitative research that generated this data aimed to present a basic portrait of:

- what motivates students to participate in the RIF, as well as their expectations regarding the program and university in general
- their perceptions of their student experience in the RIF in general, in academic as well as social spaces, including the Francophone community of Ottawa

This portrait was intended to improve our understanding of the complexity of the profiles and experiences of these students.

In April, 2010, more than 500 RIF students were invited to answer an online questionnaire[6] in the official language of their choice. Seventeen percent of these participants ($n = 37$) completed it in French whereas 83% ($n = 182$) chose to answer in English. The questionnaire asked for information on the biographical details of the students registered in the RIF. Furthermore, it served as a recruitment tool for participation in an email interview. In total, 137 participants indicated their interest in participating in the study and received the interview instructions; 24 requested it in French and 113 in English. In the end, we collected 49 interviews by email, three of which were in French and 46 in English. Moreover, seven of the interview participants agreed to take part in one of two bilingual discussion groups that took place in July, 2010 at uOttawa.

Table 1 presents the distribution of e-interview participants across various faculties, as well as of all students registered in the RIF in April, 2010. Since no questions were mandatory, some data is missing. Out of 49 interview respondents, 34 indicated they were women and four were men, while 11 of them did not specify gender according

---

[6] The questionnaire is available upon request from the author (slamoureux@uottawa.ca).

to the limited binary choice presented to them. At that time,[7] seven respondents were finishing their first year of university study, nine were in their second year, eleven in their third year, ten in their last. Eight respondents did not specify their university path, while four specified that they had complicated paths due to program changes or participation in a co-operative education program.

Table 1: Distribution of participants in email interviews among RIF students, by host faculty (April 2010)

	No. of interview participants	Actual RIF Distribution 2009–2010
Faculty of Arts	10	247
Faculty of Health Sciences	6	118
Faculty of Social Sciences	20	465
TELFER School of Management	2	104
Missing data	11	
	49	934

A more detailed version of this table appears in Lamoureux (2013, p. 113).

4. RESULTS AND DISCUSSION

For the purposes of this chapter, the email survey answers were used to reveal the areas of conflict where students found themselves in an "in-between" situation. The analysis focused on two of these areas:

- the exploration of certain elements of motivation, expectations, and lived experience of the choice of post-secondary institution, based on participant testimonies
- the respondents' perceptions of their experiences with the supplementary resources offered by the RIF

4.1. Ottawa: A Deliberate Choice for Improving French

One of the email survey questions asked students why they had chosen to attend uOttawa. In the vast majority of cases, they cited both the institutional bilingualism of the university, the perceived bilingual status of the city of Ottawa, and the *Régime d'immersion en français*. These three elements were cited by students as essential to improving their French skills and to building on the investment they had made for several years to become advanced learners of French:

> Since Ottawa is a bilingual city, I assumed that my French learning experience would extend beyond the classroom. (P3)

> I've been in immersion since kindergarten. I've invested so much that I told myself that I may as well continue in immersion for university to have the mention ["Immersion"

---

[7] Although there were 219 respondents to the survey, not all of them answered all the demographic questions.

designation] on my diploma and to maintain my skills in French, which is my second language. (P5)

I wanted to have a social life in French. (P9)

At the end of high school, I knew that in order to maintain my skills in French, I needed to be in a place where I would be obligated to use my French. (P21)

I signed up for RIF to improve my French. (P45)

These few excerpts are representative of the views of the 49 participants.

A little further into the email interview, participants were asked if they used French when they accessed university services (library, meal services, learning support services, etc.) and whether they participated in social activities in French outside the classroom, either at the university or elsewhere. With the exception of five participants, the answer was a resounding "no":

I don't know many Francophones. (P4)

My Francophone friends also speak English. (P24)

For me, the biggest challenge is improving my verbal skills and increasing my technical vocabulary in French. I'm too worried about my verbal skill level to speak French with Francophones. (P7)

I use French at my part-time job as a guide; however, I don't think I will ever feel confident enough to use French regularly. (P22)

I don't attempt to express myself in French outside of the language courses or FSL. I really hope that by continuing in RIF I can improve my French enough to feel comfortable speaking. (P3)

This feeling of insecurity was raised by at least 20 participants in the email interviews, such as P4:

Unless I'm obligated to use French at work to serve a unilingual Francophone, I don't use French, because I'm self-conscious about my English accent that I find very noticeable when I speak French. (P4)

Among the five participants who indicated using French at the university or participating in activities in French, one survey participant explained her choice as follows:

When it comes to important school issues related to my student file, I prefer to use English. Otherwise, I use whatever language I'm addressed in. I participate in many activities in French that are organized by the Community Life Service. They give me the opportunity to use my knowledge of French, but most of all, they allow me to experience Francophone culture. (P20)

She added later:

I have Francophone friends that I socialize with in French, but not as often as I'd like. (P20)

I am always proud to tell people that I'm a RIF student, that I regularly use French on campus at my part-time job (ambassador)[8] and in my volunteer work. It's important to me. I have a lot of Franco-Ontarian friends that help me improve and with my studies. (P32)

I've participated in Immersion Club[9] events and I go to conferences given in French to better incorporate French into my day-to-day life. (P1F, [trans.])

I don't use of a lot university services, apart from administrative services as needed. I always introduce myself in French because I notice that everything goes more smoothly and I get a much warmer service. I have a lot of Francophone friends that I met in the Pages program[10] during my first year and I socialize almost exclusively in French with them. It's a habit I've decided to take up in order to improve my French skills. (P2)

He added:

In my view, RIF students isolate themselves and form their own cliques, where everything happens mostly in English. They fossilize their French errors and don't improve their verbal French skills. Moreover, they do not improve their level of comfort in French environments. (P2)

This last aspect of P2's statement highlighted the tensions or risks that existed for the majority of respondents between the motivation to choose the RIF to improve their knowledge of French, and their reticence to integrate in community life in French or to take the opportunities presented to them to speak French in an authentic communication context. The weight of their linguistic insecurity caused them to resist speaking French in situations where they could choose to do so. It is equally interesting to note that more than 20 participants claimed to have no Francophone friends after one or more years at uOttawa, even though they were taking courses in French with Francophones. Moreover, they did not perceive their RIF peers as possible people to speak French with. In addition, professional experiences and classroom observations confirmed that these students spoke to one another predominantly in English, whether in French content courses or in FSL courses.

The emphasis on this tension presented program administrators with an area of focus and possibility for action. For example, in the RIF, in the context of a first-year history course given in French, students had the opportunity to participate in a peer mentoring initiative (see Chapter 9), where they were paired with Francophone students taking the same content class (Weinberg, 2013). This project allowed the Anglophone RIF students to both meet Francophones and create a social network to support them in their studies. Initiatives such as this one, which was launched in tandem by a language instructor teaching an adjunct language course and a content instructor, would have proved beneficial if widely implemented. Furthermore, since 2008, some FSL instructors

---

[8] The University of Ottawa offers a work–study program that hires undergraduate students to support recruitment efforts. These individuals give campus tours, answer questions from prospective students and their parents, and represent the university at university fairs (University of Ottawa, n.d., "Work–study program").

[9] For additional information on this topic, see Chapter 7.

[10] For more information about the Page program, see Canada, n.d., "Page program."

were including a voluntary community service experience in a Francophone community setting as a component of their course (Ambrosio, 2013). The RIF could have taken a cue from this approach, especially given that two participants in the project cited these learning opportunities as being some of their best university experiences.

How then do we incite the majority of RIF students to participate in these initiatives, and take advantage of experiences that allow them to apply their language skills in order to gain more confidence? Respondent P4, who admitted to not wanting to communicate in French because of linguistic insecurity, offered a possible solution in another part of the interview:

> In a 4th year criminology seminar that I took in French, I was forced to interact and participate in French. And by the end, I was a lot more confident in my verbal skills. (P4)

4.2. RIF Supplementary Resources

The RIF continues to offer students a number of resources, whether in academic or social settings (see Chapter 7). Analysis of the email interview answers revealed that the vast majority of participants were happy with these resources:

> What I most appreciate about RIF are the accompanying language courses. It is in large part thanks to these courses that I am succeeding in my French disciplinary [content] courses. (P3)

> It isn't that hard with everyone encouraging you and the different RIF supporting resources. Everyone should challenge themselves to participate! (P1)

> Since the accompanying courses have few students in them, it's like a little family and we help each other out. (P6)

> The accompanying courses and the disciplinary [content] courses in French really help me improve my French comprehension and my writing skills. Knowing that there's an accompanying language course that goes with a disciplinary [content] course influences my choice of courses. (P7)

> The accompanying language courses allowed me to meet other RIF students like me and afterward I see them in many other classes. (P9)

The possibility of asking for qualitative grades for a maximum of eight courses over the first two years of study is greatly appreciated by students and is considered a significant asset in the the decision to register for RIF. The following quotes represent answers from more than half of the participants:

> I also like the option of qualitative Satisfactory/Unsatisfactory grading. It's very useful! (P3)

> The qualitative grades option is very important, since it frees us of a lot of stress. The transition is already difficult enough without adding to the stress of taking courses in a second language. (P5)

Finally, for others, it was the combination of resources, both academic and social, that led to success, as expressed by P10:

My best memories of the experience were the Immersion Club activities (the trip to Carnaval de Québec!!!!) and the support of professors in the accompanying language courses. They allowed me to succeed. (P10)

However, some students had a different perspective on the accompanying language courses:

> The accompanying courses were useless — they were challenging for me to take, because I mainly wanted to talk about the subject. (P5)

For other students, accompanying language courses were not available for the mandatory courses in their program, even if they were for some elective courses. In other cases, in spite of the availability, some students chose not to take accompanying language courses, because, as P24 explains:

> Being in French courses with Francophones gave me a setting where I could use my French at all times. I really improved my skills both spoken and written in this setting, where I had to be attentive during my courses and stay focused. (P24)

Respondent P2, who needed to improve his French language skills in first year in order to be admitted to the RIF in his second year, said:

> By the time I got to my second year, even the FSL courses weren't challenging enough. For me, the RIF was a bridge that allowed me to take all my program courses in French and learn to take responsibility for my own success. The accompanying language courses were a crutch for me, just like qualitative grades. The accompanying language courses encouraged RIF students to stick to themselves too much, rather than mingle with Francophones. In order for me to improve, I had to challenge myself to live an experience like that with Francophones [without the supplementary resources or RIF peers]. (P2)

Although P7 appreciated the support from the accompanying language courses to improve her French comprehension, she would have liked "there to be tools available to support my verbal French skills."[11]

Respondent P2F encouraged future RIF students to:

> get involved and immerse themselves without hesitation in the French activities, clubs, and courses [for Francophones] to really take advantage of the experience. If you notice then that you have trouble, there are many resources available to help you. (P2F, [trans.])

She echoed P2, since, for her, the accompanying language courses limited her capacity to fully immerse herself in a Francophone environment.

This last comment by P2F put a spotlight on a second area of tension, one related to expectations regarding the purpose of the RIF. Through analysis of the participants' responses, there was the sense that some students wanted to continue to live (or, in some cases, live for the first time) the experience of an immersion program where they were separated from the majority Anglophone students, so that they could find themselves

---

[11] It should be noted that free conversation workshops led by Francophone students are available by appointment from OLBI's Julien Couture Resource Centre.

with other students with similar profiles — that is, learners of French.[12] For these students, the supporting resources available, in particular the accompanying language courses, were essential for making them feel secure in Francophone spaces such as their content courses. They wished to improve or maintain their French language skills. For them, French might play an important role in their future professional life, but that was not what motivated them. They described their student experience as different from that of Anglophone and Francophone students; in short, they situated themselves between both groups, in this third space described in Roy's work (2010) in Alberta.

However, for other students, the RIF was a "bridge" toward Francophones, content courses in French, and Francophone culture (Séror & Weinberg, 2012). They were glad that resources existed in case they needed them, but these young people wanted to immerse themselves directly in Francophone academic and social settings. They all considered French important, not only in their professional life after their studies, but also in their social lives during their time at university. They did not identify with a third space, but rather, saw themselves as integrated into two worlds. In their opinion, their student experience greatly resembled that of Francophone students in Ontario, since they had the ability to choose what best suited their needs among the university options available to them, without having to worry about language; an experience not possible for the majority of Anglophone students. Furthermore, they indicated having taken the majority of their content courses — both mandatory and electives — in French, depending on availability and course topics.

This updated notion of a space in-between, according to students' perceptions of the purpose of the RIF, has helped us understand the different opinions on and impressions of the accompanying resources being offered to them and the linguistic choices they were making day-to-day.

One last area of tension resided in access to certain supporting resources, which deserves attention. Four respondents to the email interviews were registered in the nursing program. They all raised significant difficulties in their ability to take the number of content courses in French required by the RIF. They attributed these difficulties to a lack of support from their nursing program. Although the program chose to affiliate itself with the RIF, according to these students, it did not take the RIF requirements into account when establishing the schedule of classes in French and in English. In addition, the limited number of elective courses in this program restricted the number of FSL courses that these students could take. This finding therefore revealed a tension between the obligation of meeting the requirements of a university program, and that of meeting the additional requirements of the RIF. It also underscored the limited power of RIF program administrators.

---

[12] The RIF uses the term "Francophiles" in its activities to designate RIF students and the term "Francophone" to designate the other students registered in programs delivered in French. The students do not necessarily use these terms to self-identify.

CONCLUSION

This study's main purpose was to gain a better understanding of the complexity and diversity of RIF students' lived experiences. Research by Lamoureux (2007, 2011) confirmed certain issues raised by RIF students. These were, notably, the choice to attend uOttawa to improve one's French and to have access to a larger Francophone space, and their eventual lack of participation in French activities on campus or in Ottawa more generally. Francophones and RIF students both shared a certain linguistic insecurity around these "other students" who they perceived as being more Francophone — that is, Franco-Ontarians and Quebecers for RIF students, and Quebecers for Franco-Ontarian students (Lamoureux, 2007, 2013).

Other aspects of the student experience echoed those raised in studies in North America and elsewhere regarding the transition into university studies, specifically:

- the discrepancy between the supervision in high school and the autonomy in a university setting
- the gap between expectations and lived experiences
- the difficulties in "the occupation of being a student" (*le métier d'étudiant*; Coulon, 2005) and the beginning of university life

This is what Palmer et al. (2009) had called the betwixt spaces, spaces where individuals in transitional situations carve out a place for themselves and build a new identity. However, a deeper analysis of the areas of tension inherent in this in-between space has motivated the RIF administrators to examine the discrepancy between the students' and the institution's impressions of these resources. It has also revealed the different motives and expectations of students, which explained not only their decision to participate in the RIF, but also the way they chose to live their student experience in and outside the classroom. Finally, this analysis of RIF students' paths of integration into Francophone social and academic spaces has emphasized the likely benefits as well as some limitations of the supporting resources, depending on the path chosen by students.

REFERENCES

Ambrosio, L. (2013). Apprentissage par l'engagement en milieu communautaire. In E. Yasri-Labrique, P. Gardies, & K. Djordjevic (Eds.), *Didactique contrastive: questionnements et applications* (pp. 89–102). Montpellier: Cladole.

Astin, A.W. (1993). *What matters in college? Four critical years revisited*. San Francisco: Jossey-Bass.

Bhabha, H.K. (1994). *The location of culture*. London: Routledge.

Bourdieu, P. (1991). *Language and symbolic power*. Cambridge: Polity Press.

Braxton, J., Sullivan A., & Johnson, R. (1998). Appraising Tinto's theory of college student departure. In J.C. Smart (Ed.), *Higher education: Handbook of theory and research* (pp. 107–164). New York: Agathon.

Burger, S., Weinberg, A., & Wesche, M. (2013). Immersion studies at the University of Ottawa: From the 1980s to the present. *OLBI Working Papers, 6*, 21–43.

Byrd Clark, J. (2009). *Multilingualism, citizenship, and identity: Voices of youth and symbolic investments in an urban, globalized world*. New York: Continuum.

Byrd Clark, J. (2010). Making "wiggle room" in French as a Second Language/Français Langue Seconde: Reconfiguring identity, language, and policy. *Canadian Journal of Education, 33*, 379–406.

Byrd Clark, J. (2012). Introduction—Journeys of integration between multiple worlds: Reconceptualising multilingualism through complex transnational spaces. *International Journal of Multilingualism, 9*, 132–137.

Byrd Clark, J., & Labrie, N. (2010). La voix de jeunes Canadiens dans leur processus d'identification: les identités imbriquées dans des espaces multiformes. In S.N. Osu, G. Col, N. Garric, & F. Toupin (Eds.), *Construction d'identité et processus d'identification* (pp. 435–438). Berlin: Peter Lang.

Byrd Clark, J., Lamoureux, S., & Stratilaki, S. (2013). Apprendre et enseigner le français dans l'Ontario, Canada: entre dualité linguistique et réalités plurielles et complexes. *Recherches en didactique des langues et des cultures: les Cahiers de l'Acedle, 10*, 3, 38–54.

Cabrera, A.F., & La Nasa, S.M. (Eds.). (2005). *New directions for institutional research*. San Francisco: Jossey-Bass.

Canada. Parliament of Canada. (n.d.) "Page program." www.ourcommons.ca/About/PageProgram/Index-e.html

Cashmore, A., Green, P., & Scott, J. (2010). An ethnographic approach to studying the student experience: The student perspective through free form video diaries. A practice report. *International Journal of the First Year in Higher Education, 1*, 106–111.

Cenerelli, B.B. (2013). Le modèle FCP de l'Université Simon Fraser : une immersion multidisciplinaire, expérientielle et communautaire. *OLBI Working Papers, 6*, 45–64.

Coulon, A. (2005). *Le métier d'étudiant: l'entrée dans la vie universitaire* (2nd ed.). Paris: Presses universitaires de France.

Desabrais, T. (2013). *Les mots pour le dire … L'influence de l'(in)sécurité linguistique sur l'expérience d'étudiantes de milieux francophones minoritaires canadiens inscrites aux études supérieures à l'Université d'Ottawa* (Unpublished doctoral dissertation). Faculty of Education, University of Ottawa, Ottawa.

Dubar, C. (2002). *La socialisation*, 3rd ed. Paris: Armand Colin.

Dubet, F. (1994). *Sociologie de l'expérience*. Paris: Seuil.

Durepos, J. (2014, April). *The identity of the French immersion speaker: A post-secondary context*. Paper presented at CCERBAL conference—Literacies and Autonomy of Advanced Language Learners, Ottawa.

Foucault, M. (1969). *L'archéologie du savoir*. Paris: Gallimard.

Hernandez, J.C., & Lopez, M.A. (2004). Leaking pipeline: Issues impacting latino/a college student retention. *Journal of College Student Retention, 6*, 37–60.

Kanno, Y., & Harklau, L. (Eds.). (2012). *Linguistic minority students go to college: Preparation, access and persistence*. New York: Routledge.

Knoerr, H. (2010). L'immersion au niveau universitaire: nouveaux modèles, nouveaux défis, pratiques et stratégies. *OLBI Working Papers, 1*, 89–110.

Knoerr, H. (2018). Collaboration between language and content instructors: keystone and weak link of content and language integration environments. In H. Knoerr, A. Weinberg, & C.E. Buchanan (Eds.), *Current issues in university immersion* (pp. 175–204). Ottawa: Groupe de recherche en immersion au niveau universitaire (GRINU).

Labrie, N., Lamoureux, S., & Wilson, D. (2009). *L'accès des francophones aux études postsecondaires en Ontario: le choix des jeunes.* Toronto: Ontario Institute for Studies in Education (OISE).

Lamoureux, S. (2007). *La transition de l'école secondaire de langue française à l'université: questions de changements identitaires* (Unpublished doctoral dissertation). Department of curriculum, teaching and learning, OISE/University of Toronto.

Lamoureux, S. (2011). D'élève à étudiant: expériences de transition de jeunes francophones en milieu minoritaire en Ontario. *Bulletin suisse de linguistique appliquée, 94,* 153–165.

Lamoureux, S. (2012). "My parents may not be French sir, but I am": Exploration of linguistic identity of Francophone bilingual youth in transition in multicultural, multilingual Ontario. *International Journal of Multilingualism, 9,* 151–164.

Lamoureux, S. (2013). L'expérience étudiante au Régime d'immersion en français: perspectives et constats. *OLBI Working Papers, 6,* 109–121.

Lamoureux, S. (2018). Political issues and the politics of French immersion issues in universities. In H. Knoerr, A. Weinberg, & C.E. Buchanan (Eds.), *Current issues in university immersion* (pp. 189–106). Ottawa: Groupe de recherche en immersion au niveau universitaire (GRINU).

Leclercq, D., & Parmentier, P. (2011). Qu'est-ce que la réussite à l'université d'un étudiant ? In P. Parmentier (Ed.), *Recherches et actions en faveur de la réussite en première année universitaire: vingt ans de collaboration dans la Commission "Réussite" du Conseil interuniversitaire de la Communauté française de Belgique* (CIUF) (pp. 6–9). Brussels: CIUF.

Lemaire, E. (2013). Étudier à l'université en français dans le contexte minoritaire ouest-canadien: ce que peut nous apprendre le dessin réflexif. *OLBI Working Papers, 6,* 87–107.

Mandin, L. (2010). Portfolio langagier: les finissants des programmes d'immersion se révèlent. *Canadian Journal of Applied Linguistics, 13,* 104–119.

Montgomery, C. (2010). *Understanding the international student experience.* New York: Palgrave MacMillan.

Nils, F. (2011). Comment favoriser une bonne orientation lors du choix des études universitaires ? In P. Parmentier (Ed.), *Recherches et actions en faveur de la réussite en première année universitaire: vingt ans de collaboration dans la Commission "Réussite" du Conseil interuniversitaire de la communauté française de Belgique* (CIUF) (pp. 14–18). Brussels: CIUF.

Official Languages and Bilingualism Institute (OLBI). (n.d.). Julien Couture Resource Centre. olbi.uottawa.ca/about/julien-couture-resource-centre

Oropeza, M., Varghese, M., & Kanno (2010). Linguistic minority students in higher education: Using, resisting, and negotiating labels. *Equity and Excellence in Education, 43,* 216–231.

Palmer, M., O'Kane, P., & Owens, M. (2009). Betwixt spaces: Student accounts of turning-point experiences in the first year transition. *Studies in Higher Education, 24,* 37–54.

Pilote, A., & Magnan, M.O. (2012). La construction identitaire des jeunes francophones en situation minoritaire au Canada: négociation des frontières linguistiques au fil du parcours universitaire et de la mobilité géographique. *Canadian Journal of Sociology, 37,* 169–195.

Roy, S. (2010). Not truly, not entirely—Pas comme les Francophones. *Canadian Journal of Education*, *33*, 541–563.

Roy, S. (2012). Qui décide du meilleur français? Représentations des variétés linguistiques du français en immersion. *Canadian Journal of Applied Linguistics*, *15*, 1–19.

Roy, S., & Galiev, A. (2011). Discourses on bilingualism in Canadian French immersion programs. *The Canadian Modern Language Review*, *67*, 351–376.

Schafer, P.C. (2013). *Life after French immersion: Grade 12 students' perceptions of continuing to use French after graduation* (Unpublished master's thesis). Faculty of Education, University of Calgary, Calgary.

Seidman, A. (2005). *College student retention: Formula for student success*. Westport, CT: Praeger.

Séror, J., & Lamoureux, S. (2014). Intégrer les étudiants anglophones dans le cadre d'un programme d'immersion universitaire au Canada. *Dossiers des sciences de l'éducation* [thematic issue: *Les langues étrangères à la fac*], *32*, 95–110.

Séror, J., & Weinberg, A. (2012). Construction identitaire et linguistique : le régime d'immersion en français de l'Université d'Ottawa. *Synergies Europe*, *7*, 215–230.

Séror, J., & Weinberg, A. (2013). Personal insights on a postsecondary immersion experience: Learning to step out of the comfort zone. *OLBI Working Papers*, *6*, 123–140.

Skogen, R. (2006). *Holding the tension in the sphere of the between: French immersion graduates in a Francophone post-secondary institution* (Unpublished doctoral dissertation). University of Alberta, Edmonton.

Tinto, V. (1987). *Leaving college: Rethinking the causes and cures of student attrition*. Chicago: University of Chicago Press.

Tinto, V. (2006). Research and practice of student retention: What next? *Journal of College Student Retention*, *8*, 1–19.

University of Ottawa. (n.d.). Work–study program. www.uottawa.ca/financial-aid-awards/work-study-program

Upcraft, M.L., Gardner, J.N., & Barefoot, B.O. (Eds.). (2005). *Challenging and supporting the first-year student: A handbook for improving the first year of college*. San Francisco: Jossey-Bass.

Watson, L., Terrell, M.C., Wright, D.J., Bonner, F., Cuyjet, M., Gold, J., Rudy, D., & Person, D.R. (2002). *How minority students experience college: Implications for planning and policy*. Sterling, VA: Stylus.

Weinberg, A. (2013). Parrainage francophiles–francophones à l'Université d'Ottawa dans le cadre du Régime d'immersion: pratique et perceptions. In E. Yasri-Labrique, P. Gardies, & K. Djordjevic (Eds.), *Didactique contrastive: questionnements et applications* (pp. 105–117). Montpellier: Cladole.

CHAPTER 16

RIF Students' Self-Narratives on Their Itineraries and Experiences

Aline Gohard-Radenkovic

INTRODUCTION

THIS CHAPTER PRESENTS the point of view of English-speaking Allophone students enrolled at the University of Ottawa, who chose to do part of their courses in French within the *Régime d'immersion en français* (RIF). Its aim is to analyze the representations of their experience in immersion through a qualitative interpretative approach and from a socio-anthropological perspective within the Foreign and Second Language Acquisition Theory, based on the cross-concept of representations. This analysis complements the other chapters: that is, it investigates the perceptions and life stories of various actors and co-actors[1] about and within the French immersion institutional *dispositif*.

What is different in this chapter is the way all the stories were gathered, which involved not only semi-directive biographical interviews with the various stakeholders of the academic institution but also other information using other analytical methods.

Firstly, the conceptual framework will be presented and then, the methodological framework. Finally, the students' stories will be analyzed and interpreted.

1. CONCEPTUAL FRAMEWORK: A NEW PARADIGM

1.1. Grammar of Complexity

It should be remembered that, over the last few years, a large number of governments, in the European Union and in Canada, have strongly promoted individual and collective multilingual and multicultural education. To that end, they have taken measures to encourage the various academic actors to implement it. This new deal has inevitably led to a new paradigm in the fields of language and culture; that is, the paradigm of complexity[2] (Morin, 1991, 1995), while taking into account the different dimensions underlying the investigated processes (Gohard-Radenkovic, 2012).

While the first studies concerned the political dimensions (at the macro level) or the institutional dimensions (at the meso level) and were most often carried out using a quantitative approach, more and more research is now focused on individual experiential dimensions (at the micro level), involving a qualitative and contextualized approach (Gohard-Radenkovic, 2006, 2009).

---

[1] These concepts are defined below.
[2] In the original sense of the Latin word *complexus* (what is woven together).

In order to tackle the contradictory and unstable links that individuals may develop toward language and its acquisition at various stages of their lives (Berchoud, Rui, & Maillet, 2013), researchers were led to draft a *grammar of complexity* (Zarate & Gohard-Radenkovic, 2004), to borrow Morin's expression (1991). This grammar charts the construction and evolution of a multilingual and multicultural experience, following the logic specific to mobility itineraries and from the point of view of the actors themselves, as they find themselves in immersion and try to integrate into a new environment, especially through language.

1.2. Immersion Actors Are Also Mobility Actors with Capitals

It is important here to define mobility actors and co-actors (Gohard-Radenkovic, 2009). Who are they?

> They are all those who actually move, that is, pupils, students, interns, teachers, researchers, education and administration officers, corporate or international organization executives, expatriates, war refugees, immigrants, exiles, etc. But "mobile" actors are not the only ones who play a key role in the mobility process, in the process of *their* mobility and *their* integration. Mobility actors are also all those who, in one way or another, are sought by individuals or groups in mobility: either because they work in education or language training (teachers, instructors, interpreters); or because they have other functions in the sphere of education, vocational training, social and medical services, administration, international affairs, non-profit sectors, the judiciary, etc. *They are the co-actors of these mobilities.* (pp. 6–7 [trans.; emphasis in original])

In this analysis, one cannot overlook the concept of "mobility capital" (Murphy-Lejeune, 2002, 2004),[3] which, since the early 2000s,[4] has revolutionized the links between mobility and the issue of languages. So, what does this capital consist of? To sum up:

- cultural and social capitals inherited from family and social groups
- linguistic, cultural and social capitals acquired through schooling, higher education, and vocational training
- previous mobility experiences, life abroad or migrating with the family, language study vacations, professional immersion training courses, school exchanges, holidays, and trips abroad

This mobility capital is therefore closely tied to an experiential capital but also to the creation of a multilingual and multicultural background before, during, and after the moves, which is in constant transformation. It also includes, therefore, social, cultural, or linguistic knowledge and expertise, acquired through these experiences. These mobilities concern not only international journeys, but also those from the countryside to

---

[3] Murphy-Lejeune took Simmel's (1908) concept of "stranger" and re-used it in terms of biographical experiences capital, extending it to academic mobilities.

[4] European policies promoting mobility have led to new forms of mobility, especially within the academic world, but they have also raised new issues and new migratory logics, focusing on languages and language skills.

the cities, from one linguistic zone to another in bi- or multilingual contexts such as Switzerland, Belgium, Luxembourg, or Canada.

This notion of mobility capital is also linked with another concept, which has become essential in the analysis of life narratives; that is, "the pre-dispositions toward mobility," a concept taken from Bourdieu (1982) and developed by Murphy-Lejeune and Zarate (2003) to deal with any kind of movement.

2. METHODOLOGICAL FRAMEWORK

2.1. Autobiographical Approach

As part of a qualitative process, two methods make it possible to understand the linguistic and social micro-processes at work in a given situation at a given time and in a specific context, and to assess the various stakeholders' representations, behaviours, and practices, through their written or oral stories or their interactions:

- biographical interviews (or life stories) first conducted by the School of Chicago in 1920, using an interpretative approach which involves the thematic or discursive analysis of the various life stories (Bertaux, 2005; Desmarais & Grell, 1986)
- the analysis of genuine interactions between people in a foreign language in an endolingual or exolingual context, using the tools and methods of ethnography of communication (founded by Hymes, 1962), ethnomethodology (founded by Garfinkel, 1974), and anthropology of communication (developed by Goffman, 1956)

In both cases, a qualitative approach that falls within the Grounded Theory principles (Strauss & Corbin, 2004) — that is, based on what the stakeholders say while trying to understand the meaning they give to their own life experiences — cannot, however, be just a mere description: it must go further by typifying and interpreting the processes at stake.

One must therefore try to understand the relationship that exists between the learners and the languages, both within their personal life stories and their own sociolinguistic contexts. The hypothesis is that the life, language, and mobility itineraries look like an "individual mapping"[5] that is constantly being redesigned. Since the 1990s, the reflective approach, like the language biographies[6] that had not yet played a part in language learning,[7] appeared through the European Language Portfolio as part of the principles and objectives of the Common European Framework of Reference (CEFR).[8] Learners

---

[5] This analogy is based on Richterich's "maps" concept (1998).
[6] Direct English translation from *biographies langagières*. In Europe, the terms "linguistic and intercultural autobiographies" or "life stories, language stories, and mobilities" are preferred (*autobiographies langagières et interculturelles, récits de vie, récits de langues et mobilités*).
[7] As for the life stories, they have long been used in other training and research fields: health, psychology, adult professional training, immigration, etc., but without the language dimension.
[8] The founding principles of the Council of Europe in the educational field are: gain knowledge, know-how, how-to-learn, how-to-be (*savoirs, savoir-faire, savoir-apprendre, savoir-être*) by promoting mobility so that all actors may acquire multilingual and multicultural skills for

in mobility studying in a language other than their own are called upon to acknowledge their linguistic, cultural, and social resources, their experience from/of abroad, and the strategies they use to communicate and learn in an exolingual context.

These numerous experiences (a "biographical capital," according to Bourdieu, 1982), especially those acquired through linguistic mobility, which is a move in itself, even in an endolingual context, combine previous capitals and those acquired in migratory journeys. The reflective approach has since been involved in all types of learning and training.

Autobiographies are the best approach to exploring the complex world of the relationship to one's own languages (Lévy & Hu, 2011), made up of contradictions, even tensions. Various types of autobiographical approaches have been identified (Gohard-Radenkovic, Pouliot, & Stalder, 2012):

- language and mobility maps, which enhance unique itineraries, but also allow one to highlight psychosociological processes common to these trajectories (Gohard-Radenkovic & Rachédi, 2009; Zarate & Gohard-Radenkovic, 2004)
- reflective drawings and "language portraits" (Cuko, 2016; Pungier, 2012, 2014; Robin, 2013, 2014), where learners locate their languages on different parts of the body. These "language portraits" (inspired by Krumm & Jenkins, 2001, taken up and developed by Molinié, 2009) are seen as narratives per se and lead to a reflective attitude. It is also the narrative of "linguistic incorporation" that gives each person a function, a part, a precise status at some stage in the itinerary of language users.

2.2. Multimodal Methodological Approach

The assumption of this study was that language portraits, with language and mobility maps as a counterpoint (or vice versa), are a narrative per se, offering the key events and characters that accompany an individual life story. The persons interviewed were also asked to talk briefly about a memorable experience that revealed the difficulties they faced when immersed in the language of others (here, the language of the other linguistic group) and about their strategies to cope with the situation.

To implement these three reflective approaches — language and mobility maps, language portraits, and personal narratives — a gathering with second- and third-year immersion students was organized.

2.3. A Surprisingly Homogeneous Corpus: New Immigrant Women

This randomly formed corpus[9] was quite homogeneous or, at least, had noteworthy similarities:

---

mutual understanding (*intercompréhension*, 'communication process and learning method in the field of languages'), socio-political cohesion, and employment possibilities (Council of Europe, 2011).

[9] That is, without pre-established selection criteria; they were simply required to be second- and third-year students in the RIF, with, therefore, some RIF experience, who all came on a voluntary basis.

- The 7 students were all women, which is not really surprising, since 90% of the RIF students in 2012 were female.
- All the participants had a more or less recent family history of migration (immigrant parents or grandparents) and were of different origins (i.e., Vietnamese, Lebanese, Burundian, Rwandan/Burundian, Ghanaian, Colombian, and Haitian).

It is obvious that this corpus did not really represent the entire second- and third-year student body enrolled in the RIF in 2012. However, the interdisciplinary orientation[10] required a qualitative approach. Thus, the objective was not to elaborate on the representative dimension of a sample but to grasp its significance, based on a gathered or inherited corpus (already established). According to Bertaux (2005):

> In an ethno-sociological investigation, data fulfill totally different functions [compared to quantitative investigations]. They cannot come down to statistical descriptions; they are not intended to confirm hypotheses either; they reveal how a social world or a social situation "work." This descriptive function is essential and leads toward what ethnologist Clifford Geertz calls *thick description*, an in-depth description of the social object which takes into account its internal configurations of social relations, its power relations, its tensions, its permanent reproduction processes, its dynamics of change. (pp. 24–25 [trans.; emphasis in original])

Moreover, as shown by abundant research (Gohard-Radenkovic, 2008, 2009; Murphy-Lejeune, 2002, 2003; Zarate, 1997), those who have an important mobility capital—inherited or acquired—are the ones who possess an experiential capital, consisting not only of loss and separation, but also of adjustment and recovery, which prepares them in some way for other types of mobilities or pre-dispositions to move (Murphy-Lejeune and Zarate, 2003).

This corpus was all the more significant because this mobility capital, inherited from family, coupled with a potential family language policy, played a key role in the participants' relationships with their parents' languages, and with Canada's bilingualism, as well as with their representations and expectations regarding immersion.

2.4. Organization of the Session: Initial Resistance

It was no coincidence that these seven participants, all recently immigrated Canadian women, came to the gathering. Their being paid and fed[11] was not enough to have influenced their decision to partake in the activities.

At first, their reactions were sceptical, even ironical, and they even took offense, as they said: "It does not make sense" or "Do you think we are kids?" (Instructions: draw your language portraits); "What do you expect us to do? We can't draw" or "What shall we draw? Show us!" (Instructions: draw your life, language and mobility maps).

However, as the afternoon went on, the women began enjoying participating in these diverse pictorial activities, which encouraged moments alone but also moments for sharing their creations (in pairs or in small groups), as each one in turn presented and

---

[10] In Foreign and Second Language Learning, from a socio-anthropological perspective.

[11] If it had been the only incentive, we would have had far more participants.

explained their drawings to their peers — including talking about past linguistic experiences, in their countries or abroad, or more recently, within the RIF.

3. ANALYSIS AND INTERPRETATION

It must be remembered that the purpose of these drawings (self-portraits of their bodies, and maps) was to make the participants reflect on themselves, their languages, and itineraries,[12] before assessing "other" languages and cultures, and the RIF and its actors[13] within an official bilingual context.

3.1. Language Self-Portraits Expressing Complex Relationships with Languages

What did these language portraits reveal not only about the language capital, but also about the female interlocutors' sociolinguistic imaginary world? In their portraits (see Figure 1), they marked their various languages on different parts of the bodies they had drawn:

- on the heart, beloved languages: mostly mother tongues — e.g., Vietnamese, Kirundi,[14] Kinyarwanda,[15] Arabic[16]
- languages other than the mother tongues spoken by their parents — Swahili
- on or near the head — English, for most of them
- on the mouth: immersion languages — e.g., English, French, *Franglais* (Frenglish)
- on or near the head but also on the hands or arms; that is, to find a job or better career opportunities:
    - Annelise had English and sign language marked on her head and French on her hands, as she needs it to find a job
    - Edith had English on her mouth and French on her head
    - only Marina had marked her three spoken languages (French, Arabic, and English) within the torso, all in capital letters, without making any distinction between them, thus putting her three useful languages at the same level

---

[12] This reflective approach has been called "socio-anthropological introspection" (Gohard-Radenkovic, 2004, 2013).

[13] The first names are fictitious on purpose. We will only use a few examples.

[14] From Wikipedia (n.d., "Kirundi"):
Kirundi, also known as Rundi, is a Bantu language spoken by 9 million people in Burundi and adjacent parts of Tanzania and the Democratic Republic of the Congo, as well as in Uganda.

[15] From Wikipedia (n.d., "Kinyarwanda"):
Kinyarwanda..., known as Urufumbira in Kisoro, Uganda, is an official language of Rwanda and a dialect of the Rwanda-Rundi language spoken by at least 12 million people in Rwanda, Eastern Democratic Republic of the Congo and adjacent parts of southern Uganda.

[16] This is the Lebanese version.

16. Self-Narrative Process 319

(a) Annelise's portrait (b) Solange's portrait

(c) Edith's portrait (d) Marina's portrait

Figure 1: Language self-portraits

Drawing from both their portraits and their interviews, this is how their relationships with languages could be interpreted:

- reclaimed languages: Solange (whose family, originally from Rwanda and now living in Anglophone Canada, had buried her French and only spoke English at home) chose French in her heart and would no longer have anything to do with English as her first language
- languages learned with their ears and eyes, by impregnation: Korean for Annelise
- languages learned and then forgotten: Italian for Edith, Japanese for Annelise
- languages hated and even abolished: French[17] or else Twi[18] for Solange, Haitian for Edith
- languages fantasized or desired: German, Italian, Spanish, and Turkish for Marina; German and Russian for Edith
- adopted foreign language (Solange fell in love with Dutch) or third language

This is a true "radiography" of their relationships with languages at a given time in their itineraries (they were in their second or third year of study), but their language capitals — and therefore, their linguistic resources — went far beyond the official bilingualism of academic institution: these language portraits have reveal a mental mapping of the languages that *inhabit* the students: functional languages, emotional languages, fantasized or desired languages, hidden or buried languages, discarded or hated languages, revisited or reclaimed languages, and so on.

This analysis of language portraits has revealed mobilities between different contexts (countries, regions), with movement to and from both symbolic and geographical places, as well as real mobilities between languages.

3.2. Mobility Maps Showing Refuge Strategies in a Third Language or in a Third Place

The analysis of all the language and mobility maps (Figure 2) showed that the women interviewed moved about and are still moving, for various reasons (linguistic, educational, touristic, family, migratory stays, etc.). They came and went between several contexts, be it between Anglophone and Francophone regions in Canada, or from Canada to abroad and vice versa. The moves had led to linguistic mobilities, as they carried with them the many linguistic worlds that they shared. They all spoke at least three languages, if not more, which were active or passive, inherited from their families (immigration history of parents or grandparents who came from Burundi, Rwanda, Ghana,

---

[17] Because it is the compulsory second language learned at school by all young Anglophone Canadians.

[18] From Wikipedia (n.d., "Twi"):

> Twi ... (also known as Akan Kasa) is a dialect of the Akan language spoken in southern and central Ghana by several million people, mainly of the Akan peoples, the biggest of the about 17 major ethnicities/peoples in Ghana and forms about 70% of the Ghanaian population as a first and second language.

Lebanon, Vietnam, etc.), or else which they had come across, learned, or adopted in their own interregional or international itineraries.

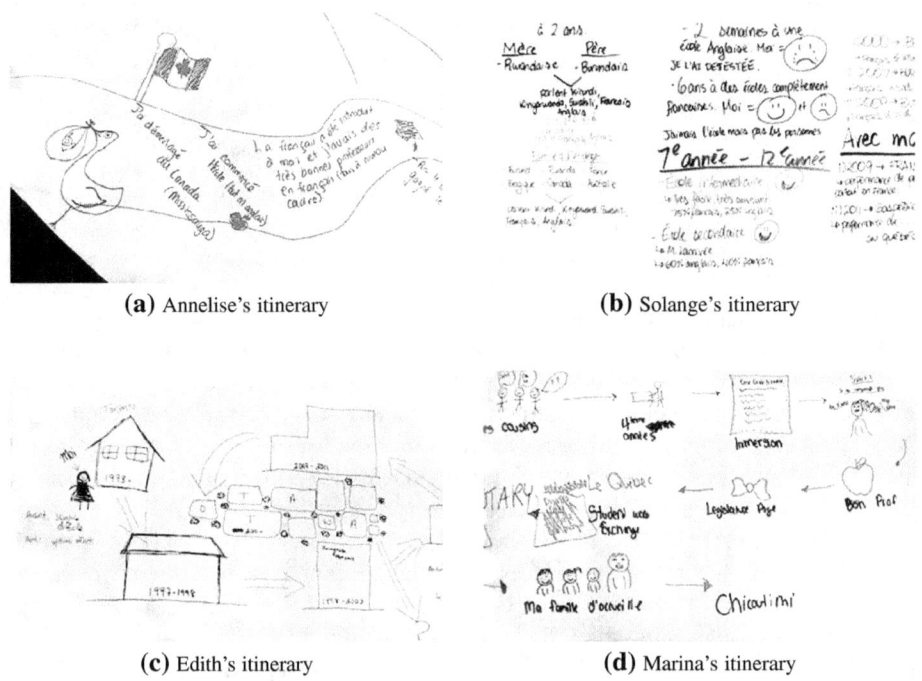

(a) Annelise's itinerary (b) Solange's itinerary

(c) Edith's itinerary (d) Marina's itinerary

Figure 2: Life, language, and mobility itineraries

So, all seven women had a multilingual and, de facto, multicultural profile, since they had been in contact with several sociocultural reference systems. This wide variety of itineraries showed that we were not dealing with students who fluctuated between two languages (French and English) in a binary mode. Deep down inside, they were living in a "between-many" situation, in multipolar mode, rather than "in-between," in bipolar mode (Gohard-Radenkovic & Murphy-Lejeune, 2011).

In response to the academic difficulties they encountered in relation to the other language of the official bilingualism, some of them developed bypass strategies, such as choosing a *third place* (for example, a linguistic or cultural stay in a Francophone country or region), which reconciled the language and culture of the close neighbour. Others chose to learn another language, a third language, or safe language (e.g., Spanish or Dutch) as a compensation strategy, even as an act of emancipation or resistance against the immersion language they had elected (in this case, French).

These third places always give meaning to situations of linguistic and academic insecurity embedded in an asymmetrical relationship (between the instructor and the student), even if North American university students are considered as clients who, therefore, have some control over the teaching and administrative staff. Diversifying places and languages, or unearthing the family's first languages, which had been buried or forbidden with a view to make integration easier (e.g., Burundi or Twi), can only improve the relationship with the immersion language, perceived by most as a missed opportunity, due not to difficulties inherent to the language itself but rather emerging from the *gaps* between the logics (and stakes) of the academic institutions and the logics (and needs) of the immersion students.

3.3. Experience Narratives, or the Individual Good Will Speech

In their oral narratives about a significant experience in class, the students accused some content instructors of refusing to understand they were immersion students, therefore non-Francophone, especially when they had to take part in discussion groups without any preparation. Most of them often felt treated like intruders, even enemies, as they represented the majority language.

Due to this instructor's presumed ill will, what emerges from all the students' oral narratives and remarks when talking about their experiences in immersion classes is a naive conception of the content-instructor-who-should-make-an-effort. The individual good will speech of the various parties and, more broadly, of the academic institution, cannot hold out against the reality of immersion for long, not unlike the unbearable intercultural innocence condemned by Giordano (2008).

These perceptions are certainly the individual projections of a politico-linguistic situation, seen by most of the actors in academic institutions[19] as one of tension, confining the students to a binary pattern (Anglophones vs. Francophones). Their complex itineraries and profiles contradict this reductive and simplistic dichotomy. One should be aware that these prevailing ideologies leading one to categorize the other linguistic group are reciprocal and seriously affect what goes on in content as well as language classes. Surprisingly enough, we did not hear many comments on the latter. While these adjunct classes were considered useful, they were, however, insufficient (not enough hours).

What do these omissions or blanks in the participants' stories mean (Bertaux, 2005)? Their process of self-exploration seems to have helped them discover that it was not only a matter of taking a language refresher course or understanding the content courses, but also uncovering more complex intimate and intersubjective realities. Moreover, they might simply have wanted to confront their own histories, immersion, and, more widely, the academic institution through this unique autobiographical approach!

3.4. Summary: Living Another Language Cannot Be Imposed

What did these language narratives say about the self-investigation process of these immersion students?

It must be remembered that the women interviewed were all in threefold immersion circumstances: linguistic, academic, and sociocultural, involving immersion experiences in another language and disciplinary culture as well as sociocultural integration

---

[19] These are other institutional stakeholders with whom biographical interviews were also conducted.

experiences—some in a Francophone environment, but mainly within an Anglophone background.

As pointed out before, there is a close link between their language itineraries and their mobility itineraries, and they all possess what is called a language capital and a mobility capital:

- the acquisition of first, second languages, etc., is closely linked to past or present experiences
- all of the women had different levels of mastery of the languages they had learned in a formal or informal context.

In this case, the students use several languages instead of shifting from one language to the other in a binary mode (French and English). And, indeed, they all have a multilingual profile.

On the one hand, living a language, even for functional purposes, can neither be claimed externally, nor be imposed upon the individual's intimate sphere of expression (Porcher, 2013). On the other hand, even if the students did not enjoy using the other official language, they managed to find loopholes and specific places to resolve tensions.

Common strategies—choosing a third place or a third language—sometimes expressed emancipation, sometimes their resistance toward the official immersion language that, although chosen, was at times difficult to grasp. These third places always gave meaning to these in-between situations of linguistic insecurity and academic uncertainty set within a de facto asymmetric relationship.

The autobiographical approach, which encouraged the students in immersion and in the process of integration to reflect on themselves, was therefore valuable in that it allowed them to express mental blocks, misunderstandings, judgments, avoidance, and rejections concerning their languages (and the speakers of the other languages), but also *coups de coeur* ('crushes'), attachments, discoveries, passions, and hopes. Beyond that, these students dared be politically incorrect, say the unspeakable, think the unthinkable, the unthought (*l'impensé*) (Laplantine, 1987).

In other words, the female narrators revealed to others and to themselves their own symbolical mapping. Even more, life stories could retrospectively make their worlds enchanting again, by renegotiating their relationship to the language of others, and, more widely, to other people as such. Reflecting back on one's life itinerary could lead to greater self-awareness.

CONCLUSION

Our assumption was that the qualitative analysis of a restricted corpus called for a *thick description* (p. 317) as well as interpretations that reveal gaps between the needs of students in mobility and the challenges of the academic institution actors.

It is clear that these Allophone students entered immersion with preconceived ideas about languages and Otherness: They already had their own visions and representations of the world, their own sociolinguistic imaginary worlds; moreover, they brought with them a multilingual and multicultural background, often acquired through various mobility experiences. As language and education experts, how do we deal with these assets?

This study also revealed that, in fact, an essentialist and functionalist (utilitarian) conception of language prevails: language and its learning process are seen as self-evident: they are naturalized (Bourdieu, 1982). Yet, any language carries with it, within it, an implicit culture shared only by initiated people who belong to a specific social group at a given time.

This shared ignorance should lead to the design of processes and schemes which take into account the Allophone students' experience in immersion (total or partial) in a context that is doubly foreign to them — or at least, unfamiliar:

- foreign to the academic background, which is a sociocultural background where they have to learn how to become students
- foreign to the language of education, while they have to master not only the language itself but also its implementation, written and oral, specific to each disciplinary culture

These students who have chosen the immersion program must therefore take on a double role, becoming students and becoming bilingual.

It is hoped that these various socio-anthropological activities of introspection will encourage the participants — starting with themselves and going toward others, from the known to the unknown — to question themselves, make assumptions about the collaborative behaviour of some lecturers and the resistance of others, while trying to understand their own values, categorizations, and behaviours, to be able to grasp the logics of other stakeholders, particularly content lecturers, so as to shift focus.

Did we succeed in making our participants question the individual good will speech on the one hand, and, on the other hand, the obvious expected good linguistic behaviours, present at all levels of the academic institution? Were we able to help them become aware of the different logics at work among various RIF actors, starting with theirs?

REFERENCES

Berchoud, M., Rui, B., & Maillet, C. (Eds.). (2013). *L'intime et l'apprendre: la question des langues vivantes*. Bern: Peter Lang.

Bertaux, D. (2005). *Le récit de vie*. Paris: Armand Colin.

Bourdieu, P. (1982). *Ce que parler veut dire: économie des échanges linguistiques*. Paris: Fayard.

Council of Europe. (2011). Common European Framework of Reference for Languages: Learning, teaching, assessment (CEFR). www.coe.int/en/web/common-european-framework-reference-languages

Cuko, K. (2016). *La classe d'accueil: un dispositif au carrefour de logiques complexes. Quand dessins réflexifs et entretiens biographiques de divers acteurs d'écoles primaires à Montréal révélent cette complexité*. Paris: L'Harmattan.

Desmarais, P., & Grell, D. (Eds.). (1986). *Les récits de vie, théories, méthodes et trajectoires types*. Montréal: Saint-Martin.

Garfinkel, H. (1974). The origins of the term ethnomethodology. In R. Turner (Ed.), *Ethnomethodology* (pp. 15–18). Harmondsworth, UK: Penguin.

Giordano, C. (2008). L'insoutenable innocence de l'interculturel. In A. Gohard-Radenkovic & A. Akkari (Eds.), *Coopération internationale: entre accommodements interculturels et utopies du changement* (pp. 161–170). Paris: L'Harmattan.

Goffman, E. (1956). *The presentation of self in everyday life*. Edinburgh: University of Edinburgh Social Sciences Research Centre.

Gohard-Radenkovic, A. (2006). Interrogations sur la conception de l'"interculturel" dans le *Portfolio européen des langues* et autres productions du Conseil de l'Europe. *Synergie-Europe* [thematic issue: *La richesse de la diversité: recherches et réflexions dans l'Europe des langues et des cultures*], *1*, 82–94.

Gohard-Radenkovic, A. (2008). Un curriculum transdisciplinaire: ses effets sur les futurs enseignants de langue en situation de mobilité. In G. Alao, E. Argaud, M. Derivry-Plard, & H. Leclercq (Eds.), *Grandes et petites langues: pour une didactique du plurilinguisme et du pluriculturalisme* (pp. 239–250). Bern: Peter Lang.

Gohard-Radenkovic, A. (2009). L'approche autobiographique dans la formation de futurs médiateurs linguistiques et culturels: de mobilités géographiques vers des déplacements identitaires. In A. Gohard-Radenkovic & L. Rachédi (Eds.), *Récits de vie, récits de langues et mobilités: nouveaux territoires intimes, nouveaux passages vers l'altérité* (pp. 143–162). Paris: L'Harmattan.

Gohard-Radenkovic, A. (2012). Contre-point: le plurilinguisme, un nouveau champ ou une nouvelle idéologie? Ou quand les discours politiquement corrects prônent la diversité. *Alterstice*, *2*, 89–102.

Gohard-Radenkovic, A. (2013). Vers une "introspection socio-anthropologique" de l'intime et de l'apprendre: contre-point. In M. Berchoud, B. Rui, & C. Maillet (Eds.), *L'intime et l'apprendre: la question des langues vivantes* (pp. 181–190). Bern: Peter Lang.

Gohard-Radenkovic, A. (Ed.). (2004). *Communiquer en langue étrangère: de compétences culturelles vers des compétences linguistiques* (2nd ed.). Bern: Peter Lang.

Gohard-Radenkovic, A., & Murphy-Lejeune, E. (Coordinators). (2011). Introduction: Mobilities and itineraries. In G. Zarate, D. Lévy, & C. Kramsch (Eds.), *Handbook of multilingualism and multiculturalism* (pp. 119–126). Paris: Éditions des archives contemporaines. (Original work published 2008)

Gohard-Radenkovic, A., & Rachedi, L. (Eds.). (2009). *Récits de vie, récits de langues et mobilités: nouveaux territoires intimes, nouveaux passages vers l'altérité*. Paris: L'Harmattan.

Gohard-Radenkovic, A., Pouliot, S., & Stalder, P. (Eds.). (2012). *Journal de bord, journal d'observation: un récit de vie en soi ou les traces d'un cheminement*. Bern: Peter Lang.

Hymes, D. (1962). The ethnography of speaking. In T. Gladwin & W.C. Sturtevant (Eds.), *Anthropology and human behavior* (pp. 13–53). Washington, DC: Anthropology Society of Washington.

Kinyarwanda. (n.d.). Wikipedia entry. fr.wikipedia.org/wiki/Kinyarwanda

Kirundi. (n.d.). Wikipedia entry. en.wikipedia.org/wiki/Kirundi

Krumm, H.J., & Jenkins, E.M. (2001). *Kinder und ihre Sprachen — Lebendige Mehrsprachigkeit: Sprachenporträts* [Children and their languages — Living multilingualism: Language portraits]. Vienna: Eviva.

Laplantine, F. (1987). *Clefs pour l'anthropologie*. Paris: Seuil.

Lévy, D., & Hu, A. (Coordinators). (2011). Languages and the self. In G. Zarate, D. Lévy, & C. Kramsch (Eds.), *Handbook of multilingualism and multiculturalism* (pp. 59–114). Paris: Éditions des archives contemporaines. (Original work published 2008)

Molinié, M. (Ed.). (2009). *Dessin réflexif: élément pour une herméneutique du sujet plurilingue*. Amiens: Encrage-Les Belles Lettres.

Morin, E. (1991). *Autocritique*. Paris: Seuil.

Morin, E. (1995). Vers un nouveau paradigme. *Sciences humaines*, *47*, 2–5.

Murphy-Lejeune, E. (2002). *Student mobility and narrative in Europe: The new strangers*. London: Routledge.

Murphy-Lejeune, E. (2003). *L'étudiant européen voyageur, un nouvel étranger*. Paris: Didier.

Murphy-Lejeune, E. (Coordinator). (2004). *Francophonies/Interculturel* [thematic issue: *Nouvelles mobilités, nouveaux voyageurs*], *5*.

Murphy-Lejeune, E., & Zarate, G. (2003). L'acteur social pluriculturel: évolution politique, positions didactiques. *Le français dans le monde: Recherches et applications* [thematic issue: *Vers une compétence plurilingue*], *July*, 32–46.

Porcher, L. (2013). À chacun sa langue. In M. Berchoud, B. Rui, & C. Maillet (Eds.), *L'intime et l'apprendre: la question des langues vivantes* (pp. 1–3). Bern: Peter Lang.

Pungier, M.-F. (2012). Croquer l'expérience ou la capitaliser? À propos d'un séjour de mobilité en France dans des journaux de bord de deux étudiants japonais. In A. Gohard-Radenkovic, S. Pouliot, & P. Stalder (Eds.), *Journal de bord: un récit en soi ou les traces d'un cheminement* (pp. 287–316). Bern: Peter Lang.

Pungier, M.-F. (2014). Étude exploratoire sur des représentations graphiques d'un stage en France par des étudiants japonais. *Glottopol*, *24*, 141–164.

Richterich, R. (1998). La compétence stratégique: acquérir des stratégies d'apprentissage et de communication. *Le français dans le monde Recherches et applications* [thematic issue: *Apprentissage et usage des langues dans le cadre européen*], *juillet*, 188–213.

Robin, J. (2013). Séjour de mobilité linguistique obligatoire dans la formation des enseignants: oui, mais comment? Le cas de la PHBern. *Babylonia*, *1*, 94–98.

Robin, J. (2014). Cartes de langue(s) et de mobilité(s) de futurs enseignants du primaire à Berne: quand une dynamique dialogique entre les corpus dévoile des processus de renégociations des représentations du français. *Glottopol*, *24*, 64–79.

Simmel, Georg. (1908). *Soziologie: Untersuchungen über die Formen der Vergesellschaftung*. Leipzig: Duncker & Humblot.

Strauss, A., & Corbin, J. (2004). Les fondements de la recherche qualitative: techniques et procédures de développement de la théorie enracinée (M.-H. Soulet, Trans.). Freibourg: Freibourg Academic Press.

Twi. (n.d.). Wikipedia entry. en.wikipedia.org/wiki/Twi

Zarate, G. (1997). Pour l'amour de la France: la constitution d'un capital pluriculturel en contexte familial. In M.-L. Lefebvre & M.-A. Hily (Eds.), Les situations plurilingues et leurs enjeux (pp. 25–34). Paris: L'Harmattan.

Zarate, G., & Gohard-Radenkovic, A. (Eds.). (2004). *La reconnaissance des compétences interculturelles: de la grille à la carte*. Paris: Les Cahiers du CIEP/Didier.

SYNTHESIS

Hélène Knoerr, Alysse Weinberg, and Aline Gohard-Radenkovic

THIS BOOK HAS SOUGHT TO RESPOND to the wish expressed by the former Commissioner of Official Languages, Graham Fraser, in his preface: in order to ensure "a learning continuum from primary to the job market," it is necessary "to collect and analyze the practices underway in order to propose a successful model of French immersion at the university level" (p. 10). The various chapters have surveyed the immersive practices at different universities across Canada and have analyzed their strengths and weaknesses at the macro, meso, and micro levels, taking into account the perspectives and experiences of all the stakeholders. We can now make an overall assessment and outline the winning conditions for ensuring the implementation of successful university-level French immersion *dispositifs*—the "successful model" called for by Fraser.

1. AT THE MACRO LEVEL

Clearly, *the legislative framework is a key driver* in the promotion of the second language. In Canada, the Official Languages Act of 1969 and the language laws of Quebec (Quebec, 1969, Bill 63; 1974, Bill 22; 1977, Bill 101) propelled the immersion wave, from children in a single school in suburban Montreal to over 400,000 students at the elementary and secondary levels across the country (Statistics Canada, 2018). "The question therefore is not so much whether it should be taught but how it can be better taught" (p. 3).

However, officially bi/plurilingual countries often operate within a federal framework, which means that education is dealt with at the intermediate levels of government and not at the federal level. In Canada, provinces are free to choose their linguistic status, and schoolboards decide whether or not French immersion programs will be implemented in primary and secondary schools. In our specific case of Ontario, the decision is made at the post-secondary level by "Her Majesty, by and with the advice and consent of the Legislative Assembly of the Province of Ontario" (as the opening phrase of the official act reads), on a case-by-case basis. For example, the University of Ottawa Act of 1965 states that one of the objectives of the university is "to further bilingualism and biculturalism and to preserve and develop French culture in Ontario" (University of Ottawa, 1965, "Administration and governance ...," section 4c). This seminal document anchors the bilingual nature of the University and ultimately led to the creation of the *Régime d'immersion en français* (RIF).

Still at the macro level, *an explicit theoretical and methodological framework* is necessary to implement a strong immersion *dispositif*, with solid linguistic and didactic foundations established through research and application. Immersion allows experts not only to revisit and question didactic and pedagogical assumptions and traditions, but also to conceptualize new approaches in applied linguistic, to renew language learner needs analysis, and to develop innovative teaching methodologies informed by both theory and practice. In so doing, immersion is contributing to the emergence of a new field: the didactics and pedagogy of immersion in higher education. New advances in research allow theories and practices to evolve, causing *dispositifs* to change accordingly — as was the case at uOttawa, where the initial sheltered model was eventually replaced by the adjunct model. But of course, each context is unique, and higher education institutions should select the model(s) best suited to their specific situation.

A final necessary condition at the macro level is *a clear conceptual distinction between immersion programs* directed toward non-Francophones (typically speakers of the majority language who want to learn the language and the culture of the second-language minority), and *other programs* integrating non-Francophone and Francophone students. The choice between these two configurations is typically driven by demolinguistic and geographic constraints, and it is important to differentiate them in order to best serve each specific content and audience.

2. AT THE MESO LEVEL

This level, at the interface between policies and stakeholders, appears to be the keystone of the system, since it crystallizes most of the key factors in the successful implementation of immersion *dispositifs* in higher education.

In terms of *administrative structure, a service is a much lighter option* than a program, tapping into existing human resources — faculty, liaison officers, registrar, mentors — and being available as an option in a variety of programs. But, while a service does not require a large staff, these employees must be top-quality professionals dedicated to serving the students — the RIF's 1700 students have regularly praised the one-on-one *personal attention* that they receive, in sharp contrast with the impersonal, take-a-number type of interactions with general university services geared toward over 42,000 students. Such individualized service comes with a financial cost, however, and institutions need to make provisions for that.

At the same time, the intrinsically administrative nature of the service must be balanced with *methodological and pedagogical guidance* provided by immersion experts in order to ensure that the right choices are being made regarding resource allocation, course objectives and content, and student evaluation. Too often, an administrator's point of view is more concerned with quantity — the numbers of students enrolled in classes — than with quality — the experience of these students — and decisions can be made in the name of financial considerations at the expense of theoretical, methodological, and pedagogical foundations. An *advisory committee involving experts in immersion* research and practice is key to maintaining the legitimacy of the *dispositif*.

Diverse learning modalities and places are essential for language learning: students learn best when they are exposed to rich, authentic environments in which they can interact and experiment with the language. Formal, semi-formal, and informal learning settings combine with enclosed academic spaces, local communities, and the world at large to provide a variety of learning experiences, whether face-to-face or virtual.

Experiential learning, community placements, and study-abroad programs are the most effective ways to acquire language and culture, as consistently demonstrated by research, and should be included in any immersion *dispositif*.

Learning language through content is best achieved in an *adjunct immersion model*, where language and content are taught by experts. *Language courses*, whether general (grammar, vocabulary, etc.) or content-based (language support classes for content courses), are essential in order to develop receptive and productive language skills as well as discipline-specific academic literacy. Similarly, requiring students to take not one third but *the majority of their content courses in their second language* will ensure that they will have enough language skills to competently function in their field, whether as graduate students or as employees in a bilingual workplace. Of course, the flexibility to customize one's academic path is appealing to students, but unless there are *standard requirements in terms of language proficiency*, the *dispositif's credibility* will be questioned.

A *dispositif* is "an intellectual, technical or material set whose function is to ensure the achievement of a project and define the role played by the actors, the associated tools and the steps needed to achieve a previously identified, and possibly pedagogical, task" (Cuq, 2003, p. 74 [trans.]). As such, *institutionalizing the relations between actors* is crucial: if the actors are peripheral to the system, they will not feel valued or involved; but if they are integrated into the system, they will be aware of the importance of their roles. Under these circumstances, *content and language instructor teams* can develop in the long term for the benefit of students and instructors themselves: these teams can invest time in co-creating pedagogical resources tailored to their courses. Similarly, experienced immersion students can act as *mentors* for their novice peers; Francophone and Francophile students taking the same content courses can participate in a *buddy system (parrainage)*, thus improving their academic success chances while also widening their appreciation of the other language and culture.

Careful monitoring and evaluation of students' language skills, at various stages in the *dispositif*, is key for its success. Research has shown that students whose language proficiency is too low when they register in university-level immersion will not persevere, no matter how high their general grade point average is (Daoust & Durepos, 2016). With at least a B2 level in the Common European Framework of Reference (CEFRL) system, they will not drop off; below that level, they can still be successful if they take a number of general and language support classes along with content courses in French. As students take language support classes over the course of their program, *language instructors must be careful to evaluate language, not content*. Upon graduating, a *recognized proficiency test* should guarantee prospective employers, both in the private and public sectors, that these students are linguistically competent professionals. *Ideally, such a test should be congruent with the levels prescribed by the public service.*

All the factors at play at the meso level share one common element: *initial and in-service training*. Because immersion in higher education is a new field, all its stakeholders need to be made aware of its unique characteristics:

- Language instructors are certified educators in second language teaching, but their training has not prepared them for the specifics of university-level immersion.[1] In content-course-specific language support classes, instructors must be able to design, on the spot, learning activities based on material from the content course but assessing language, not content. Such skills can only develop if they are taught and practiced: *mandatory training* in the form of workshops should be part of the *contract* when instructors are hired. At least part of this training could be done via online modules, which are becoming common practice in many universities requiring specific certifications from their personnel (security in the workplace, accessibility, sexual harassment, for example). The RIF's advisory committee is currently exploring such an option. Immersion *dispositifs* should also designate *pedagogical advisors* experienced in university-level immersion, who could mentor novice language instructors and assist all instructors with designing appropriate activities and tests.
- Content instructors need to be made *aware of the rationale and philosophy of immersion in higher education*, and of the challenges immersion students choose to face. They also need *access to a resource person* for suggestions on how to help these students succeed in their immersion programmes.
- Students need not only accurate *information* on what language support classes actually are (language courses, not a tutorial of the content course), but they also need *training in academic literacy*: workshops on study habits, listening and note-taking strategies, and on academic writing. These will help them develop their skills and realize that academic culture and disciplinary traditions are language-dependent.
- Administrators — whether in the registrar's office, orientation, or liaison — and service providers everywhere on campus should also be familiar with the *dispositif* and its many advantages, so that they can *provide support and encourage students to stay* in immersion.

3. AT THE MICRO LEVEL

The most striking element at this level is the importance of the *emotional dimension*, as evidenced in all the interviews of the immersion stakeholders. Researchers need to use multidisciplinary approaches to analyze the representations of ideologies as they materialize in discourse, in order to identify and understand the logics at work. For all the actors, and especially the students, linguistic, academic, social, and identity security is at the core of their experience: they need to be acknowledged as people, not as replaceable parts in the system.

This *acknowledgement* of the stakeholders is key to a successful immersion *dispositif*:

- *Language instructors need to be recognized as experts* in their field — language teaching and immersion pedagogy — in the same way as content instructors are

---

[1] Even if they did receive training for primary and secondary school immersion, such training does not help since the immersion model implemented in schools is the sheltered model, but the model implemented at uOttawa is the adjunct model.

recognized as experts in theirs, and at the same level. Too often, language specialists do not enjoy the same prestige as content specialists, even though they have the same qualifications, including up to a doctorate. The academic culture needs to be changed.

- *Content instructors should be consulted* when it comes to the immersion course offering: they should be asked whether they agree to teach a course with immersion students and they should have the option to refuse, with no impact on their career/future hiring prospects. It is a question of *respect*. Should they decide to embark on *collaborative pedagogical projects* with their language instructors, these projects *should be recognized* as valid contributions to their field and valued as such on their CVs.
- *Immersion students should expect content instructors to acknowledge the challenge they are imposing onto themselves*: they could simply have enrolled in the same program in their mother tongue; instead, their decision to pursue it in their second language commands respect, at the very least, and maybe some support and a few accommodations from content instructors.
- *Immersion administrators deserve recognition for their role as immersion champions*: they are the ones who are advertising the *dispositif* to students, parents, schools, and schoolboards; they are the ones supporting immersion students in their decisions and in their academic careers.
- *Institutions should be openly committed to immersion* and make it part of their culture. *Senior administrators*, such as rectors and vice-rectors, should recognize that immersion is the reason why students choose to come to their university, the distinctive feature that gives them extra visibility, and *demonstrate their appreciation*. One simple way would be *a reception* organized at the beginning of each term, where a high-ranking administrator would welcome *all the immersion* dispositif *stakeholders*: deans, immersion chairs, content and language instructors, and student representatives. Faculties could also create *awards recognizing exemplary content and language instructor teams*.

These and/or similar measures to recognize and acknowledge the uniqueness of university-level immersion are needed to counter the academic, linguistic, and identity (in)securities felt by all the stakeholders at the micro level:

- *Students* feel at risk academically because of the challenge of taking a program in their second language; they feel at risk linguistically because their language skills are lower than the Francophone students in their content classes; they feel at risk in their identities because they are used to being the majority in their school, their province, their country, and suddenly they become the minority and they struggle with their new Francophile identity. Initiatives such as the Francophone–Francophile buddy system, immersion mentoring, pass/fail grades, low-enrolment language support classes, and close administrative monitoring are contributing factors to fostering a sense of security in these students.

- *Language instructors experience institutional insecurity*: they have no guarantee that the time and effort they invest in developing custom-tailored activities will pay off, due to long-term course allocation. If a more senior part-time instructor requests their course, they will lose it; if the content instructor changes, readings and course notes will change as well. Administrations (and unions) should work together to ensure *stability in course allocation* in the *dispositif*.
- *Content instructors may experience linguistic insecurity if French is their second (or third) language*: they may feel threatened by their "native speaker" students or by the language instructor, who attends all classes and witnesses their linguistic weaknesses. But they may not realize that *they are role models for immersion students*, since they are living proofs that one can become *an expert in one's field in one's second language*. These instructors need institutional support, such as the Language Training Services for Academic Staff at uOttawa, which provides one-on-one tutoring, language courses, and editing services.[2]

CONCLUSION

This book has been a team effort: its contributors are involved in university-level immersion as researchers, educators, and practitioners. They have presented a detailed description of their immersion *dispositifs*, using institutional documents as well as interviews. The book has focused on the RIF in particular, a unique living laboratory for immersion in higher education, and has provided an exhaustive account of its *dispositif* at the macro, meso, and micro levels, highlighting strengths and weaknesses, and offering suggestions to successfully meet the challenges.

This has been achieved by uncovering the processes and tensions at play between official discourses promoting bilingualism and actual means, measures, and resources devoted to turn discourses into action, thus achieving a state of balanced bilingualism. Clearly, there are gaps between words and actions, and all the stakeholders interviewed in this book seem to be aware of these gaps. To bridge these gaps, we must invent spaces for meeting and mediating, find new ways of articulating services, and better align the different institutional levels and units for the benefit of the entire immersion community, starting with the students, who are the beginning and the end of the *dispositif*.

It is our hope that this book has achieved its objective, stated at the outset of this chapter: "to collect and analyze the practices underway in order to propose a successful model of French immersion at the university level." But of course, realities fluctuate, situations are complex, audiences are changing. Immersion is a multifaceted phenomenon and, consequently, it is impossible to offer a one-size-fits-all model: contextual, institutional, academic, and individual factors all interplay and must be accommodated by each *dispositif*. Immersion in higher education is an emerging field and a work in progress.

---

[2] For more information, see OLBI (n.d.).

REFERENCES

Canada. Official Languages Act. (1969). *Official Languages Act* (1969) 1970, R.S.C, chapter 0-2. www.uottawa.ca/clmc/official-languages-act-1969

Cuq, J.-P. (Ed.). (2003). *Dictionnaire de didactique du français langue étrangère et seconde.* Paris: CLE International.

Daoust J.L., & Durepos, J. (2016). *Programme de mentorat/Mentoring program: Rétention et expérience étudiante.* Internal document, French Immersion Studies [Régime d'immersion en français], University of Ottawa.

Official Languages and Bilingualism Institute (OLBI). (n.d.) Language training services for academic staff. olbi.uottawa.ca/academic-staff-courses

Quebec. (1969). *An Act to promote the French Language in Quebec* (Bill 63; *Loi pour promouvoir la langue française au Quebec*). www.oqlf.gouv.qc.ca/50ans/images/Bill_63.pdf

Quebec. (1974). *Official Language Act* (Bill 22; *Loi sur la langue officielle*. National Assembly of Quebec. web.archive.org/web/20041120120718/http://www.oqlf.gouv.qc.ca/charte/reperes/Loi_22.pdf

Quebec. (1977). *Charter of the French language* (Bill 101; *Charte de la langue française.* www.legisquebec.gouv.qc.ca/en/showdoc/cs/C-11

Statistics Canada. (2018). *Back to school by the numbers: Enrolments in French immersion programs.* www.statcan.gc.ca/eng/dai/smr08/2018/smr08_220_2018#a3

University of Ottawa. (1965). Administration and governance: 1965 University of Ottawa Act. www.uottawa.ca/administration-and-governance/1965-university-of-ottawa-act

About the Editors

Hélène Knoerr is an Associate Professor at the University of Ottawa's Official Languages and Bilingualism Institute. She holds a Masters in Didactics of French as a Second Language and a PhD in Applied Phonetics. Her current research interest is the integration of content and language in higher education, with a special focus on French. She has published numerous contributions to the field of French immersion in higher education, presented papers at several international conferences on content-based language teaching, and piloted pedagogical initiatives to improve the learning experience of her immersion students. She has co-edited three issues of the *OLBI Working Papers* (2010, 2013, 2018). She has authored several chapters in her most recent co-edited books on this subject, *L'immersion française à l'université: pratiques et pédagogies* (2016), and *Current issues in university immersion* (2018). She has also authored a number of articles and chapters in North American and European publications on university immersion.

Alysse Weinberg, now retired, was an Adjunct Professor at the University of Ottawa's Official Languages and Bilingualism Institute. She has taught French as a second language for over 25 years. Since 2006, she has been actively involved in the French Immersion Program at the University of Ottawa as a professor, researcher, and as one of its first pedagogical advisers. Her current research interests include different aspects of post-secondary immersion language learning, especially in the fields of vocabulary acquisition, listening strategies, program evaluation, and students' perceptions. She has presented papers at several international conferences on content-based language teaching and has published numerous contributions to the field of French immersion in higher education. She has co-edited three issues of the *OLBI Working Papers* (2010, 2013, 2018) and has co-edited and authored several chapters in two books — all on teaching immersion at the tertiary level: *L'immersion française à l'université: pratiques et pédagogies* (2016), and *Current issues in university immersion* (2018).

REFERENCES

Knoerr, H., & Weinberg, A. (Eds.). (2010). *OLBI Working Papers*, 1.

Knoerr, H., & Weinberg, A. (Eds.). (2013). L'immersion en français au niveau universitaire/French immersion at the university level. [thematic issue]. *OLBI Working Papers*, 6.

Knoerr, H., Weinberg, A., & Buchanan, C.E. (Eds.). (2018). Dispositifs d'immersion universitaire au Canada/University-level immersion environments in Canada. [thematic issue]. *OLBI Working Papers*, 9.

Knoerr, H., Weinberg, A., & Buchanan, C.E. (Eds.). (2018). *Current issues in university immersion*. Ottawa: University of Ottawa, Groupe de recherche en immersion au niveau universitaire (GRINU).

Knoerr, H., Weinberg, A., & Gohard-Radenkovic, A. (Eds.). (2016). L'immersion française à l'université: politiques et pédagogies. Ottawa: University of Ottawa Press.

www.ingramcontent.com/pod-product-compliance
Lightning Source LLC
Chambersburg PA
CBHW070745020526
44116CB00032B/1980